The Elusive Dream

Punta Chivato,
Baja California Sur, México
The First 40 Years

J. M. Joy

This book is dedicated first to my husband, Greg Joy, who not only introduced me to Punta Chivato but has relentlessly urged me to complete this project over the past two decades!

I also dedicate this book to my beloved only sibling, Bill Roach, who passed away at age 66 (1951-2018). He was a fearless dreamer who loved adventure and embraced challenges.
I miss you, Bill.

And I dedicate this book to my brother's first grandson, Owen William White, born 2/4/24, and first granddaughter, Eloise Claire Tonneson, born 8/6/24.

Lastly, I dedicate this to all those adventurers who have loved Baja, especially Punta Chivato, and to those who have yet to experience this magical place.

In Loving Memory of Harry Oxley
Long-time Punta Chivato Resident
Passed away at his home in Punta Chivato
Just short of his 90th birthday
1/2/1936 - 6/2/2025

CONTENTS

PART I

PART II

PART III

PART IV

Prelude

Fueled by involvement in the war in Vietnam, antiwar protests at home, the civil rights movement, and the assassinations of President John F. Kennedy and Dr. Martin Luther King, the 1960s was a time of social and political unrest in the United States. Added to that was the increasing use of psychedelic drugs, "Flower Power," and the widening generation gap. Some Americans searching for relief from the chaos escalating at home turned to Baja California, México. Although just across the U.S.-Mexican border, it felt worlds away.

This is the story of the beginnings of Punta Chivato, Baja California Sur, México, in the 1960s and its subsequent development into the new millennium. Located two-thirds down the eastern Baja peninsula, this arid point, initially accessible only by sea, was an unlikely site to construct a resort hotel. However, Dixon Collins had a dream. Once he set eyes on this location, nothing was going to deter him from moving forward. Soon, others, both Americans and local Mexicans, got involved, taking a personal interest in helping to make Dixon's dream and theirs a reality.

All the characters in this book are real. I set out to interview as many individuals as possible who were willing to share their experiences in Punta Chivato during the early years. Their voices were tape-recorded with their consent. To bring the characters more to life, their words and grammar were unaltered. By melding multiple oral recollections as well as personal letters, diary entries, e-mails, legal documents, and relevant information from newspapers, magazine articles, and books, the goal was to portray the first forty years of Punta Chivato to you, the reader, as accurately as possible.

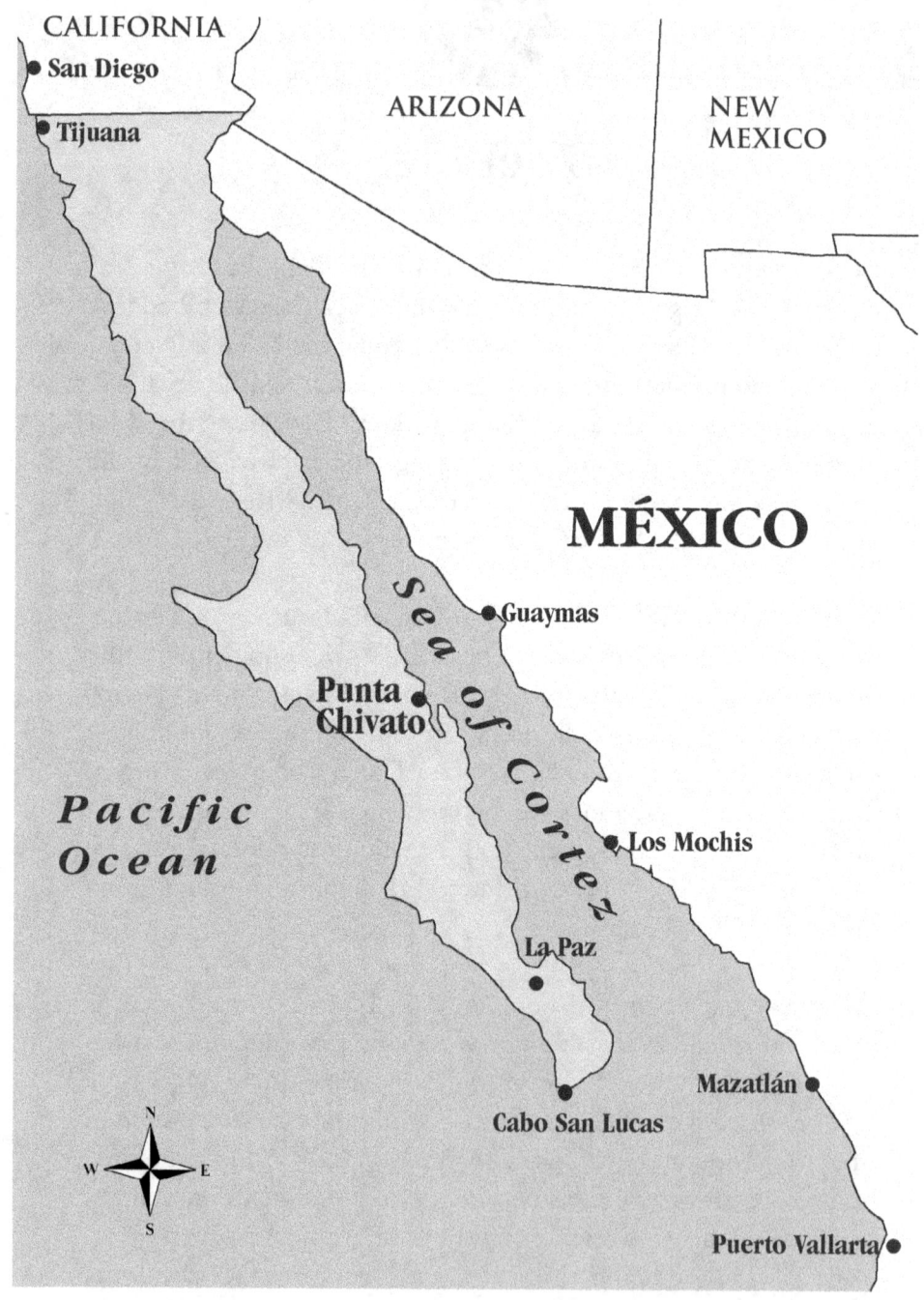

MAP 1: Baja California in Relation to the U.S. and Mainland México

MAP 2: Baja California Peninsula showing Baja 1 and Select Cities/Towns

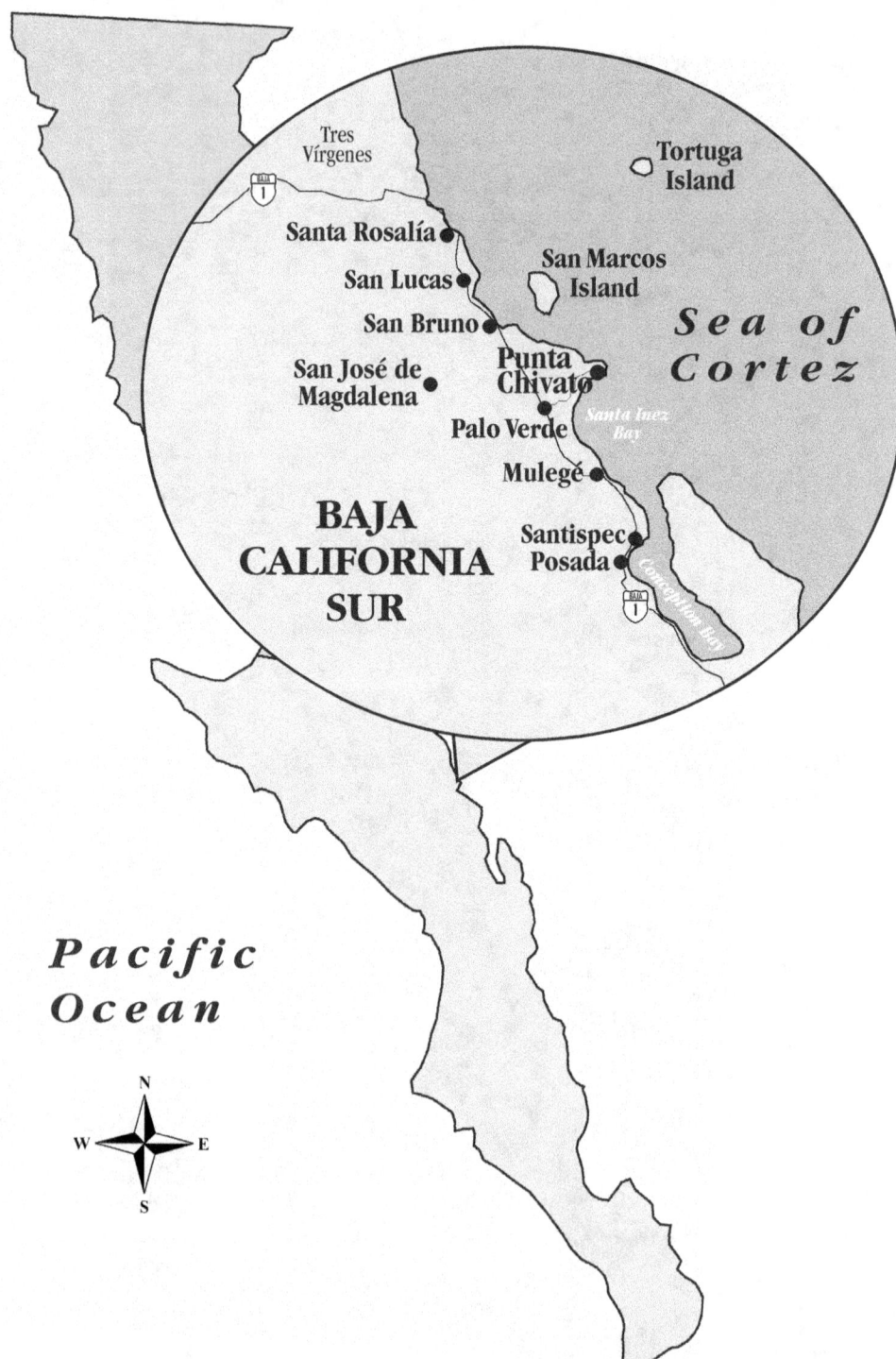

MAP 3: Enlargement of Section of Baja Sur Peninsula near Punta Chivato

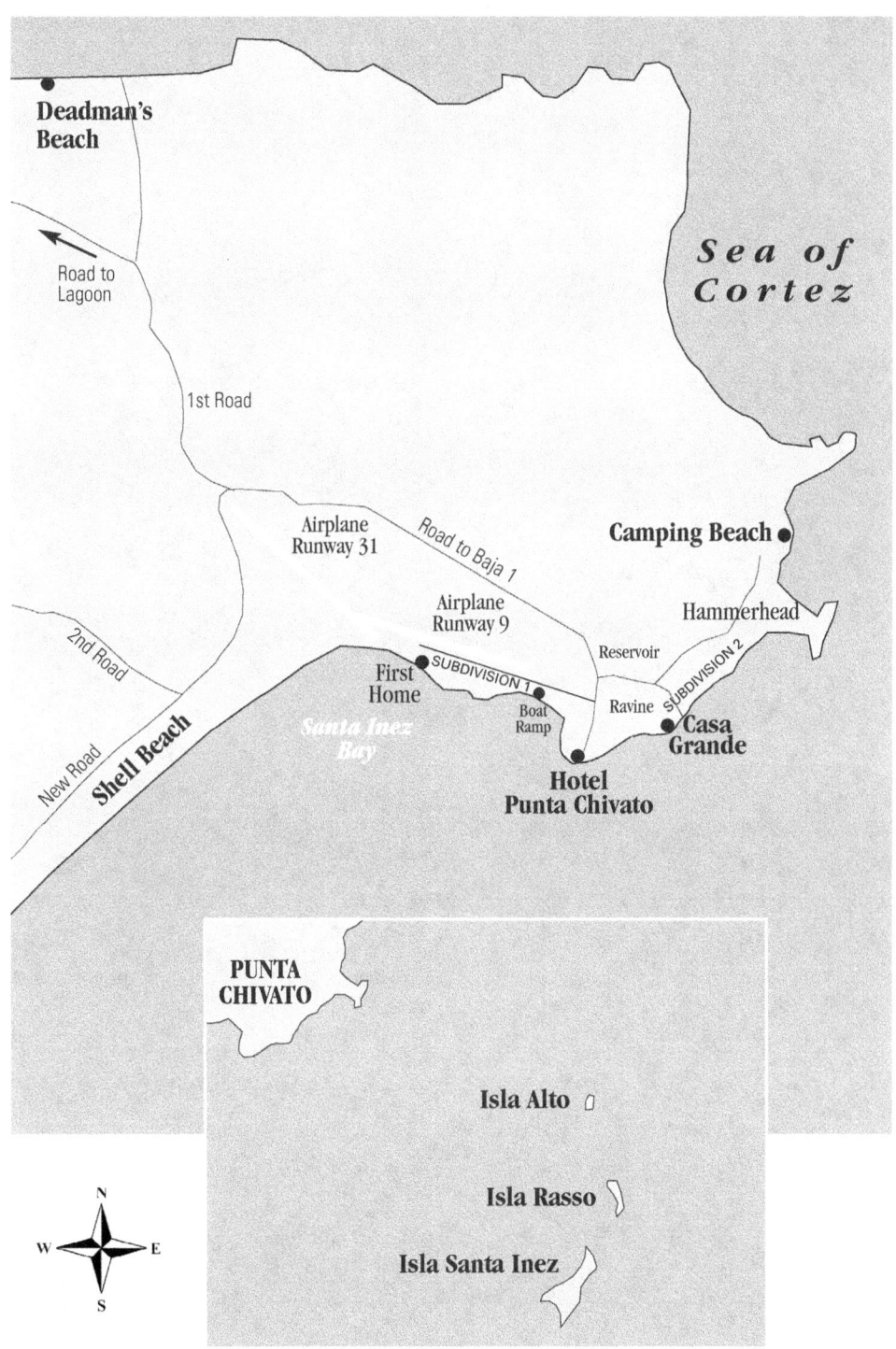

MAP 4: Punta Chivato

PART I

Chapter 1

BIG–GAME FISH IN BAJA

In the 1950s, news of plentiful, big-game fish in the waters off Baja quickly filtered northward to the United States. Don Sherwood, a disc jockey for the popular San Francisco, California, radio station KSFO, helped spread the word. He raved on air about marlin and other billfish caught off the southern tip of the Mexican peninsula near a village named Cabo San Lucas. Well-known celebrities, including Bing Crosby, Desi Arnaz, and Clark Gable, were said to frequent the area, eager to experience the excitement.

At that time, access to Baja by land was limited to a two-track dirt road that traversed the peninsula. Only daring adventurers attempted this grueling drive, those who had plenty of time on their hands and were willing to tackle unforeseen challenges. Tales circulated of severe seasonal storms, road washouts, vehicle breakdowns, limited services, and the scarcity of gas and water.

Travel by air was preferable for anyone looking for only a week or weekend adventure in Baja. However, few landing strips were long enough to accommodate large aircraft, and commercial flights were limited.[1]

Small, single-engine airplanes were increasingly popular in the United States during the 1950s. Some individuals could afford to buy their own plane, while others shared a partnership in an aircraft. These planes required shorter landing strips and could take off and land on unpaved dirt runways.

Fly-in resorts began to spring up in prime areas to take advantage of the growing American interest in Baja's game fish. Resort owners built airstrips to accommodate small aircraft. Some of the early fly-in resorts included Herb Tansy's Rancho Buena Vista near the tip of the peninsula, Ed Tabor's Flying Sportsman Lodge in Loreto, and Señor Antero "Papa" Diaz's hotel in Bahía de Los Ángeles (Bay of Los Angeles). Articles in *Western Outdoor News* by Ray Cannon, *Field & Stream* by Frank Dufresne, and *Saturday Evening Post* helped boost the appeal of these fishing resorts.

Like other avid American sports fishermen, John Bonfante was soon lured to Baja. As a successful entrepreneur in the supermarket business in central California,[2] John could afford to purchase a fiber-winged, single-engine Mooney airplane. One of the first fly-in fishing resorts in operation, Rancho Buena Vista, soon became John's favorite fishing destination. John introduced his friend, Lou Federico, to Baja on one of his trips.

John and Lou met in San Jose, California, south of San Francisco. Lou owned Fredrick Tailoring, a custom men's clothing shop he had taken over from his father. John was a long-time client. Although 13 years older than Lou, the men bonded over their shared Italian heritage and love of adventure and fishing.

On January 5, 1959, Herb Tansy, the owner of Rancho Buena Vista, was killed in a small airplane accident. John loved that resort and knew of its popularity. Although sad about Herb's death, John had an idea he wanted to run by his 33-year-old friend Lou.

"What would you think about buying Tansy's place?" John proposed as they sipped coffee one morning in a café next door to Lou's tailoring shop in San Jose, California.

John Bonfante had a commanding presence when he spoke. He was tall and distinguished-looking. With his long gray hair, he resembled a southern gentleman who had just stepped off a plantation.[3]

"I just can't believe Tansy's dead," Lou replied, taking in John's news. "Do you think it's for sale?" he added, still processing the shock of Herb's unfortunate fate.

"I think it's worth checking into," said John. "Tansy was single, and I don't believe he had any heirs who would take it over and run it."

Lou was ready for a change. He had endured four years of emotional turmoil, starting with the divorce from his first wife, Doris. Lou's mother committed suicide at the age of 51; his father died from a heart attack, and Lou and Doris's 9-year-old son was killed in a jeep accident. Later, Lou's 27-year-old girlfriend succumbed to lupus. Lou was at an all-time low. His life had stagnated. *What have I got to lose?* Lou reflected. *Maybe this will be a chance for a fresh start.*

John Bonfante and Lou Federico were outbid for the Rancho Buena Vista resort by an American named Colonel Eugene Walters, but the seed had been planted. They continued to dream about owning a fishing resort in Baja. Undeterred by their loss of Rancho Buena Vista, the two friends searched earnestly for another location.

Chapter 2

FLY-IN RESORT IN MULEGÉ

In late 1959, John Bonfante landed his plane on an abandoned but viable dirt airstrip near the village of Mulegé midway down the eastern shore of Baja, near the mouth of Conception Bay. He had flown over this area on previous trips and was intrigued by the tropical lushness that stood in stark contrast to the surrounding desert. This was Lou's introduction to the tiny, quiet village of Mulegé.

Mulegé was tucked in beside *Río de Santa Rosalía* (Santa Rosalía River), which arose from underground springs and brought lifeblood to the desert oasis. The river's banks were lined with large date palms, initially planted by local indigenous people after the Jesuit missionaries arrived in the 1700s. Fortress-like *Misión Santa Rosalía de Mulegé* (Mission Santa Rosalía of Mulegé) stood upstream on a hill above the town. The population reached as high as 2,000 after the mission was built. However, only 650 people lived in Mulegé when John and Lou arrived.

A mile and a half from the river mouth stood a federal prison called *Carcel de Cananea* (Canaanite Jail). Built in 1907, the austere, whitewashed building with high, four-foot-thick adobe walls and tall iron doors was not a typical prison. Inmates who had not committed serious crimes left at 6 o'clock each morning to work in town. The prisoners earned minimum local wages, equivalent to about a dollar a day (U.S.). They held various jobs in the village, including pruning palms, working the farms, fishing, construction, and other trades. Several of the inmates married locally. Their wives and families resided in thatched adobes around the prison or in the village.[4]

John and Lou grew enamored of the primitive town. In addition to dates, the villagers grew tropical and subtropical crops, including papayas, guavas, pomegranates, sugarcane, grapes, figs, olives, citrus, bananas, and mangoes. Farmers traveled the dirt roads along the riverbanks. Some carried wood and jugs of water on their backs. Others led burros that pulled carts of produce and wares to sell in the plaza (town square) two miles inland from the river mouth. Shops and homes, joined by shared adobe walls, lined the dirt roads around the plaza. Lush flower gardens adorned the adobe buildings. Palm-thatched roofs added to the tropical atmosphere of the village.

Río de Santa Rosalía provided easy access by boat to the Sea of Cortez. Skiffs glided over the calm river waters, followed by dozens of freeloading, squawking seagulls and frigate birds. Villagers told stories of a five-foot-long black snook, called robalo, hiding among the mangrove bushes growing along the banks of the brackish tidal estuary. Here, the fresh water from the river mixed with the saline water of the sea. Locals spoke of abundant big-game fish not far off-shore, pristine, secluded beaches, and plentiful shellfish in the 25-mile-long Conception Bay nearby.

Visitors had few choices for lodging in Mulegé in those days. Near the plaza was a colonial-style building with thick walls called *Vieja Hacienda de Mulegé* (Old House of Mulegé). It was converted into a hotel in the early 1950s by Mexican-American Octavio Salazar, who was eager to accommodate adventuresome fishermen who drove the rugged Baja roads to reach this out-of-the-way destination.[5]

John and Lou believed offering a resort with a small airstrip would provide easier access to Mulegé, and sportsmen would flock to the area. They chose to build on a hillside north of the village center and the river mouth. The twelve-acre parcel offered enough space to include a dirt airstrip.

John Bonfante and Lou Federico added two other investors to their Mulegé resort venture, brothers who ran Mexican labor camps in Hollister, California. One, Pablo Ortiz, took title to the property since he was a Mexican national.

Lou talked his long-time friend in San Jose, California, Don Johnson, into coming to Mulegé and investing in the resort. According to Don, he purchased Lou's tailoring business in San Jose after Lou left. "I ran it for a while, and then I sold the damn thing. Then, I sold a piece of property I had there. And that's where I got the money to invest into this."

However, when interviewed, Lou disputed Don's claim that he was ever a partner in their hotel in Mulegé. "He wasn't involved," Lou emphatically stated. "He thinks he was. He brought an old truck down there, an old green truck that was worth about $500, and that was his contribution. He had no cash into the place."

Just as adamantly, Don Johnson argued during an interview with the author, "I can't believe that Louie said I didn't put any money into the hotel (Rancho Loma Linda). It wasn't much, $10,000, but that was a lot in those days. Bonfante took my money."

When interviewed, Don referred to Lou Federico and the book he was writing, *One Hell of a Ride: The Life and Times of Lou Federico*, published in 2004.

"Louie has been out of here for over thirty years. What he's trying to capture is something out of me, I guess, for his own personal self to put in his book. He can't do it. People don't know who the hell Louie Federico is. You go to Punta Chivato, and people say, 'Louie Federico, who the hell is he?' They don't know. But you can mention my name, and they all know. Hell, I've been here for years." Don Johnson had indeed become a legend.

On January 1, 1961, the new fly-in resort in Mulegé was completed after having survived the hardships of building in this remote village and the great chubasco (hurricane) of 1959.[6] They named it *Hotel Rancho Loma Linda* (Pretty Hill Ranch Hotel).[7]

Reports about the new fly-in resort spread north to the United States. Guests arrived in their single-engine aircraft, ready to enjoy the informal atmosphere of the remote getaway. During the day, Lou Federico, the acting resort manager, enjoyed guiding visitors on fishing trips. Although the town grew quiet in the evenings, the resort was alive, with people dancing to Mexican tunes strummed by guitarists. Lou frequently entertained the guests by singing and playing the maracas. His audience included such well-known American visitors as John Wayne,[8] Jayne Mansfield,[9] Mayor Sam Yorty of Los Angeles,[10] actress Ann-Margret,[11] and actor Kirk Douglas.[12]

As interest in Mulegé grew, two other lodges opened in the tropical paradise. *Las Casitas* (Little Houses), a small motel and restaurant near the town plaza, was started by Fred Woodworth and his wife, Cuca Gorosave.[13] In 1961, Leroy Center, an attorney and the mayor of Redondo Beach in Southern California, built another fly-in resort near the mouth of the Mulegé River called *Hotel Serenidad* (Serenity Hotel).[14] Also, American Bill Lloyd opened *Playa de Mulegé* (Mulegé

Beach) south of the river mouth that year. It consisted of palm-thatched huts furnished with cots on sand floors and offered an inexpensive lodging alternative.

John Bonfante's dream of owning and operating a resort in Baja began to sour before the end of 1961. He held what appeared to be valid, stamped paperwork proving the transfer of property ownership from a Señor Zuniga. However, Bonfante soon learned the land on which Hotel Rancho Loma Linda was built was claimed by the local Mexican *ejido*, a sort of local commune.

Disillusioned by this turn of events, John and the other partners wanted to sell their fly-in resort. Although John and his wife, Inez, enjoyed spending time in Mulegé, they never intended to become permanent residents. Pablo Ortiz, who thought he held title to the land, also wanted out of the questionable investment.

Convinced he could gain ownership of the resort property from the ejido in Mulege, Dick Stockton, an entrepreneur from Southern California and frequent guest at Hotel Rancho Loma Linda, offered to purchase it.[15] With his Mexican partner, Frank Chaves, Stockton offered to buy the shares from Bonfante and Pablo Ortiz if Lou Federico agreed to stay as the resort manager. Lou had little choice. His life was now in Mulegé. Lou agreed to stay. By the end of 1961, Stockton had renamed the resort Club Aero Mulegé.[16]

Stockton built a home for Lou just below the resort with a river view. Later, Lou met a beautiful young woman, Lana Green, who won the title of Miss San Francisco in 1961. They married on December 8, 1963, and moved into Lou's home in Mulegé.

The hotel continued to operate for several years, but not without conflict. Financial instability and ownership changes would take a heavy toll on the once beautiful resort.[17,18]

Chapter 3

EJIDOS

To understand property ownership in México, it is important to look at México's history. Had John Bonfante done so, he may have been more wary about building the resort in Mulegé.

Land ownership in México changed dramatically when the Spanish, under Hernán Cortés, conquered the area in 1521. Previously, the Aztecs had practiced a communal system of ownership whereby land was parceled out to groups of families. After the Spanish took over, two distinct classes emerged: the white-skinned, elite Spaniards and the dark-skinned, indigenous people. Exploited by their European conquerors, the indigenous people were forced to give up their resources and land. Under the new "hacienda system," they were dependent on the Spanish landowners for their work, food, medical care, and religious worship.

Even after Spanish rule was overthrown in 1810 and México City replaced Madrid as the ruling hub of México, the gap between the social classes persisted. As the Mexican presidency passed from one general to the next, the country became even more unstable and corrupt. The wealthy elite continued to get richer, and the impoverished indigenous people poorer. By the end of Porfirio Diaz's reign, half of México's rural population worked on land owned by fewer than 900 upper-class families and land companies.[19]

The peasants, who had little hope of escaping poverty, began romanticizing rebels like Emiliano Zapata, Francisco "Pancho" Villa, Álvaro Obregón, and Venustiano Carranza, whom the government considered criminals. Under the leadership of these men, the peasants eventually revolted against the powerful ruling class. A bloody struggle started on November 20, 1910, and lasted a decade. During this time, México endured enormous destruction of property and life. Factories shut down, and currency became unstable.

Following the Mexican Revolution, the federal government in México City sought to alleviate land ownership inequality between the wealthy and the poor. In 1917, a new Mexican Constitution was drawn up. Under Article 27, the disparity in land between the "haves" and the "have-nots" was addressed.[20]

Under *La Ley Agraria* (Agrarian Law), parcels of federal and private lands were redistributed to the peasant population. The process, known as "expropriation," allowed the federal government in México City to legally claim portions of land for the working class to use. The previous landowners got no compensation and had no right to sue the government for taking their land.

Each designated group was called an *ejido*, and the members were called *ejidatarios*. The intent was to encourage these people to live on the designated land, make an income through farming, and provide food for their community. Although the ejidatarios could work the land and keep what they earned, they did not technically own the land. According to the Agrarian Reform Act, the government maintained control over any decision made by members of an ejido. The federal Agrarian Department oversaw and regulated the system, not the ejidatarios.

Although the new policy had been written into law, the government was slow to provide land to the peasants. The first elected Mexican president, Álvaro Obregón (elected in 1920), believed the working class was incapable of managing the responsibilities that would come with increased wealth and control of the land. By the time Obregón left office four years later, only 3.5% of the agrarian land owned by the government had been given to the peasants.[21]

Artists such as Diego Rivera kept the plight of the working class in the public eye. Proclaiming himself to be of white, Indian, and African blood, Rivera vividly depicted the inequities between the rich and the poor in his paintings and murals.

In 1929, a broad-based political party, *Partido Nacional Revolucionario* (PRN), was formed. Later renamed *Partido Revolucionario Institucional* (PRI), it was composed of factions from all sides, including peasants and elected politicians from the left, center, and right. Under President Lázaro Cárdenas's leadership, which began in 1934, sharing land by forming ejidos became more prevalent.

Chapter 4

DIXON FIRST VISITS MULEGÉ

Dwight Dixon Collins, who went by his middle name, "Dixon," first visited Club Aero Mulegé shortly after Dick Stockton took it over. By then, Dixon had left a job at Hughes Aircraft and started an insurance brokerage in West Covina, California. He preferred being his own boss and became a successful entrepreneur.

Dixon and a childhood friend, Dick Fritz, shared a passion for hunting and fishing. As partners in a small airplane, they often flew to Los Mochis on mainland México to hunt ducks and geese or to Lake Chapala above Guadalajara to try their luck at catching white fish. They also frequently flew to Baja.

When the long-time friends heard about the new resort with an airstrip in Mulegé, they were eager to visit. The location was particularly convenient because it was only a few hours' flight from Southern California. As an ex-Navy carrier pilot who flew AD-5s on the aircraft carrier U.S.S. Bon Homme Richard, Dixon knew how to make tricky landings and enjoyed the challenge of landing on the rugged dirt strip on the hillside above the resort in Mulegé.

Lou Federico was well integrated into the Mulegé community when Dixon Collins first arrived as a guest at Club Aero Mulegé in the early 1960s. Living in Mulegé since the late 1950s, Lou had picked up the local language and fallen in love with the Mexican people and their culture. Lou had even joined the local baseball team. Fellow teammate Saúl Davis, who would later own the popular grocery store in town, Saúl's, recalled that their baseball field was in the town's graveyard. Lou played second base; Saúl's position was catcher.

"He did pretty good," Saúl later recalled in an interview, but he remembered one unfortunate game. "We're playing, and there was a fly ball, and he [Lou] went back and fell, and he broke his collar bone."

Lou was highly regarded by the villagers, who were drawn to his outgoing, charismatic personality. Of Italian descent, Lou was short in stature and had a chiseled, Romanesque face and a strong physique; he projected an air of self-confidence. Lou was easily recognized from a distance by his Stetson hat, Texas cowboy boots, and a distinct gait that suggested he had once suffered a leg injury.

His easy-going manner, warm smile, and discerning eyes reflected a personal interest in everyone who approached him. Men gravitated to Lou because he promised adventure. Women could not get enough of his handsome features and charm. The men, women, and children of Mulegé grew to love and respect the American.

One weekend in 1963, recently divorced, 28-year-old Dixon arrived alone in Mulegé. He was greeted by a hotel employee who drove up in a jeep after Dixon landed and transported him and his luggage down the hill to the resort. After being shown to his room, Dixon wasted no time getting to the hotel bar to have a drink, settle in, and relax. It always felt good to be back.

Standing behind the bar, Saúl Davis, the Mexican bartender, gestured toward one of the wooden bar stools.

"Welcome back, Mr. Collins. How was your flight?"

"Great," replied Dixon. "Always good to hear your voice on the radio." Saúl was not only the bartender but also took control of the radio frequency, giving weather reports and greetings to incoming pilots.

"What can I get you, mi amigo? Tecate? Margarita?" asked Saúl.

"I'll have a shot of tequila for starters," Dixon replied, settling his burly frame onto a wooden stool.

"Coming right up," Saúl replied.

Saúl Davis was an excellent resort bartender. He spoke English well and had a knack for remembering the names of repeat customers. He had experience, too. Before coming to Mulegé in 1962, Saúl managed the Flying Sportsman Lodge in his hometown of Loreto, further down the peninsula.

Although Saúl was Mexican, he had an English last name, Davis. One story of how that surname came to Baja tells of English pirates landing on the eastern Baja coast centuries before. Two brothers, whose last name was Davis, decided to get acquainted with the local Indians.[22] The number of Davises in Loreto eventually grew until almost a third of the town had the Davis surname.[23]

"How's business been?" Dixon asked Saúl.

"Very good, señor," Saúl replied while setting Dixon's shot glass on a cocktail napkin. "Sometimes we get so busy the guests have to go to Serenidad."

"This area has really caught on," Dixon remarked as he sipped his drink. "You know, I've been thinking about building a resort of my own. Thought I'd ask that manager of yours to help me find a spot."

During previous trips, Dixon had gotten to know the resort manager, Lou Federico, who was ten years his senior. Like other visitors, Dixon was taken in by Lou's remarkable stories and wealth of knowledge about the area. If anyone could help him locate land for a 5-star resort, Dixon knew it was Lou.

"I don't know where you would build," Saúl stated. "When I see Lou, I'll tell him you want to talk."

Later that evening, Dixon met with Lou. "Lou, I want you to find me some land where I can build a fishing resort," Dixon said.

Removing his hat and placing it on the table, Lou replied. "I have a better idea; why don't you buy this place?"

Lou had recently heard from John Bonfante that Dick Stockton's foundry in South Gate was going bankrupt. Dick was still delinquent in his hotel payments. Lou worried about the survival of the resort he helped build. He had been part of Club Aero since its inception. He and his wife loved the quaint town of Mulegé and did not want to move.

"Buying this place would be peanuts compared to what it's going to cost to build another resort," Lou told Dixon. "You could just walk in here and...."

"No, Lou, I don't want this place," Dixon interrupted. "I want to build a bigger, first-class resort with a view. Can you find me a spot?"

Lou smiled and nodded his head with an understanding only two dreamers could share. "Sure, Dixon, tomorrow morning I'll take you there."

Chapter 5

DIXON'S DREAM

"There it is," Lou yelled over the whine of the boat motor. He gestured to a sparsely vegetated stretch of Baja's east coastline jutting into the Sea of Cortez. Along the shore, stretches of white-sand beaches gradually came into view, sandwiched between fingerlike projections of volcanic rock. The area was referred to as *Punta Chivato* (Goat Point).

Dixon Collins turned his attention from the small Santa Inez Islands offshore and gazed in the direction Lou pointed. As Lou Federico angled the Boston Whaler toward land, Dixon noted a massive dune perched above the water's edge.

As the boat drew closer, Lou pulled back the throttle, slowing the engine. "I'll beach the Whaler, and you can have a look around," Lou said.

Lou cut the power, allowing the vessel to glide onto a gently sloping beach south of the dune. The men climbed out of the boat and pulled it onto the sand. Lou wrapped the bowline around a lava outcropping.

The remote coast appeared untouched as if still waiting to be discovered. The two men walked a short distance along the beach and then climbed to the top of the close dune.

Dixon turned and faced the sapphire waters of Santa Inez Bay. Gazing past the three low-lying Santa Inez Islands, he could make out the opening to Baja's Conception Bay. The mountains on either side looked surreal, like the painted backdrop on a Western movie set.

Dwight Dixon Collins stood 6'5" tall and had the physique of a football lineman. His swagger and confidence disturbed some but convinced most that there were few obstacles he could not overcome. His dreams were as big as his stature. Ever since he visited the fishing resort in the Baja village of Mulegé, Dixon envisioned having a sporting resort of his own. He wanted to create a retreat for fishermen and hunters like himself and offer a secluded getaway for wealthy

Americans. Dixon was excited. This remote location might be the perfect spot for his dream to become a reality.

"It's fabulous," Dixon said. "This site could provide better views and access to the water than any of the resorts in Baja." Dixon held both arms straight out in front of him and sighted through them toward the sea. "If I angle the building just right, all the rooms would have ocean views," he continued, already visualizing the layout of his anticipated first-class resort. "We'd have to level this dune first," he added.

As Dixon continued his survey, he noted a south-facing, protected cove below the bluff, which would offer an ideal spot for boat anchorage. Looking slightly inland, parallel to the beach, he spotted a long, level strip of land sparsely covered with cacti and patches of grayish desert brush. A pilot himself, Dixon noted this would be the perfect location for an airstrip, within walking distance of the resort.

It was 1963, ten years before a paved roadway would connect the towns of Tijuana in the north of Baja and Cabo San Lucas in the south. There were few commercial flights to the Baja peninsula. Access for most Americans was limited to those willing to drive on primitive dirt roads, navigate a boat up the Sea of Cortez, or fly down in a private plane. Dixon knew a resort like his would need a well-maintained runway to attract the growing population of adventurous pilots.

In the distance, Dixon noticed a wide stretch of flat land perpendicular to the coastline, starting on a bluff above the water's edge and extending about a mile to the low-lying hills inland. He mused that maybe a second, longer runway could be created here to accommodate larger aircraft, even jets.

Dixon was excited as he visualized the possibilities. With easy access by private plane from California, Nevada, and Arizona, guests could quickly reach this unique location, temporarily leaving behind their day-to-day worries in the States. Here, they could fish, hunt, swim, or simply relax and enjoy the beauty and tranquility of a seaside oasis.

"Lou, this place is so fantastic. It's perfectly suited for a fly-in resort," Dixon said. He imagined the area becoming so popular that guests would someday want to build homes along the coast.

"I think Barbara's really going to love it here," Dixon said, turning his back to the sea and opening his arms wide as if to gather in the virgin land. "I'll bring her down next time; I've got to show her this place."

"Sure, Dixon, whatever you want," replied Lou. He had a hunch that Dixon's wealthy lady friend might be behind his dream of considering building a resort in Baja.

"Lou, who owns this land?" Dixon asked, eager to move forward. He knew Lou had connections to people in the area and could help him find the owner of the property he coveted for his resort.

Lou shrugged his shoulders. "Don't you think we should first find out if there's a source of drinking water before going much further?" he cautioned, knowing the importance of a freshwater source in arid Baja.

"There'll be water here somewhere," said Dixon, brushing Lou's concern aside. "I'll worry about that later. Just ask around and find out who owns this land and how much they want for it."

"Okay, Dixon," Lou said. Although disgruntled by Dixon's brusqueness, Lou felt excited about the prospect of the new resort. He had planned to build his legacy in Mulegé, but things had not panned out for him as he had hoped. Maybe Dixon's project would revive Lou's dream and leave him a more incredible legacy than he had imagined.

Chapter 6

OWNERSHIP—PUNTA CHIVATO

After visiting the point at Punta Chivato, Dixon's enthusiasm was boundless. He dreamed of having a resort that would rival anything in Mulegé. Unlike Club Aero Mulegé or Serenidad, his resort would have an unobstructed view of the majestic Sea of Cortez and be surrounded by natural coves of white sand. He envisioned building something grander than he had ever seen in all of Baja.

Dixon soon returned to Mulegé and brought his girlfriend, Barbara. She was a pretty, fair-skinned blonde, but Lou surmised it was more than her looks that Dixon found attractive. According to Lou Federico, Barbara was an heiress to the fortune of the Honeywell Corporation.[24] Dixon met Barbara at Brackett Field near Pomona, California, where he and his partners kept a small plane. Bold and adventurous, Barbara was taking flying lessons.

Described by some as "a very beautiful lady" and "first class," Barbara was recently divorced when she met Dixon. The two hit it off.

Some say Barbara would have been better off staying married to her previous husband, Franklin Otis Booth, Jr., a second cousin to Otis Chandler of the *Los Angeles Times*. Franklin would later become a billionaire after an investment he made in the early 1960s with a man from Omaha named Warren Buffett.[25]

Dixon landed his airplane on the airstrip above Club Aero Mulegé, where he and Barbara would stay for the weekend. He asked Lou to take them to the potential resort site. To Dixon's delight, Barbara was enthusiastic about the project. She marveled at Punta Chivato's unobstructed views of the Sea of Cortez and its white sand beaches covered with shells.

During a 2003 interview with Don Johnson at the Serenidad Hotel in Mulegé, he shared his impression of Barbara. "She didn't know what was going on. She just went along. And nobody had the guts to go over there and tell her. I didn't want to get involved in it. It was none of my business. I'm not the type to go around and gossip about somebody else. Barbara was a sweetheart of a gal. What she saw in that stupid idiot, I don't know."

Lou soon located two Mexicans who claimed they were partners in the land at Punta Chivato. Bastida was the government fishing inspector in Santa Rosalía, a copper mining town on the coast north of Mulegé and Punta Chivato. Gilbert Yee was someone Lou knew well, the chef at Club Aero Mulegé.

"You've got to be kidding, Gilbert. You own that property?" Lou asked in disbelief.

"Yeah, myself and Bastida, we bought it years ago," replied Yee, whose Chinese family was well-known in Mulegé. "I've got all the title papers, stamped and everything."

The two landowners were interested in talking to Dixon, and while they gathered their papers, Lou telephoned Dixon, who had returned to the United States. "You've got to come back down, Dixon. I found the owners, and they're willing to sell."

I better check into this myself, thought Dixon, not yet ready to hand over money to the alleged property owners. Dixon had an idea. He called a Mexican friend in Guaymas, a town on the west coast of mainland México across the Sea of Cortez from Baja.

"Octavio," Dixon said, "I have a favor to ask. I need to find out who owns title to some property in Baja."

Octavio Llano was part of the prominent Llano-Zaragosa family in México, descendants of the Spanish conquerors. The family owned a supermarket, a building company, and land that would eventually be the site of a Club Med. With commercial interests all over México, the affluent family wielded considerable power; Octavio's father was the federal fishing inspector for all the shrimp fleets.

Dixon explained his situation to Octavio. "I know a good attorney in México City," Octavio said. "You need to go meet with him. He went to law school with Gustavo Díaz Ordaz, who we think will be the next president of México (president 1964-1970). Good connections. I'll do what I can," he told Dixon. "It might take a while to research the title." Dixon was about to learn what was meant by getting things done in "Baja time."

Many weeks passed while Octavio spoke to officials he knew in México City. Finally, Dixon flew to the Mexican capital and met with Octavio's friend and attorney, who was Ordaz's classmate in law school. The attorney told Dixon the federal government owned the land in question; there was no record of ownership by Bastida and Yee.[26]

Within a few weeks, with the help of the México City attorney recommended by Octavio, Dixon not only met with the president of México, Adolfo López Mateos (1958-1964), but also had his signature on a document granting Dixon a 99-year lease on 4,000 acres of land.[27] Since foreigners could not legally lease property in México without a Mexican partner, Octavio Llano agreed to join Dixon in the venture. When Dixon returned to Mulegé, he was eager to share the good news with Lou.

"Hey, Lou, you'll never believe what happened. I got a lease not only for the bluff in Punta Chivato but for miles of beach and inland on both sides of it!"

Lou listened incredulously. Dixon continued, "I dealt directly with the main government office. They insisted that I buy the whole peninsula![28] I had the attorney check to make sure it wasn't ejido land. Here's the map, the paperwork—it's even signed by López Mateos."

"What about Bastida and Yee?" Lou asked, wondering what the Mexicans would do when they learned Dixon Collins had leased "their" property without them earning a cent.

"They never heard of them," Dixon replied, gesturing as if to wave them out of the picture. "All the paperwork they showed us was bogus. They never were registered in México City."

"Figures," said Lou, remembering their experience at Club Aero in Mulegé. He questioned whether one could trust any documents stamped in Baja.

"Hey, Lou," said Dixon, putting his hand on Lou's shoulder. "Why don't you leave this place and work for me? I'm going to need someone to supervise the construction, and you've already got experience building one hotel down here." Dixon sensed that with Lou's background in Mulegé, he might be the perfect choice for someone to assist him in realizing his dream at Punta Chivato.

Lou pondered Dixon's offer. As much as he loved Club Aero, he had grown increasingly discouraged by the frequent changes in ownership. Lou was beginning to doubt whether there was a future for him in Mulegé. He had no place to go but back to the United States and was not ready to leave Baja.

"If you help build the hotel and run it, we'll give you a really good wage, or you can have stock in it," Dixon added. "It's your choice."

Lou accepted Dixon's offer and opted to receive a percentage of ownership in the proposed hotel in Punta Chivato. Lou was excited about the prospect of adding another resort hotel to his legacy in Baja.

Dixon Collins was eager to return home and tell Barbara the news. As he climbed into his plane, he said, "Lou, I guess you better tell Bastida and Yee that they're out of luck."

Lou rolled his eyes and watched as Dixon's plane headed northward. He did not appreciate doing Dixon's dirty work. Begrudgingly, Lou set out to locate his friends once again, this time anticipating their not-so-welcome reaction.

"Gilbert, I've got some bad news for you," Lou said when he found the chef. "Dixon just came back from México City. They checked the records and had never heard of you or Bastida." He explained that Dixon now had papers signed by the president himself.

"Gilbert blew his top," Lou later recalled. "He wanted to kill Dixon. Since Dixon wasn't there, he got mad at me." Lou tried to calm Gilbert down, telling him not to blame Dixon but his own government. Lou recalled what happened next. "Bastida went to a government office in Hermosillo or Guaymas, I forget which, and put an embargo on the property, which means we couldn't build. Well, after we got a hold of our big attorney, he goes to the offices in México City, and the embargo went out the window. They said, 'Build.' So, we built."

Chapter 7

HOTEL PLANS & CHALLENGES

That night, after Dixon left, Lou had difficulty sleeping. All he could think about was Punta Chivato. *Where would they find water for the resort? How would they get construction materials to the site? Where would they find enough men willing to work in the desolate area?* His mind was awhirl contemplating the immense task ahead of him.

Back in California, Dixon wasted no time contacting an architectural firm in Beverly Hills, B.A. Burkess and Associates. Collaborating with architect Bill Dalziel, Dixon and Barbara discussed their ideas for the hotel. They flew the architect to Punta Chivato to look at the site and determine how best to configure the hotel on the bluff. He drew up plans for a 20-unit resort consisting of ten rooms on either side of a large restaurant and bar. The buildings would be angled so that each room and the restaurant faced the sea.

Dixon returned to Mulegé and met with Lou, showing him the plans. "This is what I want, Lou. Take a good look at them and let me know if you can handle this."

Lou felt insulted that Dixon would doubt his abilities. *Hadn't he seen the hotel in Mulegé? Didn't Dixon realize Lou could manage another hotel project?* Lou desired more than anything to have a second chance to be part of a grand resort. Dixon and Barbara had the money to spend, and Lou wanted to be the one who made their dream resort a reality.

But Lou knew constructing a hotel at Punta Chivato presented a bigger challenge than anything he had faced building the resort in Mulegé. Rolling up the plans, Lou tucked them securely under his arm. "I'll look them over tonight and let you know," Lou said with an air of confidence. He did not want to let Dixon think he had any doubts about the project. Lou walked down the hill, searching for his friend Ricardo. If anyone could figure out how to build the hotel, it would be Ricardo.

Ricardo Acosta Munguía was a man of simple means but unique talent, especially when it came to construction. Before coming to Mulegé, he had lived with his wife and children in Ensenada, in

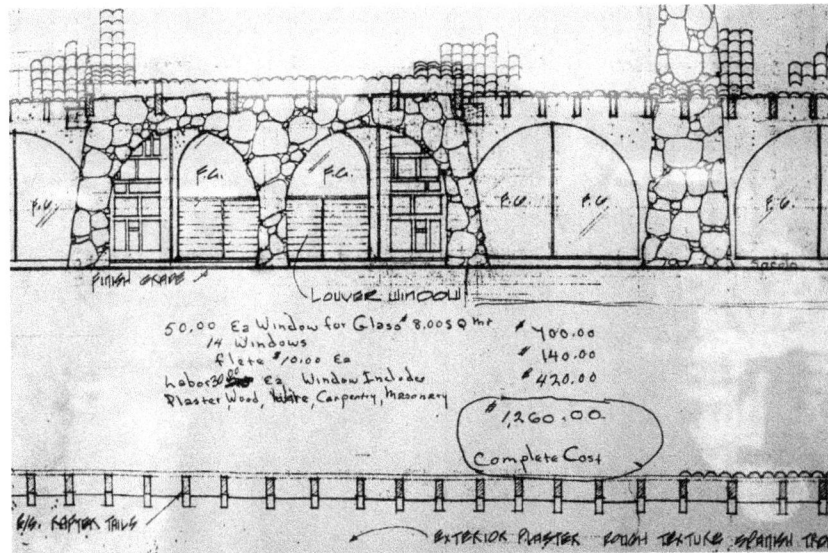

Part of original plans for Dixon's hotel at Punta Chivato with signature arches.
Courtesy Greg Joy (photo of plaque on hotel wall)

northern Baja on the Pacific side. Although not formally educated, Ricardo quickly learned the construction trade and became sought after as a builder. Lou had hired Ricardo to help with the construction at Hotel Loma Linda in Mulegé.

"Hello, my friend," Ricardo said, greeting Lou at the door of his modest home.

Ricardo and his family had grown particularly fond of the Italian with the Texan hat and friendly smile, and Lou had made a favorable impression on Ricardo's youngest children. Lou went out of his way to make the children feel important, often giving them candy or a ride in his jeep.

Lou unrolled the blueprints and laid them on the dirt floor. "These are the plans for Dixon's resort," Lou explained. "I need your input."

Over the next several hours, the two men carefully looked over each page of the plans. The Mexican nodded as Lou translated English words into Spanish and converted measurements from feet and inches into the metric equivalent. Lou could sense that Ricardo was getting as excited as he was about the project.

"This might be our big chance, buddy," Lou said, patting his friend on the back. Lou knew they would be known for miles around if he and Ricardo could pull this off. They would go down in history for building a famous resort.

Ricardo realized the resort presented him with an opportunity to reestablish his reputation as a master builder. He could still recall the day in Ensenada when he found out his oldest daughter was pregnant. He could no longer hold his head up in a town where he was once respected. Disgraced, Ricardo, his wife, and their four children piled into an old station wagon. They traveled more than 500 miles south, crossing the Baja peninsula and eventually ending up in Mulegé. Now in his thirties, Ricardo hoped to start over.

Ricardo and Lou talked into the night about the logistics of building the hotel, including finding water, a work crew, and bringing in materials.

"I told Dixon not to think of building until he found water. But he wouldn't listen to me," said Lou. "The closest water I know of is the half-mile-long freshwater lagoon about six miles to the north."

"You mean that place next to the sea?" Ricardo asked. Although he had never gone there, Ricardo had heard of the spring-fed slough walled off from the sea by a sandbar.

"Yeah, that's the one. There's no road out there, but I've pulled my boat up on the sandbar and gone hunting in that lagoon.

"We'd have to figure some way to get water from there to the site. Maybe build a road and truck the water in. At least we could use that until we dug us a well," Lou said, thinking aloud. "Do you suppose we're going to have any problem finding guys who are willing to come out there and work for us?"

"I think once we get the word out, we'll have more men than we need," Ricardo replied as he got up. He lit a cigarette and started pacing the room. "The only problem will be finding enough first-class carpenters and masons. And we'll have to provide housing," he added. "We can't expect them to travel back and forth on foot every day."

They decided to start by building tar-paper huts to house their workers and tools. A separate shack could serve as a "restaurant" for feeding the crew.

"I can ask my sister-in-law, Pedra, if she'd be willing to come out and supervise the cooking," Ricardo offered. "She needs a job and is a pretty good cook."

"She'll have to have some help," Lou remarked with a chuckle. "It's no easy job keeping up with a hungry crew."

Ricardo Acosta. Courtesy Yolanda Acosta Mesa

"What about building materials?" Ricardo inquired, suddenly changing the subject. Although he knew finding water and a crew were important, he was more interested in discussing the building project. "Are there stones nearby?" asked Ricardo, pointing to the plans that specified large rocks for the walls and majestic sweeping archways.

"Unfortunately, no," Lou answered. "The only place I know where we can get that much rock is at the quarry," a pit approximately two miles inland from Mulegé. Stones from this quarry were used to construct the hotel in Mulegé. "We'd have to get trucks up there like we did before and bring it down. Maybe we could find a way to haul it over by boat."

"It's going to require a lot of boat trips," Ricardo smiled. "Look at these plans. Rocks everywhere."

Lou knew there were many issues to work out, but he was not about to give up before getting started. The more he and Ricardo talked, the more their excitement grew. By the end of the evening, both knew that as crazy as it seemed, they wanted to tackle the project. It was late when Lou finally left; he could hear the familiar crowing of a rooster.

Chapter 8

OBSTACLES

The following day, Lou approached Dixon in the dining room at Club Aero Mulegé as he was sipping coffee and waiting for breakfast. Lou was tired but did not want to let on that he and Ricardo had been up much of the night discussing the hotel.

"When do you want to start?" Lou said, laying the plans on the table and pulling out a chair for himself.

"So, you think you can do it?" Dixon asked.

"Sure, but there's going to be some things to work out first, Dixon. I'm going to need a bulldozer to move that snow cone of sand so we can lay down a foundation," Lou said, referring to the massive dune on the bluff. Although they had not used any heavy equipment to construct the hotel in Mulegé, instead relying solely on men with picks and shovels, Lou figured it would take years to level the building site at Punta Chivato by hand. "And we'll need to build a road so we can bring in a crew and materials…and, of course, there's still the problem of getting water…"

"Hey, my brother-in-law manages a Caterpillar company in Long Beach," Dixon interrupted, afraid Lou would go off on the water issue again. "I bet he could get a used tractor for me."

"That's great, Dixon, but we've got to figure out how to get it down here," Lou replied, getting frustrated by Dixon's air of nonchalance. Perhaps Dixon thought anything was possible if one had money.

Through his contacts with former guests at the hotel in Mulegé, Lou was able to arrange transport to Punta Chivato for the heavy equipment. The guests were executives from the Kaiser Gypsum Company in Oakland, California, a business that would be instrumental in constructing the resort.

In the early 1920s, a gypsum (calcium sulfate) deposit was discovered on the island of San Marcos,[29] ten miles north of Punta Chivato Point. The barren island across from Santa Rosalía was small, measuring only 5-1/2 miles from north to south, a total of

12 square miles. Hearing of the excellent source of gypsum, the Kaiser Company decided to investigate. They eventually built a gypsum mining operation on the island, extracting the white rock and exporting it to the United States to make drywall.[30]

Peter Gerhard and Howard E. Gulick described the operation in *Lower California Guidebook*, published in 1970.

The gypsum is quarried both from the surface and from an intricate system of tunnels, moved to a long T-shaped pier by means of a narrow-gauge railroad, and loaded onto vessels by a belt conveyor and chutes.

The *USS Kaiser Gypsum* sailed out of Long Beach down the coasts of California and Baja, around the tip of the peninsula and northward into the Sea of Cortez. When it reached San Marcos Island midway up Baja's eastern coast, the vessel docked at the pier. There, they pumped water out of the ship's ballast tanks into reservoirs for use by the Mexican mining employees and their families, who lived in a small settlement in the southwest corner of the island. In 1950, the population of the island was 268.

"I know you'll think I'm crazy," Lou said when he finally got in touch with the Kaiser officials he had befriended in Mulegé, "but I need to bring down some equipment to use on another hotel project. Any chance we could work out a way to transport it on your ship?"

Lou was elated when the Kaiser executives agreed to transport the heavy equipment from Long Beach and offered to do it free of charge. The only catch was that Lou would have to find a way to get the equipment from San Marcos Island to Punta Chivato.

Dixon contacted his brother-in-law at Caterpillar and purchased used heavy equipment for the hotel project. He bought a D-6 Caterpillar tractor, two flatbed trucks, a backhoe, a dirt compactor, large generators, a welding machine, a water tank truck, Boston Whalers, and two World War II landing site craft with small, 671-diesel engines. The *USS Kaiser Gypsum* carried equipment for the hotel venture on every trip she made to San Marcos Island.

Lou also spoke with a local Mexican in the nearby town of Santa Rosalía, who was willing to rent him a WWII barge for $300.[31] This huge platform formerly held the drilling cranes used to build the docks at Santa Rosalía's harbor. Lou intended to use this to transport the equipment from San Marcos to Punta Chivato. However, since the barge had no power of its own, it needed to be towed from the island to the building site.

When the first load of equipment arrived aboard the *USS Kaiser Gypsum*, Lou was waiting with a crew at the San Marcos Island pier. The men lashed the barge to the ship and unloaded the goods. It was a slow, grueling process.

The WWII landing crafts and Boston Whalers were lowered from the ship into the water using a winch. The plan was to use these to tow the barge to Punta Chivato. But they lost the motor when the hull of one landing craft hit the pier's pilings. Fortunately, they salvaged the vessel and used it as a barge. As dangerous as the operation was, there were surprisingly few such mishaps and no loss of life.

Moving the other cargo from the ship to the barge also had its nail-biting moments. First, they had to wait until the Kaiser employees made the water-gypsum transfer. As the water emptied from the ship, its deck would become level with the barge. The timing had to be accurate. As they transferred equipment from the boat to the barge, there was the chance a cable would break or a motor would quit.

Dixon remembers paying $100 to a worker to drive the bulldozer from the ship onto the barge. "The job required perfect timing. He had to make it there before it tipped and dumped into the ocean. It was all calculated ahead of time, drawn out with chalk exactly where it had to be. It was nerve-wracking and exciting as the Mexican successfully drove the machine onto the barge. Very exciting!"

The workers attached the equipment-laden barge to the WWII landing craft by cable and slowly towed it through the sea toward Punta Chivato. This trip often took four to five hours. Once they reached the cove near the proposed building site, they offloaded the vehicles and supplies onto a rocky ramp they built up around the barge.

As word spread of the American's intent to build a hotel at Punta Chivato, many local Mexicans became skeptical. How could it be accomplished? There was not even a road leading out to that

Barge arrives at Punta Chivato with construction equipment used to build hotel. Courtesy Lou Federico

remote point. Some began to refer to it as *Punta Loca* (Crazy Point). Others hoped it would offer an opportunity for work.

Men from the surrounding towns of Mulegé, San Bruno, Santa Rosalía, San José de Magdalena, and even as far north as San Ignacio came searching for jobs. Some arrived on burros or horseback, others by sea. A few even arrived on foot. One of these was Enrique, who later became one of the cooks. Starting from Mulegé with a bottle of water strapped over his shoulder, he followed the coastline northward, fording an estuary south of the building site. "I felt sorry for him," Lou remarked, recalling the miles Enrique had walked, "but nevertheless, this is what was going on."

The men created a makeshift village consisting of tar-paper shacks with dirt floors. The workers slept on cots or directly on the sandy beach. "Some slept in their cars," remembers Yolanda Acosta, Ricardo's daughter. "Some middle-class people who had good cars drove back and forth to work."

Barrels inserted into hand-dug holes served as make-shift latrines. Later, they used jackhammers to dig holes in the rock for septic tanks and leach lines to serve the hotel.

A crude shack functioned as a "restaurant" near the building site. Ricardo's sister-in-law, Pedra, was hired as head cook and had a crew of two women and two men. One of the men, nicknamed Bocho, which means "brainy," was tall, muscular, and dark-skinned. Most of the workers avoided him when it became evident he was homosexual. Per Yolanda, other men who worked on the hotel were homosexuals.

The workers cleared land south of the proposed hotel location for an airport runway. After removing the cacti, desert brush, and rocks, the naturally-level strip was ready for a trial landing. Dixon was the first to land. Piloting his twin-engine Cessna Skymaster with big balloon tires, he easily touched down on the strip. He parked at the east end of the runway, turned off his engine, and walked up the slight incline to the building site.

"Dixon," Lou shouted, waving his arms. He had seen the plane come in and was anxious to hear what Dixon thought of the runway.

"A little bumpy but not too bad," said the pilot. "Wasn't sure I'd make it here before sundown." He and Lou shook hands. "Might be a good idea to eventually get some lights up along that runway," Dixon added.

"Sure, Dixon," mumbled Lou. Although it was illegal to fly at night in México, Lou figured that, as far as Dixon was concerned, rules did not matter here.

"¿*Señor* Collins?"

Dixon turned toward the unfamiliar voice. A worker extended his hand. "My name is Luis Sui Qui," he said, "I am happy to meet you. I am the one responsible for grading your runway."

The man was tall and muscular. His short, dark, cropped hair stood out from his head. He had straight, narrow, Asian-like eyes. Dixon was intrigued not only by the man's unusual appearance but also by his air of self-confidence.

"You do good work, Sui Qui," Dixon responded. "Glad to have you on board."

Sui Qui, one of the toughest men around, was born to a Chinese father and a Mexican mother. They raised him in San José de Magdalena, a small farming village in the mountains south of Santa Rosalía. His father was a farmer and a local healer. He practiced Chinese medicine, creating concoctions that were unfamiliar to the Mexicans.

Luis Sui Qui was proud of his Chinese heritage, but the other children often teased him when he was a young boy. As a result, he quickly developed defenses. He got into a fistfight with anyone who called him "*chino*," the Spanish word for Chinese.

Sui Qui was smart and learned how to get what he wanted. He planned to gain Dixon's respect and admiration. Introducing himself to the American was the first step. Although Lou oversaw personnel, Sui Qui knew Dixon was the one responsible for his weekly wages.

When it became time to clear the hotel foundation site, a young Mexican from the Cuesta family in Mulegé operated the backhoe to level the area. He removed truckloads of sand from the large, distinctive dune near the water's edge, drove it into the desert, and dumped it. This process took over a month to complete. When he finally cleared the site, construction of the hotel could begin.

Chapter 9

HOTEL CONSTRUCTION

It was a calm, sunny day in 1965 when Dixon Collins stepped up to address over one hundred men gathered at the newly leveled building site at Punta Chivato. The construction phase of the hotel was about to commence. Although Dixon had put Lou Federico in charge of supervising the Mexican personnel, he decided to fly down from Southern California to personally give the men a pep talk before the work began. Dixon's stature was intimidating, and the workers quickly became quiet and turned their attention toward the American.

"The hotel you are about to build will be unmatched in all of Baja," Dixon announced. "When it is done, you will have been a part of what many thought was impossible—the construction of a resort on Punta Chivato Point. You will have reason to be proud, and so will your family for generations to come."

Dixon continued to elaborate on the merits of the project. But as he looked out over the sea of brown faces, he noticed a glazed look in their eyes. Suddenly, it dawned on him: They had not understood a word—he was speaking English to Spanish-speaking Mexicans! As Dixon quickly wrapped up, he heard clapping. It started slowly at first, but soon, all the men began applauding. Sui Qui made sure of it. Dixon nodded to the men as he turned from the crowd. Not one to be embarrassed, he merely made a mental note that he should learn Spanish.

Much of the building material for the hotel was purchased from the Llano-Zaragoza family store in Guaymas on mainland México. Dixon's Mexican friend, Octavio Llano, who had helped him buy Punta Chivato earlier, participated in the family business. Some surmised Dixon felt an obligation to his friend. "Octavio was very rich with a big, big store," recounted a later employee at the hotel, "lots and lots of material was brought in."

They ferried construction supplies, including concrete, rebar, and lumber, across the Sea of Cortez from Guaymas to Santa Rosalía. Then, they loaded the material onto two flatbed trucks and transported it to Punta Chivato. Since there was no road, this journey was rough and slow.

"We put commercial 727 airplane tires on our flatbed trucks in order to drive building supplies over the sand dunes prior to building our road," Dixon recalled. Initially, they attached dual tires to the back axle. However, rocks got between the tires and chewed them up. After refitting them with single tires, the trucks traveled more easily.

When Dixon received the bill for the material purchased from Octavio's store, he complained it was "too much money," according to one employee. He said when Dixon could not come up with the money to pay the bills, Octavio replied, "O.K., I'm a partner of the hotel now." Dixon had no recourse but to accept Octavio's demand to assume part ownership to pay the debt.[32]

"God knows what Octavio Llano made out of this thing," said Lou Federico in a later interview. "He's not going to tell the truth. I'd love to know the truth. I'd like to know how Octavio came out on this thing."

As Lou had earlier suggested to Ricardo Acosta, the large rocks used in the hotel's construction at Punta Chivato came from a quarry inland of Mulegé.

"We hauled them by truck to the little wharf there at Mulegé," Dixon recounted. "The rocks were loaded into our WWII landing craft. These were like the kind you saw on Iwo Jima, bringing in the guys to the beach; the ramp would go down on the front. Once filled with rock, the crafts traveled the twelve miles by sea from Mulegé over to Punta Chivato, where we'd flop down the front, and the workers would hand-carry them to a truck onshore and haul them up to the hotel."

The landing barges also transported bricks from Mulegé to the building site. Often, they arrived broken, especially if the seas were rough. Workers solved this problem by constructing a kiln from the surviving bricks. Then, they brought in mud and poured it into molds, which were stacked in the kiln. Locally gathered ironwood provided fuel to bake the bricks.

Dixon remembered one unfortunate setback. "After 65,000 bricks had been made, a chubasco came and dumped ten inches of rain in an hour. After it passed, the stacks looked like piles of lumps. The tedious process had to begin all over."

Ricardo Acosta Munguía, the man with whom Lou Federico initially shared Dixon's hotel plans, was hired as the chief builder. Lou felt fortunate his friend agreed to take on this challenge and was confident Ricardo could get the job done. However, Ricardo needed workers, and few of the local Mexicans had experience or knowledge. "We had a real good crew but needed a bigger one with some skills," Lou recalled. So, they hired first-class carpenters and masons from Guaymas, a city 92 miles to the northeast across the Sea of Cortez. Although they earned a higher wage than the general laborers, these men initially shared the primitive living conditions of the peons.

Ricardo was not only a talented carpenter and mason, but he also was innovative. Nothing seemed too difficult for him. If they did not have the tools to do a job, Ricardo fabricated them using materials he had on hand. He supervised the construction of the huge archways that would give the hotel its unique appearance. They built forms, filled them with broken roof tiles and brick, and then poured concrete inside. After the concrete had dried, they removed the forms, textured the exterior surface, and painted it white. Ricardo often questioned the building plans. But when he offered suggestions for improvements, Lou told him to follow the plans drawn up by the Beverly Hills firm. More than once, things later had to be torn apart and redone, as Ricardo had earlier advised.

Hotel construction with signature archways. Courtesy Lou Federico

Rather than stay at Punta Chivato, Lou commuted daily from his home in Mulegé. Every morning, he took his Boston Whaler with its 17-hp Evinrude engine north across the bay. His black Labrador Retriever, *Amigo*, often stood on the bow during the 12-mile trip as if pointing the way. Since the morning waters were generally flat, Lou could crank up the speed and arrive at Punta Chivato in less than thirty minutes. "The water was like a lake," said Lou. "It was a beautiful ride."

The winds often kicked up at the end of the workday, and the trip home took longer. If the waters were too rough, Lou stayed overnight at Punta Chivato in a small office space built for him west of the hotel.

Ricardo also made the daily trip to the job site from Mulegé. As dedicated as he was to his work, Ricardo was equally dedicated to his family, which soon grew to ten children—four sons and six daughters. Ricardo felt it was important to be at home with his family in the evenings. Although he occasionally got a ride with Lou on the Boston Whaler, he usually made the daily trip in a red jeep loaned to him. Before the sun rose, he began the arduous journey along bumpy dirt roads from Mulegé to the building site at Punta Chivato. The drive was said to take him four hours one way. After a long day of strenuous work, Ricardo would climb back into the jeep and head home. This dedication did not go unnoticed by his children, who counted on their father's return every night. One of his daughters, Yolanda, was always proud to see her father coming down the road driving the red jeep.

One day, Ricardo arrived at work and noticed several bags of cement were missing. To discourage further theft, he decided to spend nights at Punta Chivato. Ricardo slept on a cot in a small building behind the construction site.

When Ricardo spent more time at the work site, his wife often visited him. Taking a flat-bottomed panga from Mulegé, she brought their baby, Victor, and teenage daughter, Yolanda. Yolanda was responsible for watching Victor so he would not get in the way. Ricardo kept a vigilant eye on Yolanda. He knew the girl's presence would not go unnoticed by the crew of 100-plus men.

Yolanda could not help but notice all the excitement around her. She loved her father's Italian friend, Lou Federico, who smiled and patted her on the head whenever he passed by. However, she hid when Dixon Collins was around. The big man was businesslike and serious and ignored the teenager. Yolanda assumed he did not like children. She watched from a distance, proud to see that the owner often conferred with her father. Although the two men knew only a few words of the other's native language, they could somehow communicate.

Dixon was absent from Punta Chivato during the week, but practically every weekend, he flew down in his twin-engine plane to inspect the progress. Sometimes, his girlfriend, Barbara, her three children, and Dixon's mother, Sibyl, flew down with him. He also sometimes arrived with women he simply introduced as "friends." Departing from Brackett Field, located near his hilltop home on 25 acres in West Covina, Dixon flew his Cessna Skymaster straight across the border without stopping until he touched down on the dirt strip at Punta Chivato. On the reverse trip, he did the same—flying straight back without clearing customs at the border.

While the hotel was under construction, Dixon and his family or guests slept in a large, wood-framed, black, tar-paper warehouse behind the hotel site. Lou hired one of Ricardo's older sons to manage the warehouse, which was called a *bodega*. As big as a house, the structure stored building materials, wheelbarrows, the radio-telephone system, and two big International Harvester generators used to produce all the electricity. Dixon often preferred to take his cot outside and sleep under the stars.

Construction of bodega behind hotel. Courtesy Lou Federico

The workers were happy to see Dixon arrive at the end of each week because he brought money to pay them. Ricardo kept track of the number of hours or piecework completed by each worker. He gave these figures to Jorge Anaya, their bookkeeper/accountant in Mulegé. Jorge showed Lou his calculations for the accrued labor and materials expenses. Then Lou called Dixon using a special radio in his Toyota pickup and told him how much money to bring down. By merely pounding a stake in the ground anywhere on the property, Lou could talk to Dixon in California.

Lou had previously dealt with Jorge and his brother, Rafael, when they worked as bookkeepers for the hotel in Mulegé. Lou had recommended Jorge as a man who was "good with figures and trust-worthy." Lou and Jorge became close friends, and Jorge often accompanied Lou on the Boston Whaler to the work site.

"O.K., Dixon, this is what you've got to bring down because you owe this much for that and the other thing," Lou recalled telling Dixon. "Anytime Dixon wanted to look at the records, all he had to do was take a look...I knew Dixon could trust him [Jorge]."[33]

Jorge's brother, Rafael, was considered a big man in the ejido in Mulegé. He was also known to be "the biggest gay in the whole area." According to Ricardo's teenage daughter, Yolanda, Jorge was also gay.

"I was in love with him, and then I found out that he was gay," said Yolanda, referring to Jorge. "He was the most well-dressed man."

Jorge's sexual preference did not matter to Lou. "I don't know whether he was gay or not," he said. "I kind of think he might have been, but he never gave me any indication of that." Lou described Jorge as "a high-class Mexican kid."

Unlike the construction workers, Lou Federico was not always pleased to see Dixon Collins. Often, his arrival spelled trouble for Lou. During the week, Lou was the man in charge, but when Dixon was there, Lou had to take a back seat. He resented being treated like one of the workers by the big man. Putting up with Dixon was tougher in Lou's mind than the physical demands of building the hotel. Often, they got into arguments, but Dixon ultimately got his way. He was the one, after all, who was financing the project.

"He was there just enough to screw everything up," recalled

Lou. "You know, building this hotel was so difficult. I don't know of another hotel anywhere that was more difficult than this because of where it was. You had to go by water, and then you got to build a rough road to get in. And then you got to put up with Dixon every weekend. I don't know what was tougher. I think it was tougher putting up with him. Because we'd go at it real good."

An unexpected visitor landed at the building site one day, an American named Jack Heron. He was a skinny, quiet fellow who ran an automotive garage in Merced, California. Some say the pressure of the business finally got to him. On the verge of a nervous breakdown, a friend suggested Jack take a trip to Punta Chivato. There, he offered his skills as a mechanic, but Jack's single-engine plane was just as valuable. With an airplane on hand, Lou no longer depended upon Dixon's weekend visits to get supplies. "I liked Jack," Lou recalled. "He stayed with us for a long time." Lou would eventually depend on Jack's help in ways he could never have imagined.

Two other major projects were simultaneously underway while the hotel was being constructed: bringing in potable water and building a road to access the main connector between Santa Rosalía and Mulegé. "We were building this hotel prior to piping in water," Lou recalled.

Getting water to the hotel site was vital to the venture's success. Lou and Ricardo knew of only one source of fresh water—a lagoon on the coast six miles to the north near Rancho San Marcos Tierra. Luis Sui Qui oversaw clearing a roadway to link the slough to the building site. With a crew of thirty men, he supervised this task. Using crude picks and shovels, the men removed cacti, palo verde trees, and desert brush from the coastal dunes. The job seemed never-ending, but Sui Qui drove the men forward.

The half-mile-long lagoon, surrounded by lush greenery and tall palm trees, was well-known as an ideal spot for hunting ducks, geese, doves, and quail. It was also known for catching pargo fish. The mouth of the lagoon was separated from the sea by a sandbar. At the upper end, it was spring-fed. If the tide was high, the slough might connect to the Sea of Cortez. Consequently, the water was salty at the top but was fresh and good for drinking near the bottom.

Lagoon north of Punta Chivato where water was initially obtained for the hotel, also popular for fishing and hunting. Courtesy Mike Morse

When the road crew finally reached the slough, they built a concrete and rock holding tank with a wooden lid at the water's edge. This structure kept the local cows from drinking out of that section.

With the road and holding tank in place, the next challenge was transporting the water to the building site. A small Homelite gas-driven pump inserted through the lid of the holding tank siphoned the water into a truck brought down on the barge from California. The precious water was then slowly transported to the building site. The trip took several hours one way, and water often sloshed out of a hole in the top of the truck's tank. At times, it arrived with only half its original load. The water that made it safely to Punta Chivato was initially stored in the truck. However, a reservoir (*pila*) was eventually built on the top of the hill behind the construction site. The water tanker was then able to empty its contents into the reservoir for storage.

Although an immediate answer to the water problem had been found, Lou continued to worry. Rainfall was sparse in this desert land, and unless a chubasco arrived, the prospect of having enough water was uncertain.

Eventually, Luis Sui Qui oversaw a well-digging crew. The men dug numerous wells by hand, some as deep as thirty feet. Cave-ins occurred, and men came close to losing their lives, all in search of water. But every time, they came up empty. The lagoon was the only source of fresh water they would find.

With a link between the hotel and the lagoon established, Sui Qui and his crew focused on clearing a road connecting Punta Chivato to the unpaved main road between Santa Rosalía and Mulegé. The desert terrain varied, consisting of sand dunes in some areas and vegetation in others.

Starting at the lagoon, Sui Qui's crew continued the road northwest. Before reaching the coastal villages of San Rafael and San Bruno, they turned the road westward, veering around or removing the distinctive Baja vegetation: Cholla, giant cardón cacti, spiny shrubs, low-spreading elephant trees, and palo verde trees bearing distinctive green trunks and branches. In one area, they followed a dry, rocky riverbed.

Painstakingly, Sui Qui's crew manually cleared 18 miles of road using picks and shovels. When they reached the main dirt road that connected Santa Rosalía to the north with Mulegé to the south, they marked the turnoff to the resort with white-washed rocks. Although the building site was now connected to the primary roadway, the 18-mile journey was still slow. It took several hours to travel one way on the rugged, dusty road.

Transporting building supplies from the United States to Punta Chivato remained no easy task. "We drove from San Diego, and it took about two weeks," Dixon said. "It was nothing but a dirt road, 500 miles of dirt road. It was unbelievable." Traveling along these roads was dangerous. Not only was the road unpaved, it was narrow. There were no service stations or tire shops along the way, and drivers had to be prepared to manage emergencies. After delivering the goods, the drivers turned north and headed back. The round trip could take up to a month.

Some materials that survived the long drive from the border did not last long once they reached the building site. Such was the case for big, plate-glass dining room windows ordered from San Diego. Arriving safely at Punta Chivato, workers carefully unloaded the glass and placed it on the sand. There, the panes were stored, propped up by 2x4s. One day, while Dixon was at the construction site, he noticed a worker shoveling sand into a wheelbarrow right by the windows. Before he could stop him, the windows fell, and every panel of glass shattered. Dixon got on the phone and ordered another batch of windows. Several weeks later, the new panels arrived. This time, they survived both the drive and the workers.

Most of the crew disliked and feared Luis Sui Qui. Some thought he was crazy, while others called him *"arma de dos pilos"* or two-faced, never knowing whose side he was on. He had a gruff disposition and intimidated the men by always carrying a .45 caliber pearl-handled pistol. Sui Qui became physically abusive at times, not hesitating to hit workers if they did not do what he asked.

Lou grew distrustful of the road-crew foreman, whose presence seemed larger than his own. He suspected Sui Qui was jealous of his position and wanted to undermine Lou and his relationship with Dixon. Lou felt the Chinese-Mexican was constantly trying to cut his throat and cause problems for him. He knew Sui Qui was one of Bastida's best friends, Bastida, the man who initially told Lou he held the title to Punta Chivato. Bastida was still angry that Dixon was able to acquire the land directly from the government. Maybe he was getting back at Lou through Sui Qui.

Luis Sui Qui was unafraid to express his opinions to anyone, even Dixon Collins. One incident involved the tiles Dixon chose to use in the hotel restaurant. The design was made in a little factory in Tlaquepaque, just south of Guadalajara on mainland México. Dixon took a sample tile to Tree Wax, an American company, and asked how to best treat the surface. They suggested a particular type of wax. However, when Dixon took it down to Punta Chivato, Sui Qui disagreed.

"No, no. I'll show you how to do this," he said. "This is our country. I'll show you how to do it." Sui Qui proceeded to mix regular wax 50/50 with diesel oil. Then, he painted the tiles with the mixture. The result was a beautiful, burnished leather look. All the tiles, including those used on the deck, were sealed with Sui Qui's unique concoction.

As much as Lou Federico warned Dixon Collins about Sui Qui's true intentions, the owner refused to listen. Luis Sui Qui had made a strong effort to endear himself to Dixon early on.[34] As a result,

Dixon would usually side with this outspoken worker. Before completing the hotel, Sui Qui's strong personality would prove too harsh and abrasive for Lou Federico and Ricardo Acosta, key players in the hotel construction.

Chapter 10

HOTEL NEARS COMPLETION

As the stylish hotel perched on the promontory overlooking the Sea of Cortez neared completion, the nickname "*Punta Loca*" quickly faded away. The impressive structure stood as an oasis in the desert. It consisted of ten suites adjoining a large dining room and bar and surrounded by lush landscaping. Green grass planted in imported soil was a unique sight in the arid region. Palms arrived from Mulegé on the same WWII landing crafts used to transport rock to build the hotel.

Panels to construct large, high-quality walk-in coolers for the kitchen were flown in from the United States in C-46 Commando transport planes and assembled at the building site. High-end poly-vinyl chloride (PVC) pipe was purchased for plumbing. When the prefabricated "plumbing trees" arrived, they were positioned and set in concrete.

Dixon's girlfriend, Barbara, chose Spanish colonial-style furnishings to complement the modern colonial architecture. Purchased in México City, the furniture, doors, rugs, bedspreads, and other accessories were first shipped to La Paz. From there, a WWII landing craft brought the goods north along the Baja coast to Punta Chivato. A ramp constructed in the harbor south of the hotel made offloading from the sea easier.

Before the resort was officially open for business, thirteen months after construction had begun, Americans began inquiring if they could stay at the new hotel. Many guests at Hotel Mulegé had grown dissatisfied with its new ownership. Although Hotel Serenidad, the other fly-in resort in Mulegé, was in operation, staying in Dixon's new resort at Punta Chivato appealed to sportsmen and those who wanted a remote getaway.

In addition to fishermen, wealthy hunters were enticed to come to Baja in search of the prized Desert Bighorn, *Borrego de Oro*, literally Golden Sheep. Inhabiting the rugged mountains above Conception Bay, this species of bighorn sheep was considered one of the four rarest in existence. Dixon, an avid huntsman himself, welcomed these hunters to stay at the hotel. Among the visitors were Harvey Gross, from Harvey's Wagon Wheel casino across the California state line in South Lake Tahoe; the Shah of Iran's brother; Steve Rhodes of the Biltmore Art Gallery in Beverly Hills; and Otis Chandler, from the *Los Angeles Times*.[35]

Otis Chandler had a passion for hunting big game and eagerly looked forward to the opportunity to add to his collection of sheep by landing a Desert Bighorn.[36] He loved physical challenges of all kinds. When Lou's wife, Lana Federico, one day spotted Otis Chandler walking along the beach at Punta Chivato collecting shells for his wife, she exclaimed, "Oh my god, what a hunk!" Chandler's 6'3," 220-pound athletic physique was hard not to notice!

Eventual pool site next to hotel dining area. Courtesy Lou Federico

As the hotel neared completion, Dixon's accountants and attorney from México City voiced concern over the mounting expenses. They were unable to account for all the money spent. When Dixon demanded his accountants juggle the figures, they got angry. "We don't need this problem," they said, returning cartons of financial files to him. Lou speculated Dixon was slipping Barbara's inheritance money into his own pocket.

Dixon's attorney called a meeting one afternoon at the Serenidad Hotel in Mulegé. Barbara, Lou, and the Mexican attorney attended. Dixon was not invited.

"What's this about?" Barbara asked, showing more anger than concern in her voice.

"It's about the hotel and the funds. We thought you should know...."

"Stop right there," she interrupted. "If you have any concerns, talk to Dixon."

Barbara abruptly excused herself from the table, and the meeting ended. She was unaware of Dixon's spending practices and didn't care to be informed. No one had the guts to dispute her. As she walked away, the men merely looked at each other. Blind faith. At least they had tried to warn her.

Dixon was spending Barbara's money before their marriage, which did not occur until January 6, 1966, in Riverside, California. Barbara was 41 years of age. Dixon was 30.

The total cost of building and furnishing the new hotel was difficult to ascertain. When Dixon Collins, Lou Federico, and Don Johnson were asked about it, their answers varied.

Lou Federico calculated the total construction costs were "less than half a million dollars. That did not include Dixon's two planes, the boats, or the heavy equipment included in the inventory."

According to Dixon, "The whole investment at those times was like $150,000 to build the hotel. That would be like a million, two million dollars now. You couldn't build that thing now. My 210 [airplane] cost me $25,000 brand new. What's a 210 today?—$250,000. It's a different world now. And Mexican labor was really inexpensive. I think we paid people 80 cents a day. Cement and everything were really, really inexpensive. Mexican products were different."

Don Johnson remarked during an interview, "That hotel over there cost over a million dollars."

While Lou could do nothing about Dixon's financial situation, he still had a job to do. Overseeing personnel was not an easy task, especially when the workforce was predominantly male. Most of these workers caused no trouble for Lou. However, when Lou hired a group of bartenders from Guaymas, there were problems. One night, Lou was awakened by a loud knock on his door.

"Lou," shouted Luis Sui Qui. "Wake up."

Lou sleepily opened his door. There stood Sui Qui and a cook he had hired from Guaymas. Sui Qui was drunk and angry, and the cook seemed anxious.

"I want to go back. I want to get out of here," the cook whimpered. "This place is crazy."

"What's the matter now?" asked Lou, rubbing the sleep from his eyes.

"Come here, we'll show you," retorted Sui Qui.

The hotel had not officially opened, so Lou thought it would be no harm to let the clean-cut recruits from Guaymas reside in one of the hotel rooms. As they reached the end room, Sui Qui opened the door and switched on the lights.

Lou could not believe his eyes. An orgy was taking place among the new bartenders and several other male employees. He was most shocked seeing his skipper's two sons.

"You're fired," Lou shouted at the startled men. "You can all go back to Guaymas as far as I'm concerned. You're out of here." Lou then grabbed the two boys.

"I'm not going to tell your dad anything right now. You'd be in real big trouble. I'm going to keep my mouth shut, but if this happens one more time, he's going to hear about it." The boys quickly dressed and hurried back to their shacks.

One day following this incident, Sui Qui approached Lou. "I've got an idea," he said. "We need women out here. I know two prostitutes (*putas*) in Santa Rosalía, and I think we can get them out here. They'll take care of the crew, plus they're real nice gals. They'll work, they'll clean—they'll do anything you want. They'll make the rooms up."

Lou thought it was worth a try. He located the American, Jack Heron, who had his single-engine airplane parked on the dirt runway.

"Come on, Jack, we need you to fly us to Santa Rosalía," Lou stated. He knew Jack would be willing to do just about anything to help.

Jack, Sui Qui, and Lou boarded the plane, and Jack flew them the short distance north to Santa Rosalía. After landing at the small airport on top of a hill near the town cemetery, Sui Qui led the men down the knoll to a brothel.

It did not take any convincing to get several women to agree to the "job." They quickly packed their suitcases, secured them with rope, and followed the men up the hill to the plane.

The women turned out to be very likable. Not only did they please the crew, but they also worked hard scrubbing floors, cleaning showers, and making beds. One employee referred to them as "My Fair Ladies." "They worked hard both day and night!"

But the solution to the problem was short-lived. Within a few months, a couple of the men fell in love with the girls. They did not want anybody to touch "their women." Some of the men even talked about marriage.

Ricardo Acosta, the construction foreman, tried to shield his children from the questionable activities at Punta Chivato. Once, he ordered two of his sons and his teenage daughter, Yolanda, to return home to Mulegé when they were visiting him at the site. The boys were old enough to realize why their father was upset. But when 15-year-old Yolanda saw a red car full of ladies pull up to the hotel one day, she ran to the cook, her Aunt Pedra, for answers.

"Men have needs," Pedra simply replied. "Sometimes, they just need to be around women."

As the hotel neared completion, Ricardo Acosta suddenly quit his job as chief builder. His reason for leaving was not the prostitutes but his dislike of Luis Sui Qui. Ricardo could no longer tolerate watching how Sui Qui treated the other workers. Although he had a major supervisory role in the project, Ricardo always considered himself an equal to Sui Qui, who, on the other hand, had an air of superiority. Ricardo fumed whenever he saw Sui Qui strike another worker. *That is not the way to treat human beings*, he thought. Sui Qui was always trying to cause trouble, saying things he should not, trying to put ideas into the other workers' heads, and making up lies. One day, an argument arose between the two men. Ricardo spoke his mind and then called it quits. He left before anything terrible happened.

When Dixon learned of Ricardo's sudden departure, he went to Mulegé and begged him to return. Ricardo politely refused. "My father was very nice with everybody," Yolanda would later explain. "He didn't use bad language. He never did." Ricardo knew he could never return to Punta Chivato as long as Sui Qui was there. "My father was respectable. But Dixon didn't give him his place." Dixon had become too dependent upon Sui Qui to let the Chinese Mexican go.[37]

Lou commuted by boat from Mulegé to the building site throughout most of the construction period. However, when his wife, Lana, became pregnant and left to visit her family in San Francisco, California, Lou spent more nights at Punta Chivato.

One day, while in Punta Chivato, Lou received a disturbing call on the Unicom radio from his friend in Mulegé, Saúl Davis. Saúl was still an employee at Hotel Mulegé, taking over as manager after Lou left to join Dixon.

"Lou, someone is in your home," said Saúl, referring to Lou and Lana's home in Mulegé. "I think he's one of Cortes's men. They may be trying to take it over." Saúl knew Lou was not fond of Manuel Cortes, the government official from México City who got involved in Club Aero Mulegé.

Lou thanked Saúl and promised not to let on how he received the news. Then, with paperwork in hand, he drove to the county seat of Santa Rosalía to talk to the officials. Lou's documents included a contract with the Mulegé Ejido for the land where his house was built. However, as Lou had earlier discovered, possession of property in México can change hands overnight despite holding papers showing "proof of ownership." Lou and Lana lost their beloved home in Mulegé. Dave and Paula Galloway eventually moved in.

When pregnant Lana returned to Punta Chivato from San Francisco, she and Lou moved into one of the hotel rooms. In June 1966, Dixon flew Lana to Hermosillo on mainland México, where she gave birth to a baby girl. They named their daughter Luana, a combination of her parents' names, Lou and Lana.

Lana and the baby returned to San Francisco to stay with her mother while the hotel was being finished. Although Lou missed his wife and newborn child, he realized their comfort was important.

Chapter 11

TROUBLE WITH OFFICIALS

Dixon was cocky and often acted as if he were above the law, both in the United States and in México. On one return flight to California, Dixon found himself surrounded by men from United States customs and the Federal Bureau of Investigation (FBI). They ordered him out of his airplane and proceeded to inspect the contents of his aircraft. Dixon was carrying two old water heaters he planned to exchange. The officials suspected Dixon was transporting drugs into the United States, so there on the tarmac, they proceeded to cut the heaters apart. When nothing was found, they let Dixon go. This incident, however, did not curtail Dixon's habit of non-stop flying. It also was not the last time he was detained.

Although seafood was plentiful locally, produce, and other supplies were needed when guests arrived at Punta Chivato. Dixon chose to purchase such items from Octavio Llano's supermarket in Guaymas on mainland México. Loading up his plane, Dixon transported the goods across the Sea of Cortez. Lou accompanied Dixon on one such memorable trip. As the overloaded plane lifted off the short, dirt runway in Guaymas headed for Punta Chivato, they heard a "whoosh" as the bottom of the aircraft hit the tops of the eucalyptus trees at the end of the airstrip.

"You've got to be out of your gourd," Lou screamed. "I don't know what I'm doing with you. It's lucky we're both not dead."

Dixon chuckled. But the flight had just started, and Lou grew tenser seeing the Sea of Cortez only 100 yards below.

"What are you doing? We could troll at this height."

"I can't get this thing any higher," Dixon responded. "The plane's overloaded. I can't get any more altitude than what I've got."

As they neared the Baja coastline, the sun set behind the hills to the west. Dixon radioed the hotel on Unicom frequency 122.8. "Punta Chivato Unicom, I'm 15 minutes out, and it's getting dark. Better get some lights on the runway."

Although flying at night was illegal in Baja, Dixon frequently left late and arrived in Punta Chivato after dark. A worker parked a Toyota jeep at the beginning of the dirt strip with its lights shining down the runway so Dixon could find it. "We'd just line it up, and we'd come right over the top of the jeep—couldn't even see any of it; it was pitch black until we were just over it. But we knew how to do it. I just lined up with the lights," Dixon later recalled.

Dixon's mother, Sibyl, answered Dixon's call on the Unicom. After confirming the Toyota was on its way to provide lighting, she said, "Dixon, I'm worried. I think you're in big trouble. Inspectors are here, and they've loaded up their jeep with cases of your scotch. They're waiting for you."

Dixon Collins and his mother, Sibyl, during hotel construction.
"Off the Beaten Track in Baja" by Erle Stanley Gardner. 1967

Sibyl, a widow, was thrilled when Dixon invited her to move to Baja and help manage the hotel. Dixon sensed her need for a change, and she was eager to help. Sibyl took up residence in the third room from the kitchen and remained there even when Dixon and Barbara were back in California.

An intelligent, take-charge person, Sibyl quickly adapted to her new role. She inspected the tables, the bar, and the rooms for cleanliness and learned how to use the radio to converse with pilots. Although she never learned a word of Spanish, Dixon was impressed by how effectively his mother communicated with the workers. When Sibyl spoke, everyone listened, even Dixon.

Dixon knew he was committing two crimes the Mexican officials would not regard favorably. One was smuggling eighteen cases of contraband American scotch, which was now in the inspectors' hands. The other was landing his airplane on an unlit runway after dark.

Sibyl met the plane as it taxied to a stop and drove Lou and Dixon up to the hotel. "You better talk to them. They want to inspect other things, too."

Dixon quickly delegated, "See what you can do, Lou. Take care of it."

Lou knew it was up to him to get Dixon out of yet another jam. He cleverly engaged the officers in a game of pool in the hotel lounge.

"What are you going to do?" Lou asked in Spanish. "Take us in and make us pay a big fine? Then what? You'll have to give it to your *comandante,* and that's the end of it. You get nothing. Why don't you just take the 18 cases of scotch and consider it a gift? We'll give you $100 on top of it if you don't file a report."

Lou's quick thinking worked. By the end of the evening, the officials were laughing and acting like contented guests. They spent the night, then got into their jeep and happily left with all the scotch and the $100 *mordida* (bribe).

However, Lou's luck at getting Dixon out of trouble was soon to end.

One day, when Dixon flew to Punta Chivato, he spotted a tar-paper shack standing on the beach in front of the hotel. He had allowed the workers to set up such temporary living quarters with the condition that once the hotel was completed, the shacks would come down. Concrete block buildings were constructed as alternative dwellings for the workers. Seeing a shack still on the beach, Dixon went into a rage over what he considered an eyesore. He quickly hunted down Lou.

"That shack's got to go. Now! The workers are supposed to be out of there," Dixon shouted. "I told them weeks ago. I don't want our guests having to look out at that."

"Take it easy," Lou said, trying to get Dixon to calm down. "We're not officially open. Besides, we don't have the permit yet from *Patrimonia Nacional.* Let it be until we get the permit."

No one was allowed to own a 60-meter-wide strip along the beach in México because it was considered federal land. However, use permits called *Patrimonia Nacional* could be granted. Dixon's attorney was in the process of obtaining such a permit so they could officially open the hotel.

"No, I want it gone now!" Dixon demanded.

As much as Lou tried to talk sense into Dixon, he would not listen. Lou suggested Dixon enlist Sui Qui's help.

"Have Sui Qui offer the guy $100 to move," said Lou. "For crying out loud, Dixon, you're a *gringo*. All you have is a tourist card. No papers. And you're telling a local Mexican to get off the beach?"

"I'll show you how to do it," Dixon retorted, ignoring Lou's comment as he abruptly turned and walked away.

Dixon found a can of gasoline and walked down to the beach. He pulled the man's cot and other meager belongings out of the shack and threw them onto the sand. Then he doused everything with gasoline, lit a match, tossed it onto the shack, and walked away.

Within seconds, flames engulfed the palm-frond roof. Dixon just kept walking until he reached his plane. He was soon on his way back to California.

It took several days for word of the incident to reach Mexican officials. Eventually, investigators arrived from Santa Rosalía and La Paz. An official from Mulegé, Señor Ugale, the father-in-law of Lou's friend Don Johnson, arrived by boat with a telegram from México City. Lou translated the Spanish. "Strangers have invaded our country and burned a Mexican off the beach. Close that operation."

Trying to buy time, Lou took Ugalde aside. "I got a mechanic over here, an American specialist that Dixon flew in. He's setting up the main generator system to operate the hotel. He's got all the wire and everything. It's going to take him three to four days before he's finished. Can't you delay this thing somehow? You're going to get me in trouble. In the meantime, I'll contact Dixon and the attorney."

"O.K.," agreed Ugalde, "I'll just tell them I couldn't find you."

"Thanks. I appreciate it."

Several days later, a D-18 landed at Punta Chivato. Two officials wearing suits and ties headed for the hotel. Lou knew there was going to be trouble. With Dixon still in California, Lou had to think fast. He quickly got his paperwork together and met the men as they arrived at the hotel.

"Are you in charge here?" one of the men asked.

"*Sí.* How can I help you?" Lou responded, trying to remain unflustered.

"We need to see your work papers."

Lou pulled out the paperwork and handed it to the official.

"These are *inmigrante* papers that permit you to be involved with Hotel Mulegé, not here. You need work papers for Punta Chivato," said the official after briefly scanning the documents.

Lou quickly explained the work papers were in transit and currently with the head of immigration in La Paz, Señor Olachea.

"Come with us," snapped one of the officers. "We'll just fly to La Paz right now and make sure you're telling the truth."

Lou, still wearing his work clothes, went to inform his wife, Lana, who had returned from San Francisco. He found her in their room in the hotel, tending to their baby daughter. Although Lou tried to remain calm, Lana could sense a problem. "I'll be back in a few hours," he said, not knowing when he would return.

After the plane landed in La Paz, the officers drove Lou to the immigration office. However, he was not invited to join the officials when they went to speak with the head of immigration, Señor Olachea. They told Lou to remain in the waiting room. Lou knew he had been set up when they returned and told him Señor Olachea knew nothing about his work papers. *Manuel Cortes must be behind this*, Lou thought. *Maybe it has something to do with Mulegé.*

"You're under arrest," the officers told Lou. "You'll have to come with us to México City so we can straighten this out."

Lou pleaded with the officials to first let him return to Punta Chivato to get a change of clothes and tell his wife where he was going. He was still wearing the work shirt, Levi jeans, and field boots he had on when they first picked him up. Surprisingly, they consented.

Lana was noticeably upset when she saw her husband packing his clothes. "Where are you going now?" she asked. "What's happening, Lou?"

"I've got to go to México City and get some paperwork," he said matter-of-factly. "It's going to take a while to square this thing away.

Dixon's going to come down and fly you and Luana back to the States. You can have a nice visit with your mother until I return." Lou decided not to tell her about his arrest.

Jack Heron had watched the plane land and saw the officials talking to Lou. He was concerned about his friend and offered to help.

"Jack, I don't know what's going on, but they're taking me to La Paz and then México City. Why don't you follow us in your plane to La Paz? Maybe I can get a ride back with you if I end up not going to México City."

Jack quickly obliged. Shortly after the DC-18 lifted off from Punta Chivato, Heron's single-engine plane did, too.

As they headed toward La Paz, the officials chuckled, "You've got a couple of real loyal maids over there. They promised to take us to bed if we'd let you go."

On reaching La Paz, the two officials took Lou to Hotel la Perla. Lou's friend Jack was sitting at a corner table when they entered the dining room.

"Why don't you ask your friend to come join us for dinner?" one of the officials asked Lou. Lou's eyes revealed his surprise. The officials had noticed Heron's presence.

The following day, the officials approached Lou with an unexpected request. "Do you think your pilot friend, Señor Heron, could fly us to Cabo San Lucas? We've got some business to do with Bud Parr."

William Matt "Bud" Parr, an American from Los Angeles, California, was involved with La Palmilla and Hotel Cabo San Lucas, two of the earliest hotels established in that popular fishing area at the tip of the Baja peninsula.

Jack agreed. In a few hours, the plane arrived at the seaport village. The men took a cab to Hotel Cabo San Lucas.

As they all sat around a table waiting for lunch at the lavish hotel, the two officials told the hotel owner, Bud Parr, that they hadn't received their fee. When Lou heard this, he understood the reason for their trip. Bud was being hit up for mordida. If the hotel owner gave them a monthly payment, they would protect him. "It's like a Mafia protection agency," Lou later explained. "You pay them regularly, and they won't ask to look at your books." Bud thought

Lou was one of "them" until Lou took him aside and explained he was under arrest and on his way to México City.

Before going to México's capital, the officials told Jack to fly them and Lou back to La Paz, where the officials directed Lou to contact Dixon.

"If you call Dixon Collins and tell him to come down here, maybe we could straighten this thing out before we have to take you to México City." Lou knew if Dixon gave them some money, they might let him go.

"Dixon," Lou said when Dixon Collins picked up his phone, "I'm under arrest, I'm in La Paz, and you better get down here because I don't like what's happening. It's because you decided to play "*el torcho*" and burn the guy off the beach." Lou was still uncertain why he was being held.

Dixon called his attorney in México City. "Under no means are you to go to La Paz, or you're going to be under arrest, too," Dixon's attorney advised him. "Wait until things clear up. Find out what's going on, and then you can go down."

For several days, Lou repeatedly called Dixon. Finally, Dixon got the okay from his attorney and flew to La Paz. A meeting was held in the immigration office. This time, Dixon and Lou were both present.

"You're doing business here in México. You're building a hotel. Let me see your papers," demanded one official.

"I don't have work papers," Dixon said. "I've got a tourist card."

"You've got a tourist card, and you're building a hotel down here? Where are your *inmigrante* papers that permit you to come down here, buy land, and build a hotel?"

"They're in transit. In fact, I paid this man right here hundreds of dollars to clear my papers," Dixon said, pointing to the head immigration officer, Señor Olachea.

No sooner were the words out of Dixon's mouth than one of the officers shouted, "You mean to say you bribed a Mexican official to cover your papers? You're under arrest! Impound this man's airplane. He's not going anywhere."

Dixon talked the officials into letting him keep his plane. He was ordered to fly back home, get some money, and meet them in México City.

When Lou arrived in México City, he was asked if he had any money. "Yeah, I've got a little bit," he responded.

"Well, that's good because we're going to let you stay in a hotel. Otherwise, we've got to put you in jail. It's a pretty nice jail; it's where we put Americans. But if you've got some money, we'll put you up in Hotel Castropol."

Lou had no complaints about his accommodations, but he was fighting mad about Dixon. Lou was in México City against his wishes, and Dixon was sitting pretty in his "mansion" in California.

After getting the approval from his attorney, Dixon finally informed Lou he was on his way to México City. He also invited Octavio Llano and Octavio's father, hoping their influence might help. But that was not to be the case. Manuel Cortes, the official they met with in México City, was too high up in the Mexican hierarchy. Cortes was closely associated with the Mexican president and appeared to have the power to do anything he wanted. Intimidating Americans for mordida seemed high up on his list.

Manuel Cortes took Dixon and Lou to a meeting with Señor Garza, who, according to Lou, acted like the FBI of México. More charges were added, including illegal possession of morphine, using a ship-to-shore radio on land, and propositioning a female employee.

In the end, Dixon agreed to pay the $10,000 fine. Most of the fine was for burning the shack, but Dixon still felt justified in what he had done. "I did what I had to do. It cost me, but the shack was gone," he later recounted.

Meanwhile, Lou, who had been under arrest in México City for three weeks, finally contacted Lana and told her the entire story. It was the day before Thanksgiving, 1967. Lana had moved back to San Francisco with their daughter, Luana, and they were staying with Lana's mother.

"Come home," she said. "Forget about Dixon and the money he owes you. We'll figure out something."

"Lana, you'll never believe it, Cortes has asked me to stay and get involved in a fantastic retirement complex in Puebla, just outside México City. It's being built for rich Americans. They know I have connections and can help get investors."

Lana would not hear of it. Lou acquiesced and booked a flight to San Francisco via San Diego. Everything Lou had worked for was gone. "I didn't have money in Punta Chivato. I had my heart and soul in it, but I got nothing for it," he later said.

The dream of being an ongoing part of the new resort in Baja had dissolved before Lou's eyes. Although he could have returned to the hotel, Lou decided to give up. He was tired of constantly battling with Dixon and Sui Qui. It was best just to leave Punta Chivato behind.

"I figured the hell with it," Lou reflected. "Get out of here. I don't need this place. I don't need this. Luis Sui Qui was somebody who told them a lot of things about the titles, about this and that. Dixon believed him but found out afterward that it wasn't true. Sui Qui didn't know. I think they found out in the end that I was right."

Lou did not care whether he ever saw Dixon or Sui Qui again. Although he lost contact with both, he would never forget them. For Lou Federico, the bitter memories continued to run deep.

In an article Lou wrote entitled "Tale of Two Hotels," he reflected:[38]

Now at age 65, I look back fondly on memories of the excitement and adventure of pioneering Baja. It was a once-in-a-lifetime experience during the early days when author Ray Cannon wrote about gulf fishing, small pueblos, and the unspoiled beauty of the country and its people. This was before roads, electricity, running water, and today's modern way of life. Tourists in large numbers had not yet left their mark and changed an area in ways that have left it clear that 'progress' is not always an improvement.[39]

View of the hotel from the sea. Courtesy Lou Federico

Chapter 12

BORREGO DE ORO

Dixon Collins was a driven man. Although his confrontation with the officials in México City set him back financially, it did not discourage him from following his dream. He made sure the work on his Baja resort continued.

With Lou Federico and Ricardo Acosta gone, Dixon relied more heavily on Luis Sui Qui, who had connections and information Dixon found invaluable. Both Lou and Ricardo had tried to warn Dixon that Sui Qui did not know what he was talking about. In their eyes, Sui Qui was dishonest and would say or do anything to win Dixon's favor. But Dixon would not listen to them. He would remain loyal to Luis Sui Qui to the end.

Before Lou left Punta Chivato, a large hole for a swimming pool had been dug directly off the veranda of the dining room. Dixon eventually completed the project, trading services with pool builders from the United States. Everything they needed to construct the pool was flown in.

Four days later, the breathtaking pool overlooking the Sea of Cortez was completed. In exchange, the builders got their fill of big game fishing and booze.

In 1966, Dixon's luxury resort officially opened. He named it *Borrego de Oro* (Golden Bighorn Sheep) after one of the most prized hunting trophies in the world, the desert ram, which lived to the

Completed pool next to hotel. Courtesy Harry Oxley

south near Coyote Bay. The resort was also referred to as *Hotel Punta Chivato* (Goat Point) after the familiar point located one mile to the north.

Dixon was proud of his first-class resort with its attractively landscaped grounds. The modern colonial building became renowned for its massive stone arches that framed the Sea of Cortez. At the center of the complex was a large, tiled dining room. This was separated from a bar and cocktail area by an immense, open stone fireplace, a welcome sight on winter evenings when temperatures might drop into the 50s (degrees F.). During the summer, visitors could enjoy cocktails on the cantilevered deck over the sea or sit by the pool only a few steps away.

On either side of the dining room were ten spacious ocean-front suites, each with a recessed sitting area and a small fireplace. Guests were supplied with mesquite and coal oil so they could enjoy a private fire in their rooms. Each room had an air conditioner, a much-appreciated feature during the hot, humid summer months. Dixon's girlfriend, Barbara, had chosen elegant furnishings for the rooms. Luxurious, queen-size beds were available in several rooms. In front of each room was a sunning area that overlooked the sea from atop the bluff. The room rates were $30 U.S./day for a single and $40 U.S./day for a double.

Dixon, always the promoter, lost no time getting the word out about Borrego de Oro. Although the resort was accessible by road, he targeted the population for whom it was built—the wealthy pilot-sportsman. Dixon was an entrepreneur, eager to attract what author Joseph Wood Krutch referred to as "the rich and footloose" in his 1961 book, *The Forgotten Peninsula: A Naturalist in Baja California*. According to Don Johnson, who purchased Serenidad, the fly-in resort hotel in Mulegé, Dixon Collins had "a gift of gab" and could "sell refrigerators in Alaska."

Private pilot Arnold Senterfitt helped spread the word about Borrego de Oro. He loved flying into México and landing at isolated dirt strips. In the early 1960s, he began gathering and recording data about these airstrips, including such pertinent facts as nearby lodging and fuel availability. When other pilots began requesting the information, Senterfitt published a simple, spiral-bound manual with his diagrams/sketches. First published in 1965, *Airports of Baja California* would later be republished, adding new airstrips in Baja and updating ones previously described.[40]

Senterfitt realized many American private pilots were hesitant about flying solo to Baja. To offer encouragement and guidance to these pilots, Senterfitt founded an organization called The Baja Bush Pilots in the 1960s.[41] His beloved Cessna 195 airplane was used as the logo for the organization. Senterfitt taught pilots how to legally cross the border between the United States and Baja, México, and how to navigate in a country that lacked radar services.[42] In addition to his flying tips, Senterfitt shared his favorite hotels and activities. He was said to have up to fifty planes on one of his guided group flights to Baja.

In the Summer-Fall 1966 edition of *Airports of Baja California*, Senterfitt only included the longer 2,400-foot runway at Punta Chivato. The one-page schematic drawing (page C-23) showed this strip as Runway 31 with a 20-foot rise going away from the gulf. It was described as having "no fuel," "no accommodations," and "resort being built." *(See photo next page.)*

After Dixon opened the hotel, Senterfitt returned to get an update on Punta Chivato for a revision of his book. This time, he listed two distinct adjacent runways. He walked the length of each airstrip using a roller to measure the distances. In the revised edition, Punta Chivato was listed on a supplement page. The primary landing

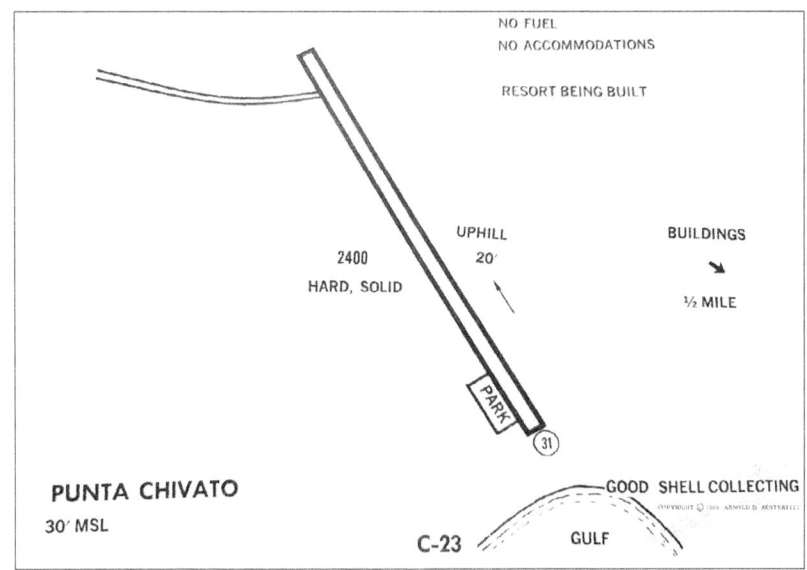

1966 Senterfitt map showing airstrip at Punta Chivato.
Airports of Baja California, Summer-Fall 1966 edition

strip was called Runway 10 (later called Runway 9), which ran east-west parallel to the beach and ended just below the hotel. It was "2,700 feet exactly," with a hard 30-foot ridge at the end. The other one, Runway 31, which ran north-south perpendicular to the far end of the main airstrip, was now recorded as 2,923 feet long. It extended from a bluff near the sea toward the inland hills.

Both landing strips were surfaced with "caliche," also known as hardpan. This material consisted of particles of sediment cemented together by naturally occurring calcium carbonate. After being ground up, the material was laid on the runway and flattened with a roller. The last step was pouring saltwater on top so it dried into a hard surface.

Additional information Senterfitt included in the supplement page for Punta Chivato was:

30 feet MSL,[43] English spoken, fuel 100,[44] kerosene, Unicom, high frequency radio, telephone, air-conditioned accommodations. Good fishing, shell collecting.

Dixon opted not to connect the two runways, which were separated by a narrow dry arroyo. Although rain was rare in this area, *chubascos* (severe thunderstorms) sometimes produced enough rainfall in the surrounding mountains for flash flooding in the lower lands. Tiny arroyos could become raging rivers within minutes. Dixon wisely decided not to take the chance of having conjoined airstrips washed out.

In November 1966, Dixon flew the publisher of *Private Pilot* magazine, Ray Rich, and his wife, Jan, to Punta Chivato in his Cessna Skymaster. Joining them the following day were Neale Perkins, manufacturer of leather and sporting goods, and writer Bob Said, who recorded their experience in an article entitled "The Good Life: a Piper under the Sun" for the February 1967 issue of *Private Pilot*.

> *The present lodge has been two years in the building, and five units are being added to the 20 already completed. Eventually another 30 units, built of adobe brick made on the site, will be constructed. Also in future plans is a natural stone tidal swimming pool directly off the veranda of the main building.*

The writer raved about the well-equipped new resort. Scuba diving, sailing, saltwater fishing, and duck hunting were available. But more importantly, he emphasized the ease of reaching the resort by private plane.

> *When people find out about this place, they'll be down in swarms. Anybody in the southwest can get here over a three-day weekend, in their own plane. And people who want to fly to Phoenix or San Diego by airline and rent a plane can get here from anywhere in the country. A week's vacation, with the weekends on each end for travel, would give you five days in this place.*

> *By the time this magazine reaches you, a 40-gpm filtered pump will be available for fueling aircraft, and airstrip plans include lengthening the present 3000-foot lighted strip to 4000 feet and paving it. The goal is to be able to accommodate corporate jets, for which kerosene jet fuel already is on hand.*[45]

Most pilots preferred landing on the shorter Runway 9 due to its proximity to the hotel. This airstrip ended next to a wide parking area and the fuel pump. Dixon put Luis Sui Qui in charge of ensuring fuel was available for the planes. The 100-octane aviation fuel was either driven up by truck from La Paz or ferried across the Sea of Cortez from Guaymas to Santa Rosalía and then driven to Punta Chivato. There, it was stored in underground tanks. The cost to Dixon for a gallon of fuel was 40 cents. He, in turn, sold it to the pilots for 75 cents per gallon. This left Dixon with a tidy profit of 35 cents per gallon of fuel sold. "They made money selling it," remembered a local Mexican who worked for Dixon.[46]

Landing a plane at night was illegal in México, a regulation Dixon knew but often violated. When he came in after dark, he tried various techniques to illuminate the runway, including using vehicles' headlights, setting out oil lantern pots, and using floodlights run by the warehouse generators. Dixon knew it was often hard to avoid arriving after sunset. He wanted to ensure his guests could land safely even if they arrived late.

In late 1967, Dixon flew in an electrician from Southern California to install lights running down both sides of the shorter strip, Runway 9. Using the hotel's radio frequency, pilots landing "after hours" could arrange to be greeted by a lit runway. Borrego de Oro became one of the few resorts where pilots felt safe to land by day or night.

Pilots rarely landed on the longer north-south airstrip, Runway 31, unless there was a strong wind from the south. However, this longer runway accommodated larger planes carrying as many as 20-30 passengers. One frequent visitor to Borrego de Oro, Bill Lear, used Runway 31 to land his self-named Learjet. When Bill was coming, Dixon made sure kerosene jet fuel was on hand.

Other notable pilots who visited Punta Chivato were Clay Lacy,[47] a native of Wichita, Kansas, and one of the first pilots to receive a Learjet Type Rating in 1964; John Conroy, who designed the Pregnant Guppy, a large, wide-bodied aircraft able to transport rocket boosters for the Apollo space program;[48] designers from Lockheed; and David Nancarrow, who opened the first Carrows family-dining restaurant in Santa Clara, California, in 1970 as the Carrows Hickory Chip Restaurant.[49]

Some of the visitors to Punta Chivato who arrived in smaller aircraft had careers as professional airline pilots. Dixon quickly got to know them on a first-name basis and enlisted their help to obtain weather reports. When making commercial flights to México City, these pilots would radio Dixon at the resort and relay information about weather conditions. This was valuable for Dixon, who had no way of knowing if a chubasco was headed their way.

Dixon was always looking for opportunities to promote his resort. When *National Geographic* magazine sent reporters to the Mulegé-Santa Rosalía area to write a story, Dixon met with them and offered his services. He spent 35 days with writer Bill DeRuse and photographer Bill Bellmack, flying support with them. One night, when they were staying at Borrego de Oro, the photographer snapped a timed photograph showing the lights of Dixon's newly acquired twin-engine Bonanza as it flew down the lighted runway, touched down, and rolled out again. Dixon included the impressive photo in an elaborate, colorful promotional brochure for his new resort. He was proud of this photo featuring this faster plane, which he had purchased to shorten his commute between Punta Chivato and his home in West Covina, California.

Perhaps the best exposure Borrego de Oro received was from Erle Stanley Gardner, aka A.A. Fair, well-known author of the Perry Mason books, which later became a popular CBS television series from 1957 to 1966. Gardener and his crew flew down to Baja in jet-engine helicopters so he could learn about this remote area. He would pen seven books about his adventures in Baja.

During one of these expeditions, a helicopter developed problems and was forced to land in Mulegé. The pilot and Gardner went to Club Aero when Dixon happened to be visiting. After meeting Gardner and hearing of the problem, Dixon offered to fly his Cessna to their camp seventy miles away and bring back their mechanic.

Later that same day, another of Gardner's helicopters developed problems. Dixon generously proposed to let one of Gardner's men fly his twin-engine Bonanza back to California to obtain the necessary helicopter parts to make the repairs. Meanwhile, Dixon invited the famous author to visit Borrego de Oro.

In his book *Off the Beaten Track in Baja*, published in 1967, Gardner includes three photographs taken during this visit to

Borrego de Oro: one of Dixon with his mother, Sibyl; another of the hotel in the process of construction; and an aerial photograph of the new resort. The text included several pages extolling Dixon's kindness as well as praising the "magnificent resort hotel" built "at a terrific expenditure of time, effort and money." Gardner described it as "a deluxe affair–a place where a person can vacation in an ideal climate, with swimming, scuba diving, hunting, and relaxation." Gardener further wrote: "We spent a fascinating two hours looking over the luxurious bedrooms, the dining room, bar and the scenic walks along the cliff. It is a pretentious place and, at the same time, a livable place."[50] Dixon's "neighborly efforts" toward Gardner would pay off handsomely as others learned about the resort through Gardner's book.[51]

Although the principal means of travel to Punta Chivato was by air, some visitors arrived by water. Big yacht races were held from Newport Beach, California, around the tip of Baja, ending in La Paz, Baja California Sur. Afterward, some yachts continued northward, anchoring in Conception Bay or in the cove in front of Borrego de Oro. Dixon and Barbara owned an all-wooden, 65-foot sloop rig they enjoyed racing.

Dixon's remote resort became a popular playground for some wealthy and well-known Americans. Young American actors and actresses came to relax and escape the limelight. Lee Marvin was a frequent visitor to Punta Chivato. During his stay, Dixon often flew him across the Sea of Cortez to Guaymas on mainland México for an evening of dining, drinking, and fun. They would return later the following day. Borrego de Oro also became a favorite retreat for John Wayne, who enjoyed big game fishing, and politician Jay Rockefeller from West Virginia.[52]

Organized flying groups, popular in the 1960s, began to visit the newly opened hotel. Members of these groups were private pilots who owned similar aircraft. Among them was the International Cessna 180/185 Club, composed of pilots flying Cessna 180s and Cessna 185s. In these clubs, private pilots learned how to cross the U.S.-Mexican border, go through customs, and safely navigate the Baja airways. They bonded in the spirit of adventure and enjoyed the camaraderie they shared in owning similar planes. Most carried a copy of Senterfitt's *Airports of Baja California* with rough diagrams showing the orientation of airstrips and information about fuel and lodging. When an updated supplement listed air-conditioned accommodations at Punta Chivato, flying groups eagerly made reservations.

One private pilot, John Fitzsimmons, who joined a flying group, would later describe his club members as "a whole bunch of Ernest Hemingways." Little did John realize that his pioneering spirit would lead him to Punta Chivato, a place he would one day call "home."

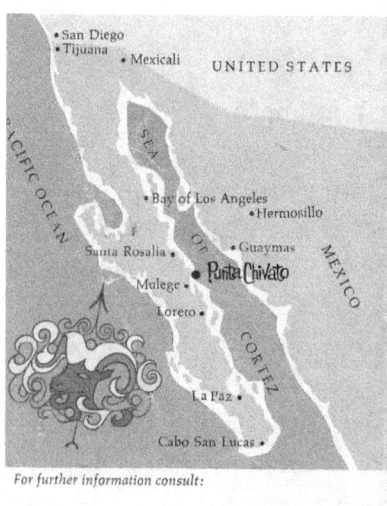

CLIMATE
Our weather is delightful in the summers; warm and balmy with a fresh sea breeze to temper the sun. In the winters, only a sweater or jacket is needed to be comfortable.

WHAT TO WEAR
Your most comfortable casuals for daytime wear, and in the evening the ladies wear slacks, shifts, and long skirts.

WHAT TO BRING
Your lotions, sunglasses, and camera are all the extras you'll need. We can provide for most everything else.

COMMUNICATION
We like to keep it quiet, but we do have a radio-telephone. You can communicate with any place in the world . . . if that's your idea of a vacation!

For further information consult:

*Back cover (left) and front cover (right) of
Dixon's hotel promotional brochure.*

Chapter 13

THE LURE OF PUNTA CHIVATO

John Fitzsimmons lived in the San Francisco Bay Area and, like many, was a fan of Don Sherwood, the popular radio disc jockey for KSFO in the 1950s and 1960s. Every Tuesday, John tuned into Sherwood's radio broadcast to hear his tales of Baja. He longed to experience firsthand the adventures Sherwood described.

While a dental student, John became interested in flying but waited until he graduated and settled down before taking flying lessons. He joined a flying club and put in enough hours to qualify for flying a Bonanza. In February of 1968, feeling like he was "cock of the walk," John was ready to make his first trip to Baja.

With his wife, Gerry, and friends Dale and Julia Dryer, John took off in a 1955 single-engine Bonanza and headed south. "The plane had the smaller tail feathers and yawed like crazy," John recalled, describing the erratic pull of the plane.

"It hardly had enough room for passengers," he added during an interview. Considering the occupants' weight and the useful load of the small plane, they were restricted to only a total of 50 pounds of luggage. "That meant 12-1/2 pounds each," John calculated. "We each had a brown paper bag with a toothbrush. That was it," he added.

The couples decided to fly to Cabo San Lucas. Proudly landing the Bonanza, John quickly realized most of the other planes at the airstrip were twin-engine Commanders. So much for his cockiness! Since it was their first trip to México, John made hotel reservations ahead of time. He chose Hotel Cabo San Lucas and received verbal and written confirmation for three nights. However, when they arrived, they were told no rooms except the expensive Presidential Suite were available. This plush accommodation was only available for two nights since Mayor Sam Yorty of Los Angeles had booked it.

Now, what are we going to do? The couples conferred. With their trip cut short, they discussed possible alternatives.

Before leaving on the trip, John had spoken to several other pilots who encouraged him to stop at Punta Chivato. With an extra day on their hands, John elected to fly north and see if rooms were available.

John landed the plane at Punta Chivato and taxied to a tie-down near the resort. Soon, a worker arrived in a Toyota truck and drove the Fitzsimmonses and Dryers the few hundred yards uphill to the stunning hotel. They were welcomed by a short, heavy-set, gray-haired woman wearing a bright, floral-print dress. She introduced herself as Mrs. Collins, the hotel manager and mother of the owner, Dixon Collins. She showed them to their rooms and invited them to the restaurant that evening for dinner.

"I thought it was wonderful the first time we came to this paradise. It was like magic. They could have served me cat crap on a stick, and it wouldn't have made any difference," Dale Dryer reminisced.

Dixon ensured the food served at Borrego de Oro equaled the superb ambiance. He made Luis Sui Qui responsible for obtaining plenty of locally grown vegetables. Once a week, Sui Qui drove to Santa Rosalía to get lettuce, carrots, chiles, radishes, cilantro, and garlic grown in his home village, San José de Magdalena, and other produce grown at ranches near San Bruno.

But by far, the most exquisite cuisine served at Borrego de Oro was found in the waters of the Sea of Cortez. Dolphin fish (*dorado*), Mexican sierra, grouper, yellowfin tuna, yellowtail, lobster, oysters, scallops, and sweet butter clams were plentiful. Giant sea turtles (*caguama*), considered a delicacy by the Mexicans and preferable to Mexican beef, were sold to the hotel by local fishermen. During storms, shrimp boats frequently pulled in south of the resort to seek shelter. The hotel restaurant was able to purchase huge baskets of shrimp for only $8.00 U.S.

In addition to seafood, the resort sometimes offered local fowl. Often accompanied by Dixon, guests hunted for ducks, doves, and quail at the same lagoon from which the hotel obtained its water. Some of the hunters proudly shared their game with the restaurant. This was a welcome treat since finding decent chicken or beef in the area was difficult.

With all this delicious, fresh food available, dinners at Borrego de Oro were memorable. Dixon hired a cook from Guaymas on the

Mexican mainland who prepared tasty dishes, often starting with appetizers of sierra chunks, fried turtle, and roast duck.

South of the hotel, a tall, brick kiln-like structure served as a fish smoker. So much yellowtail was smoked that leftovers were often sent home with the guests.

When the Fitzsimmonses and Dryers walked into the restaurant for the first time, they were enchanted. A big fire crackled in the magnificent stone fireplace, and huge turtle shells adorned the rock walls. The tables were covered with bright green, yellow, and orange tablecloths and colorfully striped cloth napkins. Vases full of flowers decorated each table. It was apparent that Sibyl or Barbara were behind these stylish, welcoming touches.

"We were in hog heaven because you could get scallops, shrimp, and fresh fish. Was it gourmet cooked? I couldn't tell you. But it was sure good as far as we were concerned," John remembered. "And, of course, the margaritas were always wonderful."

"After the fifth one, everything was wonderful," Dale Dryer added.

The hotel kitchen included walk-in coolers and an ice machine necessary for preparing margaritas. Since the hotel did not have a water purifier, drinking water was made by melting ice cubes. It was thought that once water was frozen, it became pure. This method also supplied drinking water to the hotel rooms.

Guests at the hotel had to learn patience, especially regarding food service. Waiting for a cup of coffee at breakfast often seemed like hours to the Americans. "First came the juice, which was usually Tang, and then the coffee was poured with the meal. It was no use being fussy," said Gerry Fitzsimmons. "After all, just look where we were—in paradise."

The following spring, the Fitzsimmonses and Dryers vacationed at Borrego de Oro for four nights. They came to relax and escape the hustle and bustle of life in the Bay Area. Although they met other guests at the bar with whom they shared casual conversations, they primarily kept to themselves. They relished sleeping late and rarely fished since it did not fit their late-morning schedule. A perfect day for the couples was a glass of wine and a good book on the beach. If the wind picked up, they'd find a protected niche in the cliffs.

Gerry Fitzsimmons and Julia Dryer enjoyed strolling along the shoreline, picking up exquisite shells. A long stretch of beach south of the hotel was covered with cowries, jingle shells, augers, scallops, and various cone shells deposited by the tides.[53] As Otis Chandler of the *Los Angeles Times* discovered when he visited the resort, it was hard not to take home shells as souvenirs of this paradise. Dale Dryer recalled, "The first time Julia and Gerry went down, they took a bag with them. By the time they got down to the end of the beach, the bag weighed 400 pounds! They learned you go down to the other end and work your way back."

While guests of Borrego de Oro could walk on the beach, bask by the pool, or sip a margarita while enjoying the view, Dixon made sure the hotel offered other activities. After all, he had built the fly-in resort for the sport fisherman. As author Ray Cannon, one of the early guests at Borrego de Oro, wrote, "…this grand resort is situated in the heart of one of the most exciting big and small game fishing areas in the Cortez."

Dixon bought a fleet of 28-foot, twin screw, sport-fishing cruisers from Johnny Gale, a Chris Craft dealer out of Newport Beach, California. Dixon had them all named after his girlfriend—Barbara I, Barbara II, Barbara III, Barbara IV, Barbara V, and Barbara VI. The boats were trailered across the border and 127 miles down the eastern side of the Baja peninsula to San Felipe. There, they were met by a group of boat captains from Mulegé hired by Dixon to transport them to the hotel. Surprisingly, the trip went off without a hitch, and within a week, "the Barbaras" arrived safely at Borrego de Oro.

The luxury cruisers were left in the water attached to buoys. But there were two problems Dixon did not consider: the moorings were in the sand, and it was the summer, the season of gulf hurricanes, locally called *chubascos*. The cove below the hotel was unprotected from these storms, which came from the south, bringing high winds and waves. Less than a week after the boats arrived at their destination, a chubasco came through the area, tearing all the "Barbaras" loose from their moorings and smashing them. Motors and boat parts were found strewn all over the bay.

Dixon, an insurance man, planned for the unexpected and had bought a coverage policy on the boats. He immediately called the

One of Dixon's fishing boats, Barbara IV, at Punta Chivato (Dixon Collins in shade and boatman, Rudolfo Romero, second from right with cap).
Photo included in hotel promotional brochure.

insurance company in the United States and explained what had happened. Much to his surprise, he got quick results.

"The guy arrived, looked it over, and wrote me a check for 100% of what we paid for it [the boats]. There were no questions asked," Dixon recalled. "There was no issue whatsoever. It's the second most amazing transaction that ever occurred during my entire stay in México."

With the insurance money, Dixon returned to the Chris Craft dealer in Newport Beach and reordered identical cruisers to replace the destroyed ones. They were hauled down the same way and once again moored by the hotel. A short breakwater was constructed extending off the hotel point to provide protection from the weather. The new "Barbaras," plus four Boston Whalers with 40-hp outboards, smaller skiffs, sailboats, and a catamaran, were available for the guests at Borrego de Oro.

José Ramirez, a local Mexican, was hired to manage boat rentals and sell fishing tackle to hotel guests. He worked out of a room directly across a walkway from the restaurant. It would later become the hotel office. This space also served as Dixon's mother's gift shop. Guests were enchanted by Sibyl Collins's display of jewelry, arts, and crafts from Guadalajara and other parts of México. It was hard to resist purchasing something from the hotel owner's charming mother.

For many hotel guests, this was their first experience going after big game fish. Dixon hired experienced fishermen from the area to be skippers of the "Barbaras." Rudolfo Romero and his son, Antonio, lived with other boatmen (*lancheros*) in a little house built at the top of the launch ramp.[54] Captain Romero, wearing his sunglasses and signature captain's cap, appears in several of the photos in Dixon's promotional brochure. His son, Antonio, worked at the hotel as a bartender.

Salt-water fishing was the main draw for guests at Borrego de Oro, and they did not have to go out far to catch record-breaking fish. Dixon recalled, "The fishing then, and I fished all over the world, big game fishing, never seen anything like it in my life. And it was year after year. You could get Boone-and-Crockett-sized fish. I once caught a 42-pound snook on a four-pound test line. It took me 2-1/2 hours to bring it in. *National Geographic* was there at the time and took my picture. There were sailfish, grouper, cabrilla, and yellowtail. When the yellowtail would run, the pelicans would be diving in the midst of all this broiling water, and we'd just cast into it. As fast as you could throw a line out, you'd be reeling it back in and landing a fish."

In addition to fishing gear, Borrego de Oro had shotguns available for guests who wanted to hunt. Sometimes, fishing and hunting trips were combined. Jack Heron, the pilot who showed up at Punta Chivato and ended up staying for several years, often functioned as a fishing and hunting guide. The lagoon where the hotel got its water was a favorite hunting spot. Taking the guests in a Boston Whaler, Heron instructed them how to troll for sierra and roosterfish as they headed north along the rocky shoreline en route to their destination. Reaching the ocean side of the lagoon, they anchored and hiked over the sandbar with their shotguns. There, they boarded a wooden dory with a small outboard motor clamped to its stern. The dory was kept at the site to provide hunters easy access to any part of the palm-rimmed lagoon. Ducks, geese, quail, and dove were plentiful at the site.

Dixon's well-equipped hotel had other amenities for the watersport enthusiast. Guests could rent water skis, masks, snorkels, fins,

Dixon Collins watches employee Alan Burr enter the Sea of Cortez from the stern of Barbara IV. Photo included in hotel promotional brochure.

or complete scuba-diving gear. The resort had a six-tank air compressor to keep the dive tanks full. Dixon hired a full-time dive instructor, Alan Burr, originally from Denver, Colorado. Alan, called *Alejandro* in Spanish, was usually seen wearing only his swim trunks. Noticing all his body hair, the Mexican employees called him "*peludo*" (hairy). Like Captain Romero, Alan appears in several of the photographs in Dixon's brochure: diving off the stern of "Barbara IV" with his scuba gear, holding up a giant turtle, and removing a spear from a large grouper.

"Visibility is great down there," reported one scuba-diving guest who visited the resort in the winter of 1966. "I don't think I was ever out of sight of a fish all the time I was down."[55] Not only fish but scallops, giant clams, and lobster could be found at the nearby Santa Inez Islands. Butter clams and oysters were abundant in Conception Bay to the south.

One did not have to use a scuba tank or travel far to enjoy the beauty beneath the sea. Colorful fish were plentiful just offshore. With a mask and snorkel, guests could swim less than twenty feet in front of the hotel and find lobster and scallops in the rocks.

Employee Alan Burr poses with giant sea turtle at Punta Chivato.
Photo included in hotel promotional brochure.

To highlight the beauty of the area, Dixon offered to take adventurous visitors up in his Cessna 206 airplane. The plane could seat five passengers and the pilot. These sightseeing excursions gave guests a bird's eye view of Punta Chivato and the surrounding coastal areas, including Mulegé and Conception Bay. Occasionally, Dixon flew guests to the Pacific side of Baja or over to Guaymas on the mainland for a night of partying to the sound of mariachi bands.

As word spread about Dixon's deluxe resort, more Americans flew down to see for themselves. Some guests grew so enchanted with the secluded area that they asked Dixon if they could build places of their own. Having considered this prospect when he first set eyes on the land at Punta Chivato, Dixon would nod and reply, "Perhaps someday."

Small boat passing in front of newly completed hotel.

Chapter 14

FLORENCIO

It was a sunny June morning in 2004 when my husband, Greg, and I drove up *Calle Reforma* (Reform Street) in Santa Rosalía in search of a red house with white trim. After passing a small school and *tienda* (store) on our left, we spotted the modest home of Florencio Aguilar on the adjacent corner. "This must be it," I told my husband, rechecking the handwritten directions.

As we parked our Bronco at the base of the steep driveway and hiked up to the concrete-block home, a handsome Mexican appeared. Tall, stocky, and in his late 50s, Florencio looked distinguished with his thick gray hair and bushy mustache.

"Come, have a seat," he said, gesturing toward a small plastic table with four chairs on the concrete patio. "What would you like to drink?" Although Spanish was his native language, Florencio had a better grasp of English than most Mexicans in the area.

He turned to a nearby ice chest and popped open the lid. It was filled with bright, metallic-red cans of Tecate, a popular beer in Baja. Florencio offered one to each of us, then laughed as I reached into the sack we had brought and handed him more Tecate. He filled the empty spaces in the ice chest.

With my husband and our long-time friend, Lynne Weiser, I had come to interview Florencio Aguilar and his brother, José Marcos, who had both worked at Borrego de Oro as boys.

I first met Florencio the previous winter at *El Morro Hotel* in Santa Rosalía, where he was employed as a waiter in the restaurant. Despite his large stature, he was surprisingly soft-spoken. I had hoped to interview him then, but he felt uncomfortable being interviewed at work. He suggested we meet again in a more casual setting the next time we visited Baja and graciously offered his home.

"This is my wife, Lilia," Florencio said, introducing us to a pleasant woman in an apron who emerged from the door with a platter of tortilla chips and salsa. She set them on the table and returned to the kitchen.

Inviting us to their home was a big event for the Aguilars, as evidenced by the crowd of family members who started to gather. Soon, the yard was filled with the chatter and laughter of their daughter, Jacquelin, son, Homero, and their families. Homero's wife, María, held 1-1/2-month-old Jennifer. The baby's older brother, Josue, was playing with his toy truck. María's brother, his wife, and young daughter were introduced. I started getting confused about who belonged to whom and wondered how many lived in that home! Sensing something important was about to happen, the family made a point of staying out of our way. Even the children refrained from interrupting our conversation.

Marcos Aguilar (left) and his brother, Florencio, during interview in Santa Rosalia. Courtesy Greg Joy

I turned on my tape recorder just as Florencio's brother arrived. Everyone referred to him as "Marcos." He pulled the ice chest over to the table to use as a seat. Both brothers became animated when I produced Dixon Collins's brochure of Borrego de Oro from the 1960s. Like grown-ups looking through an old high school yearbook, they began identifying people in the photographs, including a younger Marcos. Smartly dressed in black slacks, a white shirt, and a tie, the teenager stood over a table in the dining room where Dixon, Sibyl, and others were seated, awaiting their meal.

The Aguilar brothers shared their recollections of the 1960s and 1970s while Lilia brought out more goodies from the kitchen, including crackers and her homemade *ceviche* (a tangy, raw seafood appetizer). Between sips of Tecate and sampling Lilia's treats, I asked questions while relying on my tape recorder to capture the answers. *(Author's note: While the following story was developed mainly from information provided by Florencio and Marcos, a few of the details were obtained from other interviews.)*

The dining room at hotel in Punta Chivato – Marcos Aguilar, working as a waiter, stands by "sun" on the rock wall; Dixon Collins is seated at the table to Marcos' left and Sibyl to his right. Photo from hotel promotional brochure.

When Florencio Aguilar first came to Punta Chivato, he was 20 years old (born February 24, 1946). Construction of Borrego de Oro was just underway, and young men from the surrounding area had heard the Americans were hiring local men. Florencio, like Luis Sui Qui, was born in the nearby mountain village of San José de Magdalena. Work was hard to come by, but Florencio hoped to be given a chance.

At the work site, Florencio was offered a job in construction and proved to be a diligent employee. He was dependable and never caused problems. Ricardo Acosta's teenage daughter, who frequently accompanied her mother to the work site, quickly fell in love with the handsome Mexican. She admired how hard Florencio worked for her father. "He looked like Tarzan," she recalled. But Yolanda could only look at Florencio from afar and dream. Her father, the building supervisor, would not consent to his daughter being with an "older man."

Dixon was impressed by Florencio's work ethic. When the resort was eventually completed, he offered Florencio a job as a waiter in the hotel restaurant. Not all Dixon's employees were as fortunate. Only a few were asked to stay on. The majority were terminated when the building phase was over.[56]

One day, a 70-foot yacht arrived at Borrego de Oro. Owned by a retired doctor from San Diego, the lavish "floating hotel" was named *Orchia*. Dixon was delighted to entertain these guests and made sure they had an enjoyable time, including plenty of food and liquor. When the boat owner mentioned he needed a person to help him on the boat for six months, Dixon offered the services of his trustworthy employee, Florencio.

Florencio had never been out of Baja and was eager for the opportunity to "see the world." Even though the yacht only sailed between San Diego and ports in México, Florencio felt he had been offered the chance of a lifetime. He learned quickly and worked hard doing whatever was asked of him, from serving meals to showing guests how to fish. Surrounded by Americans who took vacations aboard the vessel, he rapidly learned English.

On one of these journeys, an attorney and his family from Long Beach, California, were among the passengers. David Rice and his wife, Trini, had previously visited the eastern side of the Baja peninsula and fallen in love with the unique land. They were eager to show their three daughters and two sons the area. Traveling by yacht seemed a perfect way to share the experience.

Cruising along the east coast of Baja, the captain took them into the beautiful 25-mile-long Conception Bay. The grand yacht was impressive, anchored in the waters of the popular sheltered cove of

Santispec. Fourteen miles south of Mulegé, this bay with its mangrove inlets was known for its abundance of butter clams, large *Chocolates* (chocolate-colored clams), and oysters.

Although they came to fish, the children became more interested in caves they spotted up the mountainside. They begged Florencio to go exploring with them. "I bet there are Indian paintings in those caves," said one teenage boy. Always eager to be of service, Florencio consented.

The adventurous children and their Mexican guide climbed into a dingy and went to shore. Single file, they scaled the steep mountainside with Florencio bringing up the rear. Halfway up, there was a tall rock. As Rice's teenage daughter, one of the last in line, approached from below, the rock became dislodged and began to tumble down the mountainside. Florencio quickly grabbed the girl, pulling her out of harm's way. As she cried hysterically, he attempted to calm her. Florencio realized they were both lucky to be alive.

Returning to the boat, the girl and Florencio described the incident. The captain, the owner of the boat, and the women who had remained behind listened intently. The Mexican was indeed a hero.

Later, Trini Rice approached Florencio. "Would you consider working for us? We're thinking of building a home in Punta Chivato. David has already talked to the owner. We're going to need someone to help us at the house. We'll even put in an apartment for you."

Florencio was easily persuaded and agreed to work for the Rice family. "O.K. Not a problem," he told Trini without hesitation. He had enjoyed his six months working aboard the yacht, but Florencio was ready to return to the land. As Trini grasped his hands, he smiled. Florencio knew not what to attribute his continued good fortune.

Chapter 15

CASA GRANDE

David Rice and Andrew "Andy" Lococo became frequent guests at Borrego de Oro. In less than three hours, they could fly in from Los Angeles, land at the resort's dirt strip, and be on the hotel veranda sipping margaritas. The secluded area with limited access by road, air, and sea almost guaranteed them privacy. The location appeared ideal for holding business meetings if only they could get the hotel owner to agree to their conditions. They approached Dixon Collins.

"Can we make a deal with you?" they asked. "We'll bring our people in, we'll have our meetings, and we'll pay you like the hotel is completely full. We'll stay out of your hair; you stay out of our hair, and you'll make money." To Dixon, their offer seemed too good to refuse. According to Dixon, he did not know until later he was dealing with the Mafia.[57]

The men also asked to construct a large private house on the coast near the hotel. Financed by Andy Lococo, Dixon arranged for a grand home to be built on the bluff east of the hotel. Known as *Casa Grande* (Big House), the 8,000-square-foot building was completed in less than a year at a cost of $135,000, according to Dixon. Everything for the home was flown in from the United States in a DC-3.

Casa Grande was designed in the shape of an airplane. Facing the Sea of Cortez, the "cockpit" held a living room with a large stone fireplace. Sliding glass doors flanked the fireplace and led to a tiled patio overlooking the sea. In the "fuselage" was a sizeable adjoining kitchen and dining room. On either side of the central area, the "wings" each consisted of three separate bedrooms—one for each of the Rice's five children and another for David and Trini. All six bedrooms and the living area had unobstructed ocean views. In the "tail" section in the front of the house, an apartment was built for Florencio Aguilar, just as Trini had promised.

Below the bluff on the Sea of Cortez side of Casa Grande, a concrete-rock pier was constructed for a 20-foot inboard-outboard motorboat. Dixon remembers shooting skeet off that pier. "I went to do the trigger thing, and the mechanism blew my finger out. It just ripped it to pieces," he said, pointing to a tell-tale scar.

Casa Grande. Courtesy George Powell

Once Casa Grande was completed, the Rice family made regular trips to Punta Chivato. David owned a plane and hired a pilot to transport them between their residence in Long Beach and their Baja home. According to Florencio, they stayed at Casa Grande for periods of three or four days to a maximum of one month.

Florencio served as the caretaker but was not familiar with many of the modern cleaning appliances the Rices brought down for him to use. "Mr. David Rice and Mrs. Trini had many different things for cleaning—an electric machine with a brush and a thing for polishing, a thing with wheels with a mop. Everything. It was very, very easy," Florencio remembered. "No man in Punta Chivato had one; the hotel didn't have any of these services. I was very happy." But when the Rices were gone, the caretaker sometimes encountered problems with the new-fangled equipment.

One day, Florencio went into the "special room" that held all the fancy cleaning supplies and spotted a big rubber scraper with a curve to it. "Oh, fantastic," he thought, carrying it out to the living room to clean windowpanes. "This should make things easier." But as he dragged the tool across the watered pane, two screws protruding from the scraper left large scratches on the window. "Americans are stupid," he thought, putting the foolish implement back in the cleaning room. The next time Trini came to Punta Chivato, she told him it was to be used on the floor, not the windows. "O.K., I understand," Florencio said, "I'm stupid."

Even when the Rice family was not at Casa Grande, Florencio was not alone. The bedrooms were often filled with guests. The caretaker began to look forward to the arrival of these visitors, who brought him big bags of matchbooks from various places in the United States. "I collected them," the Mexican proudly recalled. Little did he realize these guests were not just well-traveled Americans. Most were in the Mafia and used Casa Grande as their meeting place.[58]

Dixon remembered these notorious visitors. "If all the guys were coming in for a meeting or something, they stayed in the different bedrooms [at Casa Grande]. They'd also stay at our place [the hotel]. But they had their meetings over at the Casa Grande."

Rice paid Dixon $100 per month for utilities; otherwise, as initially agreed, each party avoided the other's business. "Those guys used to come down. They would fly in from everywhere—Chicago, New York. They would come down there and take over the place, and they were really fun guys," Dixon remembered. "They owned the Sands Hotel and a number of the Las Vegas places, and they used to have this rotation of hookers from Las Vegas, these very beautiful, young, bright women who were part of the big picture scene with the high rollers and all that sort of thing. They would send them down once a month, they would rotate, and it would be like R & R to come down to Punta Chivato. So, a planeload of these ladies would arrive. Sometimes, they'd stay there [Casa Grande]; sometimes, they'd stay with us at the hotel. They'd stay to themselves, and they had a great time—get some sun, lay on the beach, drink some beer, laugh, listen to the great music, do mariachi at night. Then they'd fly back to Las Vegas."

Dixon's mother, who was the hotel manager at Borrego de Oro at the time, never said anything about these strange happenings. She just acted as if she did not see them.

Dixon soon found he was getting "hassled" by police agencies and the F.B.I. "They came in a couple of times. They contacted me in West Covina [his home in California] and asked to meet. What they wanted to do was come in and bug the place because we were building homes and had sort of a relationship with some Mafia

Photo shows hotel (far right on point) in relation to Casa Grande (near center of image, to left of hotel); short runway on left. Courtesy George Powell

people—Andy Lococo and David Rice and the people who had taken over Las Vegas at the time when Bugsy Segal was killed. They [the officials] wanted to put people down there to bug the house because they had no way in otherwise without our permission."

Dixon would not give in to the officials. One day, tired of being scrupulously watched as he flew between California and his Baja resort, Dixon devised a plan. "I invited everybody up, all these different agencies, up to my house one day in West Covina." Over coffee and cookies, he confronted the officials, "Look, you guys, you're watching me on the radar, and you're trying to catch me with something. I'm doing nothing wrong. I'm not raising dope. I'm not selling dope. I'm not doing anything illegal. When I go down, it's because I've got meat or something that will spoil, and I over-fly the border. It's just damned inconvenient to stop. I'm running a business, and that's all there is to it. Now, here are my logs. You can do anything you want, but we haven't done anything illegal, except for that [flying across the U.S./México border without checking in with customs]. And I wish you'd quit bothering me, and if you want me to start stopping at the border, that's what I'll do if that's what it takes, but let's just get this over."

"Each one didn't know the other was going to be there," Dixon shared in an interview. "It was kind of funny. About a month later,

I got a bill in the mail from U.S. Customs. It said, based on what I gave them, 'You've been fined $5,000.' I sent it back and said, 'Not going to pay. Try somebody else.' Then I got another bill a month after that that said, 'O.K., we've reduced your fine to $500.' I wrote across that, 'Not going to pay. Come back up for cookies or whatever you want, but I'm not going to pay.' The last one I got was a thing saying, 'Please, just so we can close this thing—$50.' And I paid the $50 and that was the end of it. Those were great stories about things that happened. Those were the days when that could happen. Radar was just beginning to come up. We didn't have terrorism like we do now."

But Dixon's problems were not over. Soon, he faced another challenge, dealing with the Mexican government and a group of local Mexicans called *Ejido San Bruno.*

Chapter 16

EJIDO SAN BRUNO

Dixon had never heard of ejidos prior to arriving in Baja. This system of redistributing land back to the Mexican peasants was furthest from his mind as he watched his luxury resort nearing completion in the mid-1960s.

"You better make sure this land isn't ejido property," Lou Federico had warned Dixon when he first expressed an interest in acquiring the land at Punta Chivato. "Look what the ejido in Mulegé did to us," Lou said. "It came in and laid claim to the land, property that we had legally purchased."

Lou told Dixon about the problems that arose after he and his partners built Hotel Rancho Loma Linda in Mulegé. "The ejidatarios said we could make arrangements to lease back from them, but my partners sold out to Dick Stockton. When Stockton took over and renamed the resort Hotel Club Aero Mulegé, he was convinced he could reclaim the property from the ejido. But it never happened."

Under the Agrarian Law, the ejidatarios were not given title to the land they occupied. Therefore, they had no right to lease, subdivide, or sell any portion of the property. The land was still owned by the Mexican federal government.

Before breaking ground for his hotel, Dixon thought he had gone through all the proper channels. He had traveled to México City, obtained a 99-year lease, and had papers signed and stamped by Lopez Mateos, the president of México himself. Dixon even had the backing of the powerful Llano-Zaragoza family from Sonora, the Mexican state across the Sea of Cortez. However, in México, things were not always as they seemed. With the resort nearly completed, Dixon suddenly learned that his property lease was worthless. Before the 1960s, mainland México considered Baja largely uninhabitable and devoid of valuable resources. Viewed as a "poor stepchild," the peninsula was often ignored by the federal government in México City.

However, this changed as foreign investors became interested in the arid peninsula. The government saw potential profit in Baja, with wealthy Americans spending money building hotels and fancy resorts for sport fishermen. As Borrego de Oro neared completion, the time was ripe for the government to establish another ejido.

Just to the north of Punta Chivato, a small group of Mexicans lived in the coastal community of San Bruno. Many of the men worked as fishermen or date farmers. When the construction of Borrego de Oro began, some found work there as laborers. Staying at the job site during the week, they proudly returned to San Bruno on weekends with handfuls of pesos. They made more money than they were used to earning, and their income was steady. These men from San Bruno had no idea the land under the hotel on which they toiled would one day be theirs.

On June 28, 1966, by presidential decree, Ejido San Bruno was established by the federal government. Through a lottery process, a group of 27 households, referred to as Grupo 27 de San Bruno, was granted 8,630 hectares of land (approximately 21,325 acres), encompassing not only San Bruno but also coastal lands to the south. Perhaps of greatest significance, it included all the property around and under Borrego de Oro.

When Dixon learned that Ejido San Bruno was claiming the hotel property, he immediately flew to México City to resolve the situation.

"You cleared me. You checked everything. You said it wasn't ejido land," Dixon angrily shouted at a government official in México City. "Lopez Mateos even signed the papers himself. And now you're telling me your own president is a crook, and you can't do anything about it?" Dixon slammed down the papers the president had signed granting him a 99-year lease. "Now you're telling me it's owned by a group of uneducated peasants?"

But no matter how much he protested, Dixon got nowhere. His lease was now meaningless. Dixon had no choice but to deal with the new Ejido San Bruno.[59]

Dixon worked to establish a good relationship with the local Ejido. He knew life was difficult for these people, many of whom were descendants of the Yaqui Indians. They scratched a meager existence with little to no education, some living in shacks called *chozas*.

Dixon decided to try to help the local ejidatarios make money by introducing them to the poultry industry. He planned to teach them how to raise chickens, which his hotel would, in turn, buy and serve in the restaurant. They would also supply the hotel with fresh eggs. Dixon speculated the Ejido would eventually branch out and sell to other hotels and people in the nearby town of Santa Rosalía.

In the northwestern Baja city of Ensenada, there was a large chicken-raising company, Kimber Farms. Dixon hired a man from the company to come down to San Bruno and assess the feasibility of such an endeavor. After checking out the San Bruno site, the representative told Dixon it would be a good place to raise chickens. "Okay," said Dixon. "Teach us how to do it."

The expert returned and held classes for the ejidatarios on how to operate an effective chicken-raising business. He provided manuals on what to feed a chicken, starting when it was a chick, how to kill a chicken, and how to package it. He covered how to handle eggs and distribute them. The Mexicans seemed excited about their new business. Soon, chicken coops and facilities for processing the chickens were built in San Bruno. Per a later interview with Dixon, he flew a twin-engine, large transport C-46 Commando aircraft to Ensenada and picked up various kinds of chicken feed and over 3,000 chickens. He was pleased with himself for coming up with a wonderful plan.

Several months later, Dixon decided to fly over and check out the new chicken industry. Arriving in San Bruno, he felt like a hero. He was mobbed by the local people who patted him on the back, saying, "Oh, Señor Collins. *Buenos días. Buen hombre.*" He smiled and said, "Thank you very much," thinking, *boy, this is going great; this is a really good idea.* But as he looked around, he saw no chickens. "Where are the chickens?" he asked.

The men looked at each other and shrugged their shoulders.

"Don't you understand me?" Dixon said. "What happened to all the chickens I brought you?"

"Oh, the chickens," they said, "at the fiesta. The fiesta was fantastic. Señor Collins, thank you so much for the fiesta."

"What do you mean, the fiesta?" Dixon replied.

The ejidatarios explained that as soon as the chickens were big enough, they invited everybody from the nearby ranches, had a huge fiesta, and ate every single chicken.

So much for Dixon's bright idea.

Mexican Saúl Davis, who resided in Mulegé, was familiar with the concept of ejidos. During an interview, he shared his thoughts on why ejido programs often failed: "The president tried to help a lot of poor people; he tried to do good for the people. He gave the fishermen motors, the farmers money for their farms…this and that, and they shut down. He tried to give them a lot, but the people didn't come through with the program. I guess he should show us how to work before he gave us things. He tried to help. But things didn't turn out the way they should."

During an interview with Dixon Collins, he said he did not have difficulty doing business in México. "We were on the inside because the Llanos were very powerful," Dixon recalled. "Wherever we went, we were treated like royalty. The politicians loved our place. We treated them right, and we'd take them out fishing, and [they] really had a great time. We had a wonderful relationship with everybody." Even the governor of Baja would come down and stay in Punta Chivato. "He would come down there all the time," Dixon added.

But there were always payoffs known as *mordida*, literally "the bite." Ben Hunter described it as follows in his book *The Baja Feeling*:

> *It is misunderstood by Americans who refer to it as a bribe. It may be a bribe by our standards but not by theirs. Mexican government officials of all kinds, as well as policemen, accept the mordida as a legitimate (or quasi-legitimate) part of their pay. The police, for example, exist on a notoriously low pay scale and must augment their salaries in this way to survive. It is like our practice of slipping the maître d' a five-dollar bill for a special seat, quick seating, or some other favor in a restaurant. We are bribing him of course, but we call it a tip. Various Mexican presidents have sworn that they would stamp out the mordida custom, but they never succeeded. It is too much a part of Mexican life.*[60]

"Every several months, somebody would come from some department in Santa Rosalía or someplace and say, 'You need to pay us $10,000 or so many crates of alcohol,'" said Dixon. "Just about the time you make a few extra bucks, they'd come down and say, 'Can I have some more money? I would hate to take away your liquor license because you were not supposed to have it.' I truly got tired of that," Dixon lamented. "They had an innate knack for knowing exactly how much money you were making or had at a given time. They would never ask for more. They just kept you right there at the edge."

Dixon's interaction with the Ejido was limited. However, he knew he had to be vigilant. "We could expect every now and then for somebody to arrive from México City saying, 'I'm representing the Ejido San Bruno, and we think you should do this.' We'd send over ten cases of beer or something like that, and everybody got happy again. Mostly it would be for licenses, like for fishing. We would end up paying some people $5,000. It was a very corrupt time. Everything was acquired based on corruption. There were payoffs to get the leases. It was all done at a high level with people that were important in México, respected in México. They were powerful people. That's the way they did business."

Dixon realized that if he wanted something done or expedited, there was always a price tag. His run-ins were mainly with the officials in nearby Santa Rosalía and, to some extent, the Ejido. "It was kind of a game with them," he recalled. Although his right-hand man, Luis Sui Qui, helped keep the local officials at bay, Dixon was growing weary of the ongoing Mexican practice of mordida.

Chapter 17

PARTIES, PROSTITUTES, & PLANS

With Punta Chivato now controlled by the Ejido San Bruno and the Mexican government, Dixon was still determined to make it the most lavish resort on the Baja peninsula. If he needed to pay mordida or provide alcohol to the local officials in exchange for construction approvals, he was resigned to playing their game. Barbara, now his wife, passively stood by as Dixon continued to spend her inheritance on the hotel.

To accommodate more guests, Dixon built a new row of hotel units behind the water-front suites, doubling the number of available rooms. Even with the additional accommodations, sometimes the hotel ran short of beds.

"During the week, there were not many people in the hotel, but on the weekends, it was more than full," commented Chema, a Mexican hired by Barbara Collins to manage Borrego de Oro. Nicknamed "Chema," José Espinoza was born in Santa Rosalía while the copper mine was still operating. He was 30 years old when Barbara approached him. "When the hotel was full, the overflow stayed at Casa Grande," Chema recalled during an interview.

Chema, who spoke and read English, was often asked by Barbara to help translate documents. His responsibilities as manager of Borrego de Oro included all the banking, paying employees, and buying food. He lived in one of the back rooms of the hotel during his short employment. "Barbara was a very beautiful lady," Chema recalled. She was first class."

"Barbara owned the hotel, not Dixon. It was her money," Chema said. He did not have the same admiration for Dixon Collins. When asked to describe Barbara's husband, he quickly replied, "Dixon? He was second class."[61]

As visitors to Borrego de Oro and Casa Grande grew, keeping up with the higher water usage became more difficult. Dixon considered running a pipeline between the lagoon and the reservoir on the hill, but this laborious undertaking never occurred. Instead, they relied on the water truck, which, especially on weekends, had to make multiple trips to the lagoon. The truck often broke down on the rough dirt road, leaving a hotel full of guests without water.

The Mexican employees could not believe how much water the Americans used. Their reactions varied from curiosity to anger. "The Americans seemed to have a disregard for the scarcity of our precious desert resource," said Chema during an interview. "What did they do with all that water?" Some believed the wealthy Americans "threw water away" as if there was an endless supply.

The presence of drugs and prostitution at the resort did not go unnoticed by the employees. "For many years, there were no police, no *federales*, nothing. There were lots of drugs," said one former employee. "Dixon's pilot was a big dealer, *traficante*. He flew back and forth—to Las Vegas, Guaymas, La Paz, Loreto…over and over every day. Sometimes, he would bring prostitutes from Guaymas. The men were all in the Mafia. The same men, different ladies."[62]

Although Dixon denied any involvement in prostitution, he enjoyed sharing stories about the parties. Sometimes, they flew to remote locations on the Pacific side of Baja, taking Mexican mariachi bands with them for musical entertainment. "I had a Cessna 206 specially built for me with big tires so we could land on the beach," Dixon recalled. "We'd fly over to San Quintín, land on the beach, have a great all-night mariachi party, and eat lobsters from the bay."

"They were some wonderful years of my life," Dixon said, reflecting on his days in Punta Chivato. "It was a real challenge, not a game for kids. It was an enormous amount of fun."

Dixon had grand plans for Punta Chivato. "It was going to be like Cabo San Lucas is today," he reflected in an interview. "It was built to be a hotel that was ultimately going to expand. We were going to build houses." He also envisioned converting the two surplus landing craft, once used to transport the hotel's building materials, into lavish floating bars for cocktail cruises. Dixon intended to lengthen and pave the longer runway to accommodate corporate jets, and he proposed building airplane hangars. He even chose a prime piece of property on a bluff east of the hotel, where he planned to construct a home for his family. "Around the corner, there was this little private beach and a beautiful outcropping of black rock. I designed a house I was going to build out there for myself. I still have the plans," Dixon reflected.

However, Dixon realized in addition to dealing with the Mexican government and Ejido San Bruno, there were other barriers to fulfilling his dreams for Punta Chivato. "There were several weaknesses. It really needed a waterline. Without one, there was never going to be anything," he said. Also, until the proposed Transpeninsular Highway was built, connecting Tijuana to Cabo San Lucas, travel to Punta Chivato would continue to be limited primarily to those with small planes or ocean-worthy vessels.

Some believe Dixon's marriage to Barbara was starting to unravel. Although outwardly supportive of her husband's decisions, Barbara was growing less tolerant of his reckless spending habits and womanizing. Others said that Dixon's mother and Barbara left Baja around this time, disowning Dixon and moving to Arizona or New México. Some reported Sibyl's health was failing and she wanted to return to the States.

Whether it was marital issues, problems with the Mexican government, or simply lack of money, Dixon was looking for an out. In 1968, five years after he first set eyes on that desolate point where he would successfully build Borrego de Oro, Dixon had an unexpected visitor. Cleveland Benedict Crudgington, III, a wealthy man from Reno, Nevada, showed up at the hotel office and presented Dixon with an offer he could not refuse.

PART II

Chapter 18

CLEVELAND B. CRUDGINGTON

Cleveland "Cleve" Benedict Crudgington was born into affluence in 1923. His mother, Charlotte Elizabeth Benedict Crudgington, was an heiress to the flourishing American company Procter and Gamble.[63] Cleve's father, Robert Lincoln Crudgington, was a prominent pediatrician in Cincinnati, Ohio. In 1926, when Cleve was only three, his parents divorced, and he was raised by his mother and grandmother, Olivia Procter Benedict.[64] Cleve grew up among the privileged and wealthy. As is often the case, he also married into it.

Cleve's first wife, Elizabeth Stephenson, was said to be an heiress to the Otis Elevator Company.[65] She and Cleve married on February 20, 1943, in New York, where Cleve was stationed in the Navy. But Elizabeth soon became intolerant of Cleve's lifestyle and behavior. According to an article in the *Cincinnati Enquirer* dated May 16, 1944, Elizabeth "found that his apartment looked more like a cocktail bar than a place to live in, and that his friends had entrée to the place for almost any purpose." After only seven months, Elizabeth moved back to Ohio to live with her mother, Mary Cunningham Stephenson.[66] On February 1, 1944, Elizabeth gave birth to a daughter she named Mary Elizabeth "Bonnie" Crudgington. Cleve "denied being the father of their child but later apologized in writing." In May 1944, "the romance of two socially prominent young persons" ended when Elizabeth was granted a divorce from Cleve on the grounds of neglect.[67]

When Cleveland's second wife became pregnant, Cleve again insisted he was not the father and refused to give the child his name. He had the marriage annulled and paid $30,000, so his wife and the child were conveniently removed from his life.[68]

Cleve met his third wife, Phyllis Ricksen, when he was still in the Navy. She was an East Coast girl, petite, spunky, outgoing, and gorgeous. She met the tall, dashing, young sailor through a friend when he was on leave in New York. "You couldn't help but like him," Phyllis recalled. "He was the craziest guy. He was funny."[69]

Phyllis left a glamorous modeling career as a New York *Cosmopolitan* cover girl to marry Cleve in 1949 and move to a new life in Reno, Nevada. There, Cleve operated a printing company called Silver State Press. They were a popular couple in Reno throughout the 1950s.[70]

Phyllis had a son from a previous marriage to Robert Ernest Ricksen. Cleve, elated to finally have a boy in the family, adopted the 4-year-old and gave him a new identity. The boy's name was legally changed from John Gardner Ricksen to Cleveland Benedict Crudgington, Jr.

Cleve relished having a son. As Cleve Jr. got older, his father taught him to fish and enjoy boating. Frequently, they traveled to Seattle together, where Cleve showed his son how to fish for salmon. Cleveland Benedict Crudgington, Sr. was happy. Not only did he have money, but he also had a beautiful wife and a handsome son bearing his name.

During an interview, Phyllis stated that she and Cleve legally adopted Cleve's only claimed biological daughter, Bonnie, but Cleve rarely saw her.[71]

Phyllis soon realized her husband had problems managing their finances. "He couldn't hang onto a nickel," she later remarked during an interview. "Cleve spent whatever he got his hands on, and everything he invested in went down the tubes." She saw what had happened after Cleve's mother died, leaving him with two sizable trusts. Money from the first trust was spent on developing a new aluminum airplane wing rather than investing in Toni Home Permanent, considered a more secure venture.

Cleve spent the money from his second inherited trust to fund the production of a new electronic Keno machine. Cleve's printing company supplied coin wraps and Keno tickets for much of the gambling industry in Nevada. The fancy electronic machines prevented Keno employees, called "runners," from making off with the profits.

Despite receiving substantial money from his mother's two trusts, Cleve set his sights on a much larger inheritance, money from his grandmother, Olivia Procter Benedict. He anticipated his share of her trust would amount to $9 million. With that money, he envisioned building a mansion and buying an expensive yacht, two of his lifelong dreams. But unbeknownst to Cleve, his grandmother was wise to her grandson's spending habits. She devised a plan to keep him from going through his inheritance too quickly.

Cleve Jr. was boarding at Robert Louis Stevenson, a posh private boys' high school in Pebble Beach, California, when he heard the news—his great-grandmother had died. Cleve Jr. knew his father would be eager to finally get his hands on this much-anticipated inheritance. But Cleve Sr.'s dream of acquiring a lump sum quickly vanished. Grandmother Olivia Procter Benedict's irrevocable trust only allowed her grandson access to the interest.

Cleve Sr. was devastated and angry when he realized what his grandmother had done. As his grandiose plans crumbled before his eyes, so did his marriage to Phyllis. In 1962, Cleve Sr. left Phyllis and moved into an apartment in Reno. His divorce from Phyllis was finalized in 1964. Cleve Jr. was distraught by his parents' breakup. His school grades suffered.[72]

Whether it was intentional or just a coincidence, Cleve Sr. soon found another avenue to acquire money. He once again married into it. His fourth wife, Mary Williams, nicknamed "Mim," was a third-generation heiress to Dow Chemical Company, first known for manufacturing commercial bleach.

Mim and Cleve Sr. were no strangers. In fact, they had known each other for many years; she had been married to his first wife's cousin. After separating from Phyllis, Cleve tracked down Mim and began sending her flowers and love letters. He was charming and funny and soon broke down her defenses. However, Mim was reluctant to marry Cleve. She knew how easily he let money slip through his fingers. She did not want Cleve Sr. to squander her inheritance, too.

Somehow, the smooth-talking Crudgington convinced Mim they should build a home together. He chose to relocate north of San Francisco at the end of the Tiburon peninsula on Strawberry Point. Cleve custom-designed a sprawling white home and had it built to his specifications. Cleve, Mim, and her two youngest children from a previous marriage, Nathan and Heather, moved into the lavish residence. A nanny was hired for the children and provided a bedroom near the children at one end of the house. Cleve and Mim's bedroom was located at the other end.

The house on Strawberry Point was Cleve's dream come true. It had a magnificent view of the bay and the city of San Francisco to the south. On fogless evenings, one could see the lights twinkling in the distance. To Cleve, the setting could not have been more ideal. With the house completed, he set his sights on his next life-long dream—obtaining a yacht.

Chapter 19

CRUDGINGTON'S DECISION

With his Strawberry Point home completed, Cleveland Crudgington, Sr. wasted no time searching for a yacht. In 1967, in a coastal town in Connecticut, he located a 72-foot craft. Christened the *Golden Mustard*, the boat had been in wet storage for a long time and was far from seaworthy. But Cleve dreamed of having it transformed into a lavish vessel.

He paid to have the *Golden Mustard* hauled to West Palm Beach, Florida, where repair work began. The restoration took time with the boat in such terrible shape, and the costs quickly added up. Feeling he was being gouged, Cleve often argued with the men in the boatyard. Some bills he simply refused to pay. When the yacht was finally ready, the boatyard declined to relinquish it until Cleve had paid up. He did so, begrudgingly.

Unable to manage his new craft single-handedly, Cleve hired a captain and co-captain to help him bring the *Golden Mustard* around to the San Francisco Bay via the Panama Canal. Cleve Jr. thought the trip sounded fun and asked if he and his girlfriend could join them. His father agreed. Cleve Jr. looked forward to a romantic cruise basking on the ship's deck, reading a paperback, and enjoying the company of his girlfriend. But the voyage he envisioned was not to be.

As soon as they reached Nassau in the Bahamas, Cleve Jr.'s girlfriend debarked. Seasick for most of the trip since leaving Florida, she was happy to return to solid ground. Cleve Jr., however, opted to continue the journey.

As it crossed the Caribbean Sea toward the Panama Canal, the *Golden Mustard* began taking on water. Even with the bilge pumps in constant operation, they could barely keep up with the intake. Debris from the ocean had to continually be cleaned out of the strainer to keep the pumps working.

Reaching the town of Colón at the eastern entrance to the Panama Canal, Cleve Sr. had the yacht pulled out of the water so it could be thoroughly inspected. The repairmen soon found out why the *Golden Mustard* was taking on water. The strut bolts had pulled away from the rotting wooden ribs on her underside. As a result, a space had developed between the keel and the bottom of the boat.

Repairing the damaged vessel took three weeks and more money than Cleve Sr. wanted to spend. He grew irritated and took his frustrations out on the captain. In Colón, he fired both the captain and co-captain he had hired in Florida and brought on another captain to take the boat on the last leg of its journey.

Cleve Sr., Cleve Jr., and the new captain managed to successfully navigate through the inland waterways. The seas were calm, and land was always within sight. But things rapidly changed when they reached the Gulf of Tehuantepec off the southern coast of mainland México. Cleve Jr. found a set of pilot books left on the yacht by the first crew. He read about the sudden appearance of violent mountain-gap winds called "Tehuantepecers."

"Even freighters have been known to go down in this gulf," Cleve Jr. advised his father, pointing out the section he had located in the manual. "I think we should stay close to the coast."

"This is my god-damn boat, and we're going to do it my way," his father replied. "We're going to go straight across."

Cleve Jr. was not surprised by his father's abrupt response. He had experienced it many times before. Maybe his father was right, and things would turn out okay. As nighttime fell, the skies were clear and the waters calm. Even the reflection of the stars was undistorted in the glass-like ocean. It was a beautiful evening.

But around 4:00 in the morning, the seas began to get rough. The waves gradually grew. By daybreak, the surf was cresting as high as thirty feet, and the *Golden Mustard* rode up and down the big waves. The men found it harder and harder to remain on course. Occasionally, a swell broke over them, and water ran down the decks and drained out the stern. They frantically struggled to keep the *Golden Mustard* from going broadside. If that happened, the vessel would roll like a log, and they would likely perish. Far out at sea with no land in sight, they signaled a MAYDAY. However, the only people they could raise were Japanese fishermen who did not speak English.

Fortunately, the boat had twin throttle controls. They maneuvered the bow into the waves by racing one and pulling back on the other. Finally, they reached the coastal town of Acapulco.

"That was the closest I had ever been to feeling like maybe I'm not going to be around the next day," recalled Cleve Jr. "I was so sick. We pulled into Acapulco, and the hotel doctor took one look at me and the next day, I was on a plane home. I was really quite skinny at the time. I think I lost about 20 pounds. The books and suntan lotion I took along on the trip were never touched."

After a long and perilous journey, the *Golden Mustard* finally arrived in San Francisco. With his yacht home, Cleve decided to gut the inside and refurbish the cabin. He rented an apartment at The Cove Apartments in Tiburon so he could dock his boat in front and work on it. He did not live in the apartment but used it to store materials for the boat. Every day, Cleve drove from his big white house at Strawberry Point to the boat located only one mile away. There, he met up with a carpenter he had hired to help with the elaborate remodeling. Cleve Sr. was set on having brass light fixtures, mirrors in the bedroom, and a marble toilet bowl.

Although Cleve Sr. initially anticipated the entire project would take three months, the months turned into years. During that time, Cleve was evicted from The Cove Apartments after they discovered he was using it as a boatyard. He moved the yacht to Paradise Cove, a 3.5-mile drive from his home. There, the yacht remodeling project continued.

Always wanting to stand high above everything, Cleve designed a flying bridge for his yacht. From this added section above the main deck, he would have a bird's eye view of all sides of his vessel and unobstructed visibility of the surrounding seas.

Construction of this addition was a major feat, requiring cables to secure it in place. Once the task was completed, Cleve Sr. took his family out underneath the Golden Gate Bridge. The ride was uneasy as the top-heavy boat rolled and hesitated through the surf. Cleve eventually modified his design, attributing the change to the family's dogs. "You know, we can't get the dogs up to the bridge. We're going to have to lower the bridge," he said. No one in the family argued with him.

Although the *Golden Mustard* looked finished on the outside, the inside still needed work. It was during this time that Cleve began

to grow increasingly disillusioned with the United States government. With the ongoing turbulence of the 1960s, he felt the president, Lyndon Baines Johnson, familiarly referred to by his initials
LBJ, was running the country into the ground. Cleve disapproved
of the direction the United States appeared to be headed and
decided it was time to go elsewhere. Baja offered an opportunity to
invest in what he felt was destined to become the Gold Coast of the
West. Cleve was eager to move to this unspoiled paradise.

The boat's progress slowed down as Cleve Sr. put his energy into
locating property in Baja. He envisioned building his own resort
hotel and hired a pilot to scan the Baja coastline. After several days
of looking for an ideal location, Cleve spotted Hotel Punta Chivato
and its nearby runways. He ordered his pilot to land so he could
investigate. Cleve liked what he saw. *Perhaps it would be more eco-
nomical to buy an existing resort,* he surmised.

Meanwhile, because the boat's taxes were not paid, the *Golden
Mustard* was impounded at Paradise Cove and chained to the dock.
That was the last straw for Cleve. He decided that even though the
boat was not finished, it was time to get it out of the United States.
He was determined to buy the resort at Punta Chivato.

Chapter 20

DIXON SELLS BORREGO DE ORO

Dixon Collins looked up from the paperwork on his desk as a lanky, sandy-haired man entered his office. The hotel owner recognized the assertive American who had been a guest at Borrego de Oro. On two former visits, he had approached Dixon and asked if he could purchase the Baja resort. Dixon's answer was the same each time: "It's not for sale."

Dixon noticed that Cleveland B. Crudgington, Sr. had neglected to bring his girlfriend. Blonde and beautiful, Mim was not a woman Dixon could easily forget. *What did she see in Cleve, anyway?* Dixon wondered. Cleve was cold and arrogant, hardly the match for a classy woman like Mim.

"Welcome back to Punta Chivato. How was your flight?" Dixon inquired, extending his hand.

The guest set down his briefcase and shook hands. "I want to buy your hotel," Cleveland responded, ignoring Dixon's question.

"As I've told you before, it's not for sale," Dixon said.

"I don't think you understand. I want to buy it, and this is what I am willing to pay." Cleve picked up the briefcase, laid it on the desk in front of Dixon, and opened it up. Inside were bundles of money. "I'm sure you'll agree it's a fair offer."

Dixon, for once, was speechless. Before him, there was more cash than he ever imagined he could get for the hotel. "How much?" he asked.

"Enough. Count it yourself," Cleve replied.

After counting the money, Dixon smiled. "O.K., Mr. Crudgington, you have a deal."

Dixon vividly recalls that day. "It was the most amazing transaction that ever occurred during my entire stay in México, even better than getting reimbursed by the insurance company after the storm destroyed my boats, the 'Barbaras.'" Dixon refused to divulge how much Cleveland Crudgington paid him that day. He simply said, "It was the right amount of money."

Dixon relied on his friend, Octavio Llano, to facilitate a quick lease transfer to Crudgington. "Octavio knew the insiders. He came over, we signed all the papers, and the lease agreement was transferred." The smooth transition occurred without the intercession of local officials or attorneys. "Mexican attorneys are experts at stringing you along. They'll give you just enough hope and 'just one more payment, and I think I can do this,' and 'I think I can do that,' and then it just doesn't happen," said Dixon. "Octavio couldn't control the local guys 'cause that's not controllable. But as far as the big leases...."

Cleve took over Dixon's lease with the Ejido San Bruno. With it, he was entitled not only to Borrego de Oro but also to the surrounding land—4,000 hectares. He also purchased the boats, the "Barbaras," so he could continue offering fishing trips, a main attraction for hotel guests.

Bob Davis, a friend of Cleve's, remembers seeing the lease agreement. "Cleve had what was called a manuscript lease. It was a handwritten lease done in México City—umpteen pages, a thick document, very official-looking, kind of a parchment paper. It was signed by all kinds of people with lots of government stamps. It looked like a very good lease."

After signing the lease agreement, Dixon Collins packed, got into his plane, and returned to California. Although it would be twenty years before he returned to Baja, he left a lasting impression on the Americans and Mexicans he met there. "He was a real coyote," remarked an American who worked with him for many years.

"He was nicknamed the dinosaur," said Lou Federico. "He had a small head and a huge body." A female acquaintance remembers, "He was very tall, much sex appeal. Very good man. A good person." One of the Mexican workers recalls, "He had many, many girlfriends. He liked adventure and liked to fish."[73]

Soon after Dixon left Baja, David Rice sold Casa Grande to Crudgington. Some say David's wife, Trini, never liked the Big House on the bluff. She preferred staying in another home they built in Guaymas on mainland México. According to Dixon Collins, after Rice's partner, Andy Lococo, died of a heart attack, Rice moved to Guaymas to be close to Octavio Llano. "David Rice was part of the whole organization [Mafia]. I think Octavio Llano and

David formed a great friendship. David was probably getting a little protection in Guaymas," Dixon speculated.

Cleveland Crudgington moved his family into Casa Grande and took over managing the illustrious resort. The change in the hotel's name from Borrego de Oro to Hotel Punta Chivato started a new period—the Crudgington era.

In a brochure, Crudgington advertised the new name and listed his mailing address in the United States:

Hotel Punta Chivato – turnoff Hwy. #1 is 24 miles south of Santa Rosalía. Marked by a sign and white-washed rocks. 17 miles east to hotel on gulf. Deluxe accommodations include pool, dining room, and 2 airstrips. Reservations advised. Address: P.O. Box 2349, Tucson, Arizona 85702. Rates: Single $25-$30. Double: $30-$40. Baja California México—by Cliff Cross.

Chapter 21

NEW MANAGEMENT

Cleveland Benedict Crudgington leaned against the stone archway that framed the hotel terrace. He gazed out at the Sea of Cortez while a lone pelican soared above. Suddenly, the bird folded its wings and dove headfirst into the water, breaking the morning stillness as it conquered its prey. Cleve's thin lips curled into a smile as he relished his triumph. *I told Collins I wanted Punta Chivato*, he thought. *Now it's all mine.*

Aerial view of Hotel Punta Chivato during Crudgington's era.
Postcard photo, Petley Studios, Phoenix, Arizona

It was 1968, and Crudgington was happy to be out of the United States. At age 45, he was eager to start over in a country free from the turmoil of the Vietnam War and racial violence. Living in Punta Chivato was a dream come true. Cleve not only had control of a hotel, a large, water-front home, and acres of land. He also had access to miles of blue water where he planned to sail his prized 72-foot yacht.

Mexican voices in cheerful banter emanated from the hotel

kitchen as Cleve walked through the restaurant and out the front of the hotel. He climbed into his vintage WWII jeep and whistled for his dogs. Sugar, a Cocker Spaniel mix, jumped up into the passenger seat while Zarina, a greyhound, climbed into the back. The jeep with its three passengers headed up the dusty road to Casa Grande.

"Nathan, Heather, let's get going," Cleve shouted upon entering Casa Grande. "If you don't hurry up, you're going to miss breakfast."

Two handsome blonde children appeared with their mother, Mim, behind them. "You don't need to use that tone," she said quietly, ushering the children out the door. The children and dogs crowded into the back of the jeep while Mim and Cleve sat in front. Cleve revved the engine, and the jeep bounced along the rutted dirt road back to the hotel.

The new owner of Punta Chivato had a lot on his mind. Spending time with his family was often low on his priority list. He soon realized running a resort hotel was not as easy as he had anticipated. Although he hired a Mexican from Guadalajara to manage the hotel, the success of Punta Chivato rested on Cleve's shoulders. He had difficulty adjusting to the slow pace of life in Baja. Patience was not one of his strong suits.

"*Buenos días, Señor, Señora, chicos,*" the waiter greeted the family as they entered the spacious dining room. He led them past the fireplace and bar to their usual table outside on the veranda.

Several guests were already seated at nearby tables sipping coffee. They were mesmerized by the spectacular view from the veranda. The Sea of Cortez was teeming with activity. Dolphins worked in parallel rows, crowding the mackerel until their slick, quivering bodies piled up out of the water, a feast for the dolphin. As if performing for an audience, manta rays rocketed upwards from the ocean floor, broke the surface, and flipped high in the air before pancaking onto the water with a loud smack.

The spell was momentarily broken as the Crudgington family walked onto the terrace. Cleve was dressed in shorts and a polo shirt, but Mim looked as if she had stepped out of the pages of a magazine. Her form-fitting dress and diamond jewelry seemed out of place compared to the casual attire of the others. Next to Cleve,

Mim seemed short. She was a blonde, striking woman, yet appeared serious and preoccupied. The patrons never saw much of her except at meals or as she walked along the beach with one of the dogs.

Many breakfast guests were return visitors to Punta Chivato, recreational pilots and their wives and friends who frequented the hotel when Dixon Collins owned it. Since a connecting highway through Baja was still a long way off, the new hotel owner, like his predecessor, catered to these small-plane pilots.

However, some customers did not welcome the change in ownership from Dixon Collins to Cleve Crudgington. They missed the familiar greeting of Dixon's mother, Sibyl, over the radio as they prepared to land at the secluded airstrip. When the van pulled up to take the newly arrived guests to the hotel, the Mexican driver told them there was a new owner. "Dixon and Sibyl no more. Now Señor Crudgington and Mimmie," he said, referring to Mrs. Crudgington by the nickname the Mexicans used, except when speaking directly to her.

Cleveland Benedict Crudgington at Punta Chivato.
Courtesy Cleveland Crudgington, Jr.

Before leaving for Baja, Cleve had convinced Mim to marry him, informing her that living together out of wedlock would not be looked upon favorably in México. He spoke of the new life they could create together in Baja, free of the turbulent political atmosphere in the United States. He told her that together, they would build up the hotel to be the most luxurious in Baja. With Mim now his wife, Cleve had access to capital. He immediately started spending money to improve the hotel and the airstrip.

Spacious Casa Grande had ample room for the Crudgington family. With Mim's oldest daughter, Sarina, away at boarding school, Cleve, Mim, Nathan, and Heather took up permanent residence in the white stucco house. The layout was like their home in Tiburon: the children's bedrooms on one side and the parents' bedroom on the other. Between were the spacious living and dining areas. An Indian woman, Ramona, was hired as a nanny. She resided in the children's wing.

After breakfast, Mim took the children and walked back to Casa Grande. She preferred to walk along the beach rather than ride in the jeep, and the children enjoyed picking up shells.

Cleve retreated to his hotel office, but not for long. He suddenly reappeared and hurried over to a table of guests on the veranda. They stopped their conversation as the distraught hotel owner neared.

Cleve addressed one of the men at the table, whom he recognized as a prior guest at Punta Chivato. Not known for small talk, Cleve got directly to the point. "John, got any money on you?"

Looking up, the patron responded in a drawn-out, "Yeeaaaahh."

"You got $40? Loan me $40," Cleve said nervously. Although the hotel owner had money, he often was short on cash.

"I didn't know Cleve very well, but I knew the routine," John Fitzsimmons recalled. "He had approached me in the same manner on a previous trip. I figured he recognized me and looked up my name on the hotel register."

John pulled out his wallet and handed Cleve $40.

Cleve thanked him, shoved the money into the pocket of his shorts, and left the veranda. He hurried out to his jeep and drove toward the boat ramp. Within a few minutes, the guests saw him motoring one of the "Barbaras" past the hotel. He headed out to the shrimp boat moored not far off the point. The shrimp fishermen were relaxing after a long evening of seining.

John knew the loan would be repaid when it was time to check out. Cleve would tell the hotel manager to deduct $40 off their hotel bill. John also knew the hotel would be serving something special for dinner that night—fresh shrimp.[74]

Chapter 22

NEW BOSS & FAVORED WORKER

Many of the Mexican workers at Punta Chivato were not fond of their new boss. Cleve was distant and preoccupied, unlike Dixon and Barbara Collins, who were at least approachable. Mr. Crudgington had an air of superiority, a trait his employees and guests noticed. Cleve's hurried pace was out of sync with the laid-back Mexican culture. He spoke rapidly to his workers and expected them to move quickly. Cleve grew impatient and angry when work was not done immediately or supplies arrived late. He angrily stomped off when told he could expect something *mañana* (tomorrow). The promise of things arriving mañana never seemed to hold true.

But everyone quickly learned of Cleve's fondness for animals. This became particularly evident one morning when Cleve spotted a wounded seagull on the rocks below the hotel's terrace.

"*¿Qué paso?*" he inquired, turning to his bartender, Luis. "Its wing is broken. Do you know how this happened?"

"*No comprendo*," said Luis, innocently acting as if he did not understand why his boss was upset.

"*La gaviota!*" Cleve shouted, using his newly acquired word for seagull. "How did its wing get broken?"

"An accident, Señor Crudgington," Luis replied. "I didn't mean to hurt it." The bartender reached for the slingshot he had hidden on the shelf under the bar.

Seeing the weapon, Cleve flew into a rage. "God damn you, Luis! You are very, very stupid!" He then abruptly turned, walked the length of the restaurant, and crossed the walkway to his office. As his boss entered, the office manager looked up.

"How long has the bartender been here?" Cleve brusquely asked.

"One year, I believe," the manager replied.

"Figure out what we owe him and pay him off. We don't need his kind around here. Like the seagull, he is no more." Then Cleve quickly went out, climbed into his jeep, and left in a cloud of dust. His manager had the unpleasant task of notifying Luis he no longer had a job.

After that incident, the other workers began secretly referring to their boss as the protector of animals. They saw how he doted on his three dogs and took at least two of them everywhere he drove in his jeep. Cleve even let his big wolfhound lick the plates left on the tables in the hotel restaurant after the guests were gone. She particularly liked the left-over butter. The workers joked that before coming to Punta Chivato, Mr. Crudgington worked as a vigilante for animals in the United States. They said he preferred animals over people, except for one of his workers, Luis Sui Qui.

Cleve grew fond of the same Chinese-Mexican worker who had endeared himself to Dixon Collins. Luis Sui Qui quickly won the respect of his new boss. He gave Cleve advice and served as his right-hand man both at the hotel and in dealings with the government officials in Santa Rosalía. He began to affectionately address Cleve as *abuelo* (grandfather). Although too young to be Sui Qui's grandfather, Cleve was not offended. If anything, the nickname made the bond between the two men even closer.

Cleve decided trucking water from the lagoon to the reservoir on the hill was inefficient. Although he knew the costs would be excessive, he decided to build a well (*poso*) and put in a pipeline from there to the pila. It was an ambitious undertaking, but Cleve knew he could count on Luis Sui Qui to oversee the project.

The only viable well was several miles inland from the hotel. This would require miles of pipeline. Sui Qui oversaw the heavy equipment operation and decided where to dig the trenches. The other workers noticed Cleve arrived in his jeep at noon to inspect the progress. They also observed that Cleve always brought lunch to his favorite employee.

One morning, a group of planes landed at Punta Chivato, and Cleve was busy supervising the staff on how to accommodate the new guests. As noon approached, Cleve suddenly realized he had forgotten to take Luis his lunch. Climbing into his jeep, he hurried to where the pipeline crew was working.

"Luis, I'm sorry, I'm sorry," Cleve apologized as he pulled up next to Sui Qui. "I got busy with the hotel. The Bush Pilots arrived, and there was so much to do. I'm sorry I'm so late with your lunch."

"No *problema, abuelo*, no *problema*," Sui Qui replied. "I'm only bad garlic crumbs—garlic BBQ," he joked.

An onlooker might have had difficulty discerning who was the boss and who was the worker. Cleve depended on Sui Qui's advice and rarely questioned his suggestions. Although Sui Qui often helped keep Crudgington out of trouble with the local officials, his guidance would not always prove prudent.

Chapter 23

CLEVE JR.

Cleve Crudgington, Jr. was not surprised when his father remarried and moved to México. Purchasing the hotel in Punta Chivato seemed to be another one of his father's wild dreams, like buying a yacht on the East Coast and sailing it back to the San Francisco Bay. What a fiasco!

Intrigued by his father's photographs of his hotel in Baja, Cleve Jr. was eager to learn more about it. His father assured him the resort would eventually be a moneymaker. *Perhaps Dad will be right this time*, Cleve Jr. speculated. Hotel Punta Chivato had the potential to be a profitable investment. At the end of 1969, a recently-married Cleve Jr. decided to visit his father's Baja resort for the first time—for his honeymoon.

Cleve Sr. was pleased to have his namesake visit him. He put the newlyweds up in one of the hotel rooms facing the Sea of Cortez. Like the other front-row suites, it included a recessed sitting area with a fireplace. The setting could not have been more romantic.

The hotel was an ideal honeymoon getaway for the couple, especially since fewer guests than usual were staying there. While Cleve Jr. and his bride enjoyed their privacy, Cleve Sr. was dismayed by the number of empty rooms. He blamed the lack of guests on his Mexican workers who failed to maintain the airstrip. With no paved road to connect his resort to the outside world, he depended upon decent runways to attract private pilots. He would have to put Sui Qui on that crew, he thought.

One afternoon, Cleve Sr. found his son lounging beside the hotel pool, reading a novel.

"I've figured out how to attract more guests," said Cleve Sr. "I'm going to bring the yacht down here and offer overnight yachting and fishing trips."

Cleve Jr. turned from his novel and looked up at his father. "How do you plan to get it down here?" he asked.

"Well, I talked to Denny. He might be able to help me out," he said, referring to his old sailing buddy, Denny Danhurt, from the Bay Area.

"Hmm," responded Cleve Jr., reluctant to question his father's decision. He did not want to get into an argument, especially on his honeymoon.

Cleve Jr. was skeptical about his father's plan. Although the issue was not discussed further during Cleve Jr.'s honeymoon trip to Punta Chivato, the younger man would have a change of heart afterward.

In early 1970, Cleve Jr. offered to help Denny bring his father's yacht to Punta Chivato. Cleve Jr. recalled the day they arrived at the Baja resort. "When Dad met us, he was in a foul mood. He couldn't even relate to the boat, which had been such a source of pleasure for him. His mind was on other things. I couldn't even talk to him about it. It was really awful." What he had thought would bring his father joy seemed only to add to his discontentment.

Cleve Sr. was more impatient than usual and preoccupied with issues related to running the hotel. He once asked his son if he would help run the place. But Cleve Jr. quickly declined, afraid he would get sucked into another of his father's follies. Cleve Jr. would never return to Punta Chivato.

Chapter 24

PLANE CRASH

In the spring of 1970, Hotel Punta Chivato was bustling with guests who came to enjoy the temperate climate. Cleve Crudgington, Sr. was pleased. Most visitors arrived by air, a few by boat. Moored in front of the hotel was a big sailboat, the *Anita*. It was owned by a wealthy American, Mr. Lynn, who, together with his brother, were considered minor shareholders in the hotel. Rumor had it that Cleve often gave them free room and board.

One evening, Mr. Lynn was in the bar sipping margaritas while eagerly awaiting the arrival of his brother, who was piloting his Cessna 182 from Southern California to Punta Chivato. As the sun set and the skies began to darken, Mr. Lynn grew concerned. His brother, who worked in promotions and real estate, was bringing down a good friend, a Hollywood physician. *Why would he take a chance and arrive so late? He knows flying after dark in Baja is illegal*, he wondered.

Suddenly, his brother's voice came over the hotel Unicom.

"I'll be over Punta Chivato in ten minutes. Put the lights on," he said.

The workers flipped the switch for the runway lights, but nothing happened. Maybe there was a short in the wiring. The pilot overflew the airstrip.

"I need the light. I'm low on fuel," the pilot demanded. But there were no lights, no reflectors, nothing to guide him down.

Several pilots rushed out to their planes to use their radios. "You've got it made. Come on down," someone advised. "No, don't do it," said another. The pilot did a second go-around.

"Fuel out. I have to land," said the panicked pilot as he came in for his third pass. After three attempts at landing on Runway 9, parallel to the water, the 182's fuel supply ran out. The plane's engine quit over the road near the hotel. The pilot decided to ditch it into the water just beyond Casa Grande.

"Mr. Lynn's brother had two broken legs, but he was rescued

and survived," recalled John Fitzsimmons, who was vacationing at the hotel with his family and friends. Per his pilot's logbook, March 1970 was John's third flight to Punta Chivato.

The injured pilot was flown back to the States the night of the crash by a regular visitor to Punta Chivato who had a twin-engine airplane. Following the tragic accident, the pilot never returned to Punta Chivato.

The passenger in the downed plane was not as fortunate as the pilot. He drowned before anyone could reach him. Since the accident occurred at night, they were unable to get word to the officials in Santa Rosalía. According to another hotel guest, "The hotel workers packed the dead man in ice and put him in the smokehouse below the hotel until the next day when the officials could come."

It was the first of many such mishaps at Punta Chivato involving airplanes. When asked about these incidents, one of the local Mexicans said, "Those planes in the ocean? We call them 'lobster houses.'"

Chapter 25

CLEVE'S YACHT

Cleve's 72-foot yacht was an imposing sight as it sat anchored off the shore of Punta Chivato. The massive structure dominated the view from the hotel. Employees and guests wondered what the owner intended to do with it. Some speculated he brought it down purely for his own pleasure; others rumored it was destined to become a floating casino for the rich and the famous.

Cleve Crudgington's yacht at Punta Chivato.
Courtesy Cleveland Crudgington, Jr.

Oddly, Cleve paid little attention to his yacht after it arrived in Baja. Although outwardly, Cleve appeared to be financially secure, he was struggling. As much as he wanted to begin refurbishing the yacht, he did not have the money. His inheritance and Mim's were rapidly dwindling. It was rumored they spent a million dollars on the yacht and a million on the hotel. Now, the Ejido San Bruno was demanding more from them in the form of taxes. Cleve Sr. had not anticipated the never-ending hidden costs of doing business in México.

Cleve rarely stepped aboard his once-prized possession. Anchored in front of the hotel, the yacht never moved except to bob up and down day after day, week after week, month after month. Periodically, one of the Mexican workers would go out and check on it, but the primary visitors were seagulls, who soon assumed residence on the floating palace.

Cleve's yacht suddenly became foremost in his mind one summer morning in 1970. He was awakened before dawn by a loud crash outside. Cleve jumped out of bed and ran to the window. Through the darkened skies, he saw several patio chairs lying on their sides, toppled by the intense winds. Above the terrace, palm fronds danced like marionettes in the wind. Huge, frothy waves broke over the small pier in front of Casa Grande.

Cleve had been warned about the hurricanes that periodically swirled up the eastern coast of Baja during the summer. These sudden seasonal storms came up from the gulf and could travel as far north as the town of San Felipe, leaving a path of destruction. Not wanting to take any chances, Cleve followed the advice one of his workers had given him earlier in the summer. He had moored the yacht in deeper water further off the hotel point.

This must be a chubasco, Cleve thought, remembering the word the Mexicans used for violent storms. Cleve threw on his robe and ran outside onto the tiled terrace. The air hung heavy with moisture and heat.

The force of the wind surprised Cleve. Wrapping his arms around his torso, he lowered his head and rushed to the south side of the patio. Steadying himself against the trunk of a palm, he gazed out to sea. There, in the distance, he saw his yacht rocking from side to side. Although buffeted by the waves and wind, the large vessel still held its anchorage.

Cleve returned to bed but was unable to fall back to sleep. The wind grew stronger, sounding like an approaching freight train about to roar through the house. Spray from the crashing waves blew up onto the porch and hit the sliding glass doors. "I hope those anchors hold," Cleve said aloud. Mim, who lay awake, was too frightened to respond.

The yacht was anchored fore and aft in twenty feet of water with the bow facing toward the south. When the winds began to hit, they came from the southeast. Initially, the boat held its anchorage, but as the turbulence increased, the bow anchor dislodged and began to drag along the bay's sandy bottom. Slowly, the yacht turned counterclockwise, and waves pummeled its starboard side. It rocked violently from side to side as the wind and waves worked it over. Suddenly, a fierce gust hit the vessel, spinning it around like a top. In an instant, the aft line snapped, and the yacht was free.

As the sun began to peek over the Sea of Cortez and the eastern horizon began to turn yellow-orange, Cleve rose from a restless sleep. The winds had subsided, and all appeared calm. Cleve, however, was nervous. He needed to reassure himself that his yacht was still safe. Crossing the patio, now littered with broken palm fronds and overturned patio furniture, he looked south. The yacht was no longer there.

Frantically, Cleve rushed to the front of the house, leaped into his jeep, and headed toward the hotel. *Maybe it pulled the anchor and is closer to the shore*, he thought. As soon as he reached the hotel, Cleve ran through the restaurant and out onto the porch.

"My boat. Where is my boat?" he shouted to one of his workers who appeared from the kitchen.

"*Allá, en la playa*," a worker replied, pointing toward a beach south of the hotel.

Hoping he still might be able to rescue the yacht, Cleve shouted to some workers to join him. They climbed into the jeep, and Cleve drove to a bluff near the south end of the long airstrip. They saw the vessel's familiar silhouette in the distance, just south of a fishing camp. The craft was tilted on its side just offshore.

A few Mexicans had already gathered along the bluff. They became quiet as Cleve jumped out of his jeep and ran to the cliff's edge to see his beloved yacht. It appeared to be lodged against a reef just off the beach. A large gash in its starboard side caused the boat to take on saltwater and sink in only five feet of water. Cleve felt sick to his stomach. His worst nightmare had come true. He could only imagine what the yacht's once beautiful interior looked like.

In Baja, a sunken boat is considered public property. When the Mexican locals became aware of Cleve's yacht lying on its side on the reef, they were drawn to it like a magnet, including his employees. Those who speculated the vessel was used as a floating casino hoped to find money or gold onboard. Others were eager to salvage whatever they could for their houses or personal use. Although no gold was found, the scavengers hauled away ornate mirrors, furniture, marble toilets, dishes, engines, and even a lathe used onboard to make tools. Everyone wanted a piece of the luxurious yacht. Like vultures, they stripped it clean. One worker still possesses the memento he claimed so many years ago. "I only took a small thing," he sheepishly admitted, producing a pocketknife.

Cleve Jr. was shocked when he heard about the fate of the yacht. "For years, I was furious at Father for not providing a better mooring for the boat prior to the storm. After it sank, I went through a period of being really upset with him because I put a lot of my own time and energy into working on the boat. I felt that he was so irresponsible."

Later, when guests came down and inquired about the missing yacht, Cleve Sr. simply replied, "It just disappeared." He refused to go into any further detail. He did not want to think about it.

Losing his beloved yacht was both an emotional and a financial drain. But Cleve had a business to run. He needed to refocus. More than anything, Cleve desperately needed more capital to keep Punta Chivato alive.

Chapter 26

NEW INVESTORS

The pilot made a smooth landing on the east-west runway at Punta Chivato and taxied his single-engine airplane toward the hotel. Two men climbed out and waved to a nearby Mexican, who waved back in acknowledgment and headed toward them.

It was 1971. The aviator, who worked as a boat dealer in Newport Beach, and his buddy were on their way home from a fishing trip to Cabo San Lucas at the tip of the Baja peninsula. Known for marlin and other large sport fish, Cabo became a prime destination for serious anglers.

The friends loved fishing in Baja and were eager to invest in property along the coast. The day before, they had stayed at the Serenidad Hotel in the palm-treed village of Mulegé south of Punta Chivato. Serenidad Hotel, with its airstrip, was a customary stopover on their return trips from Cabo. While in Mulegé, they met with a man who showed them property for sale.

"We found a place in Conception Bay on the beach. The place is still there," one of the men remarked when interviewed years later. "We looked at it and met the owner." The dwelling needed work, but they were capable handymen. "We were going to buy it and fix it up. We had pretty well made up our minds to do that." Before making a down payment on the home, they decided to visit Punta Chivato first. They had heard good things about the resort but had only seen it from the air.

While the Mexican worker refueled their airplane, the friends walked up to the resort to look around. Cleveland Crudgington was talking to his office manager when the men entered. Turning, he smiled and greeted them.

"Welcome to Punta Chivato. Need a room?"

"Sure, how much?" asked the pilot.

"Thirty dollars a night. Best deal around," Cleve added. "The restaurant is open, and our bartender makes great margaritas."

The men relished the thought of a drink after their long flight. A margarita would hit the spot. They agreed to stay.

Cleve sent a van down to the plane to pick up their luggage and showed the men two rooms that faced the sea. After settling in, the guests headed to the hotel bar. They were greeted by the friendly bartender who poured freshly blended margaritas into large, gold-fish-bowl-sized glasses. As they drank and enjoyed the view of the Sea of Cortez out the large window, Cleve walked up. The bartender quickly began preparing his boss's favorite cocktail.

Turning to his guests, Cleve smiled. "How do you like things so far?" he said, gesturing toward their drinks and then toward the view.

"Absolutely fabulous. We've always wanted to stop here. Finally, we decided this was the time." They shared their interest in investing in property in Baja and described what they had seen on Conception Bay.

"I've been looking for some investors in this place," Cleve interjected. "Maybe you'd be interested." He told them about his purchase of the hotel and the incident with his yacht. "We've had some hard breaks, and right now, I need extra capital to keep the place running. As soon as we get things straightened out, I know this is going to be a real moneymaker."

The two visitors ended up spending the weekend at Punta Chivato. By the end of their stay, Cleve had convinced the men to invest in the hotel. Each agreed to put up $10,000, later signing promissory notes in San Diego. Cleve promised them a share of the hotel, a return on their cash investment over time, or a piece of land. "I can't sell the land yet, but it will be coming up. You can pick out the lot today if you want," Cleve added. "I can't commit to any one thing right now, but I can commit to honoring your investment."

The pilot's name was Bob Davis. He picked out a lot on the bluff above the ocean just north of Casa Grande.[75] Years later, when asked if he was ever repaid, he responded without hesitation. "Yes. Cleve paid it back, every cent. I have no regrets whatsoever. He treated me very well."

With additional capital, Cleve could continue work on the pipeline from the well to the reservoir and make payments to the Ejido. Things were finally looking up.

Like his predecessor, Cleve offered a variety of activities to his guests, including chartered fishing trips aboard the *Barbaras*, scuba gear and tanks, and snorkeling equipment. One guest at Punta

Chivato during that era, Dale Head, shared the following:

We stayed at Punta Chivato in May of 1972. My brother flew us down in his four-seater Piper Comanche. We were met at the landing strip down the hill from where the resort stood. On the east end of the dining area was the bar and there were large windows opening onto the veranda. From the bar you could see for miles over the Sea of Cortez, and we spent a considerable time enjoying the view. I recall reading Steinbeck's The Sea of Cortez, *published in the 1950s. It described fish pileups and we saw one approximately a half-mile long. A fisherman caught a Golden Grouper which was also something new for us. While we were having cocktails on the veranda one evening, the same fisherman and his guests ate one side of a large tuna and told the waiter to share the untouched portion with us. It was delicious.*

One day we flew to the Serenidad airport at Mulegé, and a taxi driver gave us a tour. We drank cool beer at an outdoor restaurant in the middle of town, and I recall a huge bougainvillea bush bursting in blooms, providing a shaded canopy over our table. We drove by the river, viewing date and citrus trees and hearing tall tales about the famous tortuava fish that inhabit the brackish waters where the river empties into the bay.

Later that day, we returned to Punta Chivato and couldn't wait to get back to the veranda. About the same time we arrived, some noisy gringos came from the landing strip to have dinner. They had been fishing to the south and were on their way back to the States. It turned out that one was a lawyer from our hometown of Prescott [Arizona] and he brought smoked shark that he'd caught and prepared during his fishing trip. It was not bad. We shared a few funny stories and off they flew. It had been a great day and under the influence of a bit too much to drink, we planned how to buy the resort, move down and run it. It never happened, but we came away with unforgettable memories of an outstanding vacation.

Because my wife then spoke Spanish quite well, she spent a lot of time chatting with the hired help and immediately became a favorite of theirs. When it was time to leave, my brother, his wife and I left with little fanfare. But as we came out the doorway to get into the van for our short ride back to our airplane, there was a line of employees who said goodbye to my wife, the men shaking her hand and the women hugging her. It was an unforgettable trip for all of us.

During Crudgington's time, an avid fisherman who later settled in Punta Chivato remarked, "People were fishing off the shore. We used to fish for dorado right past the islands out there—I remember dorado jumping everywhere. We just fished them right in the bay. Cleve knew he had to cater to the fishermen. Fishing was very good. There were pictures in the hotel of guys with marlin and sailfish."

In addition to fishermen, celebrities continued to enjoy the secluded resort. Movie stars, rock stars, and even an Olympic champion found respite at Punta Chivato. "The Doors came down and stayed at the hotel," recalled one visitor. "Everyone went skinny dipping in the pool at the hotel with them." Mark Spitz, who won seven gold medals in swimming during the 1972 Summer Olympic Games in Munich, also vacationed with his family at Hotel Punta Chivato.

Although money from Cleve's new investors helped cover hotel costs briefly, Cleve continued to face unexpected expenses. Bob Davis recalls flying Cleve to Guaymas on mainland México in January 1973. "He had tax problems. They even told him he must pay bed tax." Bob frequently acted as Cleve's pilot. In return, Cleve invited him to stay as a guest at Casa Grande whenever he came to Punta Chivato.

Visitors to Hotel Punta Chivato in the early 1970s were unaware of the pressures and challenges Crudgington faced. They were there to enjoy the secluded paradise on the Sea of Cortez and temporarily forget about their busy schedules back home. Few knew the growing rift over finances between Cleve and his wife. Operating the hotel was expensive.

Not one to admit defeat, Cleve promised Mim their cash flow would improve when the long-anticipated Baja Transpeninsular Highway was finished. This paved road down Baja was scheduled for completion by the end of 1973. Cleve was sure the new highway would change everything. No longer would he have to depend solely on guests with airplanes. With the new highway, Americans could drive to Punta Chivato from California and Arizona more easily. Cleve envisioned a hotel overflowing with guests and an end to his problems if he could only hold on.

Chapter 27

BAJA 1 & FERRY

Before the 1970s, most American visitors to Baja arrived by plane or boat. Those who drove seldom ventured past the Pacific coast town of Ensenada, 63 miles south of the U.S.-Mexican border. Beyond this point, the paved road came to an abrupt stop. Only travelers with time and a spirit of adventure continued to drive down the peninsula on the notorious Baja "road."

The narrow dirt road sometimes followed early Indian and mule trails connecting villages and water sources. Many settlement sites were in the rugged uplands of central and eastern Baja, where rainfall was more likely.

As the mining industry developed in Baja, the first wagon roads were created along the easiest and shortest pathways from the mines to the Pacific and gulf coasts of Baja. The pattern of the road swinging back and forth across the peninsula was due to an effort to use the mining roads whenever possible and to seek lower and flatter land on which to drive. Some mission settlements, like San Borja, Santa Gertrudis, Guadalupe, and San Xavier, were not included on the "main" route and could only be reached via rugged and poorly maintained side roads.

As automobiles arrived in Baja, the unmaintained dirt roadway soon became a hodgepodge of tire tracks left behind by previous vehicles. Driving was slow as one encountered giant potholes, thick dust, and bowling ball-sized rocks. The single-lane washboard road crossed through arid cactus forests, wound up and down the steep mountains of central Baja, and followed dry riverbeds. It took two hours to cover a mile along some stretches.

Early automobile travelers carried their own water, food, and shelter since lodging and restaurants were scarce. They also brought gasoline, flares, spare parts, and tools as gas stations and repair shops were limited. Flat tires were common. In areas where tire tracks created deep ruts, the higher center section of the road often sheared off oil pans or transmissions. Potholes appeared out of nowhere, ready to jar car parts loose. Less securely tied items toppled over; cans spilled their contents. The deep, soft, sandy sections of the road caused problems even for those with four-wheel-drive vehicles as tires lost traction and spun, creating deeper ruts.

"Larry Lucore made the trip on the dirt road," remarked Bunnie Adams, an early visitor to Punta Chivato. "He came all the way down to the Cape before they built the road. It took them two weeks to get to Santa Rosalía by road."

Multiple "roads" occasionally split off from the main trail. These were created by drivers who grew frustrated and searched for a better route. Subsequent travelers looked for the freshest tracks, hoping it was the "road." But even if they went astray, the alternate pathways eventually rejoined the original track.

The southern part of the peninsula was prone to flash floods during late summer and early fall. These floods could wash away entire sections of the road, and stranded travelers waited days for the waters to recede.

The adventurous travelers often encountered the rusted remains of a car or camper that had fallen victim to the rugged Baja road. Torn apart by the vibration and jolting, these vehicles refused to go further and were abandoned. Some became inhabited by cacti that took root around the disfigured metal frames and ironically added some beauty. A particular stranded, colorfully painted 1960s VW van would later be depicted in a popular Baja postcard.

The Mexican government knew that improving Baja's roads was essential to the area's development. For over forty years, Mexican presidential candidates promised a Transpeninsular Highway in Baja to encourage American tourism, create local jobs, and boost the economy. However, the needs of mainland México always took precedence.

In 1970, Luis Echeverría Alvarez was elected president of México. It is believed he was the only presidential candidate to experience Baja's road first-hand. Following a bulldozer that leveled ruts and removed rocks, he rode in a procession of limousines from the tip of Baja north to the city of Tijuana bordering California. Perhaps because of this experience, President Echeverría vowed to have a paved highway through Baja within three years.

Federal money was poured into the project, and construction

was accelerated. Thousands of men were hired to operate bulldozers and graders or to simply man shovels. A plan was devised to use as little water as possible since water was scarce. Sand, crushed gravel, and cement were mixed together. After the roadbed was spread and graded, it was sprinkled with water and rolled. Finally, a layer of oil was applied, followed by a layer of fine gravel. Day and night, the road crews worked, one crew beginning in the northern end of the peninsula and the other in the south. The goal was to meet somewhere in the middle of Baja.

Simultaneously, the Mexican government funded the construction of five tourist accommodations called *paradores* along the 400-mile rugged center section of the highway—in the towns of Santa María, Santa Inés, Punta Prieta, Guerrero Negro, and San Ignacio. These stopovers provided lodging, restaurants, gas stations, and trailer parks in anticipation of the influx of American travelers. In Santa Inés and Guerrero Negro, swimming pools were built as an added enticement.

In some sparsely populated areas, entrepreneurs from mainland México funded the construction of motels. Medium-priced hotels were erected in established resort towns like La Paz, Loreto, and Cabo San Lucas. Due to the earlier presence of luxury hotels in this southeastern peninsula, it became known as the Gold Coast of Baja.

On October 17, 1973, the long-awaited $160-million-dollar highway project was completed. President Echeverría had kept his promise. Considered one of the greatest achievements in Baja, the 1,061-mile paved road was constructed simultaneously from Tijuana in the north and Cabo San Lucas in the south. The two sections met near Rancho Santa Ynez.

On December 1, 1973, President Echeverría returned to Baja for the dedication ceremony. From the town of Guerrero Negro on the 28th parallel, the border between the territory of Baja Sur in the south and the state of Baja California to the north, he named the new highway *Carretera Transpeninsular Benito Juárez* (Transpeninsular Highway Benito Juárez) to honor a past national hero and president of México, Benito Pablo Juárez García. However, to most, the highway simply became known as Baja 1.[76]

"We thought we'd never see it," remembered Saúl Davis, a longtime resident of Mulegé and owner of Saúl's Market. "No, it never will be built. No never. We'll never see it."

Saúl credits the Mexican president with the completion of the highway. "A lot of people didn't like him, but he did some good things for the country, for Baja. He was the one who made us a highway."

But the improved road also had its drawbacks. "It's good for our economy, but with progress, you get bad things," reflected Saúl. "This was virgin country. It changed when people from other cities arrived. Bad habits and crime came. But most of us were willing to have a highway."

"The town of Santa Rosalía changed," remarked Chema, the owner/builder of El Morro Hotel in Santa Rosalía. "It changed the people and customs." But on the positive end, Chema stated, "There were so many inconveniences before the highway connected us."

Like the old road, the new, paved highway hugged the Pacific coast along the northwest, crossed the central mountains in the middle of the peninsula, and continued south along the eastern side of the peninsula. One of the biggest diversions occurred in central Baja, beginning at the 28th parallel, where the new highway bypassed the mining village of El Arco and instead crossed the Vizcaino Desert. Here, tourists were introduced to an array of unique cacti and desert plants—the towering *cardón* or elephant cactus, a tapered-candle-shaped *cirio* (candle) plant, known as the Boojum tree, and the ocotillos with their spiny, whip-like branches.

The two-lane highway vastly improved travel in Baja, but driving was still challenging and dangerous. The lanes were narrow in most sections, and there was no "soft shoulder." The ridge on which the asphalt was laid simply ended and fell away to a ditch on either side of the road. A vehicle could easily overturn if a less-than-vigilant driver let a tire stray off the highway.

Andy and Bunnie Adams, who lived in Southern California, were early travelers on the new highway. "The road had just been built; it was only like an inch thick," recalled Bunnie. "The rains came that winter, and the roads were awful." She remembers "miles of giant potholes."

Maneuvering the mountain passes was especially nerve-racking. Lanes narrowed to only nine feet wide, posing a predicament for those pulling eight-foot-wide trailers or boats. With few guard rails, there was no room for error. White-knuckled passengers occasionally spotted the mangled, rusted remains of a less fortunate vehicle resting at the base of a mountain pass. Eventually, concrete shrines began to dot the landscape along the road, placed by local Mexicans in memory of loved ones who died while traveling on the new highway.

Bunnie Adams recounted a lasting memory shared with traveling buddies and long-time friends Larry and Kathy Lucore. The couples were driving separate vehicles on the new highway. "We were going up the hill to El Rosario, and Larry had a boat trailer with their 12-foot Valco or some crazy aluminum boat on it loaded to the gills with stuff. The axle broke on the trailer. So, he unloaded everything, put the boat on top of their motorhome, which was filled with junk, including firewood, and rolled the trailer over the cliff—got it off the highway." After vacationing for ten days, the couples stopped by the site on their return trip to Southern California. "He was going to pick up parts, and the thing was gone," she said with a chuckle. "So, he said, 'Baja got it.' That was when we coined the phrase, 'Baja got ya.'"

There were no passing lanes and few turnouts on Baja 1, so it was risky to pass slow-moving vehicles. Drivers had to gingerly pull into the left lane to check for oncoming traffic and hope their timing was right. Americans were confused when they got behind truckers who flashed their left-hand turn signals to indicate it was safe to pass. Unfamiliar with this custom, tourists remained behind the truck, expecting it to turn left.

Although speed limit signs were posted, most drivers ignored them. Semi-trucks whizzed by within inches of cars traveling in the opposite direction. The ensuing air current buffeted the vehicles they passed, causing occupants to fear their car might overturn or be blown off the road.

Tourists had to be wary of local Mexican drivers unfamiliar with the "rules" of driving on a highway. In sections with no painted center line, they drove right down the middle, using the highway like a single-lane road. Some Mexican villagers slowly pulled onto the paved road from adjoining dirt roads that lead to outlying towns and ranches. Oncoming drivers slammed on their brakes as the locals nonchalantly drove onto the new roadway without looking, oblivious to other vehicles. After creeping onto the highway, they

often continued at an unhurried pace while a line of cars accumu-
lated behind them. Reaching their destination, they just as slowly
left the highway, not signaling their intentions.

At night, the risks of driving were compounded since there were
no lights along the highway. Headlights barely penetrated the black-
ness on moonless evenings, making it difficult to see ahead. The
lights from oncoming traffic were blinding, especially when the
driver could not switch to lower beams or simply forgot. Cars passed
with only one operable headlamp; others had none. At night, it was
difficult to see livestock on the road. A driver could unexpectedly
come across a cow sleeping in the middle of the highway.

Livestock also created a hazard for drivers during daylight hours,
especially in the *vados*. These were low-lying dips in the road constructed to aid in directing water runoff in the event of a sudden
storm. It was common for cows, goats, horses, and mules to wander
across the road in search of better grazing land on the other side.
As with all herd animals, if one crossed, the others would soon follow. At times, an unexpected straggler would suddenly emerge from
behind a bush into the path of a vehicle whose driver thought it
was safe to proceed.

Tourists who drove to Baja were wise to carry water, food, flares,
and spare car parts, especially along the 400-mile, minimally populated stretch across central Baja. To assist stranded motorists, the
Mexican Department of Tourism established a fleet of nine green
trucks to patrol 100-plus-mile sections of the highway. Dubbed
"The Green Angels" by Americans, these welcome vehicles carried
spare parts, gasoline, water, and powerful two-way radios. The
Mexican Green Angel drivers, who spoke some English, came prepared to fix flat tires, replace fan belts and batteries, and fix other
mechanical and electrical problems. Their labor was free; Americans
only paid for the parts. Word of these "angels" spread among American travelers and diminished their fear of being stranded alongside
the highway. They were relieved to know a Green Angel could be
expected within thirty minutes to an hour.

Some concerned locals and travelers hoped the paved highway
would put an end to the annual Baja 1000 Rough Road Race. This
motorsport race down the Baja peninsula was founded by Ed Pearl-
man in 1967. Cars, trucks, and motorcycles could enter the com-

petition. The event started in Ensenada and ended in La Paz, over 1,000 miles (1,600 km).[77] Individuals opposed to the race considered the sport a desecration of the Baja landscape. They believed the racers who sped through the countryside were tearing up the terrain rather than appreciating it. But the race would not be halted. After the paved road was completed in 1973, the event was run cross-country on a newly staked-out track.

Mexican President Echeverría followed through on another promise he made to the people of Baja; he established a second ferry line across the Sea of Cortez. Up until that time, only one ferry line linked mainland México to Baja. Begun in 1964, this line ran between Mazatlán, on the continent, and La Paz, in southern Baja. The new ferry line crossed farther north. It linked Guaymas on mainland México to the town of Santa Rosalía midway down the east coast of Baja, north of Punta Chivato.

When the first large, double-decked, white ferry sailed into the port in Santa Rosalía, locals gathered to meet it. Shop owners eagerly anticipated the arrival of fresh produce, building materials, clothing, and household supplies. Others came to greet relatives or friends who lived on the mainland.

With its capacity to carry passenger vehicles, the ferry brought to the Baja peninsula another much-desired commodity: the American tourist. This new connection to Baja was particularly popular with Arizona visitors. They could now drive straight to Guaymas and ferry their cars across the Sea of Cortez, avoiding the long journey down the peninsula.

While some travelers came prepared to camp at beaches along Baja's eastern shore, others preferred staying at quaint hotels or more luxurious resorts. Whether they arrived by ferry or car, the influx of visitors brought something Baja desperately needed—American dollars.

Chapter 28

ANGRY EMPLOYEES

The Mexican government's efforts to improve access to Baja should have elated Cleve Crudgington. Ever since he took over Hotel Punta Chivato in the late 1960s, Cleve had looked forward to the day he would not have to depend on air traffic to fill the resort. Now, the paved highway and new ferry line to the nearby town of Santa Rosalía certainly would increase his profit margin. However, as much as Cleve tried to convince himself that things would eventually get better, he began to have doubts.

Each time his cash flow started to improve, members of the Ejido San Bruno unexpectedly showed up demanding money. They claimed he owed them taxes on the water from the well, taxes on the hotel, taxes on the food he served his guests, social security for the workers, and bed tax. As the list grew, so did Cleve's intolerance of the Mexican system. There seemed to be no rules; he never knew what to expect. When the hotel owner adamantly claimed he owed no more money, the officials accused him of dishonesty and pocketing the profits. Finally, Cleve had had enough.

"I'm sure he made his problems worse with the Mexican authorities," remarked his son, Cleve Jr., during an interview years later. "If you tried to push him, he would just blow up. I'm sure that's what happened. He blew up and told them to go screw themselves."

The government officials were not the only ones hounding Cleve. One day, his boat captains came to him demanding a pay increase. These men, who were hired to take guests on fishing and diving trips aboard his cabin cruisers, the "*Barbaras*," accused their boss of being unfair.

"You're making lots of money and not giving us our share," shouted one captain. "We want a raise."

"Hey, I'm not making a lot of money here," Cleve angrily responded. "I'm giving you what I said I'd give you."

"You're a thief," the others chimed in. "If you don't give us a raise, we'll strike."

"Just try," retorted the owner.

The Mexican men belonged to a captains' union and followed through with their threat. They called their boss's bluff and walked off the job. Those clients who came for the fishing excursions at Punta Chivato soon opted to vacation elsewhere, and Cleve's cash-flow worries escalated. He felt helpless as he watched his dream of operating a profitable venture in Baja slip away.

Customarily, the Crudgingtons closed Hotel Punta Chivato for two months during the summer when the weather was unbearably hot and humid. Employees were told to take a vacation while the Crudgingtons returned north to cooler California. Mim and the children usually left a few weeks before Cleve, while he remained to shut everything down.

No one thought anything was unusual that windy morning in late July of 1974 when Cleve and his pilot boarded their plane and flew north. It was Cleve's regular summer routine—gone for two months, then back in September to reopen the hotel. That was how it had always been; they never expected otherwise.

Chapter 29

EARLY CAMPERS

It was late afternoon when the camper turned off Baja 1 onto the rutted washboard road. Nearing the end of a two-week vacation, the family was heading back home to Southern California. It was October 1974, and the paved highway had been open for a year. The family drove down the entire length of the Baja peninsula from Tijuana in the north to the sleepy village of Cabo San Lucas at the tip. There, they stayed at the famous Palmilla Hotel and fished with friends. Now, on the first leg of their journey home, they were in search of a luxury hotel on the Sea of Cortez where they could spend the night.

"Where are we going?" one of their sons asked as the tires hit a rut, and he suddenly awoke.

"Punta Chivato," his father responded. "It's out on the water. Shouldn't take too long, but the road may be a little bumpy." He knew the children were tired after the long day's drive. As the evening drew near, they were eager to find a place to spend the night.

Their father had read about Punta Chivato, one of the most expensive hotels in Baja near one of the better fishing areas. He hoped it would not be hard to find.

The road followed a dry riverbed lined with smooth rocks. Even driving slowly, the contents of the camper jostled. It was dark when they reached the ocean two hours later. Everything in the cabinets, the kids' schoolbooks, and the contents of the refrigerator were strewn across the camper's floor.

In the distance, they saw a dim light and headed toward it. They drove down a long airport runway outlined in white rock and then turned left, parallelling the water. The light came from a hotel on the bluff, barely visible in the darkness. Suddenly, a car appeared behind them. They waited as the driver got out. It was a young Mexican man clad in a T-shirt and jeans.

"What do you want?" asked the Mexican.

"Well, we came to see the hotel," the father responded.

"The hotel is not open," the Mexican replied.

Conversing in Spanish and broken English, the family learned the hotel owner had returned to the United States for the summer. He was expected back in September but still had not returned. Most employees, tired of waiting, had left to look for jobs elsewhere.

"I still hope he returns," said the man. "I'm Ramón, the hotel bartender. It's a good job."

He explained that the hotel owner had gotten into a fight with the boat captains right before he left. "Maybe he's too mad to come back," the Mexican speculated.

"Can we stay in the hotel?" the father asked, hoping the bartender could access the hotel rooms. He had read that camping on the beaches was prohibited, and he could not imagine driving back on that road.

"Why do you want to stay in the hotel?" the Mexican questioned. "You're in a camper."

"Well, can we camp here?"

"Do you want to camp here or by the beach?" asked the Mexican.

"By the beach," the wife interjected.

"Follow me," said the Mexican, pulling his car ahead. Inside, they could see a young woman and small children.

The camper followed in the pitch black of night as the car drove past the hotel along a narrow dirt road. After several minutes, they reached a big rock on the beach. The Mexican approached the American family. "Stop here. Don't go any further," he advised. "I'll come back tomorrow with tortillas and firewood." He then returned to his car and drove away. Weary from the long day of traveling, the family soon fell asleep in their camper.

The following morning, the children, ages nine, ten, and eleven, were the first to rise.

"You've got to come see this, Dad; you've got to get up," they shouted after an early exploration of the beach with their dog, Scruffy. "We've got to go fishing."

The Americans could hardly believe their luck. They were camped on a beautiful, white-sand beach with no other person in sight. To the right of their camper, a narrow strip of beach curved out into the sea, terminating in a T-shaped pattern of volcanic rock.[78] This created a perfect, shallow bay. Further along the coast, a continuation of the beach hugged the base of the bluff.

True to his word, the Mexican returned with a stack of fresh tortillas and a load of firewood later that morning. The family graciously accepted his gifts, amazed at their good fortune to have met Ramón the night before and been led to this magnificent camping spot.

The Adams family stayed at the beach for three days, only leaving when it began to rain. They did not want to risk getting stuck on the road back to Baja 1. The children, however, were reluctant to go. "Our kids wouldn't have minded if we had stayed there. They loved it," Bunnie Adams recalled. "Scruffy wore his feet out digging for crabs in the sand."

As one of the early camping families at Punta Chivato, the Adamses knew they had found a special place. As they drove away, they vowed to return soon.

Camping beach showing dunes (palapa erected later).
From Nov. 1991 video by Bill Alvarado

Chapter 30

HOTEL ABANDONED

By late fall of 1974, the local Mexicans realized Cleve Crudgington had no intention of returning to Punta Chivato. Hope and concern quickly turned to anger. The Ejido San Bruno declared Cleve's lease void, and the employees began stripping the hotel and Casa Grande. Glassware, plates, utensils, and dining room furniture were loaded into trucks and driven away. Towels, linens, beds, and sofas were taken from the hotel rooms. The employees kept some items for their own use and sold others. In time, the boat captains auctioned off all the 25-foot cabin cruisers, the "*Barbaras*." The workers felt justified in their actions, viewing their windfall as compensation for back pay they would never recoup.

Mexicans from nearby towns soon heard about the abandoned resort and joined in ransacking the once-grand hotel. Roof tiles, air conditioners, windows, doors, sinks, and toilets were pilfered. They broke glasses in the bar area, leaving the jagged shards. Unpaid invoices, files, and correspondence littered the hotel office. Other papers lay outside, picked up by the wind and carried through paneless windows. Eventually, even the pool was ravaged, its tiles cracked or broken off. "They simply took the place apart," recalled Saúl Davis.

There has been much conjecture about why Cleve Crudgington decided to walk away from his investment in Punta Chivato after six years. Speculation runs the gamut from involvement with drug smuggling to finding buried treasure to not paying taxes to simply running out of money.

Some contend Cleve had connections with the Mafia and participated in a drug-running operation. They described witnessing small planes landing on the runway after dark, even though night landings were illegal in Baja. Met by vehicles with dimmed head-lights, the aircraft only stayed briefly before departing. Others say these planes ferried drugs from South America to the United States and used Punta Chivato as a convenient midway location for hand-offs or refueling. Others report they saw strange boats arrive at

Punta Chivato Hotel abandoned. Courtesy George Powell

Punta Chivato during the night. These boats rapidly departed after transferring parcels wrapped in brown paper or plastic.

"There are lots of rumors about all the dope and girls and everything else down here. I remember all those men with their little 'nieces' at Punta Chivato," recalled one hotel guest. "I heard the hotel was used as a prostitution house for a while," remarked a later visitor. "The owner got into problems with drugs and prostitution."

Perhaps the authorities found out about a rumored operation and suspected Cleve was involved. Maybe Cleve was tipped off and decided it was best to leave immediately. That would explain his hasty departure and failure to return. Locals say Cleve was so afraid he left without taking his personal items. They found money he had left in his residence at Casa Grande.

Another explanation for the owner's sudden disappearance comes from a local Mexican, Yolanda Acosta. "This was pirate area," she recounted. "Even my grandfather, who lived to be 106, said there were gold coins buried here." She spoke of a conversation she had with one of the oldest hotel employees. "He told us Crudgington paid him to search for buried treasure. He paid him to dig holes along the beach. He dug big holes—two meters by one-half meters by one meter deep. It's true, my husband and I saw them. Holes everywhere." The employee told her that he eventually came upon the treasure—gold. "He said it was so heavy, like carrying two men to-gether," Yolanda said. The employee loaded it into a wheelbarrow and transferred it to Crudgington's plane. "He left that day and never came back. The whole town talked about this. Mr. Crudgington just took his coat and left his watch, rings, money, and checkbooks be-hind. He left everything." The employee told Yolanda it was windy that day, and the plane, loaded with the treasure, took off "funny."

Some believe Cleve was angry about the fishermen's union demanding a salary increase. Not wanting to be pushed around by union bosses, he decided he would teach them a lesson and closed the hotel so the striking boat captains would be permanently out of a job. Others say the union boss had the upper hand and gave Cleve 24 to 48 hours to get out, leading to his hurried exodus. "He just got up and left," recounted Don Johnson, long-time owner of Serenidad Hotel in Mulegé. "Left everything. Nobody knows."

According to Bob Davis, one of Cleve's investors, the owner always intended to return to Punta Chivato. "He called me that summer and said he wasn't going to open until the government gave him some relief on his taxes and he could work a better deal with them." Cleve refused to pay the Mexican government money he felt they did not deserve. "He said he would never make a profit on the hotel as long as the government kept gouging him for more taxes."

Throughout the summer and into September, Cleve tried long distance to reach a mutual agreement with the Mexican officials. But they would not back down, and Cleve, being a proud man, would not either.

A Mexican source said Cleve's employee, Luis Sui Qui, advised his "*abuelo*" (grandfather) not to pay anything to the government. As Cleve fell behind in his taxes, Sui Qui continued to tell him there would be no problem. "Luis Sui Qui was very crazy. He said, 'No, you don't pay anything to the government. You don't pay. No prob-lem. No problem.' Afterwards, many problems." When Cleve lost the hotel, it fell into the hands of the Ejido San Bruno. "They won the hotel using *chueco* (crooked ways). There were many *ratas* (rats)." Perhaps Sui Qui was part of a plan and endeared himself to his boss so the Ejido would gain control of everything the American had built.[79]

Dixon Collins commented, "Cleve had all kinds of problems with the Ejido. There's no way in hell that that guy could have ever been successful down in México because if you're going to do business in México, you have to play the game. You also have to have compassion for people. You can't just walk over them because sooner or later, somebody will get you back. And it'll hurt, and you'll lose a lot more than you'd gain by taking advantage of somebody. So, you had to be sort of an up-front guy. Cleve always put himself first. Everybody around him he saw as 'How can I use this person to feather my own nest, to get ahead?'"

Although the real reason Cleve Crudgington left Punta Chivato is still a mystery, he likely ran out of money. The government may have squeezed everything out of him, and Mim may have finally put her foot down and refused to allow her husband to invest any more of her inheritance. According to Cleve Jr., "He had gotten to the point with Mim's money where she said, 'That's it.' I'm sure that's what happened. She said, 'You cannot spend any more money on this hotel.' I'm sure they fought over it. Somehow, she probably cut him off the remaining funds that she had. I would not be at all surprised if that were the case." Cleve could do whatever he wanted as long as he had money in México. Once that money ran out, he had no more power to negotiate. He could no longer fight the battle.

"It really took a lot out of Dad when he lost the boat and the hotel," said Cleve Jr. "This was sort of like his dream going up in smoke. I think that once there was no more money, it was over for him. I think Mim had had it with him because of all the hopes and promises that went up in smoke. It was just too much."

Cleve and Mim ended up selling the house in Tiburon. A brief time later, they divorced. The chasm between them over finances had grown too deep to mend.[80]

Cleve still had his Reno printing company and moved it to an Indian reservation outside town. The government agreed to pay part of their salaries if he employed the indigenous people. But again, Cleve ran into problems. Cleve Jr. said, "There was something about this particular property that the Indians were taking back. Dad owed them money and he wasn't taking care of the property. He was suing the Indians. Mim was suing him, trying to recoup some of the money he had spent. My inheritance from my father went to his attorneys."

Mim's son, Nathan, remained close to Cleve Sr. even after he and Mim separated. Having spent so much time in Baja, Nathan had become fluent in Spanish. He married Francisca Sui Qui García, a daughter of Luis Sui Qui. "Cleve was using Nathan for something," said Cleve's ex-wife Phyllis. "All of a sudden, something happened between Nathan and Cleve. Cleve dumped him. I never knew why." Cleve Jr. added, "Anybody who's around Cleve for any length of time ends up getting dumped. Something blows up."[81]

"Everything he did, he ended up with nothing," said Phyllis. "Go from rags to riches, go from riches to rags. He was a terrible businessman. Nothing ever worked out for him."

However, Cleve Sr. was not one to readily admit defeat. In the 1980s, he returned to Baja, hoping to reacquire Hotel Punta Chivato.

Cleve would marry a fourth time to a young woman from Japan. He knew her grandfather and wanted to help her enter the United States. Running into problems, he called his previous wife Phyllis, whom he knew had contacts in Washington, D.C. When Cleve asked the favor of Phyllis, she told him she refused to "procure" for him.[82]

Eventually, Cleve managed to get the Japanese woman into the United States on a student visa. In 1990, 67-year-old Cleve married the 31-year-old so she could remain in the United States. They lived in a house in Las Vegas, Nevada, described by Cleve Jr. as "a major step down from the house out on Strawberry Point in Mill Valley."

"This house was middle-class and in disrepair. This is not the Cleve Sr. that I remember growing up. It was like his spirit had been broken. In a lot of ways, he just kind of gave up," his namesake remarked.

While living with his fourth wife, Cleveland Benedict Crudgington came up against another battle he would fight for ten years—cancer. Again, he lost. He died in 1996, shortly before his 73rd birthday.

Chapter 31

EARLY ROAD—PUNTA CHIVATO

News of the destruction of Hotel Punta Chivato quickly spread among the American private pilots who frequented the popular fly-in resort. "When things changed down there, you heard about it," remembers San Francisco Bay Area resident John Fitzsimmons. "We soon found out that Crudgington had left, and there was no place to stay anymore." Still enamored of Baja, John, and other pilots opted to fly to Baja resorts further south, like Punta Pescadero or Loreto.

With private pilots no longer coming to Punta Chivato, the remote area might have faded into obscurity. However, the completion of the Transpeninsular Highway in 1973 opened the door to a new breed of traveler to Baja, the American camper. Driving cars, trucks, or jeeps and often pulling a boat, trailer, or second vehicle, these tourists came with a spirit of adventure and a willingness to "rough it." No longer faced with countless days on a bumpy, dirt road, they were eager to explore the now-accessible Baja peninsula. All hoped to find the perfect campsite.

The most popular destinations were the shorelines, where they could set up camp on the beach and have easy access to fishing. Many preferred the Pacific side of Baja because of its proximity to the United States. Others opted to drive further down the peninsula and cross over to the southeastern coastline, where they encountered a tropical climate and warmer water. Here, the calm, clear Sea of Cortez was ideal for swimming, diving, and fishing. Fishermen were eager to snag a trophy game fish—dorado, tuna, or even a blue marlin.

After traversing miles of flat desert terrain across central Baja, motorists heading to the southeast coast suddenly found themselves descending a steep, curvy section of the highway past three landmark volcanoes known as *Tres Virgenes* (Three Virgins). Along this stretch, travelers were delighted by their first views of the magnificent Sea of Cortez before arriving at the seaside town of Santa Rosalía. Most travelers did not stop in the dirty copper-mining village except to get gas. Then, they continued down the coast, searching for the ideal camping beach.

From Santa Rosalía, the highway turned south and followed the gulf, then headed inland across the hills before descending into the palm-treed village of Mulegé. Along this 39-mile stretch, one only caught glimpses of the Sea of Cortez on the left side of the road. While some chose to stay at trailer parks in Mulegé, many continued south to Conception Bay. Here, they found picturesque coves where they could camp next to the water. In addition to camping gear, some brought small boats transported on their cartops. Places like Posada, Santispec, and Coyote Bay quickly became popular.

While camping beside the turquoise Santispec Lagoon at Conception Bay, Bill and Barbara Silzle first met Walter "Red" and Nancy Salzman. The two adventurous couples soon realized they were both from Southern California, and all were avid divers. Red and Nancy spoke about a special place they had visited in 1973, right after the completion of the Transpeninsular Highway. It was called Punta Chivato (nicknamed P.C.) and was further north.

Walter "Red" and Nancy Salzman. Courtesy Harry Oxley

"We got the lowdown on P.C. from a native at Conception Bay," recalled Red. "When we first visited, the hotel had just closed. There wasn't another camper on the beach, and the diving was superb."

As Red talked about this alternate camping spot, Bill Silzle's face lit up. He turned to his wife and exclaimed, "Barbara, I remember reading about that hotel in a brochure years ago."

Bill Silzle first learned of Punta Chivato in the 1960s. He worked for Piper selling airplanes at Orange County Airport (now John Wayne Airport). One day, he came across a brochure with a photograph of a big rock fireplace on the cover. The pamphlet described Borrego de Oro, a resort in Punta Chivato then owned by Dixon Collins.

Bill Silzle recalled being intrigued by the fly-in resort and dreamed of piloting there in a Piper Tri-Pacer airplane. But he would not realize his dream for more than ten years. "We could barely afford to buy insurance and gas for it," said Barbara. "For vacations, we drove to San Carlos Bay on the mainland with our two young sons. For years, we camped, surfed, and dove there."

With the completion of Baja 1, the Silzles decided to explore a new area. They drove from their home in Southern California to Santispec Lagoon, 13 miles south of Mulegé. "There's no surf on the Baja side of the Sea of Cortez," Barbara stated. "We went there for the diving and the shell collecting."

It was a surprise that Red had told anyone about Punta Chivato. He liked the area so much he tried to keep others from finding it. Baja 1 did not pass through Punta Chivato as it did the nearby towns of Santa Rosalía and Mulegé. To reach the area, one had to leave the paved highway and drive 17 miles on an unpaved surface. The turnoff, 19 miles south of Santa Rosalía, was initially marked by a small sign, "Punta Chivato," which hung from a 20-foot metal post on the east side of the road. "The next year we were at Punta Chivato, other campers had discovered it," Red wrote in a letter to the author. "So, my son-in-law and I removed the sign—that really cut down the traffic."

"So, how will we know where to turn off?" Barbara Silzle inquired after Red told her he had removed the sign.

"Just head back toward Santa Rosalía, and it's a rocky road on the right," replied Red. "You just have to watch the road, and at a certain place, you will figure that must be it."

Removing the "Punta Chivato" sign from the roadside kept some campers from stumbling upon the secluded area. Many, either unaware of the former resort or not believing that anything lay at the end of the primitive trail, simply drove by. However, as word slowly spread, more campers made Punta Chivato their destination. These adventurous vacationers were determined not to let a missing road sign discourage them.

Early camper Harry Oxley was unsure how to get to Punta Chivato when he first drove down in 1974. "A friend of mine told me that they had fresh-water faucets at this place called Punta Chivato and that you could camp on the beach and if you took a hose, you could go take a shower and you could have fresh water," recalled Harry, "and, you know, when you're camping in Baja, fresh water is magic." Having camped near Cabo San Lucas and La Paz, Harry knew first-hand the luxury of having access to fresh water. "We usually had to drive 40 to 50 miles to get water. So, I thought, well, I'll go to this place," said Harry. But like other travelers, Harry discovered that locating the secluded location was not easy.

"The first time I came down, I missed the road," remembered Harry. "I went all the way to the dump at Mulegé. There were two guys unloading a truck, and I stopped and asked them how to get to the road to Punta Chivato. They said, 'Go back. It's a long way back. It's where the post for the telephone line crosses the road.'"

Dennis Gardner was camping at Puerto Escondido in Loreto, Baja California Sur, when he first heard about Punta Chivato. "I had a little 13-foot aluminum boat and was having a hard time getting out to do any fishing; it was blowing pretty good every day, and the water was rolling. There was a guy who said, 'You know there's a place called Punta Chivato just north of Mulegé that is probably the best small-boat fishing spot that you'll find in Baja.' So, I pulled up stakes and went to Mulegé. I asked around about Punta Chivato, and a *gringo* guy, who turned out to be an avid fisherman, said, 'I'm camped there; you can follow me out.' He was on a motorcycle that was strictly an off-road type, so we took back roads all the way."

Dennis Gardner was shown the way to Punta Chivato on his first visit in 1974. However, he admitted it was difficult to find this out-of-the-way spot again. "Back in those days, you really had to know exactly where to turn off," recalled Dennis. "It was very confusing."

Locating the turnoff to Punta Chivato was only the first challenge these campers faced. Unlike Baja 1, the road leading from the highway to Punta Chivato was unpaved. Following the same path initially cleared by Luis Sui Qui and his road crew in the 1960s, it meandered for 17 miles through the desert before reaching the coast.

The first section of the road was rocky, following an old, dry creek bed. "It had rocks like you wouldn't believe," said Robin Converse, another early camper at Punta Chivato.

After bumping over miles of large river rock, the driver had to navigate a soft, sandy section. "Red warned us not to stop when we reached the sand, or we'd get stuck," remembered Barbara Silzle. "He also told us we'd come to a bump and would have to keep a certain speed to get over it."

Eventually, the driver came to a dirt road, a welcome sight, until it forked into multiple unmarked trails. "There were just roads going all over," remarked Robin Converse. "That was one of the comical things. You'd come to five roads, and which one is it? Nobody around. Well, that one looks pretty well traveled. Oops, this one dead ends. My God, now what do I do? We'll have to turn around and go back out. And finally, we'd get there."

Dennis Gardner made sure he had plenty of water before starting out on the road to Punta Chivato. "There were roads everywhere and no signs. You weren't sure which direction to go. I always took a couple gallons of water with me; it was so hot wandering around out there in the desert."

According to Barbara Silzle, Red Salzman had a specific way of determining the correct road. "You get to an area where there are dirt roads going in several directions. Don't turn off unless you see an empty beer can attached to a cactus or palo verde (a green, tree-like plant). It will be one or the other. Just keep looking for that. You'll go through a ranch with olive trees. Eventually, you'll see the airport and water. The beach is north of the buildings."

"Always bear to the left. That was the rule coming in," remarked another camper.

The road to Punta Chivato passed by the fresh-water lagoon

once used as the resort's water supply. Further along, a brick building and old water canals came into view. These signs of civilization might have encouraged travelers. However, on closer inspection, they realized the structures had long been abandoned. The road continued, passing groves of olive trees and towering cardón cacti, then branched and split again. Without a glimpse of the Sea of Cortez, travelers easily became disoriented.

"You got all turned around coming in there the first time," remembers Harry Oxley. "You couldn't see the water. You could see the top of San Marcos Island in the distance, but you just think that's another mountain. You think where the hell did the ocean go? I'm going the wrong direction. I'll never get to the ocean."

But as the road rounded a hill and met the long airstrip at Punta Chivato, campers knew they had finally arrived at their destination. The majestic blue waters of the Sea of Cortez were sparkling in the distance.

"That's the first place you'd see the ocean," remarked Harry Oxley, "before the airstrip. Hallelujah! Then the road crossed the runway and ended up at the beach." What became known as the Camping Beach was north of the hotel and Casa Grande.

Most campers came in two-wheel-drive vehicles and vans; some towed a small trailer. Bringing anything larger risked getting stuck, especially when crossing gullies and ditches.

The 17-mile drive from the highway to Punta Chivato required patience and stamina. "You just crept along," recalled early camper Les Conner. "You couldn't do it much faster than 3 to 3-1/2 hours. All the roads lead to the one. But you didn't know it, particularly on your first trip. My God, now what do I do? Here's three roads!"

"After about three hours of wrong turns, we found P.C. Beach," another early camper remarked. "Later, we managed to do it in 1-1/2 hours—on a good try."

Although most campers remember the drive from Baja 1 to Punta Chivato lasting anywhere from two to four hours, Barbara Silzle recalled, "The best we ever made was 55 minutes to an hour."

Barbara still remembers Red's warning before they set out for Punta Chivato for the first time. "Don't try it at night," Red advised. "You'll never get in. You'll never find the way."

If driving on the road was nerve-wracking, getting stuck or lost could be terrifying. "The old road was so bad we hardly ever saw anybody," recalled Dale Dyer. "It was so isolated that it would scare me," Jeanne Fox remarked. "I thought if something happened to you on that road, there wouldn't be anybody to find you in years. It was a terrible road. It was awful. Isolated? Isolated isn't the word for it. That was the end of nowhere."

The Adamses, who first experienced the road to Punta Chivato in the fall of 1974, decided to return to camp there during Easter vacation in 1978. This time, they invited friends to join them. In 1976, Phil Souther had built the Adamses home in Bonsall, California, where Andy practiced as a family physician. They soon became close friends. Larry and Kathy Lucore were a couple Andy and Bunnie met when their children attended the same grammar school. The Adamses and Lucores drove from Bonsall to Punta Chivato in their motorhomes. Phil and his wife, Nellie, followed in their brand-new Jeep Cherokee. The Southers camped with them for one or two days. Andy Adams noted the hotel owner had not returned and, in fact, "everything was torn out of the hotel." The only person they saw at the once-exclusive Hotel Punta Chivato was "a constantly drunk ejidatario watching it," according to Andy.

But there was something magical about Punta Chivato. Even the demolished resort and unpaved road didn't keep vacationers from returning. Stories about its beautiful, white-sand beaches began circulating among campers, family, neighbors, co-workers, and friends. Several early campers were firemen and telephone utility workers from Southern California. They had large enough blocks of time off work to drive to Punta Chivato and enjoy several days at the destination before heading back home.

"What drew us back here? Well, because there weren't a lot of people, number one," recalled Barbara Silzle. "A lot of people couldn't find it. And it was just absolutely gorgeous. Paradise."

Early camper Lynn Links echoed these sentiments in a later interview. "I loved it. A fabulous place. Quiet. Beautiful. Good snorkeling. The atmosphere. There's no place like Punta Chivato."

When asked what he thought brought campers back to Punta Chivato, Dennis Gardner replied, "Well, besides the fishing, diving, and the spirit of adventure, just wanting to get out of the norm and the rat race." On this remote Mexican point, personal difficulties, national concerns, and world problems seemed to disappear for these Americans. "The place, the view, the mountains and everything. It really hooks people in," added Dennis Gardner. "It gets implanted in your brain, and when you're not here, you find yourself thinking about it."

Author Ben Hunter captured the sentiments of many American visitors when he wrote the following:

> *Ever since we had crossed the border…México had worked a special kind of magic on us. The Watts riot, the concerns of the nation and the world, our own personal problems…job, money, house, bills, and all other concerns seemed to belong to another world, another place in time. They were no longer part of us. Neither was the future. We felt as if we existed solely in the present. We were as carefree as feathers, wafted on the warm breezes of Baja, savoring every moment. And there was a great welling of love. Love for Mother Earth, everything in it, and greater love for each other.*

Chapter 32

BEACH CAMPING

Barbara and Bill Silzle fondly remember their first camping trip to Punta Chivato. Following Red Salzman's directions, they found the turnoff and successfully navigated the unpaved 17-mile section from Baja 1 to the Sea of Cortez. As instructed, they passed the abandoned hotel and Casa Grande and followed the dirt road to the water's edge. Bill Silzle pulled their van up next to a sand dune. They got out to stretch their weary legs and looked up and down the pristine beach. Not another person was in sight; they had it all to themselves.[83]

After setting up camp, the couple unloaded their surfboards from the top of the van, carried them down to the water's edge, and glided onto the Sea of Cortez. The water was clear and warm, almost too warm for swimming. They paddled to a rocky outcropping and peered down through the pristine water. It was teeming with sea life.

Later, they returned with their snorkeling gear to explore below the water's surface. They were delighted to find lobsters and rock scallops, and they prepared a gourmet dinner. "It was absolutely paradise," Barbara recalled with a smile. For two weeks, the couple enjoyed complete solitude on the beach. "We didn't see anyone the entire time, not even a Mexican."

On subsequent summer camping trips to Punta Chivato, the Silzles often found they were the only people on the beach. "That was the most undesirable time to come," Barbara said, referring to the uncomfortable heat and humidity. But for this athletic couple, it was perfect. "It was good diving, and that's what we were here for," explained Barbara.

Not until summers later did the Silzles finally run into the Salzmans at Punta Chivato. "We didn't know them as Red and Nancy," Barbara Silzle stated about the couple who first tipped them off about Punta Chivato. But Barbara recognized Nancy by what she wore.

Barbara approached Nancy. "It's good to see you guys," she said with a grin. "My husband remembers your bathing suit." Nancy was wearing a little crocheted bikini like the one she had on when they first met at Santispec on Conception Bay.

The couples would become fast friends over the years and coordinate their visits to Punta Chivato. "The camping beach days with Red and Nancy were the happiest days," Barbara recalled during an interview.

Each year, more campers found Punta Chivato. It became a favorite vacation destination for the Adamses, Salzmans, and Silzles. Among the early campers were: Harry and Marilyn Oxley and their children, Rich and Peggy Fodor and family, Bob and Bobbie Hilbun, Les and Lucy Conner, Larry and Kathy Lucore, Phil and Nellie Souther, Dave and Norma Jacobson, John and Joan Miller, Julius and Sherrie Roastingear, Blackie and Pat August, Dennis Gardener, Robin Converse, John Siboreal, Bruce Cartmel and Jerry Henthorn. They came at various times; some preferred the summer for diving and fishing; others opted for the cooler fall, winter, or spring temperatures. For most, it depended on their work schedules and vacation availability. "Every once in a while, you'd see a family with a couple of young kids," recalled Dennis Gardner, "but for the most part, you wouldn't see much in the way of families. It was pretty much couples."

"My busiest time was during the summer," remarked Harry Oxley, who owned a motorcycle race-track business, International Speedway, Inc., in Southern California. "I had the winter off. When we first started out going to P.C. in the car, we'd stay two or three weeks at a time."

Barbara and Bill Silzle first met Harry and Marilyn Oxley when their camping vacations overlapped. "I remember Harry and his family would bring their beach chairs right out in about two or three inches of water and just sit in the water," Barbara said. "I think one time he had a shade tarp that they put out in the water so they'd be in the shade and still could cool their ankles."

Barbara remarked how ironic it was that the Oxleys drove to Punta Chivato from San Clemente, California, near San Juan Capistrano, where the Silzles lived. "We knew a lot of people that knew him," Barbara said. "But we just had never gotten acquainted because he was in the racing circle, and we weren't in that."

Some campers initially chose not to set up on the designated camping beach. Robin Converse preferred to camp in an arroyo near what would become known as Shell Beach southwest of the hotel.

"I was kind of a recluse, so didn't really hang with the other people. Nobody was on Shell Beach then. The only way you could get there was to go down by the fish camp. I'd haul ass in a four-wheel drive and just fire up one of those arroyos and get a little bit out of the wind. I camped at Shell Beach because I really liked the view better."

Les and Lucy Conner, who lived in Bakersfield, California, found Punta Chivato in 1978. Les worked for Sears and only had a two-week vacation each year. After seeing this secluded area on the east coast of Baja California Sur, they frequently spent those two weeks camping at Punta Chivato. Initially, the couple set up camp in a protected cove down the beach from the hotel.

"We didn't see one American," Les recalled of that first visit. On subsequent trips, they gravitated down to the camping beach, where they met others who vacationed there during the winter.

Les was known for smoking cigars and, later, a pipe. "You had a pipe in your mouth 24 hours a day when I was down here," reflected his friend, John Dryer, during a later group interview.

Les Conner (left) on Punta Chivato camping beach with local builder, Chaparro. Courtesy Harry Oxley

Always ready to joke, Les replied, "That came after the cigars." He then chuckled, "I was cutting back."

Dennis Gardner, who drove down to Punta Chivato from Bend, Oregon, preferred the privacy of tent camping on the hill south of the camping beach across from an arroyo. "I'd go a week without seeing anybody, except when I went into town to get ice," Dennis recalled. He remembers the first time he met Red Salzman. "I never did exactly figure out how I kept from seeing Red. Red always talked like he was here all the time. I just never saw him, even when I came for an entire summer."

While walking on the camping beach with his girlfriend, Dennis finally met Red one day. "I said 'hello,' and we shook hands," remembered Dennis. The two would eventually become life-long friends. Like the Conners, Dennis soon was a camping beach "regular."

"At some point, it seemed more practical to be down on the camping beach than it did [to be] up on the hill," Dennis said.

Harry Oxley recalled Red Salzman was the first person he met on the camping beach. Dennis recounted the fun of listening to Red Salzman and Harry Oxley bicker. Although the two men often verbally jousted, usually, it was in fun. Dennis admired an interest both men shared — diving. "I wanted to be able to dive," Dennis said, "so Red kind of took me under his wing on that and taught me everything I know."

Harry remembered another early couple who drove down from Montana, Bob and Bobbie Hilbun. They would later construct a brick barbeque near the dunes by the camping beach.

Camping on the beach was primitive in the early years. After maneuvering their vehicles through the sand, most campers pitched tents or slept in the back of their vans. The dunes on the beach formed natural camping sites that varied in size. "We always tried to get a wide space," remarked one long-time camping couple who wanted ample space to entertain other campers.

Returning campers had their favorite spots. "In the old days, if we came and someone was camping in our spot we used to pull in and stay at a 'secondary' over by the palm trees," recalled Kerry Kellogg. "We'd stay over there for two or three days. Sooner or later, our spot would open up, or another one just as good, and we'd move

Typical campsite between sand dunes at Punta Chivato camping beach.
Courtesy Dave Jacobson

over there. People didn't stay for long periods of time. Two weeks was a long time, so in two or three days, you had your spot."

Some campers, like the Salzmans and Silzles, became known as "summer people," vacationing in Punta Chivato anywhere from late July to early September. Although the diving was optimal during this time, the weather was brutal. "It was 100 degrees and 95 degrees humidity," Barbara Silzle remembered. "It was so hot you could hardly sleep at night. You'd just walk around, and the perspiration would drip off the end of your fingers, the end of your nose, and the end of your ears. It was miserable."

"There weren't many souls at the camping beach in August," recalled one summer camper. Some took advantage of this privacy. "Red and Nancy told me they used to tail-gate camp, and when nobody was on the beach, they skinny-dipped for lobster," recalled a later camper. But most remember red-headed Nancy wearing a long shirt over her bikini to protect her fair skin from the sun. Nancy's husband, "Red," whose real name was Milton, also had red hair. But, unlike his wife, Red was able to tan. One camper fondly described Red as "a little, short guy who cut a Dixie cup and put it over his nose to keep the sun off."

Barbara Silzle remembers how difficult it was to keep things cool when camping at Punta Chivato during the summer. "It was too hot in the van even though it had a pop top. We always had a shade tarp. We tried bringing a Toyota pickup. We kept all our clothes and things we wanted, food and everything inside the cab. We put a tarp over the whole top of the pickup that hung down on the sides to keep everything as cool as possible. We placed tatami mats on one side and slept on low cots because the lower you could get the cooler."

"That sand is hot, and it's white, and it just reflects up on you," stated another summer camper. "If you put up a shade, it doesn't matter; the sun just beats up off the sand on you. It can be pretty uncomfortable."

Many campers who frequented Punta Chivato during the summer were unaware of the equally committed "winter people."

"I've met people who tell me they've been vacationing here for years," one summer camper remarked, "but it was always during the winter, so I never saw them." "I didn't see much of anybody," said another, "then all of a sudden, one time, I'm down here a little earlier or a little later, and there are vehicles starting to show up on the beach."

"There were a lot of people that later on I realized were there, but I never knew them because I was never there when they were there," remarked Lynn Links, who first saw Punta Chivato by air when flying to Pescadero and Cabo San Lucas. "My first husband and I bought a Suburban, got some camping gear, and a 12-foot boat. We first drove down and camped at Punta Chivato in October 1980. It was quiet and had good snorkeling spots."

In subsequent years, the couple returned in April, May, or October, the so-called "prime times." "We never got acquainted with the snowbirds or other people who were there at different times. We didn't really know a lot of what went on at that beach because we were only there once or twice a year for very short times, maybe a week."

While "summer campers" had to endure the heat and humidity, those who came during the winter faced another challenge: the threat of a chubasco, a rainstorm, or violent squall with thunder, lightning, and often high winds. Usually, it began in the afternoon with black clouds appearing over the inland mountains. Then, the winds gained in intensity, blowing from the south.

"The 'every-5-year' chubasco would surprise us and chase us off the beach," wrote Dave Jacobson. "We were only caught once with a bad one. It blew boats and camping equipment up onto the bluff. It also flooded the area with water, making it hard to drive off the beach. Some of us had enough damage to terminate our stay. But we came back the next year."

Norma Jacobson decorated their camping space during month-long stays on the beach; later hotel owner, Bill Alvarado, had palm-fronded palapas erected to provide another amenity—shade for campers.
Courtesy Dave Jacobson

Campers who arrived between November and January quickly realized the sand dunes offered natural windbreaks against the unpredictable gusts. They came prepared to fortify their camps with tarps, posts, and plenty of rope.

"Many nights I would get up at 2:00 in the morning because all of a sudden the wind would just be blasting," remembered one winter camper. "I'd get out there and tighten down things and put up tarps we hadn't put up before we went to bed. It was a life where you expected to get up at 2:00 in the morning and take care of things."

The winds could blow continuously for days at a time. "One time it blew 25 to 30 m.p.h. for nine days," remarked a regular winter camper. Rather than go fishing, campers remained close to their base, securing tarps to protect their belongings. "You had to be out there taking care of it every day, all day long. You had to really work at it," another camper stated. "We had some really, really hard windstorms where lots of real estate changed hands," recalled yet another. "You could hardly see where you were going. It stung your legs."

Campers began to rely on each other in this rugged, sometimes hostile environment. "We were always alert and there to help rescue each other's boats if they got in trouble," remarked Lynn Links. "We did a fair number of boat rescues. It was always payback. You help with somebody else's boat, and they're going to help you with your boat."

Dennis Gardner remembered when he almost lost his 17-foot aluminum boat. "We had a south wind, so I put my boat over on the camping beach, and I left and went into Mulegé. After I left, the wind turned around and started coming more out of the northeast. Red Salzman and Russ, who owned the Critter Getter, basically saved my boat, pulled it in, and got it sheltered or hooked up."

Early campers transported their food, supplies, and boats to Punta Chivato and brought their own water. "We hauled in water in a 55-gallon drum," said Kerry Kellogg, who, with his wife, Penny, drove from Lee Vining, California, where they owned a service station. "It was work living on the beach."

Barbara Silzle remembers using salt water to wash her hair. "Before water, we had to bring it all in, so we'd wash our hair with Joy because Joy detergent worked the best in salt water. I guess there's a saltwater soap, but we didn't know about that. So, we'd use Joy detergent and washed our hair with that several times a week. Otherwise, you couldn't even get a brush or comb through it. Then we allowed ourselves about a quart of water at night, which we could rinse our body off with and rinse our hair out."

Eventually, campers located a water source at Punta Chivato. A pipe ran down from the hotel pila and crossed under the dirt road. A ravine was between the road and the hotel; next to a big tree was a water faucet. This was part of the original hotel waterline.

"We hauled water from that faucet in one- or two-gallon jugs, whatever we could carry depending on how old we were," said Lynn Links, recalling the quarter-mile walk from the faucet to the camping beach. "We hauled it physically back to camp every day from that faucet. For many, many years, we used that for all our water needs."

Early camper Dave Jacobson had a different recollection of this faucet water. He said it was non-potable. "The reservoir was not in good shape. Dead rodents were floating in it, and it had a broken cover," he wrote in a letter to the author.

"We didn't have purified water because you couldn't buy purified water in town," remembered Lynn Links. "If you'd find it in the stores in gallon jugs, it might be greener than grass. So, we used the Punta Chivato water for our needs."

Although these early campers had located a water source, they had no nearby access to conveniences such as grocery stores, gas stations, hardware stores, mechanic services, laundromats, or other amenities. The closest places to obtain supplies and services were in the towns of Santa Rosalía to the north or Mulegé to the south along Baja 1. Campers who drove to these towns to restock frequently offered to pick up necessities for other campers.

Trips to town could occupy over half a day. The drive each way took considerable time, and shopping was an exercise in patience. Campers familiar with large, one-stop, "super" stores at home found only small *tiendas* (shops), each carrying limited items, so shoppers had to visit more than one store to find what they needed. Narrow one-way roads often proved frustrating for people who inadvertently passed by a store they intended to visit. Winding one's way back took time, and parking was limited.

Most preferred to drive south to Mulegé to restock their supplies rather than north to Santa Rosalía. "We always went to Mulegé in the beginning," recalled one veteran camper. "We didn't know anybody in Santa Rosalía. The copper mine was going at that time. Santa Rosalía was not a tourist attraction of any kind. They did not like the tourists. They did not like Americans in that town."

But Mulegé catered to tourists, especially Americans. Some Americans stayed in trailer parks in the town. "I'd rarely go to Santa Rosalía," stated Robin Converse, who said that not only could food and supplies be obtained in Mulegé, but it also had a bank.

Mulegé had a big ice plant where campers drove to replenish their supply. "We'd bring down two or three ice chests and just keep them full all the time," said one summer camper. "Somebody'd be going back and forth. Boy, it was tough." Another shared, "We remember one time we drove to Mulegé to get ice (poor grade like snow), and it melted before we got back."

Sometimes, even if a camper was low on supplies, leaving Punta Chivato and driving out on the dirt road was inadvisable. "We would never go into town if the weather was questionable," Lynn Links stated emphatically.

The storms could bring so much rain it was impossible to drive on the roads. "We had a lot of wet years, real wet years, where you couldn't get out of Punta Chivato," recalled Harry Oxley. "You get in; you don't go out for about a week 'til things settle down — eight, ten days in a row in the winter."

As more campers discovered Punta Chivato, they met others who had developed a love of this remarkable place. Word was out as vacationers shared their experiences camping at this unique paradise. Early camper Barbara Silzle described the news as traveling "like wildfire."

"There were quite a group of us," said Harry.

Sharing supplies and potluck meals bonded these early Punta Chivato campers. Dealing with challenges posed by the weather and the remoteness of the location brought them even closer. At the end of their vacations, the campers often made plans for their return the following year. "Next year, same time, same place" became a familiar farewell.

Campers sharing a potluck meal on the beach at Punta Chivato.
Courtesy Dave Jacobson

J. M. Joy

Author Ben Hunter's description of his Baja camping experience could apply to many of the early campers at Punta Chivato:

> *We reached our "Secret Place" just after dark, but it was so familiar to us we had no difficulty maneuvering the camper through the sand dunes to our favorite camping spot. The moment we came to a stop and shut off the engine we could hear the music of the waves and see the sparkling fluorescence as they curled and crashed on the beach. The sky was black, splashed with stars, and a full moon hung like a giant gold coin above the horizon, making a shimmering path across the water. It was good to be "home." The morning dawned sunny and warm, and we picked up our Baja beach life as if we'd never left.*[84]

Chapter 33

FISHING

The communal meals shared by the campers at each other's camp-sites usually included fish, for it was the abundant sea life that drew them back year after year. "The best meals that we have ever eaten were on the beach at Punta Chivato," wrote Dave Jacobson. "It was fresh seafood out of the Sea of Cortez."

"Fishing was fabulous," recalled Red Salzman. "I'd say there were at least fifty times more fish when I first arrived. It would be no sport to hunt them with a gun—they didn't spook."

Although a few, like Red, preferred diving and spearfishing, most fished from 12- to 14-foot aluminum boats they hauled down on their vehicles. These boats had neither fish-finding devices nor radios. Early each morning, when the tide was high enough to float the boats, the fishermen waded into the water only a few yards from the beach camp. Starting their engines, they wished each other luck before heading out toward the sunrise, eagerly anticipating the day's catch.

Robin Converse brought a 14-foot aluminum Gregor down on top of his camper. Since he came alone, he had to figure out how to get the boat off and back onto the vehicle by himself.

Some brought small flat-bottomed fishing boats called *pangas*.[85] Harry Oxley, an avid fisherman, and Red Salzman decided to jointly purchase a panga they named the *Red Ox*, combining portions of their names. Later, Richard Fodor and Jerry Henthorn showed up with pangas, too.

Fishermen did not have to venture far off the Punta Chivato shore to get hooked up. "That was the beauty," reported Robin Converse. "Nobody went fishing out in the blue water as far as I know. The furthest you had to go was Chivato Point or up through the little islands. We never went out further than the islands. Motor around in there and then back in through up here. This place wasn't well known. That's why it was such great fishing," Robin added. "And it was the best fishing. They didn't have any bad moments then. You just didn't have them."

"Red" Salzman and Harry Oxley with diverse day's catch.
Courtesy Harry Oxley

Camper Dave Jacobson remembers first arriving at Punta Chivato with his wife, Norma, in the spring of 1979 without a boat, "20 gallons of water, a limited supply of food, and no ice." But they soon found there was plenty to eat from the sea. "Diving was good offshore," Dave recalled. "One rock, about as big as a car in about 10 feet of water, supplied us with all the rock scallops we needed. The back sides of the reefs and along hammerhead had an abundance of lobsters. Spear fishing was no challenge with cabrilla, pargo and a few sierra. Clamming south of hammerhead was excellent. So, food was not a problem." Although initially disappointed by the "derelict" appearance of the hotel and seeing no other campers during their seven-day stay, the Jacobsons were impressed by the beautiful beach, excellent spring weather, and abundance of sea life. After their first visit, they vowed to return.

On later trips to Punta Chivato, Dave found the fish were so plentiful they would often come right up onto the beach. "Roosterfish would chase mullet up on the beach, and several times we saw the roosters [fish] come up on dry land in the chase. We would push them back in the water, or they would die."

Robin Converse recalled, "There were so many roosterfish here. In the spring, you'd just put your lawn chair up on one of the cliffs, sit, drink beer, and look out in the middle of the bay. All of a sudden, you'd see the frigates [birds] piling up and diving, and you could see white underneath the frigates. Jump in your little aluminum boat and we'd go out there and fish. Big ones, real big ones. And they were all over the place. There were hundreds and hundreds and hundreds of them. They were thick."

"Red" Salzman and Harry Oxley holding roosterfish, 1987.
Courtesy Harry Oxley

Roosterfish were fun to watch but were not great eating. Although an occasional dorado, grouper, tuna, or cabrilla was caught, yellowtail was one of the more popular fish the early campers went after.

Robin Converse explained, "When I first started fishing here, the Mexicans didn't care about fishing yellowtail. They only wanted pargo and snapper and cabrilla and bottom fish. Yellowtail was a pain in the ass to them. And there were lots of yellowtail. All the yellowtail you want until you were tired of catching them. It was phenomenal fishing. We had 74 yellowtail one morning. We just let them go. Count them and let them go."

"There didn't seem to be much in the way of dorado when I

first started coming here," Robin added. "Nobody knew much about dorado. In those early days I never even saw a dorado or a tuna. But I loved to fish for yellowtail. I would go either over off the point or off the north end of Santa Inez north island. I'd be in forty feet of water. In the evening, when I would troll through there, you could just see the yellowtail and the cabrilla behind the boat racing to get to your lure. You'd just instantly hook up."

Harry Oxley remembers when the yellowtail schooled up close to the camping beach. "We used to sit on the beach and wait until we could see the big, black cloud of birds, and then we'd all get in our boats and go out there. There was a little spot I could catch a big cabrilla every time I trolled past it. It was just a good spot. There were lots of cabrilla."

"You could go out and fish all day long and have the same boil going from sunup to sundown," recalled another early camper. "You'd get so tired of catching fish. Just catch and release, catch and release."

Robin remembers fishing for yellowtail and ending up with a grouper. "You had grouper eating your yellowtail. You couldn't fish yellowtail because the grouper would eat them all the time. And that was consistent. Not just once. It was just like fishing in an aquarium."

PART III

Chapter 34

DON ZACARÍAS

On the point overlooking the Sea of Cortez, the once beautiful Hotel Punta Chivato stood in ruins. Stripped and vandalized by the local Mexicans, the resort was only fit for rats, scorpions, and centipedes. The critters wasted no time moving into the spacious residence.

First-time campers were amazed to find a hotel at the end of the long, dusty road. Impressed by its size and craftsmanship, they wondered who had built it and how the materials had been brought in. Was there a better road leading here they did not know about? Why was the hotel abandoned?

Although visitors found the interior of Hotel Punta Chivato in shambles, the surrounding landscape was surprisingly lush. The lawns and trees were green and thriving. "How was that possible?" questioned the campers. The answer became evident when they met Don Zacarías.

Hired by Ejido San Bruno, Don Zacarías was the caretaker and gardener of the property now in the hands of the Mexican commune. Although the hotel was inoperable, they wanted to preserve the landscaping that beautified the arid land.

No one recalled the caretaker's last name; he was simply known as Don Zacarías. "Don" is a word used in México as a term of respect for a man. Standing 5'8" tall, the chubby, half-shaven, gray-haired Mexican was said to have come from Guadalajara. Some early campers speculate he was well into his mid-80s when they first met him.

Don Zacarías led a simple life. He spent his day at the hotel holding a garden hose or slowly dragging it between the plants, making sure all received adequate water. He was also responsible for "guarding" the hotel and managing the water in the pila on top of the hill behind it. The Ejido paid him $10 a week.

The caretaker lived alone in one of the rooms at Casa Grande. When off duty, Don Zacarías relaxed on the veranda, enjoying his favorite drink, straight tequila.

Don Zacarías did not seem fazed by the arrival of the campers. He was happy to have company.

"Old Zacarías was full of marvelous stories," recalled one camper who was conversant in Spanish. While some viewed Don Zacarías as a drunk, others remember him as "a cool, old guy' and and "an interesting fellow." "He did more than just water the grounds," said one camper. "Zacarías acted as guide, greeter, water management, the whole ball of wax."

However, the caretaker offered little information when anyone asked about the abandoned hotel.

"I think the government and the Ejido ran 'Crudgie' off, but I don't know why," he said, referring to the previous owner, Cleveland Crudgington. "I never wanted to know, and nobody wanted to tell me. The Ejido owns it now."

If part of Zacarías's job was to keep people out of the hotel, he did not take that task seriously. Curious campers wandered over from the beach to peek inside the restaurant and the rooms. When some set up camp in the abandoned rooms, Zacarías did not interfere.

"The place looked spic and span on the outside when we got there," recalled one early visitor. "The gardener kept the red tiles out front buffed and watered the plants. Although he didn't keep the inside of the hotel clean, he never said we couldn't go inside. You could go into any room. They were all open. Some had working showers. When you moved in, you'd have to sweep the floor and dust things off, but it was pretty nice. And nobody collected any money. It was crazy."

"There was water in the pool," the visitor added, "but you couldn't swim in it. It was terrible, yucky water because nobody would ever clean it. The bar was all set up. The records were all in the office. You could just go in there and find out who stayed in the rooms. They didn't take anything when they left. It was all there. It was amazing. We went through all the records and everything."

Early hotel guest John Fitzsimmons pointed out an entry in his flight log showing he landed his plane at Punta Chivato in March 1979. "We were traveling north from Punto Pescadero to Mexicali," he explained. "It was a 'pee' break. The hotel was stripped, file cabinets open, files pretty much intact, but some correspondence was strewn about the office. A sad sight." Even then, there were rumors something was going to happen at Punta Chivato.

"We drove down with our kids at Christmas in the late '70s," recalls Dale Dyer. "The hotel was closed. We found Room 20 had a working toilet. I guess it was in concrete and too hard to get out. Room 21 still had a working shower. We parked the car on the edge of the parking lot near rooms 20 and 21 and set up camp. It was a wonderful little campsite. We had facilities for showering and all that."

Although these campers quickly discovered there was no hot water, they did not seem to mind. Any running water was a luxury in the desert, even if it meant cold showers.

One afternoon, while Don Zacarías was sprawled on his lounge chair on the terrace of Casa Grande, taking his usual siesta, he was roused by a voice coming from the direction of the beach.

"*Hola. ¿Hay alquién aquí?*" the unexpected visitor inquired, asking if anyone was there. As the visitor reached the top of the stone stairway that led from the beach to the tiled patio, he was surprised to see the heavy-set, grizzled, elderly Mexican.

Not one to be startled, Zacarías slowly reached up and nudged back his *sombrero*, the wide-brimmed hat he used to shade his face. He opened one eye and reached for the half-empty glass of tequila next to his lounge chair. This was not the first time he had been awakened from his midday siesta. Zacarías had learned by then that Americans did not share the Mexican custom and might show up at any time of the day.

The tall, well-built *gringo* was unfamiliar to Zacarías. The stranger was deeply tanned and might have been mistaken for a native if it were not for his pronunciation of Spanish.

"I'm sorry to disturb you," the American said, approaching Zacarías. He walked with a bounce in his step and wore a personable smile. "My friend and I were out fishing, saw the pier, and decided to come ashore," he added, pointing toward the concrete pier extending out from the beach below Casa Grande. Zacarías noticed the man's arms were in continual motion as he gestured to augment his limited Spanish vocabulary. "My friend is waiting with the boat. We were curious about this area and who lives here."

"Used to be lots of people, but now only me," Zacarías tersely responded. "I am the caretaker of the hotel."

"Is that building with the rock arches a hotel?" the visitor asked, motioning toward the south. "It's beautiful. Who owns it? I heard it was abandoned."

"Ejido San Bruno," the older man replied. "An American used to run it, but he left. Now it's my job to watch over it and make sure the plants get watered."

Suddenly, a voice came from the direction of the beach below the bluff, "Hey, are you there? What's taking you?"

"*Mi amigo*," the visitor told Zacarías. He motioned toward the pier where his friend, Jack, impatiently waited for him. "I better go."

"*Bueno,*" replied the Mexican, sorry his new acquaintance was leaving so soon. It was lonely living out here by himself. Days passed when he did not see or talk to anyone.

"I'm sorry, I didn't catch your name," said the American as he held out his hand to the caretaker.

"Zacarías," the old Mexican replied as he reached up to clasp the *gringo's* hand.

"I'm Bill. Bill Alvarado," the visitor said.

"Come visit me any time," Zacarías responded with a smile. "I'll show you around when you have more time."

"Thank you, Zacarías. I'd like to hear more about this place."

As he joined his friend on the beach, Bill was noticeably excited. "We've got to come back here soon," he emphatically told his friend, Jack Larsen. "I've got an idea."

Chapter 35

BILL ALVARADO

Bill Alvarado and Jack Larsen first met in Eugene, Oregon, where Bill worked as a promoter for the local newspaper, *The Register-Guard*, and Jack owned and operated a successful jewelry business.

"A group of us from the newspaper would go to the Eugene Hotel in the evenings and have martinis," recalled Bill. "That's where I met Jack." Jack rented space inside the hotel to sell his jewelry. He occasionally joined the lively group of newspaper employees for an after-work cocktail.

Bill became intrigued by the stories Jack shared with the group. Jack's life was full of adventure; he flew his own airplane and frequently traveled to Baja with his wife, Bunnie. Bill considered Jack a true México aficionado and envied his exciting life.

Bill Alvarado's arrival in Eugene in the mid-1950s had been filled with promise. Receiving a football scholarship to attend the University of Oregon, he eagerly moved north from his Southern California hometown of Covina to lend his talent to the university team, the Ducks. As a 230-pound offensive guard and middle line-backer, Bill proved to be a talented player and quickly became known in the college town. However, his playing days ended prematurely after he tore knee cartilage during a game. Bill lost his scholarship and never graduated. Not one to sit back and sulk, he went out to look for a job and soon landed a position with the local newspaper.

Jack Larsen quickly took a liking to the amicable ex-football player. He admired Bill's positive outlook in the face of his misfortune. Jack found that Bill was not only good-natured but also had infectious enthusiasm. Little did Jack know he would someday become instrumental in changing the course of this young man's life.

Bill eventually moved on from the newspaper to become a partner in the Quarterdeck Restaurant in Eugene at the corner of Willamette Street and 29th.[86] According to Mary Morss, a later friend of Bill's, "There was a partnership in that. It was Larry Anderson and Fred Beckley who was kind of the recipient of large sums of money from his father, and then Bill." While the other partners supplied most of the capital, Bill did much of the day-to-day work. The restaurant gained a faithful clientele and became a popular meeting place for service organizations and a venue for musicians.

After Bill changed jobs, he and Jack continued their friendship, meeting occasionally for drinks. One day, Bill received an unexpected phone call from his friend.

"Hey, Bill, how are you doing?" Jack inquired.

"I'm doing great," Bill replied. "Good to hear your voice."

"Say, Bill, how would you like to come with me to Baja?" Jack asked. "Bunnie can't join me this time. I'm only going down for a long weekend. What do you say? Can you get away?"

Bill worked long hours at the restaurant and rarely took vacations. He missed having time to fish and enjoy other sporting activities. Bill hoped he could take Jack up on his invitation.

"Sounds great," Bill said. "Let me see what I can do."

Bill first approached his wife, Karen, who reluctantly agreed to let her husband go on the trip while she stayed home and cared for their three young sons.

Next, Bill set about getting coverage at the restaurant. A vacation, even for a few days, would do him good. Bill found himself at the Eugene airport that weekend, climbing into the cockpit of Jack's single-engine Mooney headed for Baja.

The flight from Eugene, Oregon, to Mulegé in Baja California Sur took all day. The two men were eager to reach their destination and stretch their legs. As they followed the peninsula's eastern shore along the Sea of Cortez, Bill spotted a large structure on the coastline north of Mulegé. Jack had pulled back the throttle to begin a slow descent to the airstrip next to Hotel Serenidad near the mouth of the river that ran through Mulegé.

"My gosh, that's beautiful," Bill remarked. "What is it?"

Jack gently banked the plane to the right and looked in Bill's direction. Below, perched on a bluff, lay a large stone building with distinct archways.

"I'm not sure," Jack replied into the microphone of his headset, "but I heard it was an old, abandoned hotel."

"Wow, that's something," said Bill. "I'd sure like to see it."

"There's an old runway, but I've never landed there. Not too much going on, I imagine."

When they arrived at the Serenidad Hotel airstrip, the traditional Saturday evening pig roast was well underway. Several Americans were standing in the courtyard sipping margaritas and listening to the rhythmic strumming of guitars and voices of a mariachi band. Some lined up at the buffet table, eager to fill their plates with the freshly roasted pig and accompanying Mexican side dishes.

After unpacking the plane, Jack took Bill over and introduced him to the owner of the hotel, Don Johnson. "Don's been down here a long time," said Jack. "He was one of the original gringos in Mulegé."

Jack explained how Don first visited Mulegé in the late 1950s, was part owner of another hotel there, and later purchased the Serenidad Hotel. Gesturing toward an attractive Mexican woman dressed in a long, flowing, colorfully embroidered dress, he said, "That's his wife, Nancy."

Don Johnson and his wife, Nancy, at their hotel, Serenidad.
Photo by Brown McPherson, Discover Baja Travel Club, 2020

After introductions and pleasantries, Bill asked Don what he knew about the hotel they had flown over just north of Mulegé.

"Don told me he helped build it," recalled Bill during a later interview. "He said he wasn't sure about the runway and didn't think it was worth it to go over there."

During the weekend, Jack chartered a fishing boat, and the two friends headed north to fish near the islands in front of Punta Chivato. They caught a boatload of fish.

"We must have caught 100 or 150 pargo," said Bill. "Some of them were big. Jack was bound and determined to take all the meat home. The boat was just covered with fish. We got back and the poor deckhand cleaned, filleted, and put up all of these fish in plastic bags for us. I'm sure he expected a nice tip. He spent from two o'clock in the afternoon until dark, eight or nine at night. I couldn't believe that Jack only gave the guy $5.00." Don Johnson offered to freeze the bags of fish so they could take them back up to Oregon.

Bill returned to Eugene refreshed and excited about his experience in Baja. But unbeknownst to him, his marriage was falling apart. One day, during the busy lunchtime, a man entered the restaurant and presented Bill with divorce papers. He could not believe it. Where had he gone wrong?

Bill moved to a townhouse in Eugene, two doors down from an intriguing couple, Walter and Jeanne Fox, who moved there in 1978. "We had townhouses across the street from each other, 30 yards apart," Bill recalled.

Walter was an oral surgeon, and his wife, Jeanne, was a dental hygienist. Bill recognized Walter from the Town Club in Eugene.[87] Jeanne had met Bill at his restaurant, where she attended meetings of the United States Power Squadrons, a boating club.[88] As the couple and Bill became better acquainted, Bill was surprised to learn that Walter was not only an avid fisherman but had been to Baja.

Walter and Jeanne told Bill about a fishing trip they took aboard the *Red Rooster* out of San Diego. The trip ventured into the waters far south of the Baja peninsula. When the boat pulled into the tiny town on the tip of the peninsula to refuel, the couple disembarked. They had met another fisherman onboard who told them a plane made flights between there and the town of La Paz to the north.

"We jumped ship in Cabo San Lucas," Jeanne recalled. "It was a little fishing village at that time." Unable to find a place to stay, the couple got a ride to the airstrip located on a barren hillside above the town. The only structure there was a water tower. "The plane met us on the dirt runway," Jeanne continued. "Talk about being afraid of flying. The plane took off downhill and just managed to get up. I thought it was headed right into the ocean!" The plane arrived safely in La Paz, where Walter and Jeanne spent a couple of days before taking a commercial flight back to San Diego.

Bill told the Foxes about his fishing trip to the Sea of Cortez with Jack. He was excited to trade stories of Baja with his new neighbors. Although Bill continued to work hard, intent on making the restaurant a success, his thoughts frequently returned to Baja.

Bill Alvarado at Punta Chivato Hotel.
From Jan. 1992 video by Bill Alvarado

Bill's second journey to Mulegé with Jack was only a month after his first trip. According to Bill, Jack had made some big sales of something other than jewelry and had money to burn. Again, they spent time fishing, reeling in more fish than Bill believed possible. At Bill's insistence this time, they took a detour to Punta Chivato. It was during this trip that Bill climbed the stairway from the beach to Casa Grande and met the caretaker, Zacarías.

Chapter 36

PARTNERS AT POSADA

While working at the Quarterdeck Restaurant, Bill Alvarado met a young man enamored of Baja. George Staples was a law student who frequented the restaurant. Like Jack Larsen, George enjoyed talking to the friendly owner. Bill was an enthusiastic listener and loved hearing George's stories of Baja.

As a teenager, George became fluent in Spanish. His father, a geology professor at the University of Oregon in Eugene, taught at the University of México during his sabbatical. The family moved to México City for a year. Fifteen-year-old George immersed himself in the new culture and quickly picked up Spanish. That was the beginning of his love affair with México.

George's first trip to the Baja peninsula was soon after the construction of the Transpeninsular Highway in 1973. "I convinced my friend, Tom Miller, to drive down to Baja with me during Christmas break," George reminisced. It was not hard to get Tom to change his original vacation plans to visit family in snowy Minnesota. Against the advice of friends, they drove down in George's bright red Corvette convertible. They towed a small utility trailer carrying an inverted 12-foot aluminum boat. Crowded under and around the boat and covered with tarps were all their supplies for the week.

"People told us, 'You're out of your mind going down there to México with that car. They're going to kill you, and your wheels will be in México City. We're never going to see you or the car again.'

"But we made it to Conception Bay, south of Mulegé, where we stayed at a trailer park in the town of Posada. We fell in love with the setting on the clear turquoise bay and decided to find out if anything was for sale."

George told Bill about his meeting with Herman Morante, owner of the trailer park at Posada. "He showed us a partially built stone structure—just two walls of local rock. Nothing further had been built."

"It's an amazing location," George told Bill. "We gave Señor Morante some earnest money but need partners to help us convert it into a home. Bill, any chance you'd be interested in becoming a partner?"

Bill thought of the land, Casa Grande, and the abandoned hotel he had seen at Punta Chivato with Jack Larsen. He dreamed of turning the area back into a beautiful oasis by the sea. Maybe having a foothold in Posada would give him a base from which to operate and explore the possibilities.

"It sounds enticing," Bill said. "Let me think about it and get back to you."

Bill ultimately accepted George's offer and joined George, Tom Miller, and Phil Clapp as partners in the Posada property.

Since all the partners were either in school or working, they initially were unable to devote time to fixing up the property. In 1978, George's final year of law school, he found another investor, his roommate, William Lyons.

The two men were unlikely roommates. George was in his twenties, unmarried, and looking forward to finishing law school and starting his career. Seventy-seven-year-old William, a recent widower with three grown daughters and a son, was retired from the Navy. The common thread between the men was a love of adventure, a passion William inherited from his grandfather back on the farm in Ohio. During his military career, William lived in exotic places like Hawaii, Fiji, and New Hebrides.

William chewed on the stem of his pipe as he listened to George describe the project at Posada, an untouched region south of the small village of Mulegé. William had never been to Baja, but it sounded intriguing. Tired of the incessant Eugene rains, he was ready for a change. George's proposal to invest in the sunny locale in México could not have come at a better time. "Where do I sign up?" William interjected before George had completed his sales pitch.

William Lyons found himself involved in a five-way partnership in property in Baja with George Staples, Bill Alvarado, Tom Miller, and Phil Clapp. William was the oldest of the five, but his age did not slow him down. He was 5'7" or 5'8", wiry and strong as an ox. Trained as a veterinarian and medical doctor, he was a good one to have around, especially in a desolate place like Baja. His partners fondly referred to him as "*Viejo,* (old) Doc," or just plain "Doc," a nickname that would stick with him for the rest of his life.

The magic of Baja quickly took hold of Doc, and within a few months, he decided to leave his apartment in Eugene and become a full-time resident at Posada. Unlike his younger partners, he did not have to deal with the constraints of family or career. Financially secure, Doc had income from his military retirement and investment properties in Hawaii, Nevada, Arizona, and Moorea.

"Doc had nowhere else to go and nothing to do. It was an adventure for him. It was a great adventure," remembered George Staples.

When George graduated from law school, he decided to take a year off before sitting for the bar exam. He chose to join Doc in Baja to work on the Posada property.

George, Doc, and Tom put most of the effort into constructing the house in Posada. They hired local Mexicans to select rocks for the walls, bring in loam, and build a palm-frond thatched roof. During this time, the partners lived rustically, cooking on a Coleman stove, heating water in a bucket for showers, and using a lantern at night. By day, the men worked on the septic system and plumbing or traveled north to Santa Rosalía to purchase tiles.

When their Posada home was ready, Doc offered to provide the furnishings. "I remember stuffing all Doc's beautiful oak and leather furniture into a 24-foot U-Haul truck and driving it to the border," George recalled. "It was worth thousands of dollars. We arrived at the border on Friday night after a hell of a trip. Bill was supposed to have arranged shipping for us, but we found he hadn't done anything."

George met a man in San Ysidro, California, across the border from Tijuana, who told him he had a distant relative who owned a shipping company. Although skeptical, George felt they had no other choice. After navigating through many narrow alleys, they located Pedro's Shipping and unloaded all the furniture.

"The guy gave us a receipt and told us he would deliver it to Posada in three to four days," George smiled as he remembered the questionable transaction. "We continued on to Posada, and I could only shake my head. Such beautiful furniture. Fat chance we'll ever see it again." To their surprise, four days later, they heard a "beep, beep, beep" outside. There stood a Pedro's Shipping van loaded with all Doc's furniture. It had arrived safely without even a scratch.

Their home in Posada provided a perfect getaway. It was just a short distance off the two-lane Baja Highway via an unpaved, rocky road. Perched high up on a cliff above the majestic Conception Bay, it offered unobstructed views. Doc sat on the shaded porch for hours, smoked his pipe, and watched pelicans soar and dive for food. Occasionally, a sailboat would drift by. Doc was mesmerized by the sparkling blue waters and colorful sunrises and sunsets of this rugged land.

Much to the amusement of his partners, Doc chose an unlikely part of the house as his bedroom—the newly constructed water reservoir. Before it was filled with water, he took advantage of this extra space. The size of a walk-in closet, the subterranean concrete structure provided Doc with a cool retreat from the Baja heat. He furnished his "room" with a simple cot and a wooden crate where he stored the few personal items he brought from Oregon. In the evenings, after watching the last remnants of the pink and lavender sunset fade from the skies, Doc retired to the pila, climbing down an eight-foot, straight ladder propped against the wall. His partners would shake their heads and chuckle, referring to their strange partner as "the mole."

Doc Lyons enjoying the view from the shared Posada home (1978).
Courtesy Marge Summers

Ironically, Doc's biggest enemy in Baja was one of the things that attracted him to the area in the first place: the sun. Having lived in Florida and Hawaii for most of his twenty-year military career, Doc's light-complexioned skin showed signs of the sun's destructive power. Skin cancer lesions had begun to appear on his face and arms by the time he retired in 1963 as a captain in the United States Navy. The problem escalated during the subsequent eight years he remained in Hawaii, working as a research scientist for the Hawaii State Department. Some described him as having so many scabs and sores on his head he looked as if he had leprosy. However, Doc did not let his skin problems bother him. In fact, he often fabricated exotic stories to explain his blotchy appearance and surgical scars.

"What happened to your ear?" asked a curious fellow who was having lunch with Doc at a small café in Mulegé. "Must have hurt."

"Oh, that," said Doc, reaching up to finger the missing portion of his left ear. "Back in the days when I was in the jungles of Brazil, I was minding my own business when a snake dropped out of the tree and bit me. It was one of those deadly poisonous types, you know. I was by myself and had to act quickly, so I grabbed my knife and whacked off the ear. Thought it was better than dying alone in that jungle."

"I guess so," responded his companion, setting down his fork and wishing he had not asked. Doc had a knack for telling his stories with such a straight face that no one questioned his outlandish tales.

Chapter 37

BILL NEGOTIATES

"**I** couldn't believe my eyes. I thought it was just absolutely gorgeous," Bill said, recalling his first impression of Casa Grande. Bill took Zacarías up on his offer to give him a tour of the property during a later trip to Punta Chivato with Jack Larsen. "The house looked really good. It was big and dirty but had charm. The patio in front was tiled, and the living room looked pretty well furnished." The hotel needed major work, but Bill saw potential.

After a closer look, Bill was eager to talk to the Ejido San Bruno, the local Mexican group in charge of the hotel and Casa Grande. He asked Zacarías how he could contact the organization and was told they were holding a meeting in two weeks. "I knew I had to find a way to get to that meeting," Bill recalled.

Bill and Jack returned to Eugene, where Bill continued to work diligently at the restaurant. But his thoughts often returned to Baja and the potential he saw at Punta Chivato. *If I could get the Ejido to agree to let me buy the hotel, I could turn it into an amazing place.*

According to later visitor, Dave Jacobson, Bill was not the only American who had expressed an interest in Punta Chivato. "In the late '70s, three professional men from Oregon were making proposals with the Ejido to buy the rights to the beach, hotel, and Casa Grande," Jacobson wrote to the author. "I don't know what became of this deal, but soon after, Bill Alvarado showed up."

The Ejido San Bruno held regular meetings in a small village north of the point. Although the hotel and surrounding area were officially federal land owned by the Mexican government, the Ejido could occupy and use it for their own benefit. However, they had little interest in Punta Chivato. Instead, they grew grapes, a project sponsored by the Mexican Agrarian Department.

In an effort to help the local Ejido become financially independent, the Agrarian Department provided them with every necessity: seeds, corrosion-free stakes, wire to run the vines, money to plant and pump water, and all the essential equipment. The vineyard was set up on an elevated area south of the lagoon. In time, beautiful Thompson seedless grapes hung from the four-foot-high wires.

For the first year of production, the Agrarian Department guaranteed sales of the grapes to produce buyers. They arranged for refrigerator trucks from mainland México to transport the grapes in Styrofoam boxes. The excess grapes were laid on brown paper squares on the ground until they turned into raisins. They, too, would be picked up and shipped.

Like previous efforts to help the Ejido, the grape project was destined for failure. "There was too much money involved," Bill Alvarado recalled. It was speculated the money provided by the Agrarian Department was pocketed by the most powerful members of the Ejido.

Interest in the grapes began to wane, and watering sessions were missed. Bill Alvarado remembers the tasty produce. "We'd go over there and pick a bunch of grapes or two, and they'd say, 'Take a whole bunch. They're not selling very well. José forgot to water them." With the sporadic watering schedule, the fate of the grape project was sealed.

The Ejido blamed the weather for the failure of their crops. Bill offered a plausible excuse the Ejido might have used when reporting to the Agrarian Department. "Well, it didn't rain for so long, and we had these dust and windstorms."

"I could see what was going to happen," Bill said. "One day, I went out there, and the grapevines were not dirt brown yet, but they were camel colored."

When the Ejido quit tending the grapes, the equipment and wire were stolen by whoever got there first. "Suddenly, it just all started disappearing," Bill recalled. "Everybody free-loaded and took all of the stuff."

Per Bill, the Agrarian Department "got shafted" so often by the Ejido that they did not trust them. Equally, the Ejido did not trust the Agrarian Department.

Bill got his friend, Jack Larsen, to fly him to Santa Rosalía two weeks later to attend the Ejido San Bruno meeting. It was held in a big warehouse once used to store dates, olives, and oregano.

"I was greeted like Saddam Hussein," Bill recalled. "Here I was, a stranger coming into town asking about the hotel." Bill understood more Spanish than he spoke but could still communicate his desire to restore Punta Chivato. The Ejido told Bill they had no authority to sell or lease Punta Chivato. That permission would have to come from the governor of southern Baja.[89] Bill did not let the delay discourage him. He was learning things took time in México, and he was willing to wait.

A meeting between Bill and the governor of Baja California Sur was held in Santa Rosalía. "He was a big man with a big mustache," Bill recalled. "He spoke a little English, and I spoke more than a little Spanish, so we got along famously. And I'll be damned if the governor's last name wasn't Alvarado!"

Whether or not sharing the same last name had any bearing on the outcome, Bill said the governor was willing to sign a lease with him that day. The governor recognized that resurrecting the hotel would create more jobs for the local people. "We started talking about maids and bartenders and drivers and carpenters," said Bill.

But the lease would take time to negotiate. Bill made several trips to México City and La Paz. He met with the governor of Baja California Sur and the Agrarian Department, which represented the Ejido.

Finally, they reached an agreement. "It was a 10-year, guaranteed, renewable lease for the hotel and surrounding area," Bill recalled. "I had the strip from the end of the camping beach clear down to the estuary. I didn't pay them anything the first year. They gave me five years to create housing for the employees, and I did it in the first year and a half or two." The agreement was signed by the governor of southern Baja and the Agrarian Department.

According to letters written by Doc to his daughter Jo during the summer of 1980, the agreement was $10,000 per year for 30 years for 21,000 acres. Whatever the specifics of the lease agreement were thought to be, Bill would learn years later that they were too good to be true.

Bill sold his interest in the Quarterdeck Restaurant, but his compensation was insufficient to fund his envisioned project. He talked Jack Larsen into becoming a 50% partner in Punta Chivato. Jack did well in his jewelry business and had cash to invest. Bill planned to do most of the physical work while Jack provided the finances. Some later referred to Jack as Bill's "money man" or "sugar daddy."

Eventually, Bill brought in another minor partner, his friend, Larry Anderson. Larry was a lawyer in Eugene, Oregon, and, along with Fred Beckley and Bill, was a partner in the restaurant. According to George Staples, Bill offered Larry part ownership and sweat equity in exchange for legal counsel and help setting up a corporation. Bill offered a different story as to how Larry got involved.

"Larry became a partner by the toss of a coin. It came out heads, and he owned 17% of the corporation."[90] But getting an American lawyer to do the legal work in México doesn't work. "He was not a good Mexican attorney," Bill conceded.

Larry might have been interested in becoming more involved with the Punta Chivato project, but some speculate his wife discouraged it. The Andersons rarely visited the site.

Chapter 38

RESIDENCE IN CASA GRANDE

As the months passed, Bill Alvarado began spending less time at the Posada house during his visits to Baja. Instead, he journeyed by boat twenty-five miles north of Conception Bay to Punta Chivato. There he stayed at Casa Grande with Zacarías.

Bill claimed the biggest of the six bedrooms, Room #1, the one furthest to the left when facing the Sea of Cortez. Zacarías lived in a separate apartment above the garage, originally occupied by Florencio Aguilar.

Since the days of Dixon Collins and Cleveland Crudgington, Casa Grande had fallen into disrepair. The Big House had appliances, but nothing worked. (Bill eventually bartered with an American electrician to get the stove and refrigerator working. The electrician got to stay at Casa Grande rent-free.)

Early camper Dennis Gardner soon befriended Bill Alvarado. "There would be times when it would be just him and I here," Dennis recalled. "I would walk up to Casa Grande in the morning, almost a morning ritual, and we'd sit out in front, and we'd have coffee." In the evenings, Dennis often returned to Casa Grande and the company of its new, amiable occupant. "We'd just sit out there with a radio and a couple of chairs and a little bit of bait, and we'd catch lots of snapper and night-feeding type of fish," Dennis said, describing the early 1980s at Punta Chivato.

Camper Les Conner frequently enjoyed spending evenings with Bill Alvarado and others. He reminisced about early poker games on the terrace at Casa Grande, "…a full moon coming up over the Casa Grande between the palms and you're sitting at the table. How can it get any better?"

As Bill spent less time at Posada, Doc wondered if his friend planned to move permanently to Punta Chivato. Although not one to readily admit it, Doc missed the companionship of his partners. He had grown especially fond of Bill, whose spirit of adventure was akin to his own. They were alike in other ways, too. Both loved to tell tales of their previous escapades, both enjoyed tobacco and whiskey, and both loved to argue. Their heated exchanges often ended in a truce, but the other partners had little tolerance for their spats. One day, as Bill was about to leave for Punta Chivato, Doc approached him.

"Posada getting too crowded for you?" Doc jeered.

"Sometimes I don't think there's enough room for both of us here," Bill responded before breaking into a grin. Then, sensing his friend might be feeling lonely, Bill quickly added, "Really, Doc, you should come out and see the place sometime. It's something else. Posada's great, but this place is simply gorgeous."

"You plan on moving there permanently?" Doc prodded.

"I'd love to get that hotel up and running again," Bill continued, his brown eyes lighting up at the prospect. "It's completely abandoned except for an old Mexican guy who lives alone in the Big House just north of it. He's letting me camp out in a room at the house."

"What's he doing there?" asked Doc.

"He's sort of the caretaker of the place for a Mexican commune," Bill replied. "He spends most of his time watering the palm trees at the Big House and the lawn around the hotel."

His curiosity piqued, Doc decided to join Bill the next time he visited Punta Chivato. They went by boat from Posada since it was quicker and easier than traveling on the dusty, washboard road that led from Baja's only highway to the point. Doc enjoyed being on the Sea of Cortez and marveled at the prolific sea life—dolphins, flying fish, and boils of mackerel.

Less than an hour after leaving Conception Bay, Bill slowed the engine of his skiff as the magnificent arched stone façade of the hotel came into view. Doc spotted a big structure further up the coast, undoubtedly the one Bill called the Big House. Bill was right; this place was "something else." Doc's mind filled with the usual questions: *Who built these structures, and why had they been abandoned?*

After his first visit to Punta Chivato in 1979, Doc reconsidered where he should live. Doc knew his friend was a dreamer, but so was he. Bill's idea of refurbishing the abandoned hotel might work. Although Casa Grande and the nearby hotel were in disarray, there was potential. As usual, Bill's enthusiasm was contagious; even Doc was not immune.

Not long after his initial visit to Punta Chivato, Doc offered to move into Casa Grande with Bill and assist him in pursuing his dream of restoring the hotel and Big House.

"Doc got tired of living in the pila. He came out and said, 'I'm going to stay out here and help you,'" recalled Bill. Doc settled into the first room to the right at Casa Grande, looking out to the sea.

"He was a very, very bright guy, very old, very opinionated, and very drunk most of the time," said Bill. "He was bull-headed."

While Bill's primary concern was refurbishing the hotel, Doc focused on beautifying the yard at Casa Grande. The only plants that survived from the previous owners were transplanted palm trees. The old Mexican caretaker kept these alive and watered the lawn at the hotel's entry. Doc did not have any use for Zacarías. He noted that the Mexican would stand for hours holding a garden hose. This was not Doc's idea of hard work.

Doc eventually insisted that Bill let the Mexican go so he could have complete control of the gardening. Bill continued to pay Zacarías for his work watering around the hotel, a job Doc did not want. According to Bill, Doc preferred "to putter around the Big House."

To keep the peace with Doc, Bill later encouraged Zacarías to move out of Casa Grande and into one of three small block houses in the arroyo between Casa Grande and the hotel.

Wearing his wide-brimmed straw hat and long-sleeved shirt, Doc spent hours working outside at Casa Grande. Getting anything to grow in the parched earth was not easy, but Doc enjoyed the challenge. No one dared tell Doc he could not do something.

With the ingenuity he learned growing up on a farm, Doc devised a plan to grow a lawn in front of the house. He dug up little tufts of grass from the grounds of the hotel and carefully transported them to Casa Grande. He then soaked the tufts in a special tea he concocted before transplanting them. Little by little, he added more tufts, which gradually grew together. Doc took pride in his lawn and often worked from sunup to sundown, tending to it. He did not seem to mind the unpleasant tasks of weeding or killing the ants that resided in the new green growth.

Doc Lyons relaxing on the veranda at Casa Grande (1980).
Courtesy Marge Summers

With the lawn project in full swing, Doc gradually added other plants to the yard—twelve pineapple plants, watermelon, and cherry tomato starts. He introduced strawberry plants and bell peppers in areas next to the house protected from the wind. He even ventured into the desert and brought back aloe and local varieties of cacti.

Bill admired his old friend. He recalled one of the cherry tomato plants Doc put in the front yard. "It grew for four years. It never looked like it was going to die. We ended up with thousands and thousands, and thousands of tomatoes year after year after year."

Doc was not stingy with his produce and eagerly shared his bounty. Dave and Norma Jacobson met Doc Lyons at Casa Grande during their first visit to Punta Chivato. "He directed us to the camping beach and supplied us with freshly picked tomatoes," recalled Dave. The couple appreciated the gesture. They would later make Punta Chivato a regular vacation destination.

Although acquiring and fixing up the hotel was foremost on Bill's mind, he appreciated what Doc was doing at Casa Grande. However, Doc's role in helping Bill achieve his dream was minimal that first year. Little did Bill realize he would soon desperately depend upon his cantankerous companion.

Jack Larsen, Bill's partner, occasionally flew to Punta Chivato and stayed in Casa Grande. Although Jack was not required to provide any labor during his visits, Bill shared a story of Jack's attempt to help fix a window.

"I'll never forget the huge front windows in the living room in the Big House. They weighed over one hundred pounds apiece and should have slid." Jack wanted the windows fixed and asked Bill to work on them. When Bill said he did not know what kind of rollers they had, Jack suggested they take one window out.

"It became a disaster," said Bill. "I knew it when he was lying on his back and saw the rollers were all rusted from being right there on the ocean." After Bill suggested using a hacksaw, Jack proposed an alternate method for getting the corroded rollers off the window.

"Wait a minute, wait a minute, wait a minute," Jack said. "There's lots of ways to do things. Lots of ways to skin a pig." Bill later admitted he had never heard that phrase before. Jack went to the room he used, looked in his tool chest, and came out with a chisel and a little hammer.

"Just nip those things off," Jack said.

"Jack, I don't want to do it," Bill replied. "Right now, they're almost a permanent part of the glass."

Jack was insistent. "No, no, no, I'll show you." Jack took his chisel and TAP. "Five million pieces of glass all over the living room," Bill recalled. Jack vowed to find a replacement, and he did. A window the same size and tint arrived at Punta Chivato four months later, "The bill came to $475," said Bill. "Back then, that was really expensive."

Casa Grande (view from pila on hill).
From Nov. 1991 video by Bill Alvarado

Chapter 39

BILL'S DREAM

News quickly spread among the early Punta Chivato beach campers that Zacarías was no longer the sole occupant of Casa Grande. Soon, these campers met the transplanted Oregonians Bill Alvarado and Doc Lyons. Early camper Barbara Silzle recalls sharing dinners and meal preparation with them.

"Bill invited a handful of us over," Barbara said. "There wouldn't be more than Harry and Marilyn [Oxley], Red and Nancy [Salzman], and us [Bill and Barbara Silzle]." She added, "Casa Grande did not have electricity. We'd have to do all the cooking before it got dark. On a real dark night, we had to use flashlights to get out to the porch. Then we'd sit out there and put our feet up on the edge there and say how lucky we were and how beautiful the stars were. And it was really nice."

The meal sharing went both ways. "Bill and Doc would have dinner at our camp, and they would have us to the Casa Grande," Red Salzman shared in a letter to the author. "Bill was a great host."

On a return trip to his townhouse in Eugene, Oregon, Bill talked to his neighbors, Walter and Jeanne Fox. He could not contain his excitement about Punta Chivato.

"Bill came over one day to tell Walter about this place he found," Jeanne said. "It was when he first started getting involved at Punta Chivato."

The year was 1979. Bill encouraged the Foxes to visit him in Baja. Soon, they took him up on his offer.

"We took a plane out of Los Angeles and flew to the small airstrip next to the Serenidad Hotel," Jeanne recalled. "It was a big fishing place in those days," she said, describing the surprising number of people who got off the plane with them and stayed at the Serenidad Hotel in Mulegé. "Bill met us in his pickup and took us to Punta Chivato."

Jeanne remembered being jostled as Bill drove the last section from Baja 1 to the coast. "It was like an old creek bed for a ways and then you picked up a dirt road. It was terrible. Every time Bill would want to go into town, I would just pray that he'd come back."

Jeanne Fox described what she saw as they walked through the hotel during that first visit to Punta Chivato. "It had been cleaned out completely. Everything. The rooms. Everything was cleaned out. There was nothing in the kitchen, no furniture, no windows, no doors."

Bill invited the couple to stay at Casa Grande. They quickly fell in love with the area, and soon, Punta Chivato became their annual winter destination. They had a regular room at the Big House. Walter often offered to cook.

"If Walter did a meal, it was usually Chinese," remembered Jeanne. "He would go into town to get the vegetables and chicken or fish. Shrimp was big. He would do a stir fry with rice."

Although Walter Fox loved to cook and serve up his delectable creations, he was not as willing to share the expensive wines he brought to Baja. One early visitor to Casa Grande remembered, "Walter figured out how many glasses of wine were in each bottle and deducted that off anything he might have owed. Talk about tight. I couldn't believe it."

During an early visit, Bill introduced the Foxes to his partner, Jack Larsen, and Jack's wife, Bunnie, who were also staying at Casa Grande. Some recalled Bunnie was quite beautiful and referred to her as Jack's "trophy wife." According to Jeanne, the couple had gone into Mulegé earlier that afternoon and brought back a big jug full of margaritas from the Serenidad Hotel. "They ate and drank margaritas in their room," Jeanne remembers. "We didn't see hide nor hair of them the rest of the time."

Another Posada partner, George Staples, also came to live at Casa Grande in the early 1980s. Having passed the bar exam in 1979, George began working as a public defender in Bend, Oregon. However, he quickly grew discouraged and, according to Bill Alvarado, only practiced law for a few months before returning to Baja.

George moved into a room near Doc, and the two shared an adjoining bathroom. "He came to Punta Chivato to escape from the world," Bill surmised. George did not like to listen to people, especially his father, whom he described as "pushy." One early camper recalled, "George kind of dropped out from his previous life in Oregon and was just sort of hanging in Punta Chivato part of the time. Bill had kind of taken him in."

Many early campers described George as a nice young man. However, Doc had no patience for him. Although the two had been roommates in Oregon and partners in Posada, Doc was unhappy when George moved to Punta Chivato.

Bill recalled, "Doc just absolutely despised George. He thought George was mentally deficient, that he had some super problems that nobody could ever solve."

Doc was unrelenting. Bill acknowledged Doc Lyons was not one to change his opinion. "When Doc made a decision, he never backed off. He never said, 'Well, maybe I was wrong.'" Doc's way of dealing with George was to ignore him.

On the other hand, Bill found George's ability to speak Spanish fluently to be an asset. Most of the workers did not understand English, and Bill often needed a translator when he had dealings in Santa Rosalía. Although Bill hoped George's knowledge of law might come in useful, he soon realized that laws in the United States and México were not the same.

Chapter 40

EARLY MEXICAN EMPLOYEES

Pedro Molina grew up in Rancho San Marcos, just north of Punta Chivato. He was raised in a large Mexican family, one of ten children, five boys and five girls. Pedro was 12 years old in the early 1960s when he saw men working at the fresh-water lagoon near his town. The once quiet estuary soon became alive with activity.

One day, Pedro was fishing at the lagoon when men arrived in a truck with oversized tires. He watched as they pumped precious water into the truck's holding tank. The men then climbed back into the vehicle and headed south. Pedro saw water slosh out of the overfilled truck as it bounced along the uneven, dirt road.

When he returned home, the Mexican boy told his father what he had witnessed. Pedro learned the water was being transported to Punta Chivato, where an American, Dixon Collins, was constructing a luxury fishing resort. The resort would become Hotel Borrego de Oro.

As he grew up, Pedro heard about Dixon Collins's sale of his successful resort to another American, Cleveland Crudgington, a man Pedro would never meet. Through word-of-mouth, Pedro learned Señor Crudgington was not a nice employer. When Crudgington left Punta Chivato in the summer of 1974, Mexican workers told Pedro that the wealthy American had abandoned them, suddenly leaving without paying them. Pedro watched as the hotel rapidly deteriorated over the years. No one seemed to be in charge except for the old Mexican caretaker, Zacarías, who lived in Casa Grande.

Word quickly spread to the local villages when another American, Bill Alvarado, arrived at Punta Chivato with his dream of resurrecting the old hotel. Pedro, then a 26-year-old newlywed, decided to visit the new owner. Anticipating it would take considerable labor to restore the hotel, Pedro met with Bill and offered to help.[91]

On October 29, 1979, Pedro and his bride, Aurelia, moved to

Punta Chivato and began working for Bill. "We were only married for six months when we came to P.C.," said Pedro. "That was our honeymoon," he added with a chuckle.

Twenty-one-year-old Aurelia was born north of Rancho San Marcos in San Bruno. Like her husband, Aurelia was from a large family: five sisters and three brothers.[92]

The young newlyweds lived in one of three adobe houses built in the ravine between the hotel and Casa Grande, the one closest to the hotel. The third house, furthest up the ravine from the hotel, was later occupied by the old caretaker, Zacarías. Although small, these houses had running water and toilets.

"We came to clean the hotel," recalls Pedro. "It was all dirty. No plants. No furniture. No water. The pila wasn't good. Initially, I worked in the hotel in construction, in the garden, the rooms, all. First, I cleaned and pulled down and later put in new things, new plants, pictures."

While Pedro worked at the hotel, Aurelia oversaw keeping Casa Grande clean. Gradually, this job became more challenging as Casa Grande became the central hub of the renovation operation. Someone was always coming or going.

Aurelia Molina, one of the early employees at Casa Grande and Hotel Punta Chivato (Nov. 1991). Courtesy Bill Alvarado

Young Pedro could not have imagined the role he would one day have at Punta Chivato. The couple were not members of Ejido San Bruno and never had children. However, they became woven into the history of Punta Chivato as committed, diligent, and beloved members of the community.

Aurelia's sister, Angelita Sandoval, her husband, Miguel Romo, and their two-month-old son, Luis Romo Sandoval, followed Pedro and Aurelia to Punta Chivato the same year. Miguel was known to be an excellent fisherman but had a horrible temper.[93]

When interviewed, Pedro shared stories about other Mexicans who worked for Bill early on at Punta Chivato, including the first two managers.

"The first manager was Alberto Ramero," Pedro recalled. "Alberto left in '80."[94]

The next manager was Yolanda Acosta Mesa. Born in Ensenada in 1950, Yolanda moved with her family to Mulegé as a young girl. Her father was Ricardo Acosta Munguía, who worked for Dixon Collins as chief builder of Hotel Punta Chivato (then called Borrego de Oro) in the early 1960s. Yolanda remembers visiting her father at Punta Chivato while the hotel was being constructed.

Yolanda met Bill Alvarado in the late 1970s when she worked as the manager of Vista Hermosa in Mulegé.[95] Yolanda was employed by Paula Galloway, an American who took over ownership of the hotel after her husband passed away. This was the same hotel established on the Mulegé hillside in the late 1950s by John Bonfante, Lou Federico, and Don Johnson, initially named Hotel Rancho Loma Linda. As the hotel changed ownership, new proprietors renamed it Club Aero Mulegé, Hotel Mulegé, and then Vista Hermosa.

When interviewed, Yolanda stated, "Bill was fooling around with Paula…he came to the hotel, and he sort of fall in love with me. He was chasing me."

Yolanda was a pretty girl and was chosen "Queen of Mulegé" at age 16. She eventually moved to Arizona, hoping to become a nurse. But that dream was never realized. While in Arizona, Yolanda met and married an American. Their union was short-lived; Yolanda soon left her husband and returned home to Mulegé.

She moved into the house in Mulegé where Lou and Lana Federico had previously resided and got a job with Paula Galloway. She remembers the day Bill came to her door to offer her the manager's job at Punta Chivato.

"He asked me if I wanted to work for him and offered me more money," Yolanda said. "He liked the way I worked."

She told Bill she would have to think it over and surprised him by saying, "I have a boyfriend, and we're planning to get married."

Mateo Apodaca was a tall, local Mexican who served in the Mexican Navy. He met Yolanda when she returned to live in Mulegé. What Yolanda omitted sharing with Bill was the fact that she was several months pregnant with Mateo's baby.

Bill was not happy with the idea of Mateo joining Yolanda at Punta Chivato but finally agreed to the arrangement and invited the couple to move into Casa Grande.

"We moved to Punta Chivato in 1980," Yolanda recalled.

They occupied the little apartment above the garage where Zacarías had lived for years before being relocated to the adobe house in the arroyo between the hotel and Casa Grande.

The apartment at Casa Grande was connected to the main house via a breezeway and had one bedroom, a bathroom with shower and toilet, and a kitchenette.

"It was a beautiful place, a beautiful place," recalled Yolanda, reflecting on Casa Grande. "Other people were living there, too, Jack Larsen and his girlfriend, George Staples, and Dr. Lyon. Bill stayed in the last bedroom, the master bedroom."

Mateo enjoyed fishing and worked as a fishing guide for guests at Hotel Punta Chivato. He also studied English to become as fluent as Yolanda.

George Staples remembers Yolanda and Mateo. "They got there before I came down," he recalled. "Mateo was a handsome Mexican guy with a great voice and played the guitar." But Mateo also had a serious drinking problem.

One Saturday, when Bill had guests at Casa Grande, he went to the apartment to ask Mateo if he would come out on the terrace and play his guitar. Mateo agreed but said he first needed a beer.

"Mateo drank tequila and beer, tequila and beer," recalled Pedro. "After two hours, Mateo was crazy."

Walter and Jeanne Fox were staying at Casa Grande at the time. Jeanne remembered Mateo coming into their room. "We were not in the usual room," said Jeanne. "We were one room up. Walter was already in bed sleeping. I was at the sink brushing my teeth. Mateo came to the door. I'd known him and thought, 'Well, he's drunk.' I said something to him, and he came into the room and just stood there. I looked over at Walter and thought, 'Well, I can always scream, and he'll wake up.' Then I said to Mateo, 'You better go on home.' He went staggering back out the door."

Mateo was well over his limit and could not control himself. "He was really getting obnoxious and pushy," recounted Bill. Mateo shouted at Yolanda, grabbed her by the hair, and shoved his pregnant girlfriend into the wall. Unable to stand by and watch, Bill ran over and punched Mateo in the mouth, cutting his lip and sending him to the floor.

"I'll never ever forget this," Bill later recalled. "I still feel bad about it. Wham—right in the mouth. I think when he fell, the tile hurt him more than my punch."

Yolanda shared the story and expressed her gratitude toward Bill. "Bill had to put him in place," she said. "Mateo was *muy malo* [very bad]."

Mateo claimed not to remember the incident, but everyone at Casa Grande that evening would never forget it, including Pedro and Aurelia Molina, who had stopped by to visit with their friends Mateo and Yolanda.

Yolanda worked for Bill for about a year and a half in the early 1980s, taking time off to give birth to a daughter, Natalia, born August 28, 1980.

As vivid as that notorious evening was in Bill's mind, he did not remember much about Yolanda when asked about her years later. She made more of an impression on other Americans at Punta Chivato.

Early visitor Archie McVay described Yolanda as "an opportunist." "She got the idea that she was the queen, boy. Take care of her. She stayed at Casa Grande and expected the royal treatment." According to Archie, Yolanda's behavior quickly wore thin with Bill.

George Staples, a resident of Casa Grande at that time, minced no words. "Yolanda was just kind of a bitch," he said.

Bill did fondly remember Pepe Acosta Mesa, Yolanda's oldest brother. "He worked for me on and off," said Bill.

"Pepe was more or less Bill's kind of man there," recalled Archie McVay. "He did a lot of the maintenance there. He was always around."

"He became quite ill," Bill shared. "Liver illness. He, too, had a problem." Bill pointed out that Pepe and Mateo both had problems managing their liquor intake.

Dennis Gardner shared two memorable stories about Bill's workers. The first one began just past daylight while Dennis and Bill sat on the patio at Casa Grande, drinking coffee. "We look down the beach, and there's a fin in close to shore, like in five or six feet of water," Dennis said. They realized it was a marlin.

Bill and Dennis grabbed a couple of fishing poles, ran to Bill's car, and drove to the launch ramp near the hotel. "We jumped in his boat and went scooting around out there," Dennis recounted. "We're casting like crazy in toward shore, but we don't see him anymore." Dennis had to go to Mulegé to deal with business, so he had Bill motor back to shore.

Not soon after Dennis left, two of Bill's workers who happened to be working down by the launch ramp also spotted a fin in the nearby waters. Dennis recounted the story as told to him by Bill. "The workers see it, so they run down to the water and walk out. They're standing in water up about three feet deep or so, and they're standing very still, and here comes the marlin." One of the men reached out and grabbed the marlin's head while the other quickly wrapped his arm around the tail. "Well, the marlin just goes berserko, thrashing all over the place. They're yelling and screaming, and a third worker heard them, and he came down and jumped on it. Basically, they ended up dragging it onto the beach."

When Dennis returned from Mulegé, Bill showed him a Polaroid of his workers with the marlin. "They got it on the back of this vehicle he had. A good-sized marlin—two hundred and some pounds," said Dennis, realizing if he had not left, that marlin could have been his.

The other story Dennis told involving Bill's workers occurred one evening while Dennis was still tent camping up on the bluff near the camping beach. He was expecting his 18-year-old son, who was planning to drive from Southern California to Punta Chivato with a friend. As the sun set and the colorful sky began to dim, Dennis surmised they had been delayed. Having no way to communicate with them, Dennis eventually went to bed, trusting his son would show up the following day.

"It ended up his buddy backed out on him," Dennis said. His son took a plane to Loreto and took a bus to Mulegé. When he arrived, it was 10:00 at night, and the only person his son could find was a skinny, old, blind Mexican sitting on a park bench by the little square down towards Las Casitas. "My son walks up to him and says, 'Punta Chivato, Punta Chivato,'" said Dennis, adding that his son did not speak Spanish. The elderly man gestured down the street, then painstakingly stood up and led the stranger on a 15-minute walk to the local police station. Finding someone there, his son again repeated, "Punta Chivato, Punta Chivato."

It was midnight when the local police awakened a Mulegé taxi driver at his home and requested his services. For $25, he agreed to drive the young American to Punta Chivato.

It was close to 2:00 in the morning when the taxi driver dropped Dennis's son off at the bottom of the hill near the pila at Punta Chivato. Everything was closed. Bill was at Casa Grande, and Dennis was camped on the bluff. "It's pitch black, he has no flash-light, scared of rattlesnakes, doesn't know where the camping beach is, doesn't know where anything is, can't even see the hotel, no moon, has no clue whatsoever where he's at," Dennis recalled. Venturing a little way up the hill toward the pila, his son repeatedly yelled, "Dad, dad, dad." Fortunately, Dennis heard his voice, jumped into his car, and retrieved his grateful son.

It was not until the following day that Bill told Dennis the effect his son had had on his workers who lived below the pila. Soon after daybreak, they informed Bill of a noise they had heard in the early morning hours. They described a large figure resembling a "monster man" standing on the top of the hill, repeating, "Dead, dead, dead." They were terrified it might have been a ghost. "It was one of the very few days that everybody showed up early for work," Bill chuckled as he, too, shared the story about Dennis's son.

Chapter 41

UNFORTUNATE ACCIDENT

Bill saw the swirl of dust rising from the desert to the west. It would be at least another twenty minutes before the approaching vehicle reached Punta Chivato on the bumpy dirt road. Taking another sip of the strong coffee Doc had prepared that morning, Bill continued walking toward the hotel. It was the end of May, one of Bill's favorite months in Baja. The air and water were beginning to warm up, but the stifling humidity of summer was over a month away.

It was 1980, and Bill was eager to get the hotel up and running. With approval from Ejido San Bruno, he hired Mexican workers, including Pedro Molina, to begin the laborious task of cleaning up the rundown structure. Most workers left their families during the week and resided in small, white-washed buildings in the ravine behind the hotel. They worked hard for Bill and were happy to collect a paycheck at the end of each week.

Bill looked around the hotel and noticed his workers were already on the job. Who then could be coming out to Punta Chivato this early in the morning? Was it a visitor from Mulegé or Santa Rosalía?

"Señor Bill, Señor Bill," the driver frantically waved and shouted as the dusty taxi from Santa Rosalía pulled up in front of the hotel. "Larsen *está muerto!*"

"Slow down, slow down," replied Bill in Spanish. "What are you talking about?"

The Mexican handed Bill a piece of paper. As he stood next to the vehicle, Bill incredulously read the news about his partner:

May 28, 1980—Mooney M20J, registration: N4253H, destroyed in Cajon, California. Pilot and one passenger both killed.

Jack Larsen and his wife, Bunnie, had awakened early that Wednesday morning, May 28, in their usual room in Casa Grande, the one on the far end closest to the hotel. Bill, George, and Doc were still asleep when the couple took off in their single-engine Mooney at 05:30 and headed back to Eugene, Oregon.

George Staples recalled, "We went to Santa Rosalía the day before they left, and I flew back with Jack to Hotel Punta Chivato in his new Mooney. They took off the next day."

In a letter Doc wrote to one of his daughters, he said Jack was "supposed to be coming back to the States and put his money together."

En route, Jack Larsen landed at the border in San Diego to re-fuel and clear U.S. customs before resuming their journey. Just off Brown Field airstrip, he radioed flight service personnel for a weather report.

Low clouds were forecast in the mountains north of the Los Angeles basin. Although Jack had logged almost 4,000 hours of fly-ing time, he had not gotten his instrument rating; therefore, he was unprepared to fly into cloudy weather with no visibility. But Jack was eager to return home and apparently felt he could sneak through the Cajon Pass north of San Bernardino.

It is surmised that as the Mooney neared the pass, it became enveloped by low, fast-moving clouds. With his vision suddenly obscured, Jack could not see the fast-approaching ridge ahead. The single-engine plane slammed into the top of the mountain. It was assumed Jack and Bunnie died instantly.

As Bill ran back to Casa Grande to tell Doc the news, his mind was reeling. He remembered several scary incidents he had experi-enced while flying with Jack. According to Bill, Jack "tested his airplane every time he flew it."

Once, while they were cruising low over an estuary near Serenidad, Jack spotted a familiar sailboat. As he dipped the plane to get a closer look, they heard "snap, snap, snap, snap." "What in the world was that?" Bill asked.

"God, I don't know," Larsen replied. After landing at the Serenidad Hotel airstrip, they noticed a perfect groove on the nose cone below the propeller and on both wings. It was not until later that Larsen found out he had hit an electrical wire that broke and fell on a little island in the estuary. Every tree and bush on the island burned and power was cut off to the entire west side of Mulegé.

Bill also remembered when Jack took off from the airstrip at

Punta Chivato. He would not hit full power until the plane was three-quarters of the way down the runway. Bill was always relieved they did not wind up in the water past the end of the airstrip.

With Jack's death, Bill realized he had not only lost his friend but also suddenly lost the primary funding source for his project at Punta Chivato. Bill had spent all the money he had made selling his share in the restaurant in Eugene. Without Jack's financial backing, he was uncertain whether he could restore the hotel. Should he stay on and fight for his dream? "Although bills were piling up, I decided to keep at it," Bill said.

Doc's reaction to Bill's news was brief and predictable. "Good fucking riddance," he scoffed upon hearing the fate of the wealthy jeweler. Doc never did like Jack, and Jack knew it. When Jack was around, Doc tried to avoid him as much as possible. He thought the jeweler was up to no good and did not trust him.

Two days after receiving the news of Jack's death, Bill packed up a few belongings to begin the long drive to Eugene, Oregon. He had decided to try to keep his Punta Chivato project alive and had already devised a plan to raise new financial backing. First, however, he needed to pay his respects to Jack and Bunnie.

"Sure, you can manage the place by yourself for a few weeks?" Bill asked Doc as he loaded his bags into his truck.

"No problem," replied Doc. "Besides, it'll be nice to have some peace and quiet around this place for a while. Good luck in getting your affairs with Larsen straightened out. Can't believe you ever got tangled up with that s.o.b. in the first place."

Deciding not to get drawn into another argument, Bill climbed into his pickup. He knew Larsen's heirs would be entitled to something for Jack's share in the Punta Chivato partnership, but he had not figured out yet how to repay them. Bill was nearly broke.

"I'll get back as soon as I can, Doc," Bill responded as he waved to his old friend and pulled away from Casa Grande.

It took Bill four days to reach his destination, but he arrived in time to attend Jack and Bunnie's funeral service. The church was standing room only, as is often the case when a premature death occurs. The couple had been in their early 50s. Jack was a well-known figure in the community, having run a successful jewelry business out of the Eugene Hotel.

Bill's concern over how to repay the Larsen estate for Jack's investment in the Baja partnership was short-lived. According to Bill, Jack's daughter did not want anything to do with the hotel or anything her father had done.

"I said, 'Well, you're entitled to something, but I don't know what because I don't have anything,'" recalled Bill. "Well, that never, ever, ever became resolved. She just went blind about it."

According to Bill, the Larsens' daughter visited Punta Chivato once and did not like it. "But that was almost a precondition for her coming down, to say, 'I don't like it,'" said Bill. She closed her eyes to her father's investment and never asked Bill for any compensation.

Although there was speculation that Jack and Bunnie were smuggling something out of Baja, there was no proof. Bill later discovered they were carrying all the receipts for the expenses they had paid up to that point on remodeling Casa Grande and the hotel. The receipts were scattered on the mountain where the plane went down and were never recovered. Bill would later sorely miss these documents when he got nailed by the IRS for being unable to prove the expenses made in México.

Chapter 42

DOC'S LETTERS

When Bill drove away from Punta Chivato that Saturday morning, May 31, 1980, he expected to be gone for no more than two weeks. He left 78-year-old Doc in charge of the day-to-day operation in his absence. This included supervising the hotel employees and welcoming guests at Casa Grande.

Doc had a method for assigning work to the Mexican employees. He would never ask a prospective employee if he could do the job because the eager worker would always respond, "Yes, I can." Instead, Doc asked, "Have you ever done this?" While a worker might respond with a quizzical expression at first, he quickly caught on just to nod. Doc was averse to speaking Spanish, expecting the Mexicans to understand English.

He was excited about Bill's land lease on the eastern side of the Baja peninsula. Although Doc held a majority interest in and control of their original purchase in Posada, his focus, like Bill's, was now on Punta Chivato. That May, Doc even offered financial support of $10,000.

While Doc eagerly awaited Bill's return from Oregon, weeks became months, and he found himself dipping into his own pocket to pay the bills and cover payroll. Following are excerpts from letters Doc penned to his daughter, Jo, in July 1980, during Bill's absence from Punta Chivato:

We have the surveying all done and orally approved by the bank of México for the Banker's Trust of 30 years.

Please send the Sept. B of H [Bank of Hawaii] statement to me as soon as it arrives if it comes to you! If Bill doesn't get here by Oct. 15th I may want to pay the annual fee ... in order to hold his 30 year lease in force. I think it is $10,000/year...

No! I'm not a partner! I have no authority or responsibility, but here I am running it. The Hotel isn't open yet. It will be open about 3 months after Bill gets back here with $3-

400,000.00. I've been working on the house. It is a 6-bed-room mansion. It is comfortable—lawn, flowers, palm trees, cactus, 2 cats, 1 dog.

To reassure his family he was in the right frame of mind and happy with his life, Doc wrote to his children:

I'm enjoying every moment of life—so far. I can't see or feel that I'm senile. If any of you kids think I am then for C......sake tell me. At age 79 I could be victim of a con artist and slow witted.

I'm lazy. So! I'll sit and think about my AGE, health, enjoyment, finances, doing things and seeing results, fun, a new challenge, travel.

YES! I realize that I should want to visit you 4 "kids" and 7 grandkids and watch you all mature and grow up. Should sit around and tell war and sea stories and tall travel tales—I hereby promise to do that when I'm OLD.

Doc Lyons. Courtesy Marge Summers

During the day, Doc stayed busy. He made major employee decisions; he fired General Manager Alberto Ramero and let Yolanda Acosta go to deliver her baby, Natalia. Doc worked for hours weeding, watering the lawn at Casa Grande, and tending to the diverse garden he had planted. He kept the interior of Casa Grande clean for guests and, from time to time, washed his Chrysler. Doc also enjoyed going out diving and fishing in the Sea of Cortez and wrote the following in another letter to his daughter:

> *There was a boat wrecked off Santa Inez Island 3 weeks ago. I've been out twice to look, see, and picked up some stuff. Can still surface dive to 16-20 feet without snorkel or air. But not as easy as I could in 1944 and '45. I went down 18 feet to try for the propeller but didn't get it.*
>
> *Was out 3 miles 3 weeks ago and got into a school of about 1 square mile of porpoise—feeding—many with youngsters 3 feet long, must have been 5,000 of them. We cruised along with them for a half hour.*

Doc had a strange fascination with bugs, as suggested in excerpts from letters sent during that time.

> *Killed 1,000 ants that I found nests while weeding the lawn. Some of my guests caught a dozen scorpions one night in the house on ceilings and walls, put them in a 4" X 6" X 2" plastic jeweler's box on sand with a beer bottle cap for water and caught flies and beetles for them. Had them for a month. Watched them eat, drink, fight, kill, and eat the weaklings until only one was left. I didn't feed nor water him for a week. When I did, he gorged with water until he had a fit and passed out. I thought he was dead, but he was O.K. the next day. I killed him a few days ago when I found some prehistoric monster crawling up the wall. Looks like the front parts of a scorpion but has no tail. I'll preserve him for identification and posterity.*

But one of Doc's favorite pastimes was to sit on the veranda at Casa Grande, where the gentle breeze helped keep him cool. From this location, Doc marveled at the natural wonders of the area. One could find him there at 6 a.m. having a breakfast of decaf coffee with honey and Cremora, toast, fish, and cantaloupe. Before taking his afternoon siesta on the veranda, he enjoyed beer and crackers and often ate dinner there. In letters, Doc described the magical sights and sounds he observed:

Sunset, water is flat mirror, no breeze, misty, a thunderstorm passed going NW over the mts. 10-20 miles away. I had fried chicken, coleslaw, mashed potatoes, gravy with raspberry wine for dinner here on the veranda. Now 7:30, temp. 88 degrees, but comfortable, 4 pelicans are diving for their dinner about 100 yards out—2 fox (big) bats are darting for their dinner over the yard. Ho! Now 11 pelicans.

I'm a sitting on the veranda listening to the waves breaking over the rocks and pier. Just saw a school of porpoises (big ones 10 feet) cruise by out about 200 yards.

Manta rays are playing and feeding here now. Saw a school of several hundred frolicking in a line 200 yards long leaping out of the water 5-8 feet high, flapping their wings like a bird and hitting the water in all positions doing belly whoppers, somersaults, barrel rolls, etc. and kept it up for 15 minutes.

Lobsters are now shedding their shells. They split their shell crossways between thorax and abdomen but only on top… then double up and sort of bulge out. The first thing they do is skitter for cover—their cave. At this stage they are a nice soft morsel for many creatures including man. I have a couple of near perfect shells. Even the delicate feelers are intact.

Doc celebrated his 79th birthday that summer while Bill was away. There was no celebration in his honor. But with his unique sense of humor, Doc wrote to one of his daughters about an unusual gift that arrived in the mail.

A friend in Oregon sent me a 2-lb. pkg. of cherry tobacco and two corncob pipes and a stamp marked "BAT SHIT". I mailed back a 9 X 12 sheet of brown paper marked "Gracias" and stamped "BAT SHIT" all over it. But in spite of the stamp, I'm smoking BAT SHIT.

Doc needed to get to San Diego to take care of multiple medical issues: a broken tooth, broken glasses, and recurring actinic keratosis spots (pre-cancerous skin growths) on his hands, arms, and forehead. But he was willing to wait until Bill came back to Punta

Chivato. He wrote the following in another letter:

At the present moment I don't know how long I can be absent from here—won't know until Bill arrives. It depends on whether he has to leave again for further legal affairs and to buy equipment and furniture and supplies. Also, if he hires men to work—plumbers, painters, electricians, cabinet makers, road builders, laborers, etc. Someone must be here—maybe me!

Doc Lyons with his corncob pipe (1980). Courtesy Marge Summers

One day, as he was heading out to Mulegé for ice and supplies, Doc was approached by one of the older workers hired to help restore the hotel. The Mexican informed Doc that the former hotel owner, Cleveland Crudgington, had been spotted exiting his plane at Punta Chivato the previous day. He told Doc the man only stopped briefly, looked around the area, and left.

Doc canceled his outing and stayed at Punta Chivato, wondering if the man would return. He heard Crudgington had threatened to take back the hotel. Various thoughts went through Doc's mind. He heard the man was a Las Vegas–Tahoe–Reno type. *Could he have ties to the Mafia, C.I.A., or F.B.I.? But then again, maybe the Mexican worker just cooked up the story to gain the owner's favor.* Doc decided it was Bill's worry, not his. He chose to wait and tell Bill when he returned, which he hoped would be soon.

Doc grew weary waiting for Bill. But in a letter, he seemed to have adopted Bill's dream of restoring the hotel as his own.

If Bill doesn't get back soon with several thousand of $'s I can rent the 6 rooms here, move into the hotel and over a period of 1-2-3 years make a go Go GO of this million-dollar project.

Bill finally returned to Punta Chivato in the fall of 1980. Doc eagerly filled him in on the events that had transpired during his absence. The appearance of the hotel's previous owner, Cleveland Crudgington, in early July was of particular concern to Bill. "I got a sick feeling in my stomach," Bill stated. "It scared me pitless."

George Staples recalled the warnings they had received two weeks prior to Jack Larsen's death. Crudgington's Mexican representative in Santa Rosalía relayed the message through Bill's workers. "You guys are not ever going to open that hotel. If you try, watch your food, watch your cars, watch your airplanes. We want it back. We're going to open it."

Was it possible Crudgington had the Mexicans tamper with Jack Larsen's plane before he left that fateful morning in May? "That was my first 'oh my God' moment I had down there that made my hair stand up," George remembered.

George Staples recalled another unnerving situation that occurred while Bill was up north. One day, he was approached by a young Mexican American. "He says he wants a lot, gave me, I think, a third down, gave me $5,000 in cash in $20s, $50s, and $100s. Then I found out he was related to the previous Mexican partner and somehow had bloodlines to the people up in Las Vegas. This was shortly after Jack had been killed." George worried every time he drove back and forth from Punta Chivato to Santa Rosalía for supplies. "You've got those ridges up there, and you're thinking, 'Man, I'd be such easy pickings coming and going.' It was hairy for a while."

Bill wondered if the "mob out of Las Vegas" had any influence in taking back the hotel. "Everything just kind of simmered for about a week, and I couldn't stand it anymore. I went to the next Ejido meeting, walked in, and said, 'What happened? Crudgington was down here, met with you guys, and wants the hotel back.'"

The president of the Ejido said in Spanish, "The bastard, that son-of-a-bitch with the great big dog. The dog scared us. He was really mean. His wife was terrible. We'd never let him back in there again."

Bill was relieved to learn that Crudgington had no hold on the property and was not welcome. Bill did not have to fear competition from the prior hotel owner. The two would never meet.

Chapter 43

RAISING MONEY

Even before Jack Larsen's death, Bill was always looking for additional ways to raise capital to refurbish the hotel. He realized one nearby source of income was the growing number of campers on the beach. Why not charge a $1.00-per-day camping fee? In return, Bill would make their stay more pleasant by improving the beach and services. He decided to start by offering garbage collection.

The three residents of Casa Grande, Bill, Doc, and George, were rarely all at Punta Chivato simultaneously. Depending on who was there, one of them would periodically meander down the beach, greet the campers, and collect the nominal fee. "They didn't come down and collect every day," according to early camper Barbara Silzle.

A few campers resented the fee. Barbara remembers one particularly irate camper who worked for the telephone company. "He drove a pickup rigged for camping and really got uptight about the fee. He yelled, 'I've been coming down here for years and never had to pay anything…and now all of a sudden…'"

But most campers welcomed the chance to dispose of their trash without having to haul it back out. Having the "garbage collectors" come by in Bill's old pickup was a luxury.

On a return visit to his townhouse in Eugene in the late 1970s, Bill met a woman who would eventually join him in Punta Chivato. About a year after he took over Casa Grande, Bill urged Mary Morss to come for a visit. Mary was overcome by the beauty of the area and, in 1981, decided to stay and help Bill achieve his dream. The two moved into the apartment above the garage at Casa Grande that Yolanda and Mateo had earlier vacated.

Born and raised in Cottage Grove, Oregon, Mary was a spunky, attractive, petite blonde who was quick to offer assistance and advice. One American at Punta Chivato who knew Mary described her as "a nice person, always going 100 miles per hour."

According to Bill, Mary taught Aurelia Molina how to properly make beds at Casa Grande. Mary recalls Aurelia did not help in the kitchen. "She was more into the cleaning and tidying up."

Mary soon discovered an unexpected cost of living in paradise. "When we first got there, the only access that we had to the outside world was the little phone place on the corner in Mulegé. My first mistake was that I called collect, because I wasn't sure if the person I was trying to call was going to be home. So, I called collect, and it cost $75. I didn't call collect ever again. They accepted my call. I thought $75, oh my God, my whole month's rent."

Mary proposed a potential money-making idea to Bill—offering meals at Casa Grande one night a week. "I love to cook, and I've cooked for crowds," Mary shared, recounting the copious meals she prepared for family gatherings in her home. "So, it was nothing to me. And Bill had the restaurant experience."

Initially, they had to prepare meals without electricity. "We limped along with BBQs," Mary recalled. "I didn't have any marinade or anything, but I heard that beer tenderizes. So, I marinated the turkey with beer." Later, she realized Bill was also marinating the turkey with beer. "That turkey was really good," she recollected with a laugh. "We had lots of fun dinners."

Meals offered at Casa Grande quickly became popular among the campers. "I'd go down to the camping beach and collect…that would buy the food for dinner," Bill recalled. "We'd have no more than ten people, preferably six to eight." The cost of the meal varied from $3.50 for an "unspecial" meal to $8.00 for a "really, really special" meal, according to Bill. "It was a limited income, but it paid for the few workers that I had."

"It was like a small restaurant," recalled Aurelia Molina, who proudly took charge of cleaning up at the end of the evening.

Jeanne Fox remembers George Staples would often be at Casa Grande with his girlfriend, Lynda. The two women soon teamed up and became the "bar maids" at dinner. Jeanne recalls a specialty drink she and Lynda concocted that became popular. Using a generator-powered blender, they would "crank out mango daiquiris."

"Guests paid for their dinners, and we collected money for drinks," Jeanne added. "All the money went in a pot for Bill."

Although Mary and Bill were the primary cooks at Casa Grande, they occasionally got help from a woman named Ana, who lived in Mulegé. The sociable *señora* was known for her enjoyment of food, cooking, and her ample figure. "She made the best flan in México," Bill said. "She made it in a pressure cooker. It was absolutely the very finest, the very best I've ever had in my life."

Ana was willing to share her recipes with Bill and Mary. Sometimes, she volunteered to prepare the evening meal at Casa Grande. Ana would arrive with a girlfriend, and they would spend an hour or two in the kitchen making quesadillas and *cabrilla empanadas*[96] that were served up for dinner to their guests.[97]

A frequent visitor to Casa Grande helped promote the weekly dinners. Dr. Sordo, a physician from mainland México, flew his Piper Cub aircraft to Punta Chivato.

"He flew in with a friend. They were both very gay," Bill remembered. "His friend had the most elaborate dressing gowns or dinner or lounging wear or whatever. They volunteered to take the garbage route, collect rent on the beach, and promote dinners at the Big House. They put on such a show."

Dr. Sordo and his flamboyant friend were very entertaining, and meal reservations at Casa Grande were quickly filled. "We were making $50 a day on dinner," Bill recalled. "At that time in México, $50 a day could buy a lot of stuff. We were able to keep this up all year long because even during the summer, there were six to eight people on the camping beach, and they didn't always want to cook."

Another fund-raising concept was introduced after Bill met with his attorney friend and minor partner, Larry Anderson, in Eugene, Oregon. While discussing ways to generate money for the Punta Chivato project, they decided to offer timeshares at Casa Grande. Larry drew up the papers for the corporation Baja Shores International, Limited.

Bill put together a slide show of Punta Chivato and took it on the road, enthusiastically presenting it to philanthropic groups in Eugene and Corvallis, Oregon. He extolled the virtues of his Baja paradise, hoping to entice investors to support his dream by buying a timeshare at Casa Grande.

Jeanne Fox remembers attending a presentation Bill gave in

Corvallis. "He had slides, and he'd give his little talk about how great this place was." But putting money down on a questionable investment was a hard sell. "He really made a noble effort," Jeanne recalled.

The only ones who showed interest were Walter and Jeanne Fox. They put up two thousand dollars for a timeshare at Casa Grande. But Bill never did get his timeshare plan off the ground. "It was a real heartbreaker for him," Jeanne stated.

Chapter 44

HOTEL RESTORATION

In the early 1980s, George Staples was instrumental in cleaning up and maintaining the airplane landing strips at Punta Chivato. "A friend of mine brought in a grader, and we graded both runways, cleaned them up, and smoothed them out a little bit more," George shared. "Every once in a while, we'd get a pretty heavy rain, and they'd get rutted. We tried to keep them in pretty good shape."

As air traffic increased, Bill had another idea. Why not rent out some hotel rooms to fly-ins? This would generate additional income and attract people to Punta Chivato. There were limited rooms in Casa Grande, so Bill focused the initial hotel restoration on cleaning up a few rooms. He wanted to be able to offer additional accommodations if the demand for rooms exceeded those available at Casa Grande.

"You know, thinking what you have to do and what you actually have to do are so far apart," Bill reflected. "When I got there, the hotel was pretty much in disrepair. Nothing worked. I tried a faucet and only a little bit of water came out. Then, a whole bunch of little bones followed. I don't know what they were, maybe raccoons or whatever animals were using the reservoir as their water source. There was no plumbing; the toilets were plugged up. New water lines had to be installed."

Bill hired Pedro Molina and a handful of other local Mexicans to begin the daunting task of cleaning up the abandoned rooms at the hotel. Bill and George worked alongside them when they were at Punta Chivato. "We went room by room by room to get them livable and get the toilets working," recalled Bill.

Even Bill's girlfriend, Mary Morss, pitched in to help clean the bathrooms. "The facilities in all the rooms were horrible," she remembered. "But you just get in with a shovel and start working. You put your rubber gloves on, and away you go. We learned how to scrub."

Mary remembered when she first met early camper Harry

Oxley. "He came in when I was on my hands and knees scrubbing the bathroom, and I was just a mess. My hair was wrapped up under a scarf, and my sleeves rolled up. The next time he sees me I've showered and actually have a dress on, and my hair was brushed. He said, 'Oh, you clean up pretty good.'" Mary, always a good sport, added with a laugh, "Oh, my gosh, those were good times."

"We cleaned up the hotel rooms and started letting them," recounted George Staples. "It was a neat place to stay and a pretty view.

"We were able to put people up in either the Big House or the hotel," Bill said.

Bill began to rent out newly cleaned hotel rooms before they could get all the toilets working.

"Mary and Charles Bolls were an older couple who would stay at the hotel," recalled Jeanne Fox. "They had a room [at the hotel] but would walk back and forth to Casa Grande to use the bathroom and stuff. A lot of people did that for a long time."

"You'd see a plane coming in, and they would buzz the Casa Grande and land. It was just word of mouth," said George. "And we'd go down and pick them up, and they'd say, 'Hey, we heard we could get a room.' And we'd say, 'You bet. Come on.' And we'd feed them and show them a great time, and they'd tell other people, and it really started to grow that way."

Chapter 45

LOTS FOR SALE

Although Bill had lost his primary financial source with the death of Jack Larsen, he was not one to stay discouraged for long. Like the original owner, Dixon Collins, Bill was a dreamer. His heart was set on getting the hotel operational again.

Yolanda Acosta Mesa, one of Bill's early employees, takes credit for coming up with the idea of selling lots. "I was the one who started this building thing," she stated. "But I left before they built a house."

"She was the one that was kind of the agent for Bill Alvarado with the lots," remarked early homeowner Archie McVay. "As an American, he couldn't do that on his own."

Whether Yolanda initially gave Bill the idea or not, he decided to focus on selling lots at Punta Chivato after returning from Oregon. He felt it was the fastest way to generate the funds he needed to restore the hotel.

It took several trips to México City before Bill got the final approval from the federal government for eighteen lots west of the hotel. "The Ejido told me I could do whatever I wanted with the land," Bill recalled. "I thought it would be nice to have some houses down on the water by the airstrip."

Bill enlisted Larry Anderson, his attorney friend in Eugene, Oregon, to draw up papers for the subdivision. The price of the initial lots was $15,000 each.

"The paperwork all came through Larry Anderson's office," George Staples recalled. "The money would be paid up there. This agreement stipulated it was a land lease and explained it wasn't ownership. There was the Ejido to deal with, and the paperwork reflected that."

Bill hired a surveyor from Santa Rosalía to establish lots along the airstrip west of the hotel and north along the bluff. "He laid out the plots for the lots, shot it, measured it, and staked it," Bill said. "I spent another bunch of money that I didn't really have to get that survey." Bill planned to charge more for the lots on the bluff since they had a view.

Early camper Les Conner remembered when he first saw the white outlines for the lots. "Somebody had put chalk lines up, and I laughed," Les said. "I thought that was so funny. This is Ejido property." With uncanny foresight, Les Conner questioned whether Bill could legitimately build homes on the Mexican-owned land.

As security against the $10,000 loan Doc had earlier made to Bill, he was given his choice of one of the recently surveyed lots. He selected Lot #19 between the shorter airstrip and the sea. The lot was 100 feet deep and had 70 feet of waterfront.

Bill also offered Doc his choice of a second lot in compensation for Doc's labor and the use of his car, tools, boat, bedding, pots, and pans. Doc would eventually choose a rocky lot about 400 yards north of Casa Grande, 20 feet above the water, with a sand and rock beach. This lot had 150 feet of waterfront and was 150 feet deep.[98]

Working together, Doc and Pedro Molina laid the water pipes for the lots along the shorter runway parallel to the coast.

"Doc worked all the time," Pedro recalled. "All the time when we put in the water line, he was using the pick."

Surprisingly, Doc had a good relationship with Pedro. When asked how he and Doc communicated, Pedro responded, "Doc said, 'You need to speak in English. Spanish, I don't hear.'"

According to Pedro, Doc rarely spoke more than one or two words of Spanish to him. "I'd say, '*Buenos días*, Doc.' He'd say, 'No, I don't understand *Buenos días*. Good morning.'"

When one of the early homeowners, Archie McVay, first met Doc, he quickly formed an opinion of the old man. "Doc was so set in his ways," said Archie.

Although Archie admired Doc's work, he soon found that Doc was not one to take advice. "He was putting in that pipeline and one of my partners, he was in construction, saw what was going on," recalled Archie during an interview. "He tried to give him [Doc] some pointers on what to do there, and boy, old Doc had nothing to do with him." Doc's response was, "This is the way you do it in México."

Later, when the water lines were established, Archie approved: "It was good water. It was a little bit salty but not bad."

Once, Bill traveled to México City with $150,000 in cash. "The money was to justify everything that I'd been doing," Bill said. "That was the final rectification of the subdivisions, my permanent lease on the hotel, and to guarantee me that I wouldn't be hindered in the future," Bill explained.

He carried the money in a small tote that was given a cursory glance at the gate before he boarded the commercial airplane. "The guy opened the bag up and saw socks and a shirt and said, 'O.K.' He didn't look down any farther," Bill added. "I was sweating bullets. Being in a foreign country knowing that my life is in this little bag I'm hanging onto."

Bill disliked the shady business aspects of México. "I had to pay the guy in México City who, of course, had to pay the guys in La Paz under the table, and then he had to lie and say that he hadn't done it."

Bill felt that being a *gringo* rather than a Mexican citizen was a disadvantage. However, he considered his Spanish good enough to understand 90% of the conversation. Bill did not like some of the things they said but decided he could not do anything about it. "I didn't want to let loose something that I had started," he said.

Bill's accountant tried to talk him into becoming a Mexican citizen for years. "He wanted me to marry someone," Bill said with a chuckle. "You get married, and she goes off and lives somewhere with a nice dowry or monthly payments."

Bill recalled getting consent from the Mexican government to sell lots at Punta Chivato. "I finally got my approval, had the documents all justified, rectified, stamped, sealed and delivered," Bill shared. "But I had to have a final sign-off by the new governor of Baja Norte at that time. He wanted to meet me in Tijuana. I thought it was kind of funny. It was out of his jurisdiction. I didn't ever talk to the headman. He was in the next room. I could see him. He sent his underling in to tell me what I had to do. His underling said, 'You can have everything that you want. All we need is $1,000 a lot.' I could never challenge him because I never spoke to the governor. They're smart, they're shrewd," Bill added.

Dale Dyer remembers how he first heard about the lots for sale at Punta Chivato. "We had just flown in and saw something up on the bulletin board outside the hotel. It was a notice from Bill Alvarado announcing he was dividing lots. There was nobody here. It was just this note. We wrote our names down that we were interested in buying a lot."

John and Gerry Fitzsimmons, guests at Hotel Punta Chivato during the Crudgington years, received a letter in the mail regarding the sale of lots at Punta Chivato.

When asked how Bill got his address, John offered the following explanation: "We flew in during the period of time before Bill took over. The hotel swimming pool was empty, and the filing cabinet had blown over in the office. All the pieces of paper with previous guest names were strewn all over the place. There was no value that the local rip-off artists could see. So, when Bill got there, the file cabinet was still there. He tipped it back up and started looking through it. Anybody that had an address in the United States he sent a letter to. That's how Bill got the original mailing list to sell lots at Punta Chivato."

Following is the letter Bill sent:

Buenos Días:

I can finally give you the good news! Beach front lots at Punta Chivato are now available! Twenty-five lots, all within a few feet of beautiful Santa Inez Bay have been surveyed, staked, and lined out.

You will find enclosed two maps. The first is an area overview. The insert shows the location of Punta Chivato on the Baja Peninsula, while the larger portion shows the layout of the existing hacienda and the Hotel Punta Chivato. The location of the available lots, just south of the 3100' airstrip, is also indicated. The second map shows the physical layout of the lots. All the lots are large, 78' wide by 140' deep, with lots #1 thru #19 fronting directly on the water. These will be limited to a single story in height. Lots #20 thru #25 are behind but still have a fine view of the bay and these houses may be two story.

The criteria for construction and landscaping are in the final stages of completion and will, in general, follow the style and atmosphere of the hotel—primarily block and rock construction.

I am working with a contractor from Mulegé who will be able to offer options on construction styles and floor plans. He is aware of the local topography and building conditions as well as material availability.

Fresh water provided year-round, is already available at the hotel and will soon be piped to the lots. Federal power, coming in from Santa Rosalía, is anticipated within the year.

I have recently completed all the necessary legal steps to be able to offer these homesites. The lots, along with approximately one hundred acres, the Hacienda (the big house), and the Hotel Punta Chivato are controlled by Punta Chivato Hotel, a registered Mexican Corporation which is a subsidiary of Baja Shores International, Limited, an Oregon Corporation. The lots are being offered on a long-term lease of twenty-five years. You may, at any time during that period, rent, sub-lease, or dispose of the property just as you would in the United States.

The lots are $15,000.00. Being sold on a first come basis. Your map will indicate which of the lots are sold at the time of this mailing, but most should still be available since this is an advance mailing to the 180 individuals that have expressed a desire to have a lot at Punta Chivato when the legal work was completed. Offerings to the general public will begin in April 1981.

Please feel free to write or call with whatever questions you may have. I am looking forward to hearing from you.

Yours truly,
William R. Alvarado

Bill also promoted his lot sales to the campers. He hoped some might desire a permanent structure in Punta Chivato rather than continuing to "rough it" on the beach.

"I can still see the little 8-1/2-inch by 11-inch sheet I had to hand out to people," remembers George Staples. "Each lot was for $15,000."

Early camper Andy Adams recalls, "We found out the lots were for sale because Bill Alvarado was down on the beach telling everybody." Andy and his wife, Bunnie, would eventually take Bill up on his offer.

Dennis Gardner talked about a lot on the north bluff where he preferred to camp: "Bill told me that if I was interested in buying that lot, he could really put that money to good use. He said he would take $15,000 for it and $15,000 for Harry's lot.[99] I could have my choice. At that time, I was definitely too new to México, and $15,000 was a lot of money for me, so I said I wasn't interested."

Chapter 46

LOT SALES & HOMES BUILT

In early 1980, a Cessna 172, tail number N9748T, landed at Punta Chivato. As the pilot taxied the plane toward the end of the airstrip closest to the hotel, Bill Alvarado quickly drove out to greet the new arrivals. What a surprise to see a plane full of women, including the pilot!

Bill warmly greeted pilot Jeanne Winters and her friends. Then, he helped them unload the Cessna and drove them and their gear to Casa Grande. Jeanne's long-time friend Rich Ream would later write to the author about that visit, "The girls were dined and entertained for 3 or 4 days."

Jeanne Winters landing her Cessna N9748T at Punta Chivato (building above boat launch ramp was used by fishermen). Courtesy Rich Ream

Jeanne Winters was an unconventional woman. Leaving behind a privileged, East Coast upbringing, she ventured west and settled in Jackson, Wyoming. Jeanne smoked a pipe and used strong tobacco. She took flying lessons and eventually earned her private pilot's license.

This was not Jeanne's first visit to Punta Chivato. In November 1978, she and Rich Ream spotted the dirt airstrip while flying north from Cabo San Lucas with pilot Sam Southwick in his Cessna 185, N53044. "We were curious and landed," wrote Rich. "The place was deserted at the time except a caretaker in the Casa Grande. I think he did very little caretaking."

The following year, Jeanne again landed briefly at Punta Chivato on her way home from another trip to Cabo. Rich wrote, "Jeanne and friend flew to Cabo in our Cessna 172, 9748T. They stopped at P.C. and loved the place. Still only the caretaker."

But in 1980, Jeanne discovered the caretaker, Zacarías, was not the only one staying at Punta Chivato. She was thrilled to meet Bill Alvarado and hear of his dream to restore the once-grand hotel. She was also excited when this ambitious young man told her he intended to sell lots.

Later that same year, while Bill was up in Oregon after Larsen's death, Jeanne would become one of the first to purchase a lot in Punta Chivato.

"Jeanne ended up paying $10,000 for a lot with a 25-year lease," recalled Rich Ream. "She paid George Staples." Both Doc and George were at Punta Chivato during that time when Bill was up north.

After purchasing one of the first parcels of land in Punta Chivato in 1980, Jeanne returned to Wyoming and informed her friend Rich Ream. "The lot she bought, Lot #18, was located west of the hotel, between the smaller airstrip and beach," recalled Rich. "She asked me if I'd build a house on it, and I said, 'Yes.'" A third partner in the home was their doctor friend from San Diego, Sam Southwick, who had piloted them to Punta Chivato two years earlier.

The following winter, Rich and Jeanne flew to Punta Chivato, intent on building their dream vacation home. Doc cleaned up one of the rooms at the hotel for them to use while the house was being built. Rich and Jeanne purchased their building materials from a hardware store in Santa Rosalía. They frequently used their Cessna aircraft to transport these supplies to Punta Chivato. Santa Rosalía had a small airstrip on *Mesa Sur*, a plateau a mile south of the town center. At one end of the airstrip stood the local cemetery.

Rich and Jeanne flew south to Mulegé to shop for groceries and

Rich Ream in Punta Chivato with Cessna N9748T.
Courtesy Rich Ream

refuel their airplane. They landed at the Serenidad Hotel airstrip, where they could obtain aviation fuel, which was no longer available at Punta Chivato after Crudgington left. Frequently, the couple stayed overnight at the Serenidad Hotel to enjoy the renowned Saturday evening pig roast. "If Don Johnson ran out of fuel, we'd have to fly into Loreto," recounted Rich, referring to the next closest town that carried airplane fuel. Although using their Cessna to obtain supplies was more convenient and quicker, they also kept a car at Punta Chivato.

Rich knew how to build but hired local Mexican Pedro Molina to help with the construction. It took only three months for the first beach house at Punta Chivato to reach completion. Rich, Jeanne, and Sam had invested $25,000 in their 915-square-foot vacation home: $10,000 in the property lease and $15,000 for building materials and labor.

"Gee, I was so thrilled with the first lease or two," recalled Bill. "I was trying to find some way to generate funds to open the hotel." Bill fondly remembered Rich and Jeanne. "They went up to Wyoming every summer and came back down to Punta Chivato every winter." Their two miniature Collies usually accompanied them.

Doc Lyons had previously selected the lot next to Rich and Jeanne's on the west side—Lot #19.[100] Rich recalled Doc kept a compost pile on that lot. "He would bring over garbage and water it to keep it going. One day, I looked at our airplane and truck, and they were covered with flies (millions) from the compost pile," Rich recollected. "I finally poured gasoline on the compost and lit fire to it—no more flies.

Workers level foundation of the first house using a garden hose.
Courtesy Rich Ream

Workers pouring the foundation of Ream/Winters/Southwick home (Nov. 1980).
Courtesy Rich Ream

Ream/Winters/Southwick home under construction. Courtesy Rich Ream

Ream/Winters home with their plane and truck parked outside.
Courtesy Rich Ream

Bill sold another early lot to Frank McElrath from San Diego. Desperate for money, Bill sold it for under $10,000. "Bill was just absolute dead broke," recalled his second wife, Billie Alvarado. "He practically just gave the lot to Frank." McElwrath would not build a home on Lot #3 in Subdivision 2 until years later.

While Jeanne, Rich, and Sam were finishing their beach home, three couples from Oregon were developing a nearby lot: Archie and Doris McVay, Ray and June Nidiffer, and Don and Marge Horton.

Archie McVay lived in Brookings, Oregon, an area his great-great-grandfather had homesteaded. This family-owned acreage was located around Brookings and Harbor, Oregon. Archie loved the land and made his living from it. He and Doris had seven children and instilled a pioneering spirit in them. Every year, they hunted for moose, elk, and bears. They made jerky, and Doris baked pies using bear lard in the crust. She remarked, "That's the best lard you can use." In addition to hunting, Archie loved to fish.

"I'd been going to Baja for many years to fish," recalled Archie during an interview. "Started going down there in about 1962. That was before the highway was in. We'd fly down by commercial airplane to Cabo."

Ray Nidiffer owned C&K Markets, which operated grocery stores including Shop Smart, Price Less Foods, and Ray's Food Place. Ray was a private pilot and had a Beech Baron. He and Archie decided to land at the airstrip in Punta Chivato. "It was just vacant," said Archie. "We stayed at the Casa Grande. The caretaker was there and a fellow named George Staples. He told us they were going to develop it, make homesites."

The friends flew down to Punta Chivato several times. "There was a fellow had a boat there, and we went out and fished with him. He was a commercial fisherman. We didn't have what you'd call very good luck," Archie recalled. "It wasn't the greatest fishing as far as I was concerned. Because it was strictly seasonal for dorado. They'd usually come about July, and they'd last into November. We usually went in the wintertime. That was when we'd like to go. We got yellowtail in the wintertime, and it was more comfortable. It got pretty hot in the summer."

These avid fishermen never saw any activity that indicated lots were being developed at Punta Chivato. They soon figured George Staples did not know what he was talking about when he told them about the plan to sell leases for parcels.

An unlikely meeting led McVay and Nidiffer to reconsider building a home in Punta Chivato. On a fishing trip at a lake in Canada, Nidiffer met an angler wearing a baseball cap with "*Punta Chivato*" embossed across the front. They immediately struck up a conversation about the remote area. The man with the cap was Walter Fox, a friend and neighbor of Bill Alvarado in Eugene, Oregon. Walter told Ray that lots were finally being leased at Punta Chivato, and he had already selected one.

Walter and Jeanne Fox had put money toward Bill's earlier timeshare idea for Casa Grande. When the venture did not materialize, Bill allowed them to put the money toward leasing a lot instead. "We were buying into the lot, and we didn't have a lot of money, so we bartered," recalled Jeanne Fox. "We had a Boston Whaler that we were going to give to Bill, but he didn't need a Boston Whaler down there. Bill ended up giving the boat and trailer to his attorney, Larry Anderson, and we got our lot."

Ray and Archie wasted little time returning to Punta Chivato. As they landed on the dirt strip, they noticed stakes near the shore and realized lots were finally sectioned off.

They met George Staples, who took them to look at the parcels.

They picked out Lot #3 in Subdivision 1, near the launch ramp and boat house, east of the Winters-Ream-Southwick lot.

Initially, a few palm trees were on the lot and a boat house. "This was all tore out when we got back down there. It was all bare," said Archie. "We paid $15,000 for that lot. We thought it was a good deal at the time. We eventually signed the papers with Bill. We never dealt directly with the Ejido."

The third partner, Don Horton, was a building contractor. He produced the design for the house, which consisted of a long room and three bedrooms, one for each of the partners. Don also provided most of the building materials for the project.

"Then we started figuring out how we were going to build a house down there," Archie recounted. "It was pretty hard to get much out of those Ejidos as far as any labor. So, we decided that we'd see about hauling a house down there, you know, just in knocked-down form. We started contacting immigration and different ones there how to get something like this in. We thought you could pay so much money and we could get it in.

"This went on for, I'd say, two months. I finally got back and talked to the same woman I'd talked to before, and she said, 'Look, what you need is a smuggler. My brother-in-law happens to be a smuggler.' She gave us the phone number of this fellow.

"So, we talked it over. It sounded kind of scary, but we called him up. 'Sure,' he says, 'put everything in a 40-foot semi-van. Come to Chula Vista [California], and I'll hook right onto your van. Have it sealed, and I'll deliver it right to Punta Chivato for $3,500.' We thought that was a good figure."

They loaded everything into a semi-trailer, including the building and the entire roof, bags of cement, and a septic tank. The smuggler headed to Punta Chivato with forged papers, towing the semi-trailer. Partner Don Horton wanted to ensure everything got where it was supposed to and followed the vehicle in his motorhome. In the meantime, Ray and Archie flew ahead to await the arrival of their "home."

When the semi reached Santa Rosalía, just north of Punta Chivato, Archie was there to meet it. The smuggler pulled off the road and said, "We have to get released here."

Archie recalled getting nervous again. "I thought, 'Oh boy,

here's where we are going to get really stuck.' And this guy come out from immigration, and he had a big clipboard, and he looked at numbers. Just like he knew all about what was coming off. It had a seal on it. He looked at this here, and then he looked at the number up there and he took clippers and cut the seal off. 'Go ahead.' Not a cent. Didn't have to pay nothing."

The next obstacle was driving on the dirt road from Baja 1 to Punta Chivato. "There were some real dips in the road," recalled Archie. "Well, this semi, he couldn't make these dips. He had to go around. He got out in the sand, and he got stuck one time. Well, it happened to be right there by where this one Ejido had a tractor, a family tractor. Pulled him back onto the road, and we got on in there then. So, we unload everything right on the lot. The Mexicans showed up, and they unloaded all this stuff. We didn't know much Spanish; we only had a few words, but we had enough to get by."

The bags of cement were for the foundation, and the Mexicans said they could mix it by hand. However, Don Horton insisted on bringing down a cement mixer. Archie recounted that next border crossing.

"We load up another rig and put the cement mixer on. We come to the border, and they stopped us there. I said, 'How much?' The guy, he come running over there. 'Well, $20, make that two.' I give him $40, and I said, 'I'm just taking it down; I'm going to bring it back.' 'Oh,' he says, 'If you're going bring it back, that's another $20.' So anyway, we finally got through. We got the cement mixer down there and all the other stuff we had," said Archie.

The partners spent time in Punta Chivato in February of 1982, getting the house foundation formed and cement mixed and poured. Archie shared a photo of a visitor who came to inspect the project. "This old pelican come up and walked on our slab just after we had it poured. The pelican just hung around there. He was real interested in what we were doing."

During the construction, the partners stayed at Casa Grande. "There were just us, George Staples and Doc Lyons," recalled Archie. "We cooked our own meals at Casa Grande. We cooked for them, too. A mistake we made was with Doc. They had their own ice chest, and when we cooked, we'd just take what we needed." Doc did not approve of anyone taking items from his ice chest without asking.

Archie brought down a car they kept at the house and used to drive to the nearby towns of Mulegé and Santa Rosalía for food and supplies. Archie recalled having to drive to Mulegé to find a telephone to use.

Bill Alvarado remembered his fellow Oregonians' home construction. "That group of guys came down there and put that thing up in 24 hours. That was the second house that went up. Like overnight. They really did a number on it."

According to Archie, they made several trips down to complete the house because, due to their jobs, they could not remain for extended periods in Punta Chivato. Although they performed much of the construction themselves, they hired locals to help. Also, Archie said his two sons drove down from Oregon to put up the rafters.

One distinguishing feature of the house was its red roof. This costly addition was supposed to look like tile, was advertised to withstand 150-mile-per-hour winds, and was touted as not prone to rust or peeling. Archie was disgruntled to look up at the roof one day and see chipping. He called the manufacturer, who sent a representative all the way to Baja to inspect their product. According to Archie, "When the guy got up on the roof, he found that it was bird doo."

Doris McVay and June Nidiffer attempted to grow plants in the bare landscape surrounding their home. They dug up palm tree starts from the desert and planted the "sticks" in front of their home. "(The starts) just took off," said Archie, "it looked like a regular forest. They grew 30 to 40 feet high." Doris takes credit for this green proliferation. "I used lots of water," she said. "I just kept them watered and watched them grow."[101]

In a letter Bill wrote to Doc on February 28, 1984, he described progress on the house: "Archie McVay has completed his porch and fireplace, and a *palapa* is being built in the front yard."[102]

Although the house had three bedrooms, one for each of the partners, they rarely visited Punta Chivato at the same time. As in many joint ventures, some friction arose regarding the shared beach house. The McVays felt they did the brunt of the work. Doris was resentful of having to "clean up" after the other partners. Their "clean" did not meet her standards. "They'd come down to stay to have a little fun but not to do the work and clean up. We'd go down and clean everything up," Doris recalled.

Doris remembers hiring Aurelia Molina to help with general housekeeping. Jeanne Winters first asked Pedro's wife if she would help clean her home and recommended Aurelia to Doris McVay. While still responsible for cleaning Casa Grande, Aurelia happily agreed to extend her services to the new homeowners.

But Doris was more particular than Jeanne about how her home was cleaned. In an interview, Doris recalled, "Aurelia was the one that kind of cleaned houses. She didn't do a very good job cleaning houses. She didn't do windows. She might do the middle but no edges on them or anything."

Early homeowners Rich Ream and Archie McVay were avid fishermen and soon became friends and fishing buddies. "We were the first house up, but Archie from Oregon had started," recounted Rich Ream. "He sold us a few of his materials."

In March of 1982, Archie took a boat down to Punta Chivato. One camper remarked, "You'd go out in the morning, and those two guys were out there fishing. Every morning, they'd be there fishing."[103]

Sam Southwick, the third partner in the home with Jeanne Winters and Rich Ream, loved to go shrimping. "He'd fly in with his young son, and they'd go out shrimping," recalled Archie McVay. "He had a real nice boat, but they'd never catch anything. They'd fish and fish. Finally, one time, they went out and caught a Sierra mackerel. He was so proud of that fish. They brought it in, and Sam says, 'That is a grand fish.' He was kind of a nice guy but a real odd person really."

Bill Alvarado recounted the following story. "Dr. Southwick was the funniest guy I've ever met in my life. He was a physician, but he was also a sexologist. He had some of the damnedest stories without naming names or places. One guy came in to see him and said, 'Doc, I've talked to you a couple of times, but I've got to get down to the bare facts now. I'm having sexual relations with my dog.' According to Bill, Dr. Southwick said he was initially speechless. 'I didn't know what to say,' the doctor shared in his account. 'I looked at the guy, and all I could think of to say was, 'Oh, what kind of a dog do you have?'"

As other lots sold and homes were constructed, the new home-owners turned to pioneers Rich Ream and Jeanne Winters for help. Dale Dyer remembers seeking out Rich one evening.

"I parked our Kawasaki jet ski by the water. It was a nice, calm night. Well, the wind came up, and this big wave came, and the thing's gone. I went over to Rich's and said, 'Rich, I've got a real problem. I lost the jet ski. It's floating out there someplace. Can you take me up, fly me to look for it?' Rich looked out the window and said, 'Well, it's a little windy, and I want to tell you something about search and rescue. If you want to see that thing, you've got to get right down on the water. You can't see it from up there.' Some fishermen finally found it beached on the point over there at Conception Point."

Camper and later homeowner Bunnie Adams shared a story about Jeanne Winters and a local Mexican, Martín. "Martín was living in the little fish house by the boat ramp with his common-law wife and a few kids. Jeanne was going to fly over to Serenidad to get cigarettes. Martín was nearby, and she asked him, 'Have you ever ridden in one of these?' Being the big, benevolent *norteameri-cana* and not thinking what she was doing, Jeanne said, 'Do you want to go for a ride?' He said, 'Oh, *sí.*' He gets in the plane with Jeanne and flies over to Mulegé. When he comes back, he gets out all excited, and he tells his little *esposa* [wife], and she stabs him right in the gut. 'Don't ever do that again. Don't get in a plane with a gringa.' Martín made it to the hospital, but he never got on a plane again. Jeanne learned a lesson. You change the ecosystem here, and you're in trouble."

However, relationships with the local Mexicans were generally positive. One day on the beach, Archie struck up a conversation with a Mexican who spoke English. The man lived in Santa Rosalía and worked at the copper mine. "I told him we needed some fire brick," Archie said. 'Oh, no problem,' he says, 'I'll get you fire brick.' And here he comes with a company truck loaded with fire brick." Archie figured the man had stolen the brick since he would not accept any money. As compensation, the Mexican asked Archie if he and his family could occasionally camp on the beach in front of his home. Archie agreed. So periodically, the man and his family, including eleven children, showed up at Archie's place to enjoy the beach and water. Archie remembers they made tortillas for dinner. The family slept on the sand at night, all thirteen of them.

Archie and Doris McVay hosted a big chicken barbeque at their beach home every year. They invited all the Americans in Punta Chivato at the time and the local Mexicans, especially those from the Ejido San Bruno. Archie remembered the Mexican boys over-indulging in the free beer he provided. "They'd take all they could and take off," he recalled. "So, we had to watch them." Once, one of the Mexicans got drunk and drove off in Don Horton's car. "They eventually apprehended him and got the car back."

To further establish a good relationship with members of the Ejido San Bruno, the McVays always brought down extra shirts, pants, and dresses from Oregon. "We just had them really fixed up with clothes," Archie recounts. "Of course, we found out afterward that they were taking the clothes and selling them."

When visiting Baja, the McVays were challenged by the intrusion of critters they rarely faced in Brookings, Oregon. Once, they killed a bobcat that was lurking around their home. Wasps became a more significant issue. They crawled in and made nests, shorting everything out.

Chapter 47

CAMPERS BUILD HOMES

The seasonal beach campers took notice as the first homes were built at Punta Chivato. Many of the early campers, including Harry and Marilyn Oxley, Bill and Barbara Silzle, Andy and Bunnie Adams, Larry and Kathy Lucore, and Bob and Bobbie Hilbun, found the prospect of owning a home at Punta Chivato too good to turn down.

By the mid-1980s, the Silzles and Hilbuns had leased Lot #4 and Lot #8, respectively, both west of the hotel in Subdivision 1.[104] The next lots developed west of the hotel were leased to Larry and Kathy Lucore (Lot #13), and Andy and Bunnie Adams (Lot #10), friends from Bonsall, California, and long-time campers.

Pedro Molina helped build the Adams's home. But as Bill began to feel pressure from the Ejido to open the hotel, Doc Lyons insisted that Pedro be hired to assist with the landscaping. Pedro left the home construction business and went to work at the hotel under Doc's supervision.

Fortunately, the two got along well. Pedro remembers Doc as "a very nice person" and "very intelligent." According to Pedro, Viejo Doc was not one to sit back and supervise. "He worked all the time."

"Anytime you went up to the hotel, Pedro was watering a plant," remembered Bunnie Adams. "Andy used to call Pedro *Generale* of the *Aqua*, Water General. That was what we called him for years until Pedro started bartending at the hotel."

Gradually, more Americans leased lots from Bill and constructed homes along the Sea of Cortez in Punta Chivato. Most of the early lots were on the waterfront, west of the hotel. The parcels northeast of Casa Grande were on a bluff above the sea. Bill priced them higher since these lots were larger and offered panoramic views. Archie McVay remarked, "They say we were across the tracks down where we were. Up there [east of the hotel], those lots were a little better."

Harry and Marilyn Oxley were the first to build a home on the northeast side of the hotel and Casa Grande. They chose Lot #9 in Subdivision 2 on the bluff south of the camping beach. This area was close to where Dennis Gardner first camped. "From the hotel all the way to the camping beach, there was nothing except Casa Grande," Harry said, referring to the land between the lot they selected and the hotel.

After the Oxleys established a lot lease, they relocated their motorhome, Titanic, to their parcel. "I used the motorhome there for about seven or eight months to see where the wind was coming from, where the sun was going, and how I wanted to place the house. I had some options, it's a real wide lot," Harry recalled.

Construction of the Oxley home began in 1982. José María Navarro, nicknamed "*Chaparro*" [short], was hired as the contractor. Born in the southern Baja town of Loreto, he lived in San Lucas Cove with his wife and two daughters. As was true of many locals, Chaparro's English was limited. Americans questioned whether Chaparro had a building contractor's license. However, according to Bill Alvarado, José had construction experience. "He was one of the builders at the hotel," Bill shared. "The balcony going out in front and all the stonework. That was his work."

Casa Grande and pier (center); Oxley home being constructed (far right).
Courtesy Harry Oxley

Harry purchased a plane so he could supervise the building and flew weekly from their Southern California home in San Clemente to Punta Chivato. "I was down there from Saturday to Wednesday every week," he remarked.

The home took years to complete. In a letter Bill Alvarado wrote to Doc Lyons on February 28, 1984, he mentioned the Oxley house was "well underway with most of the foundation completed and about 1/3 of the garage walls up." He added, "There seem to be lots of serious inquiries, but so far, no cash deposits on the remaining lots."

Aerial view of Oxley home on bluff at Punta Chivato. Courtesy Harry Oxley

Les Conner and his wife, Lucy, would later purchase and build on Lot #9 in Subdivision 1, west of the hotel. Les remarked, "Harry was the first one to build a real house. People thought he knew what the hell he was doing. Because why would he put that up otherwise?"

"People saw my house and figured I must know what I was doing, so they built a house here, too," stated Harry. "I built the house I wanted. Probably no brains."

Bill developed CC&Rs (Covenants, Conditions & Restrictions) for those who leased property and built at Punta Chivato to establish uniformity in home construction. According to these CC&Rs, each home was to be single-story and 2,000 square feet, including porches. The walls were to be white stucco, and the roof was red tile. In addition, each lot owner had to plant 12 palm trees on the property. Later, homeowner Phil Souther said the Ejido San Bruno had added other restrictions. "The Ejido said that I had to start construction in six months and finish in a year and a half," he recalled.

The building rules were not always followed to the letter. Although most homes were similarly constructed, not all had red tile roofs, were white stucco, or had the specified number of palm trees. "Bill had fits about us having the metal roof," said Doris McVay, a partner in the second home constructed at Punta Chivato. "There wasn't anything that was enforced at the time," said her husband, Archie.

"I think we all started out white," said early homeowner Harry Oxley, referring to the exterior house color. "Then Bunnie Adams painted her house. She was the first one to paint her house a bright color." Harry Oxley recalled why CC&Rs were sometimes broken. "Bill needed money really bad at certain times. You give him the money, and you could build anything you wanted."

Most Americans who leased lots at Punta Chivato had no objection to the CC&Rs and willingly complied. But Bill realized he lost sales because of the restrictions. "People felt they go to México and do anything they damn want to," he remarked. Later, homeowner Greg Joy, the author's husband, offered his opinion. "There is still a lot of that going around. People feel that it's a place where there are no laws, and everything is perfect."

The water supply to each lot was from the same well used by Hotel Punta Chivato and was located on the property of Victor Manuel Velasquez Meza. It was pumped from the well through 12-inch PVC pipes to the pila on the hill above the hotel. From there, lines went to each lot. Initially, Americans who leased lots from Bill Alvarado and built homes were charged a flat fee of $30.00 per month for having water piped in. Those who leased a lot but had not yet built were charged $5.00 per month until the building commenced. They paid these fees quarterly to the hotel.

Except for water, each parcel had to provide its utilities, including electrical power.[105] Typically, this entailed installing photocell solar panels and generators. In addition, each newly constructed home in Punta Chivato had to install a septic tank and drainage system.

Communication depended on high-frequency (VHF) radios because telephone services were unavailable in this remote location. Using these radios, residents could connect with others in the area who were either in their homes or on their boats. Many home-owners made up clever call names for their homes and boats. One might hear the following broadcast:

"Taco, taco, taco, this is Sunshine. Do you read me?"[106]

This VHF communication system provided no privacy since anyone with a radio could listen in by tuning to the same frequency. If the party switched channels, the eavesdropper could do so, too. For some, this provided ongoing information and entertainment, otherwise lacking due to the absence of television.

Chapter 48

ALVARADO'S SONS

Two of Bill Alvarado's sons, Arnie and Jeff, opted to join their dad in Punta Chivato in the early 1980s. They were teenagers when Bill and Karen's divorce went through. Now in their twenties, both boys were eager to get involved in helping Bill resurrect Hotel Punta Chivato.

Many considered Arnie a bigger help than his brother. As a "contractor/builder kind of guy," Arnie took over the shop and helped train the maintenance crew.

"He was a real worker," stated Harry Oxley. "I'd give him credit for the physical portion of the hotel getting put back together."

"He could do anything," indicated homeowner John Fitzsimmons. "Very talented." Early camper and eventual homeowner Barbara Silzle added, "Arnie really pushed to get the hotel open. He got out physically and did a lot to help it."

Arnie eventually married an American woman in Baja. They had two children who were born in the town of La Paz, Baja California Sur. As a result, the children were Mexican citizens. Arnie and his family lived in the little apartment in Casa Grande when they were in Punta Chivato.

"Jeff wasn't as much help as Arnie was," stated Barbara Silzle. Jeff took over the kitchen while his brother aided in the construction aspect.

Jeff married one of Chaparro's daughters, Lupe, who was raised in the nearby village of San Lucas Cove. Lupe's father, an early builder at Punta Chivato, was hired by Americans to construct many of the early homes.

When interviewed, Mary Morss recalled Jeff's new bride. "Oh, my gosh, talk about sparkling. She has dynamite eyes, her skin is flawless, she has the most beautiful dark hair, and she's large; she's a big girl but very, very attractive, very attractive and just happy. Takes life as it comes. She was sweet."

According to a letter dated April 25, 1983, by Doc, he gave Bill a check for $5,000 "for Jeff's house." This was in San Lucas, where Jeff opened a small restaurant near a bus stop.

John Fitzsimmons told of stopping by Jeff's restaurant for breakfast one time. "They were happy to see us," he recalled. "And Jeff says, 'What do you want?' It was anything we wanted, just as long as it was eggs. Then he was gone for a while. Whatever we wanted he had to go out right then and buy. It probably cost him $10 for the food he bought, and we probably paid $25 or something. The restaurant was not successful."

Local Mexican, Florencio, who never met Bill, was familiar with his sons. "Jeff's restaurant in San Lucas was only open for two months," he remembered.

According to Dennis Gardner, Lupe later "went up and lived with Jeff in the States, and they didn't get along. Their marriage fell apart, and Lupe moved back to San Lucas."

Karen, Bill's first wife, and mother of his sons, was said to visit Punta Chivato occasionally. Per Barbara Silzle, "She would do whatever she could [while at Punta Chivato]. Maybe she'd upholster a chair in the waiting room, or she had a scrapbook that she was keeping up and it had a lot of stuff in it. They were divorced, but she came down." According to locals Pedro and Aurelia Molina, Arnie came to San Lucas in 2002 and built a home for his mother.

Chapter 49

POTENTIAL INVESTORS

Through the sale of lots, Bill finally began to generate enough money to continue refurbishing the hotel. His ultimate dream was to bring the resort back to what he imagined was its former grandeur. He knew this would require an ongoing influx of capital from leasing lots or finding another big investor.

Bill had a big heart and wanted those who purchased lot leases in Punta Chivato to be happy with their decisions. Therefore, he generously offered each potential buyer a way out. "You have one year to challenge or to feel uncomfortable, and you'll get your money back," Bill told them. He was disappointed when Americans put down money toward a lot at Punta Chivato and then changed their minds. A few came to Bill after two years had passed and asked for a full refund. But Bill stood his ground. "This is your lot. This is your payment," he told them. "Over two years have gone by, and I can't give you your money back."

According to George Staples, Bill did not always make sound business decisions. There was an opportunity to obtain major investment money from a client of Bill's attorney, Larry Anderson. The potential investors owned Angell Brothers rock products out of Portland, Oregon. "They came down and were ready to develop Shell Beach and a golf course and invest money," recounts George. "Bill just shined them on like they were nothing and they had the money, and they were ready to go."

George and several early homeowners said Bill was enamored of another potential investor, Bob Starr. Starr was a promoter out of Costa Mesa in Southern California. He told Bill he was developing a project in Haiti and was interested in Punta Chivato.

"He was going to put a couple million into Hotel Punta Chivato and become partners," recalled Bill.

An article published in the February 1983 issue of *México West* reported on a Torrance, California couple who spoke with Bill about his ambitious project and his "new partner," presumably Bob Starr:

*Don and Lois Dickson of Torrance had a talk with Bill
Alvarado, an avid Bajaphile from Oregon who has taken on
the mountainous task of trying to get Hotel Punta Chivato
going again. They related that Bill said that he has a new
partner and everything is in a "go" state as soon as the
Mexican Government approves the plans. These plans include
a boat launching area, breakwater, campsites with full
hookups, etc. The OK is expected in July, according to Bill.
At the present time, it is a lovely place for a fully contained
vehicle as well as tents, etc. Bill provides hot showers, good
drinking water from a well 5 miles away, and trash pickup.*[107]

But Bob Starr never followed through on his promise to help
fund Hotel Punta Chivato.

Following are excerpts from letters Doc Lyons wrote to one of
his daughters between April and June of 1983. Doc's frustration
with Starr is evident. In addition, Doc appeared willing to use his
own funds to keep Bill's dream alive.

*Bill to SR (Santa Rosalía) to call Starr for 6 M (million) cert.
check to SR by noon 5/1.*

*Letter from Starr. He can get 6 M peso check here by Sun.
(NO!) later I added.*[108]

*Bill told me Starr put $42,000.00 in my account in 1st
Interstate Bank of Calif. San Diego and wanted my check for
$21,000.00 in order to keep his records straight.*

I sent the check to Starr for $21,000.00 with Bill.[109]

*Letter from Starr said he sent $41,000 to my San Diego 1st
Interstate Bank of Calif. account and wants my $21,000
check back (Not $42,000.00 like Bill said.) Starr now has
my check for $21,000.00.*[110]

*Here it is 43 days since our contract was signed. I thought we
would be a beehive of action! NO! We haven't received any
$s from our financier—not even the amount that I put in on
the day the contract was signed, 5/1/83. It was to be put in
my bank on the next day—May 2nd.*

I get the report via Bill and Starr's secretary that Starr has been under doctors-dentist orders with abscessed jaw. I want to believe it. BUT I've been hearing excuses for about 2 years from him. I'm tired of it. I think it is time to use the expression I heard my dad use on his neighbor Mr. Poulass in 1909 after they had dickered 3 months on which would sell his farm to the other. They were sitting on two stumps down in our new ground when I was surprised to hear Dad say, 'We've dickered long enough. Shit or get off the pot.' Poulass got off. We sold to someone else and moved to West Lafayette April 3, 1910.[111]

"He [Starr] made all these promises, but no money ever showed up," said long-time Punta Chivato homeowner Harry Oxley. "Every Thursday, the money was going to be there. 'When are you going to get the money, Bill?' 'Next Thursday.' They had the champagne ready and everything. The money never came. Bill didn't have any money, and what little he had went into the place."

Archie McVay remembers Bill frequently looking into the sky and shouting, "I hear a plane. He's coming in! But Bob Starr, his financial savior, never showed up."

"I was going down on the beach and collecting garbage and money from campers to try to keep us running," said George Staples. "We weren't getting any cash infusion from the States at all. Bill kept saying, 'Oh, we've got this Starr who's going be a big investor, big wheel.' He never came through. Bill never got anything from Starr. That was another one of those major, major decisions where Bill just blew it."

Years later, Bill shared his disappointment in this would-be investor. "Bob Starr was the biggest dreamer I've ever known. He knew everybody with zillions of dollars. He kept proposing that he could put three or four million dollars into Punta Chivato and really make it special. Boy, get your hopes up and knock your feet out from underneath you. It was all just a big sham."

Chapter 50

ILLEGAL LANDINGS & CONTRABAND

As in Dixon's time, it was illegal in Baja to land a single-engine air-craft at night. However, like the previous hotel owner, some pilots, either thinking they were invincible or due to poor planning, ended up flying into Punta Chivato after the sun had set.

Early homeowner Rich Ream remembered the occasional night landings at Punta Chivato, "We used to line up a few cars at night along the airstrip with lights on for night landing."

Dale Dryer told of the chaos created by "cars coming from every direction" to use their headlights to illuminate the runway. "People would just park their cars along the side of the runway," he said. "I guess it was a little confusing."

Archie McVay recalled an even simpler method used to guide the pilots down. "At night, some planes would come in, and they'd [people on the ground] run out with flashlights. You know, you're not supposed to fly at night. But they'd go out with their flashlights or their cars."

Bill thought the system of everyone flocking to the runway was "scary" and finally devised a procedure. "You people stay away," said Bill. "We have a procedure [emergency procedure]."

The system was simple. Using the longer airstrip since it had more room, Bill had two cars positioned at the start of the runway facing each other and one car down at the end. The pilot "would land, touch down where these were, and head for that light," re-called Dale Dryer.

Bill thought pilots who dared to land after dark were foolish and dubbed them "the night riders." He created a unique way to chastise them. "We headed up to the hotel and engraved a glass, put their name on it as a 'night rider', and I put the number on it, like Number 15, Number 42."

Bill remembered Harry Oxley picked up one of these "night riders" on his airplane radio at 7:00 or 8:00 at night. Harry's plane was tied down at the end of the short runway near the hotel. The pilot was asking for the Santa Rosalía tower.

"Harry gets on and says, 'Buddy, I don't know where you're going, but there is no Santa Rosalía tower.' And he said, 'Yes, there is. We're having a Rotary meeting there tomorrow morning, and I'm booked to land at Santa Rosalía tower.'" Harry reiterated, "I hate to tell you, but there is no Santa Rosalía tower." By then, planes were no longer landing on the 3,000-foot runway in Santa Rosalía, which never did have a tower.

Bill added to Harry's story about this pilot. "Harry said, 'Let me put it this way, we're at Punta Chivato, and you're somewhere over us, and unless you land here, you're a dead man.' He needed fuel. He was almost out of fuel, and he was trying to get to the tower. Harry finally convinced him that we would put cars on the runway, and he would talk the pilot down. The guy made it in, taxied up to the end, got out of his plane, and said, 'Where's the bar?' He was drunk. He went up to the hotel. No 'thank you,' no 'oh, my God, I'm thankful that you guys were listening.' He got drunker than a skunk at the bar, spent the night, got in the plane the next morning, and took off. Nobody ever saw him again. Somewhere out there, he's drunk or he's dead."

This character was not the only intoxicated pilot who showed up at Punta Chivato. Bill told of a pilot who landed on the short airstrip parallel to the water. He "taxies up kind of close to the hotel, gets out of the plane, gets this sack, and unscrews it and glug, glug, glug. And he's drinking booze, and it's 8:30 or 9:00 at night. And he obviously had been drinking quite a bit."

Another memorable "night rider" became terrified as he approached the longer runway. "He just flat wouldn't land," said Bill. "He'd pass, make another pass. We had a lot of cars down there then. Probably ten or twelve. The strip was lit; I mean, not perfect, but it was lit. He finally got on the radio and said, 'You know, I think I'll go to Loreto.' I said, 'Well, O.K., but if you fly down to Loreto and land at this time of night, you don't get past go; you just go right to jail.' And he landed."

It was conjectured that some pilots who landed at night were engaged in drug running. Punta Chivato was uniquely positioned between mainland México and Baja at one of the narrowest parts of the Sea of Cortez. The presence of an airstrip there would have been appealing to smugglers.

Yolanda Acosta, who lived with Mateo in the apartment in Casa Grande after Zacarías had left, frequently saw planes land in the early mornings. "I was pregnant, just a few months, so I couldn't sleep," she said. "Early in the morning, I was up. I saw a plane landed on the big airstrip at that hour. It was dark. It's there, and it takes off. Very quick."

Upon further investigation, a huge fuel tank was found hidden in the bushes. According to Yolanda, Mateo and Doc Lyons got the tank into a truck and brought it to Casa Grande. "They [those in the plane] never, never came back," she recalled.

Yolanda stated she confronted her boss, "Bill, are you involved with them?" Bill denied having any involvement. "Somebody was involved with that," said Yolanda, "but we never find that out.

Archie McVay affirmed Bill's innocence. "There were quite a few things during the time when we first went there and before we got there, where they'd have activity in the drug trade," Archie shared. "I don't know of any of it that went on as far as Bill was concerned. I don't think he was involved."

Early homeowner Rich Ream wrote about an event he experienced in Punta Chivato. "One day, we were informed not to leave P.C. for a couple of hours. A couple of jets later landed on the north-south runway. Also, a bunch of police cars showed up. The jets were throwing something out of the fuselages which we thought were 'bodies.' Later, we drove to where they landed and discovered they were plastic fuel containers marked 'Made in Colombia.'" Early camper and homeowner Les Conner years later showed the author one of these containers he saved in his garage as a souvenir.

Desperados had no qualms about arriving at Punta Chivato in broad daylight to engage in their dubious activities. Mary Morss remembers one day in the early 1980s when a plane landed on the long airstrip. She jumped into her little red Bronco and drove down to greet the people and transport them to the hotel. As she drew closer, Mary noticed two planes, a larger one and a smaller one on the other side. People were "taking stuff from the smaller plane and putting it in the bigger plane."

"I get out of the truck, and around from the plane came a short American guy dressed in a vest, khaki shorts, and Birkenstocks," Mary recalled. "As he's walking towards me, he pulls this gun and puts it right in my face, and he said, 'If I were you with that pretty little face of yours, I'd turn right around and get back in that truck, drive away and forget someone landed.'"

"Well, the problem with me was my body was saying, 'Go back in the truck,' but my mouth wouldn't shut up," Mary said.

"You can't do this," she protested. "We're opening up, and we can't have this kind of activity going on."

"Then this tall guy came around and said, 'Why don't we just take her with us?'"

"I've got people at the hotel; I can't go anywhere," Mary nervously said to the man.

In retrospect, Mary wondered if the guy thought, "Oh my god, we don't want her with us anyway; she's nuts. She's really nuts."

Mary finally turned around, got back into the truck, and headed to Casa Grande. Bill was curious when she pulled up twenty minutes later with no one in the car. Her eyes were wide, and she appeared to be in a state of shock.

"What happened?" Bill inquired, "Did you meet the people?"

"Yeah," Mary stammered, "they pointed a gun at me and told me to go away or I'd be dead. So, I went away."

While the couple considered what to do next, Mary got out a pen and an 8-1/2-inch by 11-inch piece of grid paper and wrote down every single detail she could think of, including the plane's tail number. Eventually, the plane took off.

It was not until the following day that Bill drove out to the area where Mary met the plane.

"We found a 100-gallon gas tank, pump and all, off in the brush," Bill remembered. "Doc confiscated it and put it in the back of his pickup so he could have gas all the time."

"I never turned in the plane number or description, but somehow Bill later figured the plane was leased," said Mary.

"Approximately three to four months later, the same plane came in," Bill remembered.

One evening, Mary was sitting at a back desk in Casa Grande that served as their office. A Coleman lantern provided light. "I hear patter, patter, patter, patter," said Mary. She looked up and saw a large, muscular man standing in the doorway. She immediately recognized him as the one who had pointed the gun at her.

"He said, 'Do you remember me?' and I looked at him and said, 'Yes.' He says, 'Am I welcome?' And I said, 'Yes if you came with an empty plane.' And he said, 'Yes, I did.'"

Mary invited the man to come in and sit down. He proceeded to tell her he had stayed at the hotel before. "He said he didn't want any harm to come to me and didn't really want to shoot me, but they had to make their connections."

Bill remembers meeting the American, who he learned was from north of San Clemente in Southern California. "He was around a number of times since then. He was probably importing drugs to the U.S.," Bill speculated during a later telephone conversation with the author.

"One of the trips he was down, he asked if he could borrow a blanket," Bill said. "I realized later he had it full of dope because as he was leaving, I drove him down to the plane, and he went in and placed the blanket in the plane."

Before Bill turned to leave, the man handed him an envelope and said, "Oh, here, by the way, take this." As the plane took off, Bill opened the envelope. To his astonishment, inside were ten $100 bills. "Oh, I'm an accomplice!" Bill remembered thinking. "But I really needed the money then, too."

On another occasion, Bill returned to Punta Chivato from a trip to San Diego and found "the place was just a twitter." Earlier, a big plane had landed, and drugs were off-loaded. Bill learned that *federales* lined both sides of the airstrip. The plane took off, the *federales* left, and another truck drove away. "Everybody thought I knew all about it, and that's why I got out of town," Bill said.

Early camper Dennis Gardner shared the following. "Bill was approached to put aviation gas out on the runway to supply people who were trying to run drugs through here. They could come in at midnight or 1:00 in the morning in their private plane, gas it up, and continue on their journey."

Occasionally, boats carrying marijuana would pull up at Punta Chivato. Bill remembered one such incident. "We had two young guys, I would say late teens, maybe early twenties, that pulled up in front of the Casa Grande. And they were high," Bill said. "They were yelling and hollering and crawling up and down the steps. They had a whole panga this deep in marijuana, clear back to where they were sitting back by the motor. They picked it over at Conception Point. It was growing wild down there. They had, I don't know, 300 or 400 pounds of it. It was still green. I didn't buy anything from them, so they took off and went to Santa Rosalía. Pulled right into the harbor and started yelling about marijuana for sale."

Sometimes suspicious-looking packages were seen bobbing in the Sea of Cortez off the coast of Punta Chivato. The author remembers seeing such a square bundle in the water during a trip with her husband to San Marcos Island in their panga. Atop the brown, twine-bound parcel sat a pelican, innocently standing watch!

Bill shared the following story about an acquaintance who turned out to be a marijuana grower from California.

"I was up in San Diego and wanted to borrow money just to make payroll. He called me at the hotel and said, 'What are you doing?' And I said, 'I'm up here trying to get a loan.' 'Well, let's have lunch.'"

"So, we were having lunch, and he said, 'How much money do you need?'"

"I said, 'I need $3,000 and I don't know if I can pay it back.'"

"Here," the man said, handing Bill the money.

"I said, 'How soon do you want this to be paid back?'"

"Wherever you can."

"This was before I knew he was a dope dealer," Bill added. "He grew marijuana for years. He later turned the business over to his son. After he was out of business, he told me how he tapped into the Sonoran water system and ran lines two or three miles into the forest and made all kinds of money."[112]

Early camper Barbara Silzle shared a story about the first person she and her husband, Bill [Silzle], met while vacationing during the summer at Punta Chivato. She told of a young man who landed a small, private plane on the short runway at Punta Chivato. "All of a sudden, there's a car there, a pickup; an old Mexican pickup comes in," said Barbara. The pilot climbed into the truck and was driven to the launch ramp. The driver unloaded his passenger, a boat, dive gear, and an ice chest. "Wow!" thought the Silzles, impressed by the service this pilot received.

Later, the couple learned that the pilot, Robert Russell Brown, nicknamed "Russ," was a surfboard manufacturer from Newport

Beach and owned Russell Surfboards.[113] According to Barbara, Russ told them the pickup driver was Ejido San Bruno's president. "I keep my stuff in his garage," Russ told the Silzles, indicating the ejidatario's garage was near the town of Palo Verde. "He watches for me. I circle my plane, and then he puts everything in the car and brings it to me."

"How come?" Barbara asked curiously. "What do you do for all this service?"

"Well, I've been helping him with his ranch," Russ told Barbara. "I've got trees for him. I fly stuff down for him that he wants."

One day, Barbara and Bill saw Russ return from a diving excursion. "He pours big buckets of water over himself at the launch ramp. We're here for ten days, and he's just taking a shower every time he goes out!" Barbara exclaimed.

Unable to contain themselves, the Silzles confronted Russ, "Where are you getting this water?"

"It's right at the end of the dock," said the pilot. "There's a spigot there."

"So, we got in our boat and went over there with a jeep can and said, "Oh, this is absolute heaven!" Barbara recalled. "That's when we first found water. And why the water was there? I guess for the fishermen. We always felt like we were kind of sneaking it, but we didn't know. Nobody said you couldn't."

Although they never surfed together, Russ and the Silzles shared stories about the sport they loved. They all enjoyed diving, as well. "One reason he was so nice to us," said Barbara, "was while he was diving, the anchor of his boat broke loose, and my husband went out and helped him get his boat and then helped him, who was almost out of breath. He was very grateful."

They grew concerned when the couple no longer saw Russ at Punta Chivato. They called Russell Surfboards when they returned home to San Juan Capistrano, California.

"Russ isn't going down anymore. He's burned out," said the person who answered the telephone.

"We said, 'What do you mean?'" recounted Barbara, wondering how anyone could grow tired of Punta Chivato.

"All of his equipment got burned up. Somebody didn't like the Ejido, and they burnt the whole thing. So, he's not going down," the person on the telephone explained.

Barbara and Bill later heard rumors that drugs were involved. "I don't know the whole story," Barbara added, unwilling to speculate about the surfboard maker's affairs. However, she readily shared the story about the first person they saw camping at Punta Chivato and the "luxurious" treatment he received when he arrived there.

Chapter 51

BILL PURCHASES RANCH

Accessibility to potable water was always a concern on the arid Baja peninsula. Bill still used the well installed when Cleveland Crudgington owned the hotel in the 1970s. With the anticipated increase in guests at the hotel and newly purchased lots, Bill was eager to locate an alternate water source.

An adjacent section of land, about a kilometer from the existing well, was private property owned by a local farmer, Manuel Moreno. In one of Doc's letters to his daughter, dated June 12, 1983, he mentions the rarity of such a piece of land, one not under an ejido.

> Bill and I are going to look at a 320 acre ranch up near our water well this P.M. It is one of the scarce pieces of private property in Baja or México—I think only 5% of land in México is privately owned.

Señor Moreno had put the ranch up for sale, and Bill was eager to purchase it as an investment. According to another letter Doc wrote about a month later, Bill was third in line as a bidder on the property. The first and second bidders were Mexicans. Doc was not thrilled with Bill's idea, except for the prospect of acquiring another well with a diesel pump.

> The land is no good for grain or vegetables. However, the location, WATER, trees, and buildings are good…A salesman tried to sell it to Bill for $40,000. I have a $24,000 price and will check on it again in 3 wks. The auxiliary water supply may be an asset to the hotel. The ranch and building lease or rent should pay the interest and taxes. I'm not too much interested or excited. It will take much work.[114]

Bill got the property but did not recall the price when asked. "I think Doc had a little money that he put into it," speculated early camper Dennis Gardner.

Bill allowed Manuel Moreno to remain on the property as caretaker. Although, according to his writings, Doc did not think the arid land was suitable for growing crops, it did have an established olive grove that Manuel helped to sustain.

"Boy, did we get a ton of olives off of it," recalled Bill. "And the old man, Manuel, did all the curing of the olives. So, it worked out real well. I told him we would go 50-50 if he would process the olives. And he said, 'Sure.'"

"We had great olive crops," Bill added. "He cured them and then sent them on their way to La Paz for sale." "We made some pretty good money. For the season, we made $800 to $1,000, and this was after he got his share. So that was extra money for him."

The additional well proved vital to Punta Chivato. Bill recalled when the first well started pumping out water that looked like "chalk." He speculated a nearby city project might have caused the change. "We thought it was the well that Santa Rosalía was drilling up near the highway that clouded the water in our well," Bill said. "But it was our fault. We had a gentleman who was supposedly tending the well, and he just let the engine run out of oil and burned it up."

"That was a fiasco," Bill remembered. "We had to run about over 400 feet of pipe to connect it [the newly acquired well] to the reservoir at the hotel. But anyway, we got water again until we could get a new engine."

Only two areas in Baja were known for having experts who could fix pumps: Via Constitución, 207 miles south, and a place above San Ignacio to the northwest. Both had extensive agricultural lands for raising tomatoes and "pumping authorities."

Bill made numerous trips to Via Constitución and took a member of the Ejido each time. "I had the expense of taking down someone to oversee all of this and he didn't know his left ear from a prune about pumps. It cost zillions of dollars."

After several months, Bill was informed, "Number one, this pump has been beat to death, and number two, all the impellors have been worn out from sand from this last excursion and also from just years of use." Bill remembers he was told the pump had been too close to the bottom of the well.

"The well pump itself, which is down at the end of the shaft, had broken off, and it was hitting the sides of the raw earth and sucking all of this [dirt]." After the pump was reinstalled above a layer of gravel, the water came out almost clear. "Whatever it was had settled out or was pumped out."

At some point, Bill decided to sell a half-interest in the ranch to an unlikely partner, a British woman in her sixties. The woman had relocated to the United States and lived in Escondido, California. Although the author never learned the circumstances of their meeting, a strong friendship developed between the two.

"Barbara would drive down by herself," Bill stated. "That was kind of a challenge. She was older and didn't have a whole lot of trust in people. But she made it down year after year."

"She always wanted to invest down there," Bill continued. "I asked her if she would like to invest with me on this property. And she said, 'Sure.'" Bill did not recall how much Barbara paid him but thought it was around $6,000.

"I don't remember how Bill got tied up with the English lady," remarked George Staples when interviewed. "It seems like it was after I left full-time that took place." George later returned to visit Punta Chivato with his bride, Lynda. George said Bill drove him out to see the ranch.

Bill's long-time Oregon neighbor and friend, Jeanne Fox, also was not privy to the complete story about the ranch partnership. "I never really knew the history of that," she said.

Dennis Gardner, who occasionally took the English woman out fishing, recalled, "Bill sold half the ranch for $10,000 or something like that to this English lady and started billing her 'X' number of dollars a month. That helped to get the hotel open."

Although Dennis described the woman as "a real neat lady" and "a real kick," he was more impressed by her 35-year-old daughter, who occasionally visited Punta Chivato with her mother. The daughter resided in London, where she owned a bookstore on Piccadilly Square. Her focus was collecting rare books.

While Dennis was uncomplimentary about the mother's appearance, referring to her as a "bulldog," he remembered her daughter as a "fairly attractive lady, shapely." He considered both women as "nice" but said the daughter was "very unpopular for some reason."

"Bill did some kind of timeshare with the mom and the daughter," recalled Dennis Gardner. "They paid him like $2,000 in advance, and for five years, they stayed at the hotel for two weeks each year. Free room and meals or something like that."

Dennis got to know the woman and her daughter over the years. Once, he offered to drive the daughter from Punta Chivato to her mother's home in Escondido, California. "We had some wine and dinner." The woman told Dennis that she was sending Bill $600 a month to pay her half of the diesel fuel to supply water for the ranch's olive grove.

Dennis liked Bill and always considered him a friend, but he did not think Bill was a good business partner. "Bill's putting it to you," Dennis warned the British woman.

When Bill eventually left México, he gave the deed to the ranch to his son, Jeff, who entrusted it to his girlfriend, Lupe Navarro, a Mexican citizen. "Her dad, Chaparro Navarro, was a good friend," said Bill.

"They [the Moreno family] have the ranch now," Bill stated during a later interview. "They talked Lupe out of it. They took it back. They have title to it. She made some money off it. It really, really upset me 'cause I trusted her with the papers. They just came and took it [the ranch] 'cause I was out of the country. Lupe didn't hold onto it. That sure didn't work out."

Florencio Aguilar, a previous employee at the hotel, recalled the situation differently. "Bill lost the ranch due to delinquency in payment. "They say that Bill didn't pay his half anymore, so when the owner, Manuel, died, the family of Manuel Moreno took it back."

Florencio lamented that the once productive *aceituna* (olive) ranch was dead. "When Mr. Manuel Moreno had it, there were much olive trees," Florencio recalled. He offered two explanations. "Now it's dead because Mr. Bill didn't put water on the trees. Another problem. After a plague of insects, possibly *gusano* (worm), the roots died, and therefore, the trees died. All of them."

The author was unable to follow up on what happened to the British lady or her daughter.

Chapter 52

MIKE MORSE

One morning in 1983, Bill was awakened by an unexpected knock on the door of Casa Grande. It was 4:00 a.m. *This could only mean trouble*, Bill thought, as he awoke from a deep sleep. Doc's skin cancer seemed to be getting the best of him, and he had left for San Diego to have more lesions excised. *Had something happened to yet another friend? Or did one of Bill's workers or a camper get hurt?* Bill dressed and rushed to the front entrance. When he opened the door, he saw a tall blonde *gringo* with an older man.

"Hi, I'm Bill Alvarado. Can I help you?" Bill asked, extending his hand toward the young stranger.

"I'm Mike Morse, and this is my dad," he replied. "Sorry to bother you, but we just got here and need a place to stay."

Bill opened the door wide, graciously ushered the pair in, and showed them to an available room in Casa Grande. Little did Bill know the bond he would later develop with this first-time guest.

"Bill and I just clicked," Mike recalled. "Bill saw I had a whole pocketful of $100 bills, and we've been best buddies ever since," he added with a grin.

Born in 1949, Mike Morse was 34 years old when he first set eyes on Punta Chivato. He lived in Poway, twenty miles east of San Diego, California, and worked as a house painter. An avid fisherman, Mike learned about Punta Chivato from a friend who shared stories of catching big sea bass, an abandoned hotel stripped by locals, and a purported history of drugs and prostitution.

Some who later got to know Mike were surprised he brought his father to Punta Chivato. "I don't ever think he was raised with him," remarked Jeanne Fox. "Mike hadn't known his dad that well when he was young. They'd been estranged when Mike was growing up. I think he lived with his grandparents."

"Mike's dad was an intense man," recalled Mary Morss. "He was very intelligent. He mastered five languages. He was a fabulous, amazing man, and Mike respected him. I was fond of them both."

Unfortunately, Mike's father later had a stroke and lost his ability to converse. But this did not stop Mike from bringing him to enjoy the magic of Punta Chivato.

"I was there when he learned to say, 'Mary,'" said Mary Morss, fondly remembering one Christmas Mike arrived with his father. "We were singing "We Wish You a Merry Christmas," and he was going, 'Mary, Mary.' Mike was fantastic with him, but it was in a joking way. That's what his dad needed."

After his first visit to Punta Chivato, Mike was hooked. He often returned to the area, extending his visits from five days to a month. In exchange for staying at Casa Grande, Mike offered to help paint the inside of the hotel. He had experience from his work in Poway.

At Punta Chivato, Mike soon became known for his enthusiasm for fishing. "Mike was more animated with his arms than I am," Bill recalled. "He just bounces around, and gosh darn, he wants everybody up at 4:30 in the morning to go fishing."

Mike Morse with a grouper. Courtesy Mike Morse

But after a full day of fishing, Mike's energy was spent, and he needed time to recharge. "He collapsed because he was so worn out," added Bill. "'Don't talk to me. I don't want to hear anybody.

I don't want to see anybody,' he'd say."

Bill and Mike fished together on several occasions. Bill described when he, Mike, and a friend Mike brought down from Poway fished off Tortuga Island, 27 miles from Punta Chivato Point.

"The yellowfin tuna were really running, and we caught the big ones. I don't know how many were there—30 or so. And they were all nice fish. They were all 20-pound-plus fish." With the boat full of tuna, the trio headed back to Punta Chivato.

Suddenly, they spotted a marlin jumping twenty yards away. Bill put out a couple of marlin jigs. "Mike had a big, big rig that he always wanted to catch a 300-pound grouper on," Bill recalled. "That's what he had out in the water."

The marlin hit Mike's line, and he began reeling. "I said, 'Mike, Mike, let it run a ways. You can't bring in a hot, 250-pound fish like that.' He cranked it right up to the side of the boat, and that thing goes up in the air and comes splashing down, and the fourth time it jumped like that, it hit its tail on the gunnel. You're looking up at this big fish. So, we told him he could never fish for marlin again as long as he lived," Bill said with a chuckle.

As Mike began to spend more time at Punta Chivato, he became known by the campers and early homeowners for his big heart and good-natured personality. He always had a joke to tell and cigarettes in his pocket to share.

From the time he first showed up in Punta Chivato in 1983, Mike wanted to become a permanent resident. He picked up odd jobs wherever he could. "Mike survived down there in a very interesting way," one early homeowner commented. "He's worked for everybody that would give him a project to do...sometimes he did things he didn't like to do or didn't agree with, but he's a survivor," remarked Les Conner. "Mike had done Bill a lot of favors hauling down stuff."

According to Pedro Molina, Bill trusted Mike enough to put him in charge when Bill would leave for the United States to purchase food for the hotel, glasses for the bar, or other items. Mike would later sell t-shirts at the hotel. Doug Moranville, who owned a t-shirt printing business in Bend, Oregon, produced the shirts.[115]

Bill helped Mike buy Lot #2 in Subdivision 1 in trade for his work. As on many lots, a garage was the first structure erected. "He had a desk in there, his fishing tackle, a bunk, and all sorts of stuff," noted camper Lee Links.

Les Conner stated that Bill needed names to put on the lots for the Agrarian Department in La Paz to validate the leases. According to Les Conner, that is how Mike Morse's name ended up on the lease for that lot.

No matter what played a part in Mike Morse having a place to call home at Punta Chivato, the tall *gringo* was proud to have it. A fishing buddy of his who lived in San Diego planned to become a partner with Mike.

Mary Morss described Mike as being "very nervous and high energy." Others described him as "hyper." Mike made social calls but never stayed long. "He always wanted something to tell," remarked John Fitzsimmons. "You don't tell him anything you don't want to have just passed right on." On the other hand, Mike was the guy to talk to if you wanted to get information around the beach quickly.

Mike endeared himself to those at Punta Chivato by his willingness to help people. "If you needed anything, he always tried to accommodate you," Penny Kellogg stated. "Mike has always been very nice and tried to help." John Fitzsimmons described Mike as "one of the most well-meaning individuals down here."

"He would do anything," added John's wife, Gerry.

Chapter 53

TILE FACTORY & ICE HOUSE

One potential revenue-generating project Bill Alvarado began in early 1984 was a tile factory. He thought it would become a lucrative business with the anticipated increase in homebuilding at Punta Chivato. According to Harry Oxley, Bill "egged" him into purchasing the equipment from a tile factory in Via Constitución. Harry got Red Salzman to partner with him to finance the project.

Bill asked Chaparro to build the tile factory in the ravine between the showers and the hotel. Chaparro and his crew of local workers first constructed a ramada, an open building with a roof of palm branches. They set up two tile presses and two soaking troughs under the ramada. A drying platform was set up nearby. The tiles were manufactured using cement. They tinted the tiles brick red by swirling paint into the wet cement mixture. After pressing the tiles, the workers laid them on the drying platform to harden.

Tile factory at Punta Chivato (1984). Courtesy Harry Oxley

"I used to go over there and watch them," remarked camper Kerry Kellogg, "just because I was amazed at what they could do. Out in the middle of nowhere, a tile factory and all that tile."

Chaparro used these tiles for flooring in many of the homes he built at Punta Chivato. John Fitzsimmons and Robin Converse pointed out a distinguishing feature in their floor tiles. "You'll see a flaw in each tile," said John, "Little marks. If you go into anybody's house that has this tile, you'll see this flaw in it. They all came out of that same mold."

In a letter Bill sent to Doc in February 1984, he mentioned the tile-making project:

"Two tile presses have been put in place below the showers, and we've produced about 200 square meters of tile—hope the stuff sells—the quality is far superior to anything produced in Mulegé or Santa Rosalía."

After the tile "factory" had been in operation for three years and produced thousands of tiles, Harry Oxley and Red Salzman confronted Bill. "Red and I saw a lot of tile go out of the tile factory, but we didn't see a peso come back," Harry recounted. "We really got upset one day; it finally came to a head. We sat Bill down, and we said, 'We gotta do something.' We paid $4,000 for the tile factory. Bill gave us back $2,500 out of his pocket. That was the end of our tile factory adventure."

Bill tried to keep the business open, but he could not make a profit. "It went belly up," he said. "A couple of the block molds and one of the presses from that tile factory are in Eugene," Bill added.

Another one of Bill's failed endeavors was an icehouse at Punta Chivato. Andy Adams remembered both experiments. "I don't know if the tile factory was before or after his icehouse," Andy said during an interview.

"It was an experiment on my part," Bill recalled, referring to the icehouse, "because we couldn't produce enough ice. We could produce ice cubes. My plan was to buy ice blocks at the ice plant in Mulegé, bring them out, and put them in there. Never got going."

Bill would later buy ice machines for the hotel, which solved the ice problem.

Chapter 54

IMPROVED SERVICES & ROAD

Bill Alvarado never stopped thinking of ways he could generate money to fund the restoration of Hotel Punta Chivato. "The campers down on the beach provided a good supply of our income," recalled Bill's girlfriend, Mary Morss. However, although helpful, the money derived from camping fees and dinners at Casa Grande was not enough. Bill decided to offer more amenities. He hoped to bring more Americans to Punta Chivato and persuade them to purchase lots.

Bill had already provided trash cans and garbage pickup for the beach campers. Next, he installed three outhouses with primitive pit toilets near the base of the bluffs by the camping beach. Campers who came in cars, trucks, or vans used a combination of the outhouses and their own port-a-potties.

Harry Oxley posing next to outhouse installed at camping beach.
Courtesy Harry Oxley

Before Bill built the tile factory in the ravine between the hotel and the road to the camping beach, he constructed primitive showers nearby for the workers. Two side-by-side showers were built of corrugated iron adjacent to a water faucet. A garden hose ran up across the top of the structure, and a shower head was attached to the end.

Dave Jacobson, who labeled the water from the spigot as "non-potable," was nonetheless appreciative of this convenience. Despite the questionable quality of the water, he said, "The water and showers were quite welcome." As more water ran through the system, it became clearer.

Lynn Links described the limited privacy of the shower. "There were at least a couple of peek-a-boo holes in the metal between the two showers, but who cared?"

Barbara Silzle also remembered the lack of privacy in those crude showers. "If you hung around, you could sure see through," she said.

Crude shower in ravine near tile factory. Courtesy Harry Oxley

Les Conner recalled using a shower near the Sea of Cortez down below Casa Grande. "You could take a shower there. I never saw anybody walk by," he remarked.

For winter campers, the public showers could be especially unpleasant. "You were not only showering in cold water, but it was drafty because it was open in the top," remarked an early camper. If it was windy, not only were you "freezing to death," but during the walk down the unpaved road back to the camping beach, "the wind would blow dirt on you, so you might as well not have had a shower."

Barbara Silzle remembered doing laundry at these showers with Nancy Salzman. "Nancy and I would go over there with a tub, and we'd wash clothes. And it was terrible as far as these wasps were concerned because they would just be thick there by the water. She always worried that we'd get stung. We never did. We washed what we could there."

Bill Alvarado knew he had to improve the road from Baja 1 to Punta Chivato so camping trailers would have better access. Campers had tried to drive larger vehicles to Punta Chivato with little success. The original road built by Lui Sui Qui in the 1960s was insufficient for trailers or vehicles with long hangovers. Many got stuck navigating the bumpy old road and traversing the numerous water run-off dips called *vados*.

"I can remember the first trailer that I ever saw at the beach," recalls Barbara Silzle. "It was kind of a camper-like thing. We all said, 'Boy, wait till he goes out.' We'd all stand back and bet how many times it would take. Oh, my God. You could hear everything come out of the cabinets when he finally made it. It took him several times. Really, that was part of the fun of being on the beach."

With approval from the Ejido San Bruno, Bill contracted with Rudolfo Vargas to construct a new entry road to Punta Chivato. Vargas lived in Santa Rosalía and was employed as the head of the Mexican highway department in that area. He provided a grader and trucks.

"It was one of those horrible situations," recalled Bill Alvarado. "Wherever we graded, it became dust. We ended up almost with a riverbed going up to Punta Chivato for the first four miles." In some sections, to keep the dust down, crushed seashells were laid on the roadbed.

Starting at the small settlement of Palo Verde on Baja 1, the new, graded road initially followed an existing section. According to Les Conner, the decision to bring the road through Palo Verde was made because the Mexican government had already provided a rough dirt road connecting Palo Verde with Tierra San Marcos, located north near the fresh-water lagoon. After passing through a section of *saguaro* cacti, the new road veered to the right, away from the existing road and toward Punta Chivato.

"The road was much improved," recalled George Staples, referring to the new twenty-kilometer section from Baja 1 to Punta Chivato. "It was widened so two cars could pass, and they put in culverts."

Early camper Harry Oxley, who first drove a van down to Punta Chivato, decided to drive in a motorhome when the new road was in the process of construction. "I got about one-third the way in. That's as far as they had gotten on the road; they were still working on it. I had to go out and around the other way."

The new road from Baja 1 to Punta Chivato was still frustrating to navigate with bigger rigs. The Oxley's motorhome, fondly named "Titanic," would soon have permanent residence in Punta Chivato. "I went in twice with the motorhome, and the second time, I just left the motorhome there," Harry Oxley remarked. "I said, 'It's not coming back out again.'"

Identifying the turnoff to the new road was easier than finding the turnoff for the original road to Punta Chivato. Although most of the inhabitants of Palo Verde were olive ranchers and lived away from Baja 1, some structures on the Transpeninsular Highway served as landmarks.

"There's a water tower, two buildings, and a tree. Everything else is brown," one camper said, describing the landmarks along Baja 1 at the Palo Verde turnoff. "This is the green area. Turn left."[116]

"We'd tell people to go to mile marker number 156," explained Dale Dryer.

Later, a "Hotel" sign was erected on the highway, which helped unfamiliar campers locate the new road to Punta Chivato. But early campers like Les Conner were not so anxious to let others learn about the special spot.

"I wanted to tear the signs down when they first put them up to let people know how to get in here on the road," he said. Many, like Les, appreciated the new road but were concerned about others flocking to the secluded vacation area they had grown to love.

By 1983, Bill had raised the beach camping rate from $1 to $3 per day. George Staples, Doc, or Mary would walk to the beach to collect the fee. Later, one of Aurelia's brothers, Ramón, was hired for this job. With the improved road from Baja 1, garbage services, and three pit toilets on the camping beach, Bill felt justified in asking Punta Chivato campers for this increase.

Some campers resented the $2 increase in cost and moved further down to camp at Shell Beach. Others drove in late, camped overnight, and left early before the fee was collected.

However, most established campers appreciated the convenience of the new services. The Silzles and others went directly to Casa Grande when they arrived at Punta Chivato. They told Bill how long they planned to camp and paid him upfront. "We'd come in and say, 'We're going to stay ten days,'" said Barbara Silzle.

The new road from Baja 1 made it easier to get to Punta Chivato by vehicle. "It was a shorter run and no rocks," said Robin Converse. "It only took about 45 minutes to get to the highway, which was a great improvement."

John Fitzsimmons remembered a hair-raising drive he, his wife, Gerry, and Dale and Julia Dryer made with George Staples in his pickup truck. "I've never been so scared in all my whole life. He just floored it over the new road. We got out to the highway, and George said, 'God, 34 minutes! That's as good as I ever get!'"

George shared that he traversed the road at even higher speeds. "I think I made it in fifteen minutes to the main road, averaging 45 or 50 miles per hour," he stated. Although parts of the new road were wide enough for two cars, it was just one vehicle wide in sections.

"I'd be running 50 to 60 miles an hour out that road, and the dust would go a million feet in the air. There were blind corners because of the cactuses and the mesquite. It was rutted, and you'd have to bank high. You'd come just flying down there looking for dust," George Staples remarked.

Given his reckless driving, one would imagine George Staples might have been involved in numerous accidents. However, he recalled only one mishap:

"I made that trip so many times. Only one time I got in a wreck. Had some tourists coming out. On that type of a road, you can do one of two things: either anchor it full trying to stop, or you simply bale and get off the road. Well, I had a guy coming at me. *Where are you going? What are you going to do?* Well, I slammed on the brakes, and he slammed on the brakes we ended up crunching a little bit. We decided we'd eat our own damages."

As with all well-traveled dirt roads, it did not take long for the new road from Palo Verde to Punta Chivato to become rutted like a washboard. George Staples recalled a newcomer who drove in on the road. "I was up in the office, and it was about 8:00, and this guy comes in, 'My God, what a road,' he says. 'I understand there's a new road in here now. Where is it?' I had to tell the guy, 'You just came over it.'"

With the entry road now accessible to trailers, Bill decided to make the camping beach more accessible. Early campers remember a particular dune at the entrance. "You couldn't bring a trailer out. The hill was as high as my door top," shared one regular camper. "People had so much trouble getting out of the camp after they got in."

Campers pitch in to help get trailer unstuck on camping beach.
Courtesy Harry Oxley

Many relied on the assistance of other campers to avoid getting stuck. "The night before someone was going to leave, we'd get all the cans: coffee cans, beer cans, any can and get salt water and sprinkle the road down to make it damp enough where it settled," remembers Barbara Silzle. "Then we'd all stand back and see if the guy was going to make it or not."

Eventually, Bill Alvarado had one of his workers level the sand hump with a bulldozer. Although the camping beach was now more accessible to trailers, negotiating the road was still not an easy task.

The arrival of trailers brought an additional problem to the camping beach: the disposal of wastewater, called "gray water."

"People handled their gray water in different ways," recalled Lynn Links. She used dishpans outside their recreational vehicle (RV) for dishwashing. "We dumped it out into the dunes," she added. "But a lot of people ran their gray water through their RVs, and they would dig holes, and that gray water was just going down into sumps in the ground there."

Managing the "black water" was another matter. This term described the wastewater from the RV toilet stored in a tank under the rig. To accommodate the campers, Mary Morss and Bill brought a "honey wagon" down from Portland.[117]

"We'd make our two-day trip down," recalled Mary. "In the back of the truck, we had this thing that you could roll out and pump out the stuff from the trailers and then put it back in the truck and haul it off. So, you learned the humility of it all. I didn't know that I was going to be the 'Agua Negra' [Black Water] girl."

Kerry Kellogg remembered a local Mexican, Ramón, who arrived with a blue "honey wagon" one day. "They had to put it in the back of their truck. They would take about twenty gallons at a time. It was one of those mañana [tomorrow] things. 'Ramón, I need my black water hauled.' 'Mañana, señor.' Ramón would never come down."

"So, I decided I was going to make one," Kerry Kellogg continued. "I asked Ramón before I did it because I didn't want to take one of the jobs away from the Mexicans. In fact, I was going to bring it down here and just give it to him. It would have made his job so much easier to take it over there and get rid of it. Then he could charge whatever they were charging; I think it was 20 pesos at the time. I was going to give it for their enterprises. But we just started doing our own."

In the late 1980s, when Lynn Links began taking a trailer to Punta Chivato, she and her second husband, Lee Links, used Kellogg's honey wagon. "Kerry Kellogg brought it from home. It was a good-sized, plastic gas tank mounted on an axle and two wheels. It had a handle that you could attach to the ball. We had to dig a ditch to get the tank down low enough for gravity to take it from our holding tank into the honey wagon. The waste was dumped into it through the top. It was a learning process. More of it usually got on you than got into that thing."

"Sometimes there would be errors, and then there'd be a lot of odor on the beach," remembered Kerry.

Getting the black water into the honey wagon was the first step. From there, it had to be driven a half-mile mile to the dumping station. "That old dumping station was in bad shape," Kerry recalled. "There was no hose for washing up." One time, the honey wagon was too heavy. It broke off, and one side of it went into the tank. "It took three, 4-wheel drives to pull that thing out."

"The bad part about it—nobody ever fixed it," said Kerry. "I told Bill, 'I fell in your tank over there. You ought to send somebody over there to fix it.' Bill replied, 'We'll take care of it later.'" Bill eventually installed a dump station down the hill from the pila near the end of the short airstrip.

The Kelloggs kept their honey wagon in storage and welcomed any camper who wanted to use it. "We were really primitive," remembered Lynn Links. "Basically, you would do yours, bring it back, and the next guy would do his. We all used it."

In retrospect, Kerry remarked, "If we had a dollar for every time that thing's been used…We should have rented it out. We should have had a little deal that says 'For Rent' on it. But we would have been run out of the country for enterprising."

Early beach camper Jerry Henthorn, a retired fireman, brought down a motorhome that some say had a red velvet interior. When Jerry started dating a young Mexican girl, Adela, and they became serious, Bill Alvarado offered advice: "Jerry, you're not just marrying her; you're marrying her and her family." As Bill predicted, Jerry got married and soon moved his motorhome off the beach to the town of San Bruno, where his wife's family lived.

It was not until the mid-'80s, after the tile business went out of operation and the showers in the ravine were closed, that Bill began to provide potable water on the beach for the campers. Barbara Silzle remembered how grateful they were.

Bill also allowed campers access to water at Casa Grande. In a letter to Doc dated February 1984, Bill wrote:

"I found a pipe embedded in the outside wall next to the garage door—put a faucet in—makes it lots easier for campers to 'fill up.'"

Bill Alvarado raised the cost of camping on the beach to $4 per day as he provided more amenities for the campers in the 1980s. Long-time camper Lynn Links remembered Bill offered a discount if you camped at Punta Chivato for longer than a month. "I think if we stayed four weeks, we'd get a fifth week free," she stated, recalling the cost was then up to $5 per day. "So, it was less than $5 actually if you were staying for a length of time," she added.

Early camper Dennis Gardner speculated that Bill must have brought in $800 to $1,000 from camping fees during certain months.

Just as Bill had hoped, more services brought more campers each year to Punta Chivato. But his overall dream was to restore and open the hotel. All fees from the beach campers, room rentals, dinners offered at Casa Grande, and sale of lots would be used for that purpose.

Fish cleaning station next to new 20′ wide concrete boat launch ramp on right (a later amenity). From Nov. 1991 video by Bill Alvarado

Chapter 55

CAMPING BEACH STORIES

Lynn Links did not recall meeting Bill Alvarado when she camped at Punta Chivato in October with her first husband, Dave. "He [Bill] was there probably the second or third time," she stated.

Lynn was an adventurous woman. Even after her divorce in 1983, Lynn made Punta Chivato camping beach her vacation destination.

"I started coming down camping on the beach by myself in '84, but only then for short times," she said. "I only came down when I could get away from work for 10 to 14 or 15 days. I would come down twice or maybe three times a year. Sometimes, I brought work with me. I worked while I was there. But I was a loner. I wanted to be away from people. I didn't want stress."

Early camper Dennis Gardner does not remember meeting Lynn until 1985. "She was by herself. It was rare for a woman to show up by themselves. Definitely not much of a place for single women."

Lynn drove her Suburban down the Baja Peninsula from Southern California to Punta Chivato. Once there, her favorite camping spot was "a little slot" on the south end of the beach. "I loved the view of the mountains there, and it was private," she recalled. "There wasn't a lot of people coming and going."

In those days of "tailgate camping," Lynn rigged her vehicle for both sleeping and meal preparation. "I had a platform in the Suburban, and all my kitchen stuff was underneath," she said. "I had a sleeping platform up above."

Lynn remembered walking or driving to the area by the tile factory for water. But rather than use the communal shower in the ravine by the hotel, Lynn preferred the solar shower she set up at her campsite. "I could sun shower there at that spot without worrying about anything," she recounted. "There weren't that many people."

Lynn gives credit to camper Barbara Silzle for giving her the idea for a solar shower. "Barbara would stay by herself part of the time in her trailer," Lynn recalled. "She had her little sun shower set up in the back. Barbara's was the very first one of those I ever saw with tarp covers set up on square pipe frames. It made a real impression on me." Eventually, several other campers constructed solar showers patterned after Barbara Silzle's.

Although Lynn tended to keep to herself in those years, she could not help but meet other campers. "Virtually, I didn't know hardly anyone socially except Red and Nancy," said Lynn of those early days. "You couldn't be there and not meet them. They were very personable. They knew everybody who was around. Nancy, especially in later years, liked to sit and talk. That was when she was less active. I was a single woman on the beach, and some people have different attitudes about you because you're a single woman. Red and Nancy were good to me."

Lynn Links shared the following impression of the Salzmans: "In the earlier days, Nancy was a lot different, of course. Red was always kind of Red. He always was kind of Jewish. Everybody knew that Red had plenty of money, but Red was always scrapping and scrounging and reusing things. Nancy was very active. She was a great freediver. She'd go out there and get those lobsters. Red and Nancy were lobster diving almost every day. They were very, very physically active. Day after day after day after day, the two of them would go out diving. They originally had a small boat. When I met them, they had just gotten their trailer. They were just Red and Nancy. They were younger then," Lynn reminisced. "All of us were younger at one time. And we all were more active when we were younger."

"Red and Nancy Salzman were just real, real die-hards," recalled Bill Alvarado. Even George Staples, one of Bill's partners at Posada and early housemate at Casa Grande, fondly remembered the early camping couple. "He ["Red"] was reputed to be worth about eighty bezillion dollars," George said. "Oh, just loved those people. They were a treat."

Lynn Links introduced her second husband, Lee Links, to Punta Chivato in the late 1980s. On a driving vacation to the tip of the Baja peninsula, they detoured to camp at Punta Chivato on the way down and back. "It was a six-week trip," Lynn recalled. "It was in the hot months. It was during late July and early August."

On later trips, Punta Chivato became their "go-to" destination. Initially, they drove down at various times of the year and camped in a van. When they could haul down a trailer, they kept it parked on the beach and began to extend their stays.

Lynn described their year-round, thirty-foot-long beach camp at Punta Chivato. "We had solid tarp on the north side, and we had shade cloth on the other two sides, and we had the trailer out on the west side. We were basically almost like a house down there."

Lee Links (1992). Courtesy Harry Oxley

After Bill installed public showers on the beach, Lynn and Lee continued to prefer the solar shower they set up in the corner of their camping spot. Their shower was warmer than the public showers due to the tarps surrounding all sides and the top.

There was another reason the couple chose not to use the public beach showers, especially in the spring. "Eastertime was when the Mexicans would go in there and leave dirty diapers and stuff in the showers," Lynn said. "All those kids were in there playing in the showers, and they would poop in the showers, and the showers would just be a total disaster."

Leaving their beach camp unoccupied was never a concern for

the couple. "We didn't worry about people stealing from us when we were in town," Lynn remarked. "I always had the kitchen set up outside," she said, describing how their fishing tackle and kitchenware were left exposed. "All those years on the beach, nobody ever touched a thing of ours. We never lost anything at Punta Chivato."

Others voiced the same sentiment. "There was never any concern of things being ripped off," stated Kerry Kellogg. "The most honest beach I was ever on."

Some campers, however, were not as fortunate. "I tried leaving my stuff down there all year long," said Dennis Gardner. "Red tried it. It didn't work out too good. We had some break-ins."

One vacationer recounted another camper, Helmut Zwick, who was the victim of a thief. "Helmut had his fishing poles ripped off one night. He had left his fishing poles in his boat tied up in the cove in front of the beach. When he got up the next morning, Helmut found the fishing poles were gone. God, he was heartbroken. Got in his boat and started going around the point, and he found the fishing poles lying in the water out there. Whoever stole them must have got scared and dumped them in the water. He washed them all up, and they were fine. Never had any problem at all with them. He was very lucky to get them back. From then on, everybody took their fishing gear out of their boats."[118]

Some early campers, like the Oxleys and Silzles, who later brought down a motorhome and trailer, respectively, did not feel comfortable leaving their rigs on the beach when they returned home to California. They preferred to store their vehicles on the bluff by Casa Grande, high above the water and away from beach traffic.

Bill Alvarado later attempted to alleviate the concern about theft by providing a storage unit where campers could leave their trailers. Unfortunately, this solution backfired.

"That came to a grinding halt when the *federales* came out and wanted to search all of the trailers that were in storage," Bill recalled. "Before I could even say 'yes' or 'no,' they just started breaking into them—all storage cabinets and the trailer houses down there. The *federales* planted marijuana. Two of the workers saw them when they took marijuana into one of the trailer houses and then came back out holding up this sack of marijuana. They confiscated the trailer, but they never took it away. I don't know what they really wanted except money."

The camaraderie of the camping community at Punta Chivato became vital when inclement weather descended. In winter, there could be winds from the north called "northerlies." During the summer, July through September, winds could come up in the afternoon, causing problems at the boat launch ramp. Summer campers also were concerned about chubascos.

"This place can be very intimidating," remarked early camper Robin Converse. "You've got to watch the weather."

"You had to be prepared down there for everything. You could never relax for a minute if you had a big camp and you had everything outside like we did," stated Lynn Links. "Everything we owned was out there just about. We had to be on top of it all the time."

Many campers pulled their boats out of the water at the end of the day. Some left their boats anchored between the reefs in front of the camping beach or just offshore near the boat launch ramp south of the hotel. However, when windstorms came, these moorings often did not hold. The anchors would pull clear, sending the boats adrift.

Dennis Gardner remembers more than once waking up in the middle of the night when the winds were blowing 50 to 60 miles per hour. Boats left in the water threatened to flip over as the wind whipped up big waves.

"There were lots of times you would get up at 12:00, 1:00, 2:00 in the morning, and we would literally work until 6:00 in the morning, 'til daylight, getting everything out," he said. "Everybody always pulled together."

Dennis reminisced about one morning he frantically helped to recover other campers' boats following a strong wind. "It was almost like a fun part of it," he recounted. "As long as there was no serious damage, or nobody got hurt. [Afterward] you'd go into the trailer and have a big robust breakfast, pancakes and eggs and hot chocolate."

After Bill set up residence in Casa Grande, campers and homeowners often congregated at the Big House for shelter and reassurance until the winds and rains subsided. Dennis remembers once counting fifty individuals at Casa Grande and thinking, *Where'd all these people come from?*

Dennis Gardner described a frightening situation that arose early one morning while he was still camping on the bluff. It was at a time when there were few campers. He had anchored his 17-foot Gregor aluminum boat offshore.

"I had my boat down there in what we'll call Harry's Cove, south of the camping beach, south of the sand spit," said Dennis. "Harry's boat was over at the main camping beach, and Bill was here."

It became dark over the mountains, and the wind suddenly started blowing out of the north. Dennis and Bill rushed to the camping beach and pulled Harry's boat out of the water. "His boat filled up with water, and things got a bit wet," said Dennis, "but we managed to get everything out and dried off."

When Dennis returned to his trailer parked above the beach, he found his girlfriend fast asleep. The wind had not disturbed her. Dennis described the winds blowing from 35 to 40 miles per hour out of the north. A terrifying event occurred in the morning after his girlfriend woke up and the two were having breakfast. "All of a sudden, I'm looking out at the water, and everything just flattens out," Dennis said. The wind picked up again and changed direction, blowing seventy miles per hour from the south. Then, "the rain came down in buckets."

Dennis looked out the window toward the sea to check on his boat, but the rain obscured his view. "I'm barefoot, in a pair of shorts and no shirt, and I manage to get out the trailer door, which was not easy because I was pushing it against the wind," Dennis recalled.

With rain pelting him, Dennis jumped off the bluff onto the beach and ran to the cove where his boat was anchored. Both anchors had pulled free, and his boat was drifting near shore and filling with water.

God, I wonder where Harry is? Dennis thought, knowing he could not single-handedly recover his boat. *I wonder where somebody is. I really need help.*

At that moment, Bill Alvarado was visiting Harry Oxley at his trailer on the beach. While chatting over mugs of coffee, the two suddenly thought about Dennis's boat and ran to the cove.

"We're sorry," Bill apologized to Dennis when he arrived on the scene. "We forgot all about you. The wind turned around. We didn't even think."

"Harry was like this wild banshee," Dennis said, remembering Harry's eagerness to help. "It didn't matter if he broke his leg on the way to my boat. It was like the Marines had landed."

The threesome got a rope and tied one end onto the bow of Dennis's boat and the other onto Bill's four-wheel drive. Waiting until there was a pause between the waves, Dennis and Harry spun the rig around. Bill punched the accelerator and drove the boat onto the beach. "It had some holes in the bottom," Dennis recalled. "It was a bit trashed, but we managed to repair it over a period of time."

When there were heavy storms at Punta Chivato, the rain washed clay down from the mountains toward the camping beach. As it traveled downhill, the slimy mud covered the road and threatened campsites.

Dennis Gardner witnessed rain and high tides turning the camping beach into a quagmire, so Harry Oxley could not drive his motorhome out. His rig sank into the mucky road and was buried up to its axles in the sludge. "We hooked three 4-wheel drives onto it and couldn't budge it," recalled Dennis. "We probably had like twenty guys there with shovels." Dennis worked barefoot so he would not lose his shoes in the slime. "You're barefoot and shoveling like crazy and pushing, and these three trucks were pulling," said Dennis, remembering their effort to free Harry's motorhome.

Finally, a tractor pulled up to the scene. "Someone brought down a tractor from the Ejido," said Dennis. The questionable farm tractor was about 50 years old with big rear tires. Hooking a chain onto Harry's motorhome, the tractor driver put his archaic machine into gear. "Putt-putt-putt-putt-putt just pulled it right out," Dennis remarked with a laugh.

Lynn Links described a storm they experienced one night around 2:00 a.m. while camping on the beach next to Charlie Gastelum, fondly referred to as "Charlie Tuna."

"All of a sudden, in the middle of the night, we had this humungous thunderstorm, and it just dumped. Rained on us like you wouldn't believe."

The sand at their campsite was hard packed since Lynn and Lee had camped there for extended periods. They erected a large tarp to cover the outdoor area. But the flat tarp would not drain naturally. So, the couple punched nine or ten drain holes in the "roof" and placed buckets under each hole. Then, they had to deal with the runoff.

"You start with bucket number 1, you take it and haul it out onto the beach, and you dump it because you have to haul it away from the camp; otherwise, it will just flood back in on you," Lynn recounted. "So, we got this chain going. We haul bucket 1, bucket 2, bucket 3, 4, 5, 6. By the time we get to bucket 9, bucket one is full again." The bucket brigade worked for almost four hours. "By the time we're done, and the rain eased off, we had just both sort of had it," Lynn continued.

"About 5:00 in the morning, dawn is starting to crack. I go over to Charlie's and said, 'Hey Charlie, you got any Kahlúa? I need a drink of Kahlúa really bad.' So, Charlie and I are there drinking Kahlúa. Charlie never let me live that down how I needed a drink of Kahlúa because I was so tired of dumping buckets. But it was part of beach life. You had to do it. Lee and I dumped buckets more than once down there on the beach," said Lynn.

Another method the Linkses used to help keep water out of their campsite was to dig a trench around their entire camp, encircling both outdoor space and their trailer. "We had these great projects—ditch-digging," Lynn said with a chuckle. "My husband, Lee, always inspired all these people to go out and do all this ditch digging. All these guys got their exercise that way." They left the moat up year-round, only re-digging when necessary. When the surf flooded the beach during high tides, the ditch helped to divert the water. Likewise, runoff from the road would go into the trench and soak in rather than come into their camp when it was raining.

"We were always trying to defeat Mother Nature. But you can't do those things to Mother Nature because she doesn't go along with those programs," Lynn reflected during a later interview. "But it kept everybody active and kept everyone young."

Lynn shared stories of the camaraderie between the campers at Punta Chivato in the 1980s and 1990s. One common social gathering was weekly potlucks on the beach. "We just couldn't eat like that," said Lynn, recalling the volume of food available at these shared meals. "We would go once a month or something, but we just wouldn't go to weekly potlucks." Lynn and Lee opted to go and be sociable at cocktail hour before the potluck.

One memorable beach potluck was the Kelloggs' "deviled egg party." This idea stemmed from the fact that whenever anyone brought a plate of deviled eggs to a potluck, they would "disappear in twelve seconds," according to one camper. By asking everyone who came to their potluck to bring a tray of deviled eggs, they hoped the availability of this popular hors d'oeuvre would last longer. "There must have been ten different types," remembered Lynn Links, who attended that potluck. "We pigged out on deviled eggs." In addition to the deviled eggs, Mexicans Hector and Mari Aguilar arrived with barbequed *carne asada* (roasted meat). This Mulegé couple would become close friends with many of the beach people.

Barbara Silzle spoke of another event that brought the beach campers together. When the Oxleys were still vacationing on the beach in their motorhome, Titanic, Harry Oxley would occasionally hold a "movie night."

"We're going to have movies," Harry would announce.

"Movies?" someone would reply, figuring Harry was about to tell another joke.

"Yeah," Harry replied, "This is going to be movie night. I brought some tapes." He would bring out a small television and plug it into a generator behind his motorhome.

"Everybody would bring a beach chair, and Marilyn Oxley would make a big bag, like an Alpha Beta bag, of popcorn," recounted Lynn Links. "We'd sit down, and they'd pass the popcorn around. Oh, I guess maybe only eight or ten of us at the most. But that was movie night. That was really uptown."

Some campers began to complain because Harry's movies always showed motorcycle racing—his business and interest. A few not so subtly suggested he consider bringing other movies down from the States to share at "movie night."

Harry Oxley remembers hosting Thanksgiving dinner at the Oxley camp one year. "We put up a big tarp and smoked a turkey, and it rained and put our fire out. We had a hell of a time."

Camping on the beach was not for the faint-hearted. In addition to the scarcity of amenities and seasonally harsh weather, campers had to contend with various local critters.

"Animals that visited us on the beach were raccoons (at night), kangaroo rats (when you're eating), bats (at dusk), and, of course, the yelping coyotes (when you're trying to sleep)," wrote Dave Jacobson.

"At night, the coyotes would sit on the bluffs (where the houses are now) and howl," he added. "A rock or two in their direction made for better sleeping." Dave Jacobson once even spotted a mountain lion perched on the side of a cliff off the beach south of Punta Chivato.

Raccoons would come onto the beach after dark, hoping careless campers had left food out. "If you left a banana or an avocado outside overnight, you had hell to pay in the morning because the raccoons would smear it all over your whole camp," remembered Lynn Links. "They would get into our dishwater because we left our dishwater out on the table. You had to learn how to handle those characters." Lee and Lynn had their cat, Moricito, with them on the beach, but "he'd never challenge them [the raccoons]."

One would not expect a cat to tangle with raccoons, but a dog in camp was a more probable deterrent. Lynn Links shared the story of a couple, both pilots, who came to camp at Punta Chivato with two large dogs. They brought a big bed and set it up on the beach; at night, the dogs would sleep at their feet. But the raccoons were tenacious and undeterred. "One night, the raccoons got into their place and just tore it up," Lynn said.

Less menacing were the kangaroo rats, which would come down from the dunes above the camping beach. Barbara Silzle remembered these small critters had hindquarters like a kangaroo and a tail with a large tassel. She, therefore, referred to them as "tassel-tail mice."

"They were so cute," she said. "I never saw one walking. They were always running or hopping."

Barbara was not the only camper who took a personal liking to these friendly critters. The campers began to identify specific "tassel tails" and personally claim them. While gathered at night around a campfire, the kangaroo rats would scurry among the campers, eager to pick up any dropped crumbs. Following is a frequent scenario:

"Oh, here they come," one camper might announce after the first kangaroo rat appeared, illuminated by the light of the campfire.

Another camper would drop a few pieces of oatmeal to attract the creature and then proclaim, "Just a minute, that's not mine. Mine just comes over for oatmeal," as the critter hopped toward another camper in search of a different handout.

"Well, I'm feeding mine Ritz Crackers," someone would say.

Someone else would join in, "I'm feeding mine wheat germ." Then, the campers would challenge each other's "tassel tail" to determine whose could jump highest.

Barbara recalled one tiny creature coming and nibbling her husband's toe as he was sitting on the beach. "They got so friendly that Nancy [Salzman] and I could put our hands down, and they'd come and crawl right onto your hand. Of course, you had to have some food there. We just had so much fun."

Other nightly visitors to the camping beach were three-inch crabs. When the Silzles started camping in a trailer at Punta Chivato, Barbara Silzle sewed together tatami mats and placed them in front of the door to keep sand out. "At night, those little crabs would come up from the beach, and they'd crawl all over those mats," said Barbara. "It wasn't that they bothered you, except for the scraping-like sound on those mats."

More formidable creatures at Punta Chivato included rattlesnakes, scorpions, jellyfish, and stingrays. Of the four, the last was the most common. Stingrays often nestled under sand in the shallow waters at the shoreline. One had to look closely to notice their presence; sometimes, only a ray's two eyes were visible. A common verbal warning a camper might hear upon entering the water was "shuffle your feet." The motion of the water was enough to scare the stingrays, which rapidly swam away. However, unsuspecting waders got stung on the foot or ankle. The pain was instant and very intense. The remedy was putting one's foot into a container of hot water, which denatured the protein in the venom.

American campers became acquainted with the Mexicans who routinely came to Punta Chivato to camp during Easter holiday week. The Kelloggs remembered meeting Hector and Mari Aguilar from Mulegé in 1983. "A great couple. Just fantastic," Kerry Kellogg recalled. He [Hector] speaks English very well. He's awful good, he'd sure tell you," Kerry jokingly added.

They also met other local Mexicans who would arrive at Punta Chivato for the Easter celebration. "They would all come out here and party. It was a week-long party," said Kerry Kellogg. "They'd bring all the beer with them and the music; they'd play and dance and have a good time. It's when palapas, sun umbrellas constructed of palm fronds, were still on the beach down here. And, oh my gosh, I'll tell you, they know how to party. We really had a lot of fun."

Bunnie Adams remembered a group of six male Mexican officials from Santa Rosalía and Guerrero Negro who came out every Easter and partied. "Andy asked them where their wives were," Bunnie said. One official replied with a chuckle, "Somebody has to go to church for Easter."

Overall, the American campers at Punta Chivato were cordial toward newcomers. "In those days, there was a lot more turnover of people on the beach," said Lynn Links. "People were just coming and going all the time. "We'd welcome anybody who looked like they might be lost or might have questions," said Lynn. "Like, 'How much do we pay?' 'Where do we pay?' 'Where do we get water?' We were there to answer all those questions for anyone who came in."

However, Kerry and Penny Kellogg received a lukewarm welcome the first time they showed up in the early 1980s. The Kelloggs arrived by boat, unlike the ten to twelve campers already on the beach, who had driven there. The couple camped at Santispec on Conception Bay and were fishing near Punta Chivato when they ran into trouble.

"One of the tanks that we had on the boat was contaminated so that we couldn't use the gas," said Kerry. "We saw all these people over here on this beach and decided that we'd go in there and see if we couldn't get some gas. Well, by the time we come into shore, there wasn't hardly anybody who would even talk to us. They just acted like we weren't even around. It was kind of a strange feeling. I went up to the first campsite, and I told them that I needed some gas. 'Well, we don't have any gas to spare.' I said, 'Well, it's kind of an emergency. We'd kind of like to get home. We're going to be back here tomorrow. We'll just fill your can up and bring it back.'"

"Nope. Nope," was the answer they got.

In desperation, Kerry remembers going to Casa Grande, where he met Doc Lyons and George Staples. "Doc Lyons was a different kind of guy," recalled Kerry. "He'd had cancer, and his nose was gone, and his ears was all chopped up and everything. Nicest man you ever met, but you didn't know how standoffish he would be. They would give me five gallons of gas if I delivered a message to their house in Posada at Conception Bay."

The Kelloggs agreed to the deal and got the gas they needed to motor back to their camp at Santispec. The following day, they decided to take their Ford pickup and drive from Santispec to Punta Chivato to return the five gallons of gas to Doc and George. "There were three couples, four people in the back of the pickup and two in the front," Kerry recalled. "It was very hard to find the road coming in here because there were so many roads that come into Punta Chivato." In addition to the passengers in the back of the pickup, they brought aluminum chairs. "By the time we got to Punta Chivato, there wasn't one of those chairs that was any good because the road was so rough that it just collapsed them."

In later years, the Kelloggs drove to Punta Chivato in their Ford pickup with a big overhead camper. Behind it, they pulled their boat, which had a Volvo inboard motor. They launched the boat from the launch ramp and anchored it in front of the camping beach. "We came down here, and we camped at the far end of the beach, and we didn't have to get too friendly with all the snobbies down there," Kerry said lightheartedly. "No, they turned out to be really nice people," he added with a smile.

"Sometimes it blew so hard, the spray would come up here," said Penny Kellogg, referring to the camping beach. In 1983, she and Kerry brought down a bus. Although more confident with the larger vehicle than their overhead camper, Penny remarked, "I was really scared. We've had some sleepless nights."

Not only did the Kelloggs make Punta Chivato their destination of choice, but they also soon introduced Betty and Lester Bell to the area. The Bells were their neighbors in Lee Vining, California, where they ran a sporting goods store. "It was really like a general store," Kerry clarified.

Mike and Conna Melton first camped at Punta Chivato in April of 1983. "We had our 20th wedding anniversary down here," Mike said. "Someone on the camping beach brought us a bottle of champagne, and Bill Silzle shot off fireworks."

Barbara Silzle remembers meeting Mike and Conna on the beach, where they pitched a tent. The couple, who worked for a grocery store, decided to retire early and move to Punta Chivato. "My husband looked at them. They were forty or something like that," said Barbara. "He said, 'Boy, I hope you've got it figured out.'" The couple became regular beach campers for six and a half years. "There were a lot of nice people there that we met," said Mike, "and some not so nice."

Septembers were notoriously the stormiest times of the year at Punta Chivato. Lee and Lynn Links recounted a memorable storm during an *El Niño* year in September 1998. "This El Niño brought us a flood that we had never seen before," remembered Lee.

About ten camps were set up at Punta Chivato Beach, including the Linkses's, Salzmans's, Acosta's, and Charlie Gastelum's. The first thing the Linkses witnessed was a surge coming onto the beach. Then, a boat in the water by the camping beach broke free from its mooring. While Lee Links and others ran out to rescue the loose boat, Lynn drove over to check on their boat anchored off the boat launch ramp. Reaching the launch site, she noted the surf was so high no one would be able to safely back a boat trailer down the ramp. Lynn had to anxiously wait until the tide went down before she could get their boat safely out of the water.

The Linkses had earlier moved two vanloads of gear from their campsite to a storage locker on higher land in anticipation of the storm. Bill rented these storage spaces for $300 per year.

The following day, while standing in camp talking with Charlie Tuna, another surge flooded both their camps. "We had a freezer outside," recalled Lynn. "Lee runs over, and we grab the freezer, which was up on 4 x 4s. We put it up in the trailer."

"It was high tide, but high tide when the level of the sea was higher than it's ever been," said Lee. Within less than an hour, not only the camps but the road above the beach were flooded.

Although water covered the road, the ground was still solid enough for the Linkses and other campers to drive their trailers from the camping beach to higher ground. Lee and Lynn parked their trailer in Bob and Lynda Davis's side yard on Lot #2, Subdivision 2. High on the bluff, they hoped they were out of harm's way. "Then a torrential rain hit us," said Lee.[119]

"Red and Nancy stayed down until after it started to rain," said Lynn. "They didn't go out that night. Red was stubborn. They stayed in there until the last dog was dead." Although the Salzmans had a more challenging time getting their rig off the beach the following day, they eventually succeeded. Like the rest, they moved their trailer to higher ground, parking it behind Rich and Peggy Fodor's home on Lot #8, Subdivision 2.

The Linkses removed their camp from the beach, except for the pipe framework, empty gas cans, and the AstroTurf they used for rugs on the sand. The following day, they drove their van back down to the beach to retrieve whatever they could from their campsite. The couple remembers it was difficult to drive, and when they tried to walk, it was like "walking on a Slip 'n Slide" due to the slimy clay. "It was almost totally impossible," Lynn recalled. "This clay was so nasty that you just couldn't walk on it. You couldn't stand up on it. It was terrible stuff."

They found their AstroTurf buried in clay washed down from the mountains by the rain. "It was well buried," said Lynn. "We weren't about to dig it up."

Days later, they returned to their campsite to remove the AstroTurf and salvage any items left on the beach. Unfortunately, luck was not on their side when trying to drive away. "The van slid off of the road and went into the ditch on the side," remarked Lee. "We couldn't get the damn thing out." Ruben, a local Mexican, and Mike Morse were soon on the scene to help. "The two cars finally pulled the van back onto the road and out of there," said Lee, remembering someone took a photograph.

Lynn vividly recalled the odor at the beach after the storm. "That beach smelled like you wouldn't believe," said Lynn. "We had all those outhouses that had been re-dug and relocated over all the years. That beach smelled like a sewer after all that rain. It was bad. All that gray water and all that stuff came back and haunted us.

After I went back down to that beach and I smelled that, I never wanted to go back. I told Lee we would never live on that beach again."

Chapter 56

ABUNDANCE OF SHELLS

As terrifying and destructive as the storms were to campers and homeowners at Punta Chivato, they left an amazing treasure in their aftermath. Just a short distance southwest of the hotel, the beach was covered with shells dredged up from the Sea of Cortez and deposited in an array of various shapes, sizes, and colors. The area became known as "Shell Beach."

Barbara Silzle, an avid shell collector, was enthralled by the variety of unique shells she discovered at Shell Beach after a storm hit Punta Chivato. "The beach was stinking as heck," Barbara said, recalling the newly washed-up shells with dead or dying creatures inside. Beautiful lion's paw scallop shells, cones, cowries, murexes, turbans, and olive shells littered the beach. "We did some of the best shelling on that trip that we ever did," said Barbara.

Shell Beach would become known as a shell collector's paradise. Bob Davis, who first visited Punta Chivato during Cleveland Crudgington's era and later built a home, stated, "People came from all over to go down shelling there. I've met people who had shelled all over the world, and they said this was one of the best places. They really thought highly of it."

Hazel Harris, a single woman, was known for the collages she created from shells she found on Shell Beach. Lynn Links first met Hazel on the camping beach in the early 1980s. Lynn was in her 40s, and Hazel was in her 60s. "Hazel was one of the really fabulous fixtures on the beach for a number of years," said Lynn. "I always enjoyed Hazel. She was an absolute inspiration to all of us."

Hazel would drive by herself from Reno, Nevada, to Punta Chivato in a small motorhome built on a van chassis. When it eventually wore out, she showed up with another one. Sometimes, her sister, Betty, who lived in Oakland, would drive down with her.

Lynn Links recalled the spry, self-sufficient woman. "Hazel would be trotting by your camp early in the morning with her fishing rod. She went out to the point of the hammerhead to catch her triggerfish for the day. By God, Hazel would go out on that point, and she would catch their dinners."

Hazel walked from the camping beach down to Shell Beach to collect shells almost daily, which she fashioned into stunning shell collages.

"There was one of her shell collages in the hotel," said Bill Alvarado. "It was a beautiful, big one. Just a gorgeous thing." Others who claimed to have one of Hazel's masterpieces were Mike and Conna Melton, Marge and Jere Summers, and Kerry and Penny Kellogg.

For years, Hazel returned to camp at Punta Chivato. "It's just amazing that she, at her age, could drive all the way down in that little motorhome. She had to be in her eighties," remarked Bill.

Even when Hazel began to have trouble walking, she continued to come to Punta Chivato, sometimes driven down by her son or grandson. "She had a limp, a little difficulty in walking, and you'd never know it from all the things that she did," recalled Mary Morss during an interview.

Hazel later moved to Petaluma to be near her son, where she resided until her passing. But this spunky, adventurous woman remains alive through her creative shell collages, the material provided by the chubascos that came through Punta Chivato.

During an interview, Archie McVay remembers when he and his wife, Doris, first went to Shell Beach, and "those shells were just piled up." He observed Mexicans coming in and scooping up the shells. "They hauled them out of there by truckloads," recalled Archie. He said many of the shells ended up in La Paz.

"As you go into La Paz all along the road out there, there was several little factories there making odd little knick-knacks," Archie shared, "little things that stick on the refrigerator and that. And all those shell things." Archie speculated that making the shell trinkets was part of a work arrangement subsidized by the Mexican government. "I think the Americans were probably at the bottom of it," he said. "It was done through the Americans for the Mexicans—the higher Mexicans."

Storms at Punta Chivato revealed other treasures in the area. Dave Jacobson wrote about finding fossilized shells and "a few fossilized shark teeth up to three inches in length." These were exposed when torrents of water cut through the shale buttes above the beach, exposing embedded sea life that turned to stone thousands of years ago. "I've heard of some of the beach campers finding arrowheads in the area, but we didn't find any," added Dave.

Later, some campers, including Char Willett, who would live above Shell Beach with her husband, Will, avidly searched for arrowheads around Punta Chivato. She proudly displayed her framed collections on the walls of their motorhome.

Chapter 57

RESTORING THE HOTEL

From the time Bill first set eyes on the abandoned hotel at Punta Chivato, his dream of renovating it to its original grandeur never faltered. Despite trials, disappointments, and an uncertain cash flow, Bill focused on cleaning up and refurbishing the hotel. The tasks seemed endless—purchasing generators, kitchen appliances, refrigeration units, furnishings, and making general repairs, but nothing could deter Bill from his goal, no matter how long it took.

"The hotel was just totally, totally, I mean, you wouldn't think you could even rebuild it," remarked George Staples. "It was so filthy. The roofs were gone. It was just in terrible shape."

Not only was the hotel stripped of all its furnishings, but the building itself was in disrepair.

George Staples remembered when the hotel pool was cleaned up. "We got the rattlesnakes and tumbleweeds out of there and, eventually, got the swimming pool filled."

Although it was known that some ejidatarios and other local Mexicans pilfered the hotel after Crudgington left, it was not common knowledge that American visitors also helped themselves to parts of the hotel.

"We came upon Americans who were chipping the tile out of the restaurant," remembers Mary Morss. "I said, 'You can't do that.' They said, 'Yes, we can.' The man pulled out a book that showed different airstrips in Baja. The page listing Punta Chivato airstrips marked the hotel as 'abandoned.'"

"We had to tell people this is not abandoned anymore. It's ours, and we're improving it." Mary explained. "It's going to be better, and we're going to connect them [the airstrips] and eventually do all these wonderful things."

One day, Bill witnessed Americans blatantly helping themselves to things from the hotel.

"I bought probably $200 worth of flowers and plants and shrubs and things and spent the better part of the weekend planting," Bill recounted. "I took a break and had a warm beer. We didn't have any refrigeration. I was trying to do something with the dining room area. I walked out of there and up the ramp because I heard something. There was this couple digging up the flowers."

"I said, 'Hey, what are you doing?'

"The man replied, 'We're going to take these home.'"

"Those are mine," Bill said, incredulous at the audacity of these people.

The man boldly replied, "They can't be. This hotel has been abandoned for years."

Bill informed the couple that he was fixing the hotel and had just planted the flowers. "Did you notice the dirt was fresh, and they've been watered?" Bill added.

"Well, I thought maybe the old guy who is around here decided to do something. But I wasn't going to let them just die here in the desert," the man said.

"They were visiting from Mulegé, Santa Rosalía, or someplace," recalled Bill. "I finally convinced them. They just left them there, dug up. They didn't even replant them. They were Americans, which made it even worse."

Bill would later have coconut palms and eucalyptus trees planted around the hotel. Over the years, the coconut trees produced coconuts, which many hotel guests enjoyed. The eucalyptus trees grew to over forty feet tall. Of course, regular watering was necessary for all the vegetation to thrive in the desert.

As much as possible, Bill purchased building supplies from the towns closest to Punta Chivato, particularly Mulegé. "I had a good relationship with the lumber company," said Bill. "We bought a lot of stuff there." Mulegé had other important services, including a telephone for outside calls, banks, and *cambios* for money exchange.

Bill initially preferred to shop in Mulegé but later favored Santa Rosalía. "When we first got there, the banks were in Mulegé," Bill said, "but I guess Santa Rosalía, wanting to win over all the commerce, took all the banks out of Mulegé. Makes it hard to shop in Mulegé." The money exchange was also taken out of Mulegé.

According to early homeowner Rich Ream, difficulty in obtaining one vital piece of equipment delayed opening the hotel. "Bill had trouble getting a large motor generator to supply the power needed to run the hotel. He was always having trouble, mainly with the diesel generator. I felt sorry for Bill trying to make a go of P.C.," Rich wrote.

Locating reasonably priced equipment for the hotel and transporting it across the U.S.-Mexican border was rarely without incident. Bill shared his experience purchasing and bringing air conditioning units into Baja.

"A guy had an ad in the *San Diego Tribune*[120] for air conditioners—*One or ten, $200 each*. So, I called him and said if I could get a deal, I'd like thirty or forty."

Bill dickered with the dealer and got the price down to $125 apiece. "The price was very, very right," Bill said. "I knew they would have been $450 or $500 apiece. Some of them were new."

Bill purchased 48 air conditioners and borrowed a trailer to haul the units to Punta Chivato. His trip was delayed while the broker he hired at the border and Mexican officials completed the necessary paperwork. "It was expensive and time-consuming because the trailer sat in the storage yard for about a week," he recalled.

Finally, with receipts in hand, Bill hooked up the trailer full of air conditioners and drove it across the U.S.-Mexican border. "I go through the checkpoint, no problem," said Bill.

But as he traveled further south on Baja 1 and entered the town of Maneadero south of Ensenada, Bill was pulled over by a uniformed man. "The guy raised his hand and said, 'May I see your papers for your cargo?'"

Smugly, Bill complied, knowing he had all the necessary paperwork, including the serial number for each air conditioner. "He goes back and looks at the air conditioners. Every one of them. Then he comes back and said, 'O.K., now may I see your transfer license for your trailer?'"

"What? You're kidding me!" Bill exclaimed.

"No, I'm not," the man replied.

"What's this going to cost me?" Bill asked, aware of the frequent practice of mordidas or "bites" in México, a slang term referring to bribes.

"$200," the man answered.

Having just $220 cash in his wallet, Bill said, "I just can't do that because I won't have enough money for gasoline."

"Well," the man said, "let's make it $150."

Bill reluctantly paid the man and was finally on his way. But when he reached the next town, the same thing happened.

"I said, 'There is absolutely no way I'm paying. Everything I have is legal, and it's Mexican because it's been imported. You're not getting a penny from me because if I give you one penny, I'm not going to be able to get this stuff down to where it has to go.'"

In retrospect, Bill figured there was some conspiracy going on. "I think one guy called the other because this guy also asked for $200," Bill said.

Sometimes, crossing into Baja from California went more smoothly than anticipated. Bill remembers purchasing a freezer for the hotel kitchen at Punta Chivato that was like an ice cream truck freezer. "Put it in the back of the truck. Drove across the border with it. And they inspected everything, you know. Never mentioned the freezer," Bill added.

In addition to the potential obstacles of crossing the border and getting through official and unofficial checkpoints along Baja 1, the road itself was another impediment to safely bringing supplies to Punta Chivato.

Mary Morss shared an incident during which a delivery truck was bringing roof tiles for Casa Grande through the mountain pass above Santa Rosalía. In this area, Baja 1 became steep and narrow with hairpin turns. It had no guardrails as it snaked through the mountains known as the *Tres Virgenes,* the three virgins.

"The brakes went out on one of the first delivery trucks we had to come put the roofs on. Somehow, the brakes were lost. I don't think that anybody was killed or anything, but it tipped the load off, and the contents just slipped down into oblivion. One of those hills going down into Santa Rosalía is nicely tiled with Chivato tile," Mary added with a laugh.

Bill gradually began to add hotel furnishings, stoves for the kitchen, and seating for the dining room and pool areas. He was thrilled by purchasing numerous fiberglass tables and chairs in San Diego. "I was able to get them for $3.50 apiece," Bill exclaimed. The used items purchased in the United States were hauled via Baja 1 to Punta Chivato. "He worked like a trooper," Jeanne Fox remarked about Bill's nonstop work ethic.

Jeanne recalls she and Walter helped Bill transport articles from Oregon. "A hotel in downtown Portland changed their bedding," Jeanne said. "Bill purchased them, and we picked up a whole bunch of sheets and comforters and drove them down to Punta Chivato."

Mike Morse also eagerly offered Bill his assistance. In addition to helping paint, Mike began to bring things down from the United States to refurbish the hotel. While doing a painting job at the Quail Inn at Lake San Marcos near San Diego, he discovered the hotel was undergoing a remodel. They planned to buy new furniture.

"Wait a minute. I know someone that needs it," Mike told the owners of the inn. After calling Bill and clearing the purchase with him, Mike negotiated for the furniture and bedding. He drove his purchases to Punta Chivato.

"Mike brought down all the curtains for the rooms," said Bill Alvarado. "I think he had a deal with a cleaning company or something. People bought new curtains and didn't want these. Mike paid for having them cleaned and then brought them down. He did so many things he just didn't have to do. What a guy."

Some remember Mike later donating a vehicle and a boat for hotel use. "He was always bringing something down for Bill," remarked Jeanne Fox.

Mike would eventually move to a small home in the ravine once occupied by the old caretaker, Zacarías. He married a local Mexican woman, Magdalena, and became the father to her children from a previous marriage.[121]

Chapter 58

CARING SPIRIT

People who got to know Bill Alvarado admired his enthusiasm and positive approach to almost every situation. Campers, pilots, workers, and others who met him at Punta Chivato described Bill as a person who "saw the good and potential in everything," "never turned away a soul," "made you feel like a long-lost brother," "didn't have a mean spirit in his body," and was "sensitive to a fault, sacrificing his own direction to be gentle and receptive to someone else's need."

Known to treat his employees well, Bill provided housing free of charge for workers and their families. Although he paid his employees what the Mexican government deemed appropriate hourly wages, Bill also gave them Christmas bonuses, vacations, and other benefits.

Jere Summers recalled the employees' morning schedule. "The workers would come in and start about 7:30 in the morning or so, and at 9:00, they would go to breakfast. Everybody would quit. It was like a siesta in the afternoon."

Pedro Molina remembered having no problems with his boss. "He was a good person," he said, "I worked for Bill for 14 years."

Bill came to the aid of both Mexicans and Americans who encountered medical crises while at Punta Chivato. One common injury was getting snagged by fishhooks.

"I was always asked to take fish hooks out of people, whether it was in their feet or their head or wherever," Bill recalled. "Fishhooks, treble hooks. I sure learned a slick way. They wouldn't even know it. I'd take a 40- or 50-pound, 80-pound monofilament and run it through the barb, or two of them, 18-20 inches, give it slack and pow."

During the interview with Bill, Greg Joy, the author's husband, a physician and an avid fisherman, added, "Bill, there's one other step. You had to push on it." Bill confirmed that added step of pushing down on the hook's shank before he pulled it out.

Tarantulas were among the natural inhabitants of the arid land around Punta Chivato. One day, a tarantula bit Hector, one of Bill's workers. Terrified he was going to die, the employee immediately found Bill.

"Common thinking was if a tarantula bites you, you're going to die right now," said Bill, explaining Hector's fear.

While Bill had someone take Hector to the hospital in Santa Rosalía, he quickly figured out a way to quell the fear of the others on the beach. Bill caught another tarantula and let it crawl up his arm and across his shoulders. "Everybody was just petrified and started backing up," Bill recalled. "They knew I was going to die." But Bill knew a tarantula's venom was weak, and he had no fear of letting one crawl on him. However, his action did little to quell the anxiety among his workers.

Bill did not shy away from stitching up people who came to him with large gashes. He shared the story of a Mexican boy who was hit in the head by a cable while working on a shrimp boat off the coast of Punta Chivato.

"That was ugly," Bill said, "because it was a couple of days before he came in." Bill tried to shave the boy's hair away from the wound. "God, golly! Half the hair was bent inside the wound," Bill recalled.

"I had Xylocaine, so I numbed him pretty good before I started stitching," he said. Bill admitted not knowing how to do sutures but forged ahead and performed the job. "I sewed it up like you'd sew up a tear in a shirt or something."

Next, Bill split a piece of aloe vera from the garden at Casa Grande, put the juicy side on the wound, and wrapped up the Mexican boy's head. He told the shrimper to return in about a week, and he would take the stitches out.

The injured boy did not return for a month. "The bandaging looked like something a garage lackey would wipe his hands on," Bill remembered. "It was terrible. It had come undone a number of times. It was just black. I carefully picked up one end; I didn't want it to stick or hurt, and it just came right off. And there was just a pink, ragged, jiggety line going down his head. It was perfect! Perfect! I cut one end of the stitch, grabbed it in the middle, pulled it a little bit, then grabbed the other end, and it came right out."

Harry Oxley recalled that the shrimping boat donated the large broken cable to Bill. He repurposed it as a sturdy tie-down for private airplanes. For years, the cable was used by airplane pilots to secure their aircraft parked at the end of the shorter runway closest to the hotel.

When the bar in the hotel reopened, Bill tended to those who got injured due to intoxication. He shared the story of one *gringo* who came to the hotel on a mini-bike and "practically drank us out of booze."

"He was a real chugger—probably 15 or 20 drinks in about an hour and a half," said Bill. "Then I hear rrrmmrrmm…I said, 'What? Don't get on that bike! It could be a disaster.'"

"I can make it," the man yelled just before the vehicle flipped over. Other people standing outside in the dark witnessed the accident.

"He was a ground-up hamburger mess," Bill said. "Not only the side of his face was scraped but also his knees and his chest because he wasn't wearing a shirt." When they removed the man's tennis shoes, even his big toenail was torn.

Fortuitously, a nurse was staying in one of the hotel rooms. She was standing near Bill at the time of the incident. "I'll help you clean that sucker up," she offered.

Bill was steaming mad. "I'd take out a piece of gravel and cuss at him," Bill remembered. "I told him how stupid he was. I never seen such a dumb bastard in all of my life."

According to Bill, the injured man did not use congenial language, but the biker eventually appeared humbled. When Bill and the nurse finished cleaning up his road rash, "he walked away, head down, back to the beach where he was camped."

Bill not only stitched up the wounds of others but also his own. In an interview, he shared the following story.

"I had two little boys that I hired to pick up tin cans and broken glass and stuff like that. I'd take them out at 9:00, and I'd pick them up at noon, a three-hour day. They did a really good job. They gathered up hundreds of pounds of tin and glass.

"I went out to pick them up, and this little boy said, 'I cut myself really bad.' I looked, and it was enough to bleed, but it wasn't deep or anything. So, I took him back and put a Band-Aid on.

"He really didn't want to go to work the next day. And I said, 'Well, it's up to you. It's your dollar and a half.'

"'O.K., I'll go,' he said because his mom told him he had to go.

"He'd gone back out there, and I went to pick him up, and they had all these bags, and I threw them into the pickup, and I hit my lower leg. There was a piece of glass sticking out. It cut pretty good. I said, 'Oh, I've got to go home and take care of that.' I went home and stitched up my leg."

Two or three days later, the same little boy cut himself again. When Bill picked him up at noon, Bill asked, "What happened?"

"Oh, nothing, nothing," replied the boy. After noticing the stitches in Bill's leg, the boy decided he was not badly hurt after all.

Bill was ready to assist people who sustained minor scrapes and cuts. When a more severe injury occurred, Bill made sure to get the individual to the small hospital in Santa Rosalía.

"When Chaparro cut his finger off, I trusted Mary to take him and his finger into the hospital," Bill said.

"Another injury that required a trip to the hospital occurred at Casa Grande. Bill was with Pedro's brother, Ramón, in the garage at Casa Grande, filling propane bottles when "the whole inside of this double garage turned into a ball of fire, even the cobwebs up in the corner." Bill recalled, "A five-gallon can that I was filling the small bottles with was on fire. I had to reach in and turn that off." As a result, Bill's eyebrows, arms, and legs got singed.

Ramón sustained extensive burns from the explosion. Bill put ice on him and got him to the hospital in Santa Rosalía. There, Ramón's burns were covered with a gel, and he was "wrapped from head to toe."

Bill remembers covering himself with aloe when he returned home. "I was in misery for about four or five days," he stated. His skin blistered from head to toe. "I'll never forget having an itchy forehead and a patch of skin come off my forehead. Skin falling off everywhere."

However, Bill's suffering was minor compared to Ramón's, whose burns kept him off work for 1-1/2 months. "That poor guy," said Bill. "I ended up with just one scar." Despite his injuries and missing eyebrows and eyelashes, Bill continued to work. "You have to keep going down there."

In October of 1992, Ramón had another life-threatening injury. In an interview, Bill recounted the tale.

"One of the beachgoers came up and told me the water line to the shower was broken. I went down to the camping beach that evening, and I'm looking around for an easy fix. I finally found part of a broom handle to use as a plug. Water was everywhere, and it was dark. I waded back to the shower, put the plug into the pipe, taped it in, stopped the leak, and got the water flowing.

"The next day, I sent Ramón down to repair it. He walked back in there where I did, steps down, reaches down to get the plug out and turn the water off, and a rattlesnake bites him on the toe."

Ramón killed the snake and then drove to the hotel to tell Bill.

Bill asked someone to take his employee to the hospital in Santa Rosalía. Later, Ramón was driven north to the hospital in the town of Guerrero Negro where he received anti-venom shots. He spent three days at the hospital and was off work for a long time.[122]

Mary Morss recalled Bill was often late for appointments because he was "either talking to someone or helping someone." She stated he quickly adopted the concept of "mañana."

"The philosophy of mañana does not necessarily mean tomorrow," Mary Morss said. "It just doesn't mean today." Bill embraced the term. "If you invited him to dinner and you wanted him to be on time, you better tell him an hour early because it was pretty difficult for him," said Mary, acknowledging Bill's problem with punctuality.

Bill's caring spirit was particularly evident in a letter he wrote to his dear friend, Doc Lyons, on February 28, 1984. Doc had traveled north and was staying at the Plaza Hotel in San Diego. He planned to receive more medical treatment for his skin cancer, a problem he battled for years. Bill expressed his concern about Doc's long absence and updated him on the recent happenings at Punta Chivato. He knew Doc was as eager to return to the Baja point as he was to have his verbal sparring partner back. The following are excerpts from this letter.

Dear Doc!

I'm really anxious to hear from you—I've tried unsuccessfully to get a report from the hospital and the Plaza Hotel says that you will be back in your room about now 2/28—please drop me a note. I'm really concerned.

Good news from Manuel at the Bank—the Bank Trust on the house is ready for final disposition. Our cost will be $225,000 pesos—If I get another lot leased I'll make the payment.

The septic tank at the Hotel is now about ¾ dug. I really feel sorry for the guys digging in the solid rock—it's rough.

I've rented 2 rooms in the Hotel for a month, that will help keep the wolves away for a while. Had a good week at the house—3 rooms rented for 5 days each so I do have a cash flow.

Camping has fallen off quite a bit. We had 9 days of continuous wind at about 25-30 m.p.h. It really became a little boring. Planted a few strawberry plants and bell peppers in areas around the house where I felt the wind was less severe. Charlie and Mary [rice farmers] along with a host of other people from years past have all inquired about you.

Haven't been fishing since you left, but I really don't think I've missed much, a few yellowtail have been caught, but the wind has kept everyone off the water.

The tomato plant outside your room is about 5' high now and I've probably taken close to 50 tomatoes so far and believe me, it is loaded with tomatoes —it is really doing well.

I'm enclosing a reduction of the subdivision maps prepared by the local architect and approved by all the departments necessary to legalize it and set us free to lease lots and start building—Hope you find them interesting.

Please drop me a note or call Harry Oxley in San Clemente. He will be returning around the 13th of March by car and bring things for the Hotel project as well as his house.

Doc, I miss you—very much. I need someone to yell at or have yell at me![123]

Lots of love, Bill

Chapter 59

PIG FARM

Before the hotel opened, Bill and Mary Morss decided to move from Casa Grande into one of the back rooms of the hotel. Mary helped Bill with bookkeeping, did the banking in Mulegé, and continued working with him to provide dinners to guests at Casa Grande and the few open hotel rooms. Bill remembers the rooms at the Big House were the first to receive air conditioning units. "When I got a generator for air conditioning, people preferred to stay at the Big House," Bill said. "Getting air was really something."

Hotel Serenidad's pig roasts were well known to *gringos* who visited Mulegé and the surrounding areas. Every Saturday, guests mingled on the Serenidad patio, sipping margaritas and swaying to the tunes of a mariachi band. The aroma from the roasting pig wafted through the courtyard from the outdoor spit.

Bill and Mary often discussed having their own pig fiestas at Punta Chivato someday. They conferred about side dishes they might provide—coleslaw, beans, and rice. But they knew the hotel kitchen needed to be completed before any fiestas could occur.

The couple knew where they could obtain the pigs. Once, while shopping in Mulegé, they met an American couple who owned a pig farm. Their ranch was located halfway between Punta Chivato and Mulegé, just west of the Baja highway.

"One day, I'd been in town [Mulegé], and I had a skirt on, and I had my nylons on and my high-heel shoes," recalled Mary as she shared the story. Mary always dressed up when she went to Mulegé or Santa Rosalía. Nothing irritated her more than to see American women in town wearing shorts. She felt they contributed to the negative opinion Mexicans had of them.

Mary was well known by the locals in Mulegé. Her smart dress and outgoing personality made it easy to like her. She usually parked her truck at the service station and walked through the small village doing her errands. Mary fully trusted the men at the gas station. "They would fill my tank, wash it, and take my vehicle around to the repair people if necessary. I knew they would always take care of me." She even recalled leaving jewelry and money in her car. It was always there when she returned.

That day, earlier than usual, Mary finished her business at the bank and met with their accountant at his office at the end of the street. She had been fortunate not to find the usual long line of customers at the bank. Each person took a number and waited for a teller to call them forward. An hour's wait was typical.

Before picking up her truck, Mary made her usual stop to greet Ana, the Mexican woman who occasionally drove out and helped cook at Casa Grande. Mary was ahead of schedule as she drove up the grade out of Mulegé. Heading north on Baja 1, she decided to take a detour and visit Walt and Nora, the pig farmers she and Bill had met in Mulegé.

"Walt had a gigantic grin that went from ear to ear," Mary said. "He and his wife, Nora, were incredible people."

Walt and Nora were delighted to see Mary and invited her to join them for a drink before she headed home. During their conversation, the topic of raising pigs in Punta Chivato came up again, and Mary decided to take Walt up on his offer.

"I can take a couple of pigs today," Mary said. "I've got the truck."

"Well, there they are," Walt said, gesturing to two piglets in the pen nearby. "Go get them."

"Me? Me?" Mary asked, wondering if she had heard Walt correctly.

Her questioning quickly turned to determination as she rose to meet Walt's challenge. "You know what? I can do that," she said as she removed her high heels and headed to the pigpen.

"Pigs are not easy to catch," Mary said, recalling the ordeal. "Walt sent one of his workers to help me and then just sat laughing and hitting his knee."

After struggling to get the piglets into gunny sacks, the worker lifted them into the back of Mary's truck. One had wriggled out of its sack by the time she arrived in Punta Chivato.

Bill reached into the truck to retrieve the loose piglet. "The pig was fighting mad," Mary said, "and pigs bite, by the way."

Bill and Chaparro built a little corral. They had previously discussed where to set up the pen when raising pigs was just an idea. They quickly constructed an enclosure for the piglets up the ravine from the workers' housing.

"We ran a water line out there, so they had water all the time," Bill said. "They had lots of food from the garbage."

The piglets grew, and the two became twelve in less than four months. The hotel was still not ready for guests, but they often served barbecued pork at Casa Grande. Too soon, the supply grew faster than the demand.

"We ended up with close to 40 pigs," said Bill. "That's a whole bunch of pigs. It got to the point I had to buy pig food for them." Since it didn't serve the intended purpose of increasing revenue, Bill decided to get out of the pig-raising business.

Chapter 60

INVALID LEASES

In 1984, the Americans who had, in good faith, given Bill Alvarado money to lease property in Punta Chivato learned their 20-year leases were invalid.

"All of sudden, they come over from México City and say, 'These are all illegal,'" remembered early camper Les Conner. "They said you could only lease property from the Ejido," he added. "We all leased our properties from Bill!

When Bill obtained his original lease for the run-down hotel, Casa Grande, and the land at Punta Chivato, he assumed he had done everything required. As Zacarías had advised, Bill first met with members of the Ejido San Bruno regarding the land. They, in turn, informed him the permission would have to come from the governor of Baja California Sur. Subsequently, Bill set up an appointment with the governor, who, according to Bill, approved and signed his lease. When Bill was told to speak with the Agrarian Department in La Paz, representing the Ejido, he set up meetings and followed through. Bill thought all was properly settled. He truly believed he had a legal document for a renewable, 10-year lease for the hotel and the surrounding area. Bill had already completed one stipulation of the lease: to build housing for his Mexican employees.

The signed agreement did not mention that Bill was not allowed to sublease lots. In fact, he recalled the Ejido telling him he could do whatever he wanted to with the land. So, he went to Santa Rosalía, where he hired a surveyor to lay out two subdivisions at Punta Chivato.

According to Bill, everything seemed to be going well until officials in México City heard that Bill was leasing lots. As a result, the Mexican authorities decided to pay Bill a visit.

"The Ejido and the Mexican government came in and said he [Bill] had no right to lease that property," said Les Conner.

According to the officials, the lots had to be leased from Ejido San Bruno. The leases could only extend for three years, not 20 or 25, as Bill promised the lessees.

Under what was referred to as *Contratos de Asociación en Participación* [Contract of Association in Participation], Mexican law allowed outside investors to partner with an ejido and the Agrarian Department for no longer than three years. At the end of this term, the ejido and the Minister of Agrarian Reform would determine whether the investor was meeting his/her obligations of making improvements to the land. If not, the Mexican authorities could abruptly revoke the lease and confiscate any structure built on it.

"Can you imagine renewing your house?" Les Conner exclaimed in an interview. "You're at the mercy of the Ejido every three years!"

But this was what the Mexican Constitution had always required. The Americans, including Bill Alvarado, had been misled. Unknowingly, Bill had illegally subleased the lots.

The homeowners at Punta Chivato had varied responses to the unwelcome news. Some pointed to the Ejido San Bruno as the instigator. "The Ejido was trying to get the money back from Bill that we paid him," remarked Harry Oxley.

Others saw Bill as the reason for their illegal leases and said he should fix the problem.

"We flew Bill to La Paz several times to meet with an official from México City to get our leases straightened out," indicated Rich Ream, who, along with Jeanne Winters and Sam Southwick, had leased the first lot at Punta Chivato. But often, when Bill arrived in La Paz, the official he was scheduled to meet did not show up for the appointment.

The Americans who leased lots at Punta Chivato were angry to suddenly learn their leases were illegal. "They didn't get their X's taken care of," said Bunnie Adams. "The permissions from the government weren't there."

Bunnie gave Bill some credit. "He did have it [the lots] surveyed. He did have that done right."

The homeowners decided to meet with local Mexican officials to resolve the issue. "We would meet with the San Bruno representatives and Mexican lawyers to clear up the matter," recalled Rich Ream.

One of the biggest issues Bill and the Americans did not understand was the importance of getting final approval from the federal government in México City. The Americans expected the documents would be forwarded to México City for final approval, but the leases never left the Baja peninsula. Many documents did not pass beyond the local government in Santa Rosalía or the state government in La Paz, Baja California Sur. Although the papers were stamped "official," they were not legally registered. American investors had been assured their documents were signed and recorded when, in fact, their paperwork was invalid and would not hold up in court if challenged. Local or state officials frequently told the investors their documents could not be located or were "lost."

Foreigners who wanted to invest in Baja were particularly at risk. Most did not speak the language or know Mexican real estate law. When they were told all documents were in order, the Americans blindly took a local Mexican official's word for it.

When some documents passed through the channels without incident, clients and their attorneys were advised to be quiet and "not rock the boat."

Early homebuilder Archie McVay tried to enlist the help of an attorney from La Paz who had a relationship with the head of the Agrarian Department there. This official recommended the home-owners work together.

"I don't know what his retainer was; it wasn't that much," stated Archie. The attorney said he would work with the Agrarian Department in La Paz.

The head of the Agrarian Department "was a very intelligent guy, but he was very non-committal, too," recounted Archie. "He said the only way to make it work was to go through the bank, have the bank handle it, all the proceeds. Not have individuals. He says, 'It would never work in México. 'Cause everybody's holding their hand out for a take somewhere along the line.'"

McVay could not convince the others in Punta Chivato to buy into his idea. "The rest of them wasn't interested in it," he said. "Too many of them get into it, too many factions, and it didn't look like it was going to work out.

Archie felt Bill Alvarado might be blocking the idea of the homeowners banding together and getting land approval through an agreement with a Mexican bank. "He [Alvarado] didn't want this to happen because it would have taken him out of the picture."

The man from the Agrarian Department "told us out flat—Bill was gone," McVay continued. "He was on the way out. They didn't know how soon, but he [Bill] wasn't going to be there very much longer."

The federal officials who visited Punta Chivato, bringing the initial news of the illegal leases, concurred. They said they planned to evict Bill because he sold all these illegal leases. "However, there's no problem for you other people," they assured the homeowners. "All you have to do is work with the Ejido."

George Staples, who had left Punta Chivato by that time, recalled, "Things started falling apart because Bill was just mismanaging things.…Government guys were getting out there and were getting PO'd." George indicated the Mexican government was also angry because Bill "wasn't taking care of taxes."

According to Archie McVay, many of the lessees nonetheless stuck with Bill. "Rich [Ream] and them went along with Bill."

One homeowner who sided with Archie was Andy Adams. "He [Andy] was all for it. He said, 'That's the only way to go,'" McVay recalled. "He understood the fact that if we could have got this through the bank if it [the leases] had been turned over to the bank, it would be with somebody who would have been responsible and would have made a permanent thing of it," said McVay. "That was my understanding. We just kind of lost interest."

Partly due to their invalid leases, the Americans began to discuss forming a homeowners' association.

"While we were there, the homeowners tried to have an association," said McVay, "but they couldn't get organized." He remembers having a meeting at his home in Punta Chivato. "It'd end up with everybody shouting and yelling. We'd have a meeting, and then everybody'd talk, and then [Phil] Souther would say, 'It's all wrong. It has to be my way.'"

Although the homeowners were initially upset by the unexpected visit from the Mexican officials, things did not seem to change in Punta Chivato. Bill continued to sublease lots as he had always done. Some of the original Americans who leased parcels from Bill and then decided to leave the area turned around and sold their invalid leases to new, unsuspecting American buyers.

Chapter 61

HOMEOWNERS' ASSOCIATION

On Easter week of 1985, the early lot lessees held an organized meeting at Punta Chivato. Initially, the group decided to call themselves *Punta Chivato Asociados*. This would eventually be changed to Punta Chivato Homeowners' Association, later referred to by the acronym PCHA. Andy Adams was selected as its first president.

During the first meeting, the attendees voted to establish an Emergency Fund at Punta Chivato. Its purpose was to cover unexpected, urgent situations and "to subsidize projects that will be beneficial to all of the lot/homeowners." It was decided to assess $100 per lot/homeowner to establish this fund.

The second PCHA meeting was held on Easter week of 1986. It was a holiday week for most homeowners still working in the States. With extra days off work, they could go to Punta Chivato and attend the meeting. The weather was generally mild during the spring months and conducive to travel.

A board was selected for the year. The 1986-87 board consisted of Andy Adams, Archie McVay, and Kathy Lucore.

The following individuals were present at the second meeting:

Archie & Doris McVay	Lot 3	First Division
Barbara Silzle	Lot 4	" "
Bob & Bobbie Hilbun	Lot 8	" "
Larry & Kathy Lucore	Lot 13	" "
Richard Ream & Jeanne Winters	Lot 18	" "
Phil & Nelly Souther	Lot 12	Second Div.
Rich Fodor	Lot 8	" "
Bill Alvarado		

After the meeting, Andy followed up with a note to all who could not attend. He informed them the former Emergency Fund had been renamed Punta Chivato Lot/Homeowners Association

Fee. By then, $1,100 had been collected, which did not include every homeowner.

The PCHA's initial focus was largely benevolent and social. The association gave the Punta Chivato baseball team one hundred dollars to help defray the cost of their uniforms. The team consisted of men from the Ejido San Bruno. A barbecue was planned for the Ejido in February 1987. Homeowners Archie and Doris McVay agreed to head up that endeavor, an event they would fund on their own for a couple of years.

Security was also a concern. At the PCHA 1986 annual meeting, building a caretaker's home was discussed. This person would be hired to "watch all of our lots and homes." [124]

Potentially contentious issues, like the leases, were not discussed at the early meetings. One board member wrote: "I think I can speak for most of us when I say we're in Baja to fish and enjoy the sunsets, not to get political, but we do need to be a little organized to make things more pleasant for all of us." [125]

However, as with most organizations and gatherings of people with different agendas, the PCHA eventually became political. Over the years, the organization got involved in contract negotiations, lot transfers, payment for water delivery, and other concerns. The American investors felt such matters could be managed more effectively as a group than as individuals.

In the early 1990s, individual water meters were installed, so each homeowner was charged for the water used rather than the earlier set fee of $30.00 per month per parcel. Ejidatario Victor Velasquez initially oversaw reading the meters. The cost to the homeowners for water was $1.00 U.S. per cubic meter used.

As more homes were constructed at Punta Chivato, inquiries about the accuracy of the water meter readings increased. Punta Chivato homeowners eventually took over reading the water meters from the Ejido.

For years, Jere and Marge Summers performed this service on the first of each month. After determining the amount each homeowner owed the Ejido for water, Marge, who served as treasurer of the PCHA for several years, wrote out a check from the local homeowners' association bank account. Then, she sent bills to the homeowners, hoping they would pay promptly to keep the account solvent.

The condition of the water delivery system, including the well, pipes, and generator, was brought up to the PCHA. To tackle these concerns, a water committee was formed in 1992 consisting of select members of the Ejido San Bruno,[126] the Punta Chivato home-owners,[127] and hotel owner Bill Alvarado.

The meetings were amicable and productive. A re-built 30-KW diesel generator was ordered and installed inside a newly constructed covered generator room next to the well site. The Ejido consented to putting in separate water meters on the camping beach, Casa Grande, and the hotel. They agreed they would pay closer attention to disparities between water costs and homeowner usage. Some homeowners who had lush gardens surrounding their homes were often charged less than homeowners with minimal landscaping. Checking for leaky pipelines became more routine.

In a letter to the Punta Chivato Asociados dated December 23, 1992, then-president Harry Oxley reported improvements he observed at the well.

> *I was very surprised that it [the pump house] had not only the roof on but filters on all the windows to keep the dust out. The floor had been scrubbed clean. The generator was very clean, apparently wiped down recently. The entire area had been cleaned up and there was a trailer with a caretaker and his family living on the premises.*

However, the availability and delivery of the precious commodity of water would continue to be an issue in the arid desert community of Punta Chivato.

Chapter 62

EARLY HOMEOWNERS LEAVE

The McVays, Nidiffers, and Hortons enjoyed their beach home at Punta Chivato for several years. But in 1986, they decided to sell it.

"You know, I kind of saw the writing on the wall," said Archie. "It was getting so we was having a hard time."

George Staples offered his opinion as to why these partners from Oregon left. "They were more interested in the process of putting something together rather than sitting around and enjoying the fruits of their labor. It was a challenge to them, and they did it. Then they kind of lost interest and ended up getting rid of it."

Ray Nidiffer was acquainted with Art Oberto, a sausage maker from Seattle, Washington. Art's company made "Oh Boy! Oberto" beef jerky, which Ray sold in his grocery stores. One day, Ray told the sausage maker about the beach home he and his partners had for sale in Punta Chivato. Art expressed interest.

Not long afterward, Art Oberto and his wife, Dorothy, drove their motorhome from Seattle to Punta Chivato to look at the property. "Oberto just drove up here with his motorhome," said Archie. "He wanted the house real bad. It was kind of odd. He said, 'Add this to my junk money,' and started writing a check out. This was his mad money." The Obertos paid $75,000 and took over the lease.

Archie and Doris McVay would visit Punta Chivato once again in the mid-1990s. They stayed as guests of the Obertos in the home they had helped design and build ten years earlier. Archie noticed Art Oberto was still driving the old car Archie had brought down to use at Punta Chivato.

In 1984, Rich Ream and Jeanne Winters added another bedroom, bathroom, and large garage to their home, an additional 753 square feet. However, health concerns caused the couple to leave their dream home in Punta Chivato. Jeanne had emphysema and once had an attack while in Baja.

"She was flown out by Medivac, and it was horribly expensive since they didn't have insurance," said homeowner John Fitzsimmons. "They just realized that they couldn't do that very many times. The doctor said she shouldn't live here. She needed to be near medical treatment," added John's wife, Gerry.

In a letter Rich Ream later wrote to the author, he explained, "Jeanne was ill from emphysema, and I had to have a pacemaker. We all thought the fun of going to P.C. and Baja was the fun of flying a little airplane. We really loved P.C. and felt badly about having to leave. I have many fond memories."[128]

Jeanne Winters on the beach below the hotel (early 1980s).
Courtesy Rich Ream

In March 1991, the Ream-Winters-Southwick home on Lot #18 of Subdivision 1 was sold to two pilots from Northern California, Tom Rosen and Tom Ryan, for $80,000, which included the home and the land lease. An additional $2,400 U.S. was paid to Ejido San Bruno as a lease transfer fee.

The house and their boat became known as Tom-Tom. The partners added a solar power system within the first month. Later, they added guest rooms and a bath, increasing the living space by 450 square feet. They and their families continue to use it to this day.

Chapter 63

HOTEL CELEBRATES REOPENING

"It didn't seem like the hotel was ever going to get open," commented early camper Dennis Gardner. "The work there was progressing so slowly, and of course, Bill didn't have two nickels to rub together to speak of. Then, all of a sudden, things started happening. Everybody was kind of excited about it."

Early camper Dave Jacobson remarked, "Bill put a lot of work into the project and did a great job. Slowly the hotel was remodeled and finally opened, mostly to fly-ins."

Punta Chivato Hotel reopens under Bill Alvarado.
Courtesy Harry Oxley

Pilots who owned small aircraft arrived as members of flying clubs. Other fly-ins affiliated with philanthropic organizations came to provide medical services to the local Mexicans. Dentists who flew small airplanes and a group known as the Flying Samaritans periodically arrived at Punta Chivato.[129] Mexican families from neighboring communities would travel long distances to receive the free medical services these charitable associations offered.

Bill Alvarado recalled a boy receiving the gift of sight. "They had a pair of glasses made for this little boy, and he put them on, and it was just stunning. Everybody got choked up. He looked at his hand. He looked at his fingers. And he looked around the room, and he looked at his mother and father, and he didn't know them. His mama starts crying, and I start crying, and everybody started crying. This little boy had never been able to see detail in his life. That was one of the most heart-rendering things I've ever seen."

While the official opening date of Hotel Punta Chivato varies depending on whom one consults, the most likely estimate was in the fall of 1986. By that time, Bill was there alone; Mary Morss had moved back to Oregon, George Staples had left and gotten married, and Doc Lyons had passed away.

When interviewed, early workers Pedro and Aurelia Molina said the hotel opened in September 1985. "There was a big party, music, the swimming pool was open," said Pedro. He remembers Harry Oxley and his son, Brad, attending the opening.

Harry Oxley concurred that the celebration was in September but was unsure about the year. "Brad and I were down here," Harry said, confirming his son was with him. "Our house was finished. We were staying in our house. We went down to the hotel and swam in the swimming pool and drank champagne to inaugurate the opening of the hotel."

The author surmises the official opening of Hotel Punta Chivato occurred in September of 1986 based on the following evidence: a quote from a visiting couple and a dated announcement put out by the PCHA.

"Julia and I had come down in June of 1986," Dale Dryer shared during an interview. "The hotel was not open."

An article printed in the Punta Chivato Homeowners' Association newsletter dated June 6, 1986, reported:

> For some time, Bill has been renting rooms at the hotel, but it is not officially open yet. We were told he plans to open it, with services, in October. We were also told that the International Airport, being built between Santa Rosalía and Punta Chivato is supposed to open in December. As you know, this is Baja, so this schedule is subject to change.

When the hotel reopened, there were 30 rooms: 20 water-front rooms and 10 rooms in the back. Room rates at the hotel started at

$18 per night. If the hotel filled up, six additional rooms were available for guests at Casa Grande. An undated brochure listing Bill Alvarado as proprietor of Hotel Punta Chivato indicated he later increased the rates. Waterfront room rates were listed as Single $40, Double: $50; back-room rates were Single $35, Double: $40. Each extra adult was $10 per night and $5 for each additional child. All rooms were listed as having fireplaces.

In each hotel bathroom was a small indoor garden with a skylight. "They had, for some bizarre reason, pomegranates growing in those and odd plants," recalled Bunnie Adams.

Bill remembered some guests brought down wine as "their contribution to exchange for bartering."

"We did a lot of bartering," Bill added. "Some came down and always had the same room."

Shrimp boat offshore from hotel; fresh shrimp cost $2.00/kilo or could be bartered for with beer, cigarettes, or Playboy magazines.
Courtesy Dave Jacobson

As in earlier days, some visitors arrived with two or three boxes of Playboy magazines to give out to the workers. "They'd trade those for shrimp," said Bill, referring to the swap between the shrimp fishermen anchored near the hotel and the magazines' owners.

Bill hired some of his construction workers to stay on and work at the hotel after it officially opened. Pedro Molina was one of them.

"When the hotel was open, I was working in the garden, and Bill asked me if I'd like to work in the hotel," Pedro recalled. "I said 'yes.'"

Pedro first worked as a waiter in the dining room. Later, Bill asked if he wanted to work at the hotel bar. Pedro's wife's brother worked as the bartender but spoke little English. Pedro did not know how to mix drinks but was more conversant in English than his brother-in-law. The two employees were able to learn from each other. "I like the bar better than working as a waiter," Pedro said. In time, Pedro became known for his potent margaritas.

Long-time Punta Chivato employee, Pedro Molina, working at hotel bar.
From Nov. 1991 video by Bill Alvarado

While the bartenders had a tip jar, the waiters tended to make the most in tips from diners' money left on the tables. The waiters rapidly picked up English since it led to better tips from the Americans. "They worked at it, and some of them got pretty darn good," Bill remarked. In addition to Pedro, Bill said Saúl and Hector also learned to speak English while working as waiters at the hotel.

Most other employees did not speak English. They complained to Bill, saying they should get part of the waiters' tips. They wanted the money placed into a pool to share the gratuities among all the workers.

To help make the distribution of tips more equitable, Bill put a box on the desk in the reception office for all gratuities. As guests checked out, they would put money into the locked box. Once a month, Pedro oversaw opening the box and counting the contents.

Then the money was divided among all the employees.

"That didn't work very well," Bill remembered, "because each employee felt they had a different value than the other guy." Wanting to avoid being in the middle of the conflict, Bill decided to turn the whole thing over to the employees to work out. The only tips the reception office kept track of were those left by guests staying in rooms at the hotel.

Bill Alvarado with the author in Punta Chivato Hotel gift shop (1987).
Author's photo

Early on, Bill had a satellite television installed in the hotel dining room. "We really gathered in people then," said Bill, indicating many were beach campers. "It wasn't too long before they started coming to the hotel."

The television was usually tuned to sports, especially Monday night and weekend football. Then came the World Championship Fight. The dining room was overflowing. "We had, I think, every male from Santa Rosalía and Mulegé," Bill said.

"All the buildup. The fight was supposed to start. But somehow, the order didn't go through, and we didn't get it," recalled Bill.

In retrospect, Bill realized they could have had a guy come out for "$20 or $25 bucks" and "do his magic with the box." But Bill had decided to go the less expensive route, ordering the broadcast for $10.

"I drove down to Mulegé faster than I've ever driven in my life and got on the phone," Bill recalled. The satellite phone lines were down, and he could not get through.

"You talk about 150-200 guys inside at the time waiting for the broadcast. They were mad. I just knew the whole place was going to crash down," Bill recounted. "But they were pretty congenial about it. I bought them all drinks."

Chapter 64

ACTIVITIES & CELEBRITIES

As in the early days of Dixon Collins and Cleveland Crudgington, Bill Alvarado made sure Hotel Punta Chivato offered assorted options for guests. Some preferred to lounge beside the pool with a book or cocktail in hand, while others chose to sign up for one or more available activities.

Bill provided chartered fishing trips aboard his boat, *Sea Ray*. Employee Miguel Romo ran the boat and functioned as a fishing guide. Guests could rent gear to snorkel in the shallow reefs for clams, rock scallops, and lobster. Many chose to relax under a palapa on the beach and enjoy leisurely dips in the warm, clear waters of the Sea of Cortez.

Guests who learned Bill was a game hunter sometimes asked to participate in one of his hunting excursions. While living in Oregon, Bill had taught himself how to hunt with a bow. Bow hunting took him years to learn, but with diligent practice, Bill became proficient. When he came to Punta Chivato, he brought his bow, and when time permitted, he enjoyed hunting for doves and other birds at the lagoon near San Bruno. However, few of his guests were bow hunters. They preferred rifles. Bill recalled a private pilot from Southern California who flew down in his Cessna 210 and stayed at the hotel.

"He wanted to go dove hunting," Bill said. Bill knew there were quail, dove, and ducks at the lagoon north of Punta Chivato. The only problem was the man planned to come down when doves were not in season. Reluctant to disappoint his guest, Bill contacted the police in Santa Rosalía to see if he could get special permission.

"Are you going to be there?" asked the policeman who took Bill's call.

"Yeah," said Bill.

"How many days did you want to hunt?"

"I don't know. Probably two," Bill responded.

"I'll come out and have lunch on you."

"O.K.," Bill said.

The policeman arrived at Punta Chivato with a signed document that read, "Special Open Season."

"It just needed the names of the people who were going to be hunting," Bill recalled.

Word quickly spread that the hotel at Punta Chivato had reopened. "Both the Phoenix and Tucson newspapers had full-page, full-color stories about the hotel," Bill recalled, pleased with the advertisements in these large Arizona cities. Fishing publications also featured the reopening of the Baja resort. Articles appeared in circulars mailed by the flying groups. Eventually, write-ups about the newly restored hotel appeared in commercial airline magazines.

Traveling to Punta Chivato by private plane was enjoyed by many flying clubs.
Courtesy Harry Oxley

"We had people from all over Europe who came," said Bill. "They read about it in magazines…I was surprised at the number of French that came in there," he added.

Dennis Gardner remembered when ten single women from the French swimming team visited the hotel. "They were all skinny-dipping in the pool and jumping on everybody's laps and looking for single men," he said. "I was always a day late and a dollar short, that's for sure."

Many, including local officials, used Punta Chivato to engage in activities they wanted to keep covert. "I had a lot of government people come out to have lunch or to have dinner and brought a girlfriend," Bill said. "*Segunda frente*. If you're married and you're running around, if that's any kind of lasting relationship, that's your second front."

Bill shared a story of two women who were at the hotel bar one evening. "These two really pretty, early-20s gals were sitting at the bar; it's getting late, but they still held the attention of four or five guys," recalled Bill. "They were buying them drinks and asking, 'You want to go for a walk on the beach? Do you want to go swimming?'"

Bill continued, "Finally, one gal says to the other, 'You know what? It's getting late. We better get to bed.' The other one says, 'You're right, dear.' Then, a 30-second lip lock. Talk about some disappointed guys!"

Bill was not shocked by what he saw. Gay employees at Hotel Punta Chivato were common.

"We had a gay guy working for us," Bill added, "who probably was the best employee you ever had as far as public relations and customer satisfaction."

Tucked away on the eastern Baja peninsula, Punta Chivato offered a safe place to spend a secluded vacation out of the public eye. As word spread, some well-known personalities visited the hotel.

"We had a number of celebrities that stayed there," Bill said. John Wayne and Shirley MacLaine signed the guest book, which sadly seems to have disappeared, according to Bill.

Bill remembered when Jacques Cousteau arrived in a single-masted boat. "Maybe half a dozen of the members of the expedition stayed at the hotel," said Bill. They told Bill about a deep dive they had done in one of the trenches two-thirds of the way to Guaymas across the Sea of Cortez off mainland Mexico. The water temperature was hot, 112- or 115 degrees Fahrenheit, and the sea life there was entirely different from anywhere else. "They have these little starfish-like things that move real fast," Bill recalled hearing. "Just weird-looking fish. All of them hover around the steam holes where the hot water runs bubbling up. It was just fascinating."

Another memorable guest was actor Denzel Washington. "He was unusual because he was black, and not many black people came down to Punta Chivato," said Bill. The hotel proprietor struck up a conversation with the quiet young man and remembered Denzel as "fascinating...This was before anything big happened to him," Bill added.[130]

Several individuals interviewed by the author remembered when a well-known pop and movie star arrived. "Olivia Newton-John stayed here for three or four nights," Bill Alvarado recalled. "She was quite a character."

Known for hit songs in the 1970s, including "I Honestly Love You" and "Don't Stop Believin'," Olivia Newton-John starred as Sandy in the film adaptation of the Broadway musical *Grease*, opposite John Travolta in 1978. In 1981, she released her popular song "Physical," which later was included in her exercise video and became a hit in aerobics classes.

Mexican builder Raúl Luján recalls meeting Olivia Newton-John in Mulegé. She had bought property there and was interested in building a beach home.

"We took her and her husband to Punta Chivato in John's boat, the *Don Juan*," Raúl said, referring to Punta Chivato homeowner John Lyddon. According to Raúl, who constructed homes at Punta Chivato, Newton-John wanted to look at the houses he had built. "She loved the way we were building with the old beams from Santa Rosalía and all the antique stuff," Raúl said, referencing the large wooden beams he used from the old copper mill in Santa Rosalía.

Bill Alvarado and Mike Morse were walking on the beach en route to Mike's living quarters when the *Don Juan* carrying Raúl, Olivia Newton-John, and her husband, Matt Lattanzi, pulled up near the boat ramp. Mike Morse vividly recalled the reaction of Olivia's husband.

"Her husband was a real wuss," Mike remembered. "He's bitching and moaning, 'Get up closer, more up on the sand. I don't want to get my feet wet.'" Her husband had good reason for this request; he wore dress shoes.

According to Bill, Mike was eager to meet the famous singer-songwriter-actress.

"Olivia Newton-John, she's ready to go," Bill remembered. "So, Mike says, 'Hey, I'll give you a lift.'" Mike spontaneously reached out, and "Olivia Newton-John hops into his arms, and he carries her up the beach and turns left, away from the hotel," said Bill, noting that Mike's garage was in that direction.

"Mike, where are you going?" Bill yelled after him, not knowing what prank his friend would try to pull this time.

"Home," Mike said.

Mike later described the event. "As a joke, I started to run with her toward my room as if I were going to take her there and have my way with her for the evening. Then I tried to stop, but my feet stopped, and my body didn't. I fell forward on the sand and landed on my elbows. I was on top of her, face to face, eye to eye. I thought that she was going to be mad, but she burst out laughing.

"She was giggling and laughing," Bill recounted with a smile. "Her husband did not appreciate the humor."[131]

Celebrity Olivia Newton-John with Mike Morse at Punta Chivato.
Courtesy Mike Morse

Bob Davis recalled when the rock group *The Doors* came down and stayed at the hotel. "Everyone went skinny dipping in the pool," he said.

Actor Larry Hagman, who played oil baron J.R. Ewing on the long-running 1980s television series *Dallas*, and Major Anthony Nelson in the 1960s sitcom *I Dream of Jeannie*, was first introduced to

Punta Chivato by the Cessna 185 Flying Club. After his first trip,
the actor, then in his 50s, became a frequent visitor in the mid-
1980s and early 1990s.

An article in the March 1992 PCHA newsletter, *Chivato Charla*,
recorded:

> *Fly-in of about forty 180's and 186's over Mar. 5-8, included
> Larry Hagman and his party. Nice to have you people enjoy-
> ing our oasis.*

Mike Morse was one of the few who did not know the actor.
Never too proud to share a funny story showing his naiveté, Mike
told of meeting Hagman at the hotel. "He would come up to the
bar and say, 'Hi, I'm J.R. I'm from *Dallas*,'" Mike said. "I thought
he was from Dallas, Texas."

But most guests were thrilled to see the well-known television
star at Punta Chivato. "He could talk to those old ladies at the hotel
and just make them melt," shared one homeowner. "Larry had the
gift of gab, and he could talk to anybody about anything."

"Everybody wanted to get their pictures taken with Larry
Hagman," recalled Bill. "There were people at the hotel all the time,
and he'd stand with his arm around them, and they'd take a picture."

Celebrity Larry Hagman and Betty Bell (1992). Courtesy Betty Bell

Betty and Lester Bell flew to Punta Chivato with the Cessna 175 Club in 1992 and met Hagman. "It was our 50th wedding anniversary," said Betty, proudly sharing the photograph of her standing next to Mr. Hagman. "We [Betty and Lester] were married June 29, 1942," she added.

"I have a flag that he signed with everyone that was in the 180/185 club that was down there," Bill said during an interview. "It's a world peace flag."

Bill occasionally solicited the help of homeowners to take his hotel guests fishing. One day, Bill asked homeowner Robin Converse to take Larry Hagman. Robin was an excellent fisherman but tended to keep to himself.

"Bill, I don't want to do it," Robin told Bill. "I don't want to charter."

"But you have to," Bill said.

"No, I don't have to. I'm not going to do it," Robin adamantly responded.

Desperate to please his guest, Bill went to Robin's house and asked again for the favor.

"Well, come up and meet him," Bill finally said to Robin.

So, Robin agreed to meet Larry Hagman at the hotel. "I went up and introduced myself," Robin recalled. "I was sizing him up, and he was sizing me up, and he had some good humor."

"Look, I'm not going to charter for you because then you'd run me. It's my boat, and I run the boat," Robin told the actor. "That's the way it is. So, if you can understand that all you have to pay for is the gas, we'll go fishing."

To Robin's surprise, fishing with Larry Hagman was more enjoyable than he had anticipated. "He had a great time fishing," recalled Robin. "He was a very good fly fisherman. But he used conventional tackle. It was kind of tough for him. I kept teaching him. Pretty soon, he started to get it."

The two got along well during that first fishing trip and later became close friends.

"Every time he'd come down, he'd stay at the hotel, but he'd come over here," recounted Robin. "Everybody was somewhat standoffish about me. I had that reputation, I guess," Robin continued. "Larry loved it. He'd sit here. He drank a lot of beer, but he also smoked a fair amount of pot. He was a fun guy."

Bill recalled that Hagman started drinking beer early in the day. "He'd get up at 5:30 in the morning or so to go out fishing with one of our homeowners," Bill said. "First thing he'd do is pop two beers."

"He was funnier than hell," Robin remembered. "He had you peeing your pants and laughing all day long fishing. He was hysterically funny. He was quite a guy. He'd been around the block more than once," Robin added.

Robin described one memorable fishing excursion out by Punta San Marcos with Larry Hagman and his son, Preston. Fishing guide Miguel Romo went along to assist. Robin remembers when Larry hooked up and thought he had a yellowtail on his line.

"Larry, you don't have a yellowtail on; it's a big squid," Robin told him. "I don't want that in the boat. I don't want to mess with the stain and everything. It's a pain in the ass."

"Oh, no, no," Larry said, sure that what he was reeling in was a yellowtail.

"Trust me, it is," said Robin.

To prove his point, Robin allowed Larry to continue reeling. When the squid broke the surface, it released its defense mechanism. "It just laced them [Preston and Miguel] with ink, about five gallons or so. It was a big squid," recalled Robin.

"Yeah, yeah, you're right," Larry conceded after seeing the squid and watching the ink spray.

"I've done this before, Larry," Robin responded. He remembered Larry got a big laugh out of that.

Robin became such close friends with Larry Hagman that Larry invited Robin and his girlfriend, Pat, to his son's wedding in Southern California.

"It was in Newport or right about there. Put us up in a beautiful, high-rise hotel. It was first class," Robin recalled. "When the limousine came to pick us up, there was Larry and Peter Fonda."

Robin remembers they were all smoking reefers. "We rolled right up in front of the church, and he said, 'No, I don't want to get out. I want to take a couple hits.'"

"O.K., Larry, it's your show," Robin told his host.

"We copped a good enough buzz, and the limo driver came

around, and we walked into the church and did the deal," said Robin. "Went to a nice reception, and Pat and I caught a flight out of there the next day." "He [Larry] had the ability that he could get totally snockered during the day, and you would never know it."[132]

Chapter 65

BILLIE BRUSH

Around 1985, before the hotel officially opened, Dick and Billie Brush brought a trailer to camp at Punta Chivato. The couple had both worked for the United States Forest Service and were enjoying retirement. Billie retired in 1984. "Dick said Billie got a better retirement," remarked Bunnie Adams. "Billie had money."

"She [Billie] wasn't a people person," recalled early camper Dennis Gardner. "The general feeling of everybody I knew on the camping beach was pretty much that she'd scare anyone away from wanting to stay there."

"I remember he [Dick] seemed like a very nice man," said Dennis. "Billie didn't seem to treat him all that nice. Their relationship seemed a little trite," Dennis reflected.

Unfortunately, Dick got into an accident while riding an ATV in Baja, sustaining an injury to his cervical spine. He was transported to a hospital in the States and eventually recovered enough to return to Punta Chivato. But according to people there, Dick was different. "When Dick returned, he was never the same," remarked Bunnie Adams. "I think he was having trouble with depression," recalled Dennis Gardner.

Some speculate Bill Alvarado had begun to hook up with Billie during her husband's recuperation. "Bill ended up sneaking Billie away from him," recounted George Staples. "That was kind of a messy deal."

According to Dennis Gardner, Dick Bush "went out and bought an airplane one day and went flying the next and crashed it." He did not survive. Some thought Dick's accident was suicidal, that he was aware of his wife's infidelities. Some believed Billie told her husband about her interest in Bill. Wherever the truth lies, Billie Brush and Bill Alvarado soon became a couple.

"I don't know at what point Mary split and Bill got tied up with Billie," said George Staples. He remembers returning to visit Punta Chivato, and Bill was with Billie. "It must have worked," George said during an interview, "because they've been together ever since."

Although Bill stated Mary left Punta Chivato a couple of years before he and Billie became involved, Les Conner recounted seeing Mary in the hotel parking lot. "She's coming back with her stuff," Les said. "Chaparro's coming in, and he whispered, 'Billie's in the room. *Mucho problema.*' I guess that night she [Mary] went to Serenidad," Les added, referring to the Serenidad Hotel in Mulegé.

Billie recalls Mary's exit from Punta Chivato. "Mary left when I was down there," Billie said. "She left in 1986, I think. She left right at the very busiest time. She packed her bags and took off before Christmas."

Whatever happened, most believe Mary left Punta Chivato because she caught Bill in indiscretions and lies. Everyone was aware that Bill liked women.

Campers at Punta Chivato were sad to see Mary leave. Many had known her since they first started driving down to stay on the beach and had enjoyed her meals at Casa Grande. Mary was personable and friendly, but they described Billie as serious and businesslike.

"Almost all liked her [Mary]," long-time Punta Chivato employee Pedro Molina recalled, referring to the campers. "With us, Billie was not a problem, but with other people, it was, with the Americans on the beach. They didn't like her [Billie] much."

Dennis Gardner said Billie "seemed totally out of place. She had an accent, maybe Texan. She was kind of a cowgirl. Kind of hard."

Güero Alaníz, a local Mexican who would later open a small market in Punta Chivato, remembered Billie seldom spoke to him. "She didn't like to chat. I chatted, but she didn't say anything. She almost never tried to speak Spanish."

At the hotel, Billie noticed Bill was "running around like a chicken with its head cut off trying to take care of everything," and she was eager to assist. "I was absolutely bored out of my mind," Billie said during an interview. "I had worked all my life; the job I had was a busy one. I traveled all the time, did training courses, and held seminars all over the country. I was just always on the go, which is what I liked."

One day, Billie approached Bill as he sat behind the reception desk at the hotel.

"Can you use some help, Bill?" Billie asked. "I wouldn't mind helping you out if there's something I can do."

"That would be wonderful," Bill responded.

So it was that Billie Brush began to help Bill Alvarado with the administration of Hotel Punta Chivato.

"Billie had some insurance money," said Dennis Gardner. "All of a sudden, there was a new boat and motor for Bill and a couple of little things straightened around at the hotel. The next thing you know, she's sitting at the front desk!"

Homeowner Lucy Conner shared the story of a friend who was visiting her and made an innocent mistake. Thinking Bill was still dating Mary, her friend approached the woman sitting at the hotel reception desk.

"Hi Mary, it's nice to see you," she said.

"I'm not Mary. I'm Billie."

Realizing her blunder, Lucy's friend quickly retorted, "Oh, that's right, you're the good-looking one."

Billie enjoyed helping Bill and loved her new role. "I never got lonely," she said. "There was always too much going on, and I was always busy. You know, if Bill was gone to the States, I ran the place 24/7. If he was at Chivato, there was always stuff going on, always things to check on, always some problem, or this or that or the other."

Billie began to speak on the radio to pilots landing at Punta Chivato or just passing through the area. "I even talked on the radio to some commercial pilots once in a while," Billie shared. "Tried to talk them into stopping to see us."

Greg Joy remembers flying with a pilot friend to Punta Chivato. During a conversation years later, Greg told Billie how she sounded over the radio when the plane was over the top of Punta Chivato and his friend had announced his intention to land. "All of a sudden, your voice came on, and it sounded like *2001: A Space Odyssey*," Greg recalled. "You sounded like Hal. This very, very sexy, very smooth voice." Billie gave them the wind direction and cleared them to land. "My friend said, 'I gotta meet that gal.'"

Chapter 66

BILL & BILLIE ENJOY FISHING

It felt like they were busy from morning to night running Hotel Punta Chivato, but Bill and Billie occasionally got away. "If the hotel wasn't real busy and all of the boats weren't out, we'd go out in a boat and fish once and a while," recalled Bill. "We didn't do it all the time; it just depended on how busy it was and what was going on." The least busy time at the hotel was in the summer when it was "100 degrees and 95 degrees humidity...Just the diehard fishermen were about the only ones who came," Bill remarked, "the people who knew the fishing was good."

Billie talked about their pre-sunrise excursions, "What we'd do is get up early, hop in the pickup and drive over to Deadman's Beach and fish for about an hour or so and then come back and go to work." Billie enjoyed catching roosterfish and corvina, which, to her, "looked like trout."[133]

Sometimes, Bill and Billie took the boat further out into the Sea of Cortez to search for sailfish. They looked for porpoises, which indicated that billfish were nearby.

Dennis Gardner saw the couple out fishing and noted Billie never looked the part. "You'd see her and Bill out fishing, and she'd be wearing a long dress, like a gown and a big bonnet. She just looked like some southern belle that was just totally out of place in a boat in Punta Chivato."

Bill and Billie shared one unforgettable experience when they were out tuna fishing. The fishing had not been good: "The fish that had been caught that day were all little footballs," according to Bill.

After trolling to the north end of San Marcos Island, Billie got a "hit."

"Billie, get that damn fish in because there's more out here," Bill urged after Billie fought for 15 to 20 minutes reeling in the fish.

Tired, red-faced from exertion, hands white from constant reeling, Billie begged Bill to help. But Bill wanted Billie to experience the satisfaction of bringing in the catch by herself.

"She finally got it up to where I could see it," Bill said. "Holy smokes! She caught a 65-pound sailfish!"

"Just about killed me," Billie added, remembering she was through fishing not only for the day but for the rest of the week. "My muscles were so sore I could hardly bend my arms."

Billie's sailfish ended up being mounted and proudly displayed on the office wall at the hotel. "I don't know who ended up with it," said Billie, still curious about the disappearance of her prized trophy fish. "Somebody got off with it."

Bill shared the following story of reeling in a blue marlin when he and Billie were out fishing in the Sea of Cortez:

"I was lying in the bottom of the boat asleep," Bill recalled. "Billie was running the boat. I heard the reel go. I jumped up and picked it up, and by this time, half the spool was gone."

"Chase it, Billie, chase it!" Bill said excitedly.

"What?" Billie responded, not having seen the fish jump.

"Turn and follow the fish," shouted Bill.

"Where's the fish?" Billie asked.

"Over there!" Bill said, pointing in the direction of the marlin. Bill narrated the story: "Billie turned the boat around just as it's getting down to the last 10 or 12 turns on my reel. I start cranking and cranking and tried to gather line back. She's running towards the fish. I gained half the spool back, maybe three-quarters. Then the fight was really on because it became a tug-of-war. I wasn't sure if he was winning or not. But it felt like it."

Bill ended up radioing the hotel and asking for another boat to help him gaff the marlin once he could reel it in, a feat which took a good hour. "It was a big one," Bill recalled, estimating the marlin was 400 to 600 pounds. Billie stated it was "as long as our boat."

A young Mexican worker finally arrived in a hotel boat and pulled alongside to give Bill a hand. But just as Bill grabbed the leader and attempted to raise the fish, the marlin opened his mouth and got away. Bill was not disappointed he lost the marlin. "At least we got to see it," Bill beamed. "I got my thrill out of it."

Although Bill often released his catch, Billie remembered once they brought in a marlin and served it at the hotel. Another time, they gave one to their workers.

One frequent recipient of Bill and Billie's fish was Don Hielo, a Mexican Bill hired to help maintain the yard after Don Zacarías and Doc Lyons were gone. "I told the Ejido I needed a gardener," Bill said. "It was getting out of hand. I couldn't take care of it all. So, he [Don Hielo] came out, and we talked for two minutes, and I said, 'You're hired.'" Bill recalled the gardener loved eating fish but did not have the opportunity to get on the sea. "So, we usually gave our fish to him."

Not only had Bill taught himself to hunt with a bow while he lived in Oregon, but he was also a self-taught fly fisherman. At first, Bill did not have a fly rod at Punta Chivato and fished with regular jigs for dorado, yellowtail, and billfish. Then, he received a gift from one of his guests.

"A guy came down, a very good fly fisherman," Bill recounted. "He could cast a full line."

Bill and his guest started talking about their shared sport. This guest became a regular visitor to Punta Chivato, and Bill spent time with him every time he flew in.

"You really enjoy fly fishing, don't you?" the man remarked during one of his early visits to Punta Chivato.

"Yeah, I do," Bill replied. "A big mistake; I didn't bring a fly rod down."

"Here," said the guest, handing Bill not only the fly rod but the reel, line, the whole thing.

Bill was delighted. "That was just marvelous," he remarked, remembering the kind gesture.

With a fly rod, Bill would enjoy using blue and whiteflies and casting in the shallows over rocks for smaller fish. He said he had not had luck catching larger fish with his new rod.

Chapter 67

MACHO

Billie Brush was in Oregon visiting her mother when she decided to buy an unusual present for Bill—a bobcat kitten. "Bill had said so many times to me that he wanted a bobcat," Billie stated, defending her decision. While at her mother's home in Albany, Oregon, Billie read an advertisement for bobcat kittens in the Sunday morning newspaper. She called the owner and learned he had four, all just days old. According to the owner, the kittens needed weaning from their mother early, or they would not bond with a human. He was hand-feeding them.

"I took my mom with me, and we drove down there," recalled Billie. "Here were these little guys all in a box." The cost was $500 apiece. Although a couple of bobcat kittens were already promised to someone, the owner allowed Billie her pick since he had not yet received any money from the first buyer. She chose the smallest one. They would name him "Macho."

"He told me what kind of formula to fix for the bottles," said Billie. "You get little jars of baby food and a dry mixture and goat's milk, and you mix this stuff up and give it to him." Billie immediately went to the store, purchased all the necessary ingredients, and was soon hand-feeding her newly acquired bobcat kitten using a bottle given to her by the seller.

After a brief trip to Eugene to visit Bill's son Arnie and his family, Billie drove to San Diego en route to Punta Chivato. Along the way, she periodically stopped to feed Macho or put him on the ground so he could take care of his business. "He was so cute and so sweet," commented Billie, who quickly grew attached to the kitten.

Billie drove with Macho to the hotel in San Diego, where she and Bill often stayed. She decided it was best not to tell the hotel management about her furry companion. After getting settled, Billie called Bill in Baja. During a later interview, Bill recounted the following conversation.

"I bought you something," Billie said after Bill answered the telephone.

"What's that?" Bill asked.

"A bob-o-lynx."

"A what? I can't understand you," said Bill.

"A bob-o-lynx," Billie reiterated.

"What's a bob-o-lynx?"

"It's a cross between a bobcat and a lynx," Billie explained.

Still not sure what Billie was trying to say, Bill wrapped up the conversation and assured Billie he would meet her in San Diego.

"I drove up to San Diego and met Billie, who was holding the ugliest kitten I'd ever seen in my life," Bill recalled.

During a later interview, Bill continued to describe his first impression of Billie's gift. "He had a head that was bigger than his body," Bill said. "It kept falling over on its nose. I wondered what we were going to do with a bobcat."

The couple drove across the U.S. border into Baja without any problem. "They didn't even know I had him," said Billie. Macho stayed down in his little bed and snoozed. "He was so good," Billie recalled. "He was the cutest thing there ever was."

When they reached Punta Chivato, Bill and Billie carried Macho to Bill's room at the hotel—number 25, in the back, furthest from the ocean.

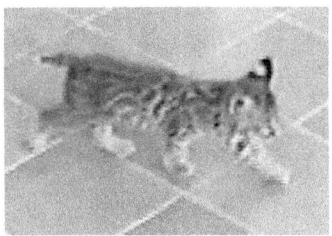

Macho as a kitten at Punta Chivato Hotel. From Nov. 1991 video
by Bill Alvarado

In the mornings, Billie carried Macho to the hotel reception desk where she worked. "I'd take him to the office and hold him with his little blanket and give him his bottle," Billie reminisced. "He bonded with me within days because I was his mother," she added. "I was the one that fed him all the time, several times a day. He was a delight."

Bill had a tail-less female Russian Blue cat who gave birth to a litter of kittens soon after Macho arrived. When the kittens grew old enough to venture away from their mother, they took note of the larger, curious-looking "cat." Bill recalled the day he let Macho outside, and the kittens fearlessly approached the odd-looking cat. "The kittens were pretty agile and wanted to come over and jump on him," said Bill. "It was really fun to watch. Lots of laughs."

Eventually, the mother cat took a liking to Macho. "I have a picture of the two of them walking side-by-side, leaning on each other," Bill said. As Macho got bigger, Bill put him on a leash. On occasion, Bill would see the mother cat "grab the leash and haul him around."

Bill hoped Macho might eventually be their "control mechanism for the *mapaches*," referring to the nightly invasion of raccoons at the hotel.

Bill and Billie Alvarado with Macho. Alvarado Christmas photo 1992

"We had so much fun watching him grow up," Bill later remarked. However, several of the homeowners at Punta Chivato did not share the couple's sentiment, especially as Macho grew bigger.

"We knew Bill loved cats, but we thought it was stupid, not a good idea," said one homeowner. "Seemed like Bill had enough problems without having a wild cat."

Eventually, Bill and Billie decided Macho needed a mate. They learned that a family in the town of Guerrero Negro had a female bobcat. The owners had gotten it when it was a baby. "They took it home and just fed it rice and beans," said Billie. "When we found out, we went up and asked to buy it. I can't remember what we paid for it. We got it and took it home." They named the female Rammie.

"Macho was absolutely beside himself. Livid with rage," said Bill, describing Macho's reaction when introduced to Rammie.

Bill and Billie quickly learned bobcats are solitary animals, only associating with each other for breeding. "They don't like each other, and they have their own territories," Bill explained.

By that time, Macho was living in a cage Bill erected by a tree next to the hotel. "We kept them separated for quite a while," recalled Bill. "When we did put her in there, he wanted to tear her to pieces. He never did warm up to her."

Most of the homeowners at Punta Chivato never warmed up to either of the bobcats.

Chapter 68

ATTEMPTED HOTEL TAKEOVER

In early 1987, a small group of homeowners from Punta Chivato secretly met in Orange County in Southern California to discuss taking over the hotel from Bill Alvarado. They had heard Bill's lease was up, and the Ejido San Bruno might not renew it. "Andy Adams, Phil Souther, and Tony Hasso planned to run it and have Tony be the onsite manager," explained one homeowner.

Bill's lease required him to complete certain improvements during a specific period. Confident he was compliant, Bill was surprised when the Ejido questioned renewing his lease. "I just brought down a new generator and had done some pretty major work around there, trying to put in a new septic system. I'd bought new uniform shirts for all the workers, those that worked in the hotel and those that worked in the shop. I connected the airstrips and got medical attention for the people and eyeglass attention," Bill said. "I had far exceeded every requirement."

Some of the younger Ejido members told Bill there was *no problema*," and assured him he would be granted a new lease after his existing one expired. However, when Bill found out some homeowners were plotting to take over the hotel, he grew concerned.

The dissenting group of homeowners arranged to have the Mexican military visit Punta Chivato to prove Bill had not fulfilled his lease requirements. "They sent the Mexican military with guns and everything out there to search all the rooms. It didn't do any good. They were full of guests," Bill said.

Bill was not the only one troubled by this news. Punta Chivato homeowners, including the first ones to build at Punta Chivato, Jeanne Winters and Rich Ream, questioned their fellow homeowners' intentions to take over the hotel. Following is a letter they mailed to PCHA president Andy Adams:

Dear Andy,

Many disturbing rumors have been circulating in Punta Chivato concerning the past and present actions of the officers of our Assoc. We are very concerned that our interests are not being fairly represented. Consequently, we feel it is time to have a Homeowners meeting in order to separate fact from fiction, to discuss the actions and proposals that have been made to various Mexican agencies, and to elect officers for the coming year.

We do hereby call a Punta Chivato Homeowners' Assoc. meeting to be held in Punta Chivato on Sat. April 18th, 1987, at 3:00 P.M. at Jeanne Winters' home. This date will allow time for everyone interested to plan, and or, make arrangements to come.

Sincerely,
Jeanne Winters
Rich Ream
Robin Converse
Robert Hilbun
Bobbie Hilbun
Mr. & Mrs. Dennis Millard (Dennis helped write this but had gone to La Paz, J.W.)
c/c all lot owners

Jeanne Fox heard about the homeowner conflict from Rick and Patsy Shoemaker, a couple from Eugene, Oregon. Like the Foxes, the Shoemakers owned a lot at Punta Chivato. "We were friends of Bill's, so we didn't get involved," said Jeanne. "I think the architect [Phil Souther] and Andy perhaps wanted to get in there and develop the whole property, do what Bill eventually did." Jeanne Fox sympathized with Bill's difficulty getting together the money needed to finish the hotel. "He was just going from hand to mouth," she said.

Doc's daughter, Marge Summers, who took over her father's lots at Punta Chivato after he died, received the following letter from Jeanne Winters urging her to come to the next homeowners' meeting or at least express her wishes about the hotel situation.

Wed., March 3, '87

Hi Marge,

2 reasons for the enclosed letter: I want to keep our assoc. out of the Hotel business, and I don't think two of our officers, Andy Adams and Kathy Lucore, can do this, or want to.

If you can't get down for the April 18 meeting, we should think about your giving me your proxies so that new officers can be elected.

Take care, Jeanne

As scheduled, a Punta Chivato Homeowners' Association meeting was held on April 18, 1987, during Easter week at the home of Rich Ream and Jeanne Winters. Although the author could not locate the minutes from that meeting, Harry Oxley summarized the heated debate.

"Andy and Phil Souther, and Tony Hasso were all working on a project to take the hotel away from Bill. I guess they thought they were going to make a zillion dollars. We had a horrible disagreement over it, a big monster row." Harry told the gathered homeowners, "I came here to relax and enjoy myself, not to run a hotel. I don't think the association should be involved in this."

By the end of the meeting, Harry Oxley was elected the new president of the PCHA. Any talk of running the hotel appeared to have been rejected, and the issue was no longer seriously considered.

It was a scare for Bill, but he ended up having his lease renewed. "They didn't get the hotel," Bill recounted. "Souther ended up having to get rid of his place, thank God. And Adams, he can go to you know where, too, where he deserves to be."

Chapter 69

LEASES REVISITED

The Americans who came to Punta Chivato were enamored of its beauty and dreamed of living on the Sea of Cortez. They trusted Bill Alvarado when he offered the original land leases and believed their stamped paperwork was valid. They assumed a signed lease was legal, just as it would have been in the United States.

In 1984, when these Americans were informed Bill Alvarado had no right to lease them the land at Punta Chivato, they were shocked. However, they assumed their concerns were over when nothing came of the situation. Bill continued to offer land leases. Three years later, however, the same issue resurfaced.

On November 15, 1987, Punta Chivato homeowners Harry Oxley, Jeanne Winters, and Robin Converse met with Ejido San Bruno representative Julian Vargas, the Ejido council, and Señor Juan Manuel Muro, the representative for the Agrarian Department in México City. The meeting was to discuss drawing up another lease for the Punta Chivato leaseholders.

After the meeting, Harry Oxley, then president of the PCHA, wrote a multi-page letter to the Punta Chivato homeowners.[134] In it, he explained the specifics of the new lease proposed by the Ejido San Bruno and the Agrarian Department.

Contrary to the previous federal representative who arrived in 1984 and informed the homeowners their original leases with Bill were invalid, Señor Muro told them those original contracts were legal. The plan was to replace them with different leases.

Each new lease would be between the individual homeowner and the Ejido San Bruno, eliminating Bill Alvarado and Hotel Punta Chivato from the transaction. This new partnership agreement, *Contrato de Asociación en Participación* (Association Contract in Participation), would be for a term of 20 years.

After signing the contract, those who leased one or more lots at Punto Chivato would have one year to start building. If the homeowner did not start building in one year or complete construction within three, the Ejido could cancel the contract and repossess the property. The new contract could also be terminated if the homeowner intervened in the Ejido's business or if both parties agreed to terminate it.

"Basically, it was a land-use agreement from the Agrarian Department for a three-year lease and a 17-year business agreement," Les Conner later explained. Once the building had started, "you had three years to construct the house, and you had 17 years to recoup your investment," Les Conner clarified. "Our responsibility was to construct a house."

The proposed lease required all plans for new homes to be submitted to a commission formed by the homeowners and the Ejido members. Construction could not commence until the commission authorized and approved the plans.

Per the new agreement, the Ejido had the first opportunity to bid for labor and services for home construction. However, the Americans were only obliged to use local labor and materials if their "price and quality was as good or better than what you can solicit elsewhere."

Services previously provided by Bill, such as water, roads, airports, and electricity, were not included in the new contract and would remain the responsibility of the Hotel Punta Chivato. Any negotiations regarding these amenities would be directly between the leaseholders and the management of Hotel Punta Chivato, that is, Bill Alvarado.

Señor Muro said he was authorized to allocate thirty new contracts for the thirty lots Bill had leased. Once the leaseholders had signed, the federal representative promised to send the contracts to México City for final approval. Signing the new agreement would nullify the original contract made with Bill Alvarado.

The proposed new lease agreement was not a simple transfer from the original lease. The Americans were to complete an application that included an estimate of their lot's square footage and proposed home. Those who had already built on their lot needed to provide their current square footage. Any additional construction for an airplane hangar, extra parking for vehicles, or an extra garage for boat storage had to be listed. The Americans were reminded that the federal zone was not incorporated as part of their square footage and could not be leased.[135]

Harry Oxley's November letter highlighted several areas of "severe" concern to him and the other Americans present at the meeting. One issue related to the date on the new lease. "We felt that the lease should be dated upon signing and not backdated to the original lease time as specified in the new lease," Harry wrote in his letter.[136]

The new lease proposal included an additional cost per year and an annual percentage increase over the term of each contract. The ejido proposed $1.50 a day, plus an 8% annual increase. "That comes up to in excess of $25,000.00. This is obviously unacceptable!"

Harry's letter continued:

We have proposed that the Ejido consider a $1.00 a day or $365.00 a year with a 2 or 3 percent a year increase. That still works out to $10,000.00 over a 20-year period, but that seems much more acceptable.

Another concern was the cost of the lease at the end of the twenty-year term. The contract called for a guaranteed lease renewal if the lessee had conformed to all the terms. However, the price of the lease renewal was not indicated. The Americans were informed that the cost at the time of renewal could not be written into the contract—it just could not be done.

The lessee could transfer the property to another individual before the end of the twenty-year agreement as a sublease, or the Ejido could approve the transfer and write a new lease. If a homeowner chose not to renew at the end of the twenty-year agreement, the contract specified a period of 60 days to move out.

In the case of death, the contract would go to the heirs specified by the homeowner. If the property was destroyed by an act of nature, such as a hurricane or earthquake, the Ejido could draw up a contract for a new lot.

The Americans questioned the fairness of the proposed system for settling disagreements. Per the new contract, all disputes would be settled by cooperation between the Ejido and the homeowner. If the issue could not be resolved, the Agrarian Department would arbitrate. The document stated the lessees would have to accept the

Agrarian Department's decision and waive any right to go to a higher authority such as the courts.

Harry also expressed the following in his November letter to the leaseholders at Punta Chivato:

> *We are waiving our rights to the legal process and accepting the arbitration of the Agrarian Department, which represents the Ejido in the first place.*
>
> *Obviously, none of us have the right to accept or reject any offer, but we will make our best effort to present you with something you can live with.*

On the evening of November 18, 1987, a follow-up meeting was held with the Ejido San Bruno and the Agrarian Department representatives. The Americans present were Harry Oxley, Jeanne Winters, Robin Converse, and Larry and Kathy Lucore. After three days of mulling over the information they received at the previous meeting, the Americans shared their concerns about the lease and offered potential solutions. They hoped they could sway the Ejido to make some clarifications and changes to the proposed contract.

The Ejido representative, Julian Vargas, did not want to back down from the proposed additional fees of $1.50 a day plus an 8% annual increase on each lease. After a long debate, participants decided to meet again the following evening. The Americans still had not seen an English translation of the new proposed lease. The Ejido's translator, Beto, had not been available. Larry Lucore was waiting to hear back from a translator in San Diego. Reading a translation of the new lease in English before signing was important to the Americans.

At 4:00 p.m. on November 19, 1987, Harry Oxley heard a knock on his door. When he opened it, there stood Julian Vargas and Señor Muro. They informed Harry that Beto was still unavailable to translate the document. In addition, Julian said there was no use holding another meeting that night to discuss the amount of the yearly assessment without more leaseholders present.

The meeting was rescheduled for December 5. All lessees were encouraged to attend to discuss the proposed new lease with Julian Vargas and Señor Muro. In bold letters, Harry wrote to the American homeowners:

IF YOU POSSIBLY CAN, PLEASE BE HERE ON THE 5TH. THAT WILL PROBABLY BE THE MEETING THAT DETERMINES THE TERMS OF OUR NEW CONTRACT WITH EJIDO SAN BRUNO.

"We all met together up there at the hotel," recalled Dale Dryer about that day in December 1987. "We had been here three years and had just finished paying off the house."

The discussion went back and forth regarding the specifics of the agreement. Afterward, everyone had to sign papers. Although not stated in the lease agreement, Dale Dryer remembered, "Part of those negotiations was Julian Vargas claiming he was going to get a truck every year." Les Conner echoed that understanding, "Julian wanted in good faith for us to give him a new truck every year."

After the establishment of new leases by the Ejido San Bruno and the Mexican Agrarian Department in 1987, the Americans understood that real estate transactions made in the United States and those made in México, particularly Baja, were different. Once again, the leaseholders received documents that appeared to have been authorized by the Mexican government. The pages of their leases had signatures and many official-looking stamps, just like the original lease papers. However, were these new leases indeed valid?

For transactions to be legal in México, they had to go through the proper channels in México City. Although Señor Muro made a point of assuring the Americans he would do this, his follow-through was later questioned. Les Conner believed all 33 documents were sent, but some were not returned.

In 1989, when Greg and Pam Joy were interested in building in Punta Chivato, they hired an attorney from México City to review everything before construction commenced. The lawyer investigated in both México City and La Paz. He informed them the leases had been sent to La Paz, the capital of Baja California Sur, but not to México City.

"Our lawyer went back to México City and called me and said, 'Listen. You're not going to get any better than they're negotiating right now. It's not going to be okayed across the pond [in México City], but it's going to be okayed in La Paz. Don't get me involved in that. I'll just mess it up.'"

"Too much was at stake for the Ejido to have the homeowners leave," Greg Joy speculated. "Somehow, Julian Vargas, a very clever man, worked to have the leases recorded in La Paz. They were never sent to México City."

The lease issue would not come up for another six years, at which time considerable changes would be made to Mexican real estate laws.

Chapter 70

WINDSURFING

As windsurfing became popular, sailboarders soon found their way to Punta Chivato. Due to its location and topography, the winds off the point offered ideal conditions for avid so-called "board heads," especially during the winter months.

In the summer, winds along the eastern side of the Baja peninsula generally came from the south or southeast. However, when high-pressure weather systems developed over the southwestern United States in winter, the winds came from the north. From December through February, the north winds could be strong and last up to a week. While not conducive to fishing, diving, boating, or kayaking, they provided excellent speed sailing conditions and lured enthusiastic windsurfers.

Jutting out into the Sea of Cortez and having a relatively flat topography, Punta Chivato offered an area with strong, steady winds. In addition, the sandy beaches along the shores of Punta Chivato allowed boarders to rig their sails and enter the shallow water easily.

Bill Alvarado took notice of the increasing number of people who arrived at Punta Chivato with windsurfing boards and colorful sails. He decided to provide an on-site sailboard operation and used Excursions Extraordinaires out of Eugene, Oregon. They loaned out equipment and provided instruction. In addition, this company offered package windsurf trips. Boarding a DC-3 from Brown's Field Airport in San Diego, California, guests were flown to the dirt airstrip at Punta Chivato.

A brochure about the company listed consecutive weekly tour dates from December 19 to 26, 1989, through February 17 to 24, 1990. The cost of each tour was $795 for windsurfers and $545 for non-windsurfers. The price included lodging and three daily meals at Hotel Punta Chivato, unlimited use of boardsailing equipment, and instruction in technique.

The Windsurf Baja Center, commonly referred to as the "windsurf shack," was set up between the hotel and the boat ramp. Here, the latest windsurfing equipment was available—boards and sails of all sizes. Walk-ins who did not arrive as part of the Excursions Extraordinaires package deal could rent gear. This luxury afforded those already proficient in the sport the option of leaving their cumbersome gear home. In addition to windsurfing equipment, the concession offered mountain bikes, snorkeling gear, and kayaks for rent.[137]

Windsurfer heading out from beach; Hotel Punta Chivato in background.
From 1991 video by Bill Alvarado

The following was in the company's promotional brochure:

The Windsurf Baja Center at Punta Chivato represents the best of Baja México! With Baja's sunny climate and incredible expanses of pristine, warm water…you have the ingredients for one of the most popular winter windsurfing destinations in the world!

Novice windsurfers were encouraged to arrive at the windsurf shack in the morning when the winds were milder. More advanced speed-sailors came out after mid-morning when the winds picked up. The Santa Inez Bay off Punta Chivato offered flat water conditions, preferable for beginners and speed sailors alike. The reaches could be several miles long parallel to the beach. Advanced windsurfers who wanted the challenge of sailing waves could venture further north.

Windsurf sails provided by Excursions Extraordinaires at Punta Chivato.
Courtesy Greg Joy

A support boat was available to help tow the windsurfer and equipment back to the beach if a sailboarder got into trouble.[138] This was extremely important since the winds blew offshore, and any sailor in trouble could be blown further away from shore into the Sea of Cortez. Windsurfing can quickly become dangerous, especially if the boarder's ability does not match the wind conditions.

As an avid windsurfer, homeowner Greg Joy remembers windsurfing at Punta Chivato one day in November in the 1990s and getting involved in a rescue that almost proved fatal. "After a day of good windsurfing, I packed up my gear because the wind was way too strong," he recounted. "The sand was blowing in our eyes." An American wearing shorts approached him.

"My girlfriend has done a stupid thing," said the concerned American. "She got on her board, and she can't get the sail up, and she's floating out toward somewhere."

The camper explained that his girlfriend was a brand-new windsurfer and unfamiliar with sailing in such high winds. She had launched her rig from the camping beach, not knowing the waters off that area could be choppy and the winds strong. Her boyfriend kept an eye on her, but she disappeared as the winds picked up. Frantically, he drove to the hotel to ask for Bill's help.

Bill radioed his boatman, Miguel Romo. The young man was to meet him at the boat launch.

"I got a wetsuit on; I'll jump in with you," Greg told the camper when Miguel arrived with the boat. Surprisingly, Miguel headed the boat right to the woman. "It was amazing," Greg later commented. "I was trying to plot where she would go with my sailing experience, and I would have gone totally to the wrong place. Miguel knew exactly where the person was."

Greg went over the side of the boat to help the woman. "Even though we were drifting out, she didn't want to come aboard unless the sailboard was on the boat because she just paid for it and wasn't going to let it go," said Greg. "So, we got her in the boat, and I helped get the board on. During the process, the waves made it dangerous. Miguel let the boat drift away leaving me in the water while they secured the woman and her board."

"Miguel came back for me fast, but he didn't see me. He was about to whack me with the front of the boat," recalled Greg. "Miguel then cut the engine while I pushed the boat away. The waves were large, and I was being pushed up above the level of the gunnel and down in the troughs. Miguel took off again to avoid hitting me and I lost track of them again."

This scenario occurred several times. "I got worried," said Greg. "I didn't understand what was going on. He would go away for two or three or four or five minutes. He'd come back, and the same thing happened."

Miguel was notorious for his temper, and he grew angrier with each failed attempt to get Greg back into the boat. The thought crossed Greg's mind that Miguel might leave and not return.

Miguel did not speak English and could not convey to Greg that the boat's engine was malfunctioning. Miguel put the bow rope over the side. "So, he's trying to drive up past me so that when the engine quits, I'll grab it," Greg later recounted. "Of course, every time I see him coming up, I think he's nuts, and I push the bow off.

"Finally, somehow, they get the information to me that the engine's dying," said Greg. At the next pass, Miguel throttled back, and Greg grabbed the rope and pulled himself into the boat. Then the engine quit. It would not idle.

Miguel could not get the engine going again, and the boat with four people and the girlfriend's windsurf gear began to drift. Miguel quickly got out the anchor, lowered it into the water, and focused on getting the motor going.

"The girl and her boyfriend onboard began to go nuts," recounted Greg. "The guy was sure he was going to freeze to death."

Bill Alvarado grew concerned when Miguel did not return in the expected amount of time. He decided to take another boat and go out to look for them. "He gets very close to us but doesn't see us," recalled Greg. "Bill went all the way to Conception Point and back and missed us because the sun was going down, and he was looking right into the sun, and we were, of course, in the sun's light." Bill returned to the hotel.

The sun set, and darkness fell. *I'm sure we're going to spend the whole night here*, Greg remembered thinking.

Miguel spotted shrimp boats a distance away, picked up an oar, and started waving it at them. "I thought he was crazy," said Greg. "There was no way that those guys were going to see him. But the shrimp boats gradually turned, came around, and found us."

The foursome eagerly climbed aboard the shrimp boat and were provided shrimp and brandy to help warm up. Meanwhile, the shrimp boat captain got ahold of Bill on the radio. Bill motored out again, got everyone into his boat, and towed the faulty boat back to Punta Chivato. "We'd had enough Don Pedro brandy to make getting back onto the boat very difficult. This was probably the most dangerous part of the ordeal," Greg later jested.

Once they returned to the beach, Greg stayed and helped Bill and Miguel tie off the boats while the couple left. Greg went home and later returned to the hotel for dinner with his wife, Pam. In the restaurant, a football game was being telecast. "I can remember the Rams were playing the 49ers," recounted Greg, who grew up in La Habra Heights in Southern California and was an avid Rams fan at the time. "The Rams couldn't get into the Super Bowl, but the 49ers could if the Rams didn't beat them, and the Rams were ahead. As soon as I arrived, the Rams fell apart, and the 49ers won."

While Greg and Pam were eating dinner, the windsurfing couple Greg had helped earlier came past their table. The boyfriend leaned over and said to Greg, "What took you so damn long?" Neither Bill nor Greg ever received an acknowledgment or a "thank you" from those campers following that risky windsurf rescue.

"Bill was like the Punta Chivato Coast Guard," said Greg. "He just did it without question. He'd get in the boat and risk his life in the middle of the night."

Chapter 71

BILLIE & BOYS DEPORTED

"In the fall of 1989, the Ejido, especially Julian Vargas, raised a big stink about me and Arnie and Jeff working at the hotel," recalled Billie Brush. "We didn't have our green cards, which was true. All we had was visas." According to Billie, the hotel was doing well, and the Ejido president, Julian Vargas, wanted to get rid of as many Americans working there as he could. "He went to La Paz to get me, Jeff, and Arnie kicked out of the country."

Although Billie and the Alvarado boys went to plead their case in La Paz, the capital of Baja California Sur, they were told to leave México. Billie felt it was "absolutely horrendous" to leave Bill alone at Punta Chivato.

Billie drove to San Diego, where she lived with friends for several months while trying to regain access to México. "I immediately contacted a Mexican attorney in México City that delved into immigration problems," said Billie. "She flew in and out of San Diego all the time and said she'd fly into San Diego and meet with me."

On the agreed-upon day, Billie met with the Mexican attorney. She took a Mexican friend with her who spoke excellent English. "I wanted to make sure that somebody could hear everything and understand everything," Billie recalled. During the meeting, she explained her predicament—she and Bill's sons had been working at Punta Chivato without green cards and were "booted out of the country" by the president of the Ejido San Bruno.

"How do I go about going back down with legal paperwork?" Billie implored.

"I can do it for you, but it will take some time," the attorney responded. "It will cost you $4,000. I want two of it now, and I'll wait and get the other two when I get all the paperwork for you. If I don't get the paperwork for you, then I'll give you your $2,000 back."

The attorney explained to Billie, "You know things get tied up on this desk and on that desk; things move very slowly."

Billie had no alternative. She gave the attorney $2,000 and then waited to hear back from her.

"She kept in touch with me by phone," said Billie. "That was in November, and by April or May of the following year, she had all my legal paperwork." The attorney returned to San Diego and again met with Billie. After receiving documents granting her re-entry into México, Billie gave the attorney the additional $2,000 as agreed upon.

Billie knew if she tried to return without the proper paperwork, she would have another confrontation with the president of the Ejido. "I didn't want to ever have a problem again with Julian," she said.

Billie finally returned to Punta Chivato six months after being deported from Baja. Bill's sons were also eventually allowed to reenter Baja.[139]

Chapter 72

RAÚL LUJÁN

One weekend in 1989, a King Air landed on the airstrip at a secluded ranch five miles from San Francisquito in northeast Baja California. The beautiful ranch, said to have been once owned by actor John Wayne, was now the property of three of Wayne's friends from Newport Beach, California. They planned to turn it into an exclusive retreat.

John Lyddon, the pilot of the King Air, came to the ranch to speak to a young home builder named Raúl Luján.

"We were in the middle of nowhere," recalled Raúl, who described the ranch as being at the end of a tiny dirt road 120 kilometers from the Bay of Los Angeles (Bay of L.A.). "Everything had to be delivered from the Bay of L.A. or Guerrero Negro, which was five hours away through the mountains," said Raúl. "Sometimes, we didn't go out for two to three weeks."

The Mexican builder became accustomed to seeing private planes fly in and out of the ranch. "All rich guys landed their jets in Hermosillo and flew in in King Airs or little planes to the ranch," Raúl remarked. "It was quite an experience to build there," he added. But he was surprised when the pilot of the King Air approached him.

"Want to have a few beers?" the pilot asked. "I want you to build me a house."

"I don't know you," Raúl responded, surprised by the brashness of the pilot. "Who are you?"

"Oh, I'm a friend of the owner here, and I've been checking you out," said John Lyddon. "Jump in the plane and let me buy you lunch. I want you to see my piece of property."

John ended up flying Raúl and his engineer partner, Francisco, south to Punta Chivato, where John had leased two adjoining lots between the short runway and the Santa Inez Bay, Lots #14 and #15 in Subdivision 1. John Lyddon, whose primary residence was in Bakersfield, California, was in the oil business.

"That day, I enjoyed meeting Bill Alvarado and saw the job he was doing at the hotel," Raúl recalled. "He invited me to come back and spend a weekend there."

Raúl was familiar with the Conception Bay/Mulegé area south of Punta Chivato. As a teenager, he camped there with his family. Later, after Raúl got married, he took his family to vacation in Mulegé once a year. "We always thought about someday having enough money to retire early to this area," Raúl said.

Raúl knew Punta Chivato existed at the end of a dirt road off Baja 1, north of Mulegé. But he had never ventured out there before. The day John Lyddon flew Raúl Luján to Punta Chivato would begin a long association and friendship between the two men.

Raúl Obregón Soberanes was born in 1959 in the northwestern state of Sinaloa on mainland México. He was his parents' first child. A second son, José, was born in 1967. Raúl's father's family roots were in Guanajuato and Sonora, México. His ancestry included Álvaro Obregón, the president of México from 1920 to 1924.

Raúl was 12 years old when his parents separated. He and his brother moved in with their grandmother in the state of Sinaloa, where Raúl completed *secondario* (high school). The boys' father eventually died in the state of Sonora.

Their mother relocated to start a new life in Via Constitución in Baja California Sur, México. She met and married Señor Luján, who owned a ranch in Via Constitución and ran a store in Tijuana called *Cinco y Diez* (Five & Ten). Mr. Luján eventually adopted Raúl and his brother, re-registering them with the name "Luján" in place of "Obregón." The Lujáns had a son together whom they named Chris.

After high school, Raúl moved to La Paz for schooling. Later, he returned to the mainland, where he enrolled in a civil engineering school in Aguascalientes, a city in the interior of México.

In the late 1970s, after Raúl's parents sold their ranch in Via Constitución, Raúl moved with them to Rosarito Beach on the Pacific side of northern Baja California. Raúl commuted from Rosarito Beach to Tijuana (about twenty miles northeast), where he continued his schooling, switching his major from civil engineering to architecture.

Raúl disagreed with his parents' decision to sell the ranch, and friction developed between them. They refused to help him financially, so he began to work part-time. Not owning a car, Raúl took the bus from Rosarito Beach to school in Tijuana. He never received his degree.

Raúl began working full-time for Carlos Teran, a developer in Rosarito, a coastal resort town ten miles south of the U.S.-Baja border. Raúl was hired as the hotel manager of Tito del Mar, a complex founded by Carlos Teran that included not only a hotel but also a residential area. Raúl soon began contract work building houses. Although both Raúl's parents were fluent in English, his English improved through working for Americans in Rosarito Beach.

One of the homes Raúl built at Rosarito Beach was for a couple from the United States. They had leased a home in the area for years but, now retired, they wanted to reside there permanently. Raúl soon met the couple's daughter, Kim, a single parent with two young sons. She and Raúl fell in love and were married in 1980. Raúl officially adopted Kim's two sons, Bobby and Jeffrey, and they were given the Luján surname. In 1989, Raúl and Kim had a child, a daughter they named Rebecca.

Through Carlos Teran, Raúl met an architect and an engineer from the Palm Springs area in California. They were creating an exclusive compound in Rosarito Beach named *Castillos del Mar* (Castles of the Sea). Raúl went to work exclusively for them, under the architect's supervision.

In the mid-1980s, Raúl was hired to build a home for Bruce Eicher, a well-known lighting and artistic designer in the Beverly Hills and West Hollywood areas. Raúl attributes much of what he learned to Bruce Eicher, who in 1963 established a design firm in West Hollywood called Bruce Eicher, Inc. Raúl recounted the Baja California home he constructed for Eicher. "It took four years to build this mansion on the beach. Everything was built with antiques that he bought in México and put together to build his dream house. We did a real great job on it." The architectural effects and details inspired Raúl. He took note of the antique furniture and lighting Eicher incorporated.

"He [Bruce] invited me to work with him and learn the business and become his partner," said Raúl. "We were the first antique designer shop in Rosarito Beach, named Sticks and Stones." Raúl enjoyed traveling to southern México to buy items for the business. "Designers and people that are building in California come down to Rosarito Beach to buy stuff for their houses—tiles, antique furniture," Raúl added.

"Originally, Sticks and Stones was just a warehouse and finishing facility—carpentry, some stone carvers, that only worked for us," explained Raúl. "Ninety-five percent of the stuff that we had in the stores was exclusively to be shipped to showrooms."

Before faxes, texts, and e-mails, interested businesses could only view the warehouse inventory using a catalog. "We had a catalog with every item from a doorknob to a door or a fountain—everything was numbered and photographed three times," said Raúl, indicating there were catalogs "in my office, one was in the factory or warehouse, and the other catalog was in the L.A. office." Sales were generally made by telephone, referring to the catalog. "I could not tell people we would sell to the public," Raúl added.

However, there were exceptions when the warehouse was opened to exclusive clients. One Sunday morning, a beautiful woman who was always trying to buy things directly came to the warehouse, hoping to purchase some items. She was thrilled to find Raúl there and asked if she could come in and look around, hoping to make purchases from the warehouse floor. Raúl checked with his partner and got permission to sell directly to the woman.

The woman was a designer and antique collector from Newport Beach, California. She ended up buying a substantial number of accessories, hand-carved stone, old boards, and antique furniture. The following week, she returned and bought more, requesting that Raúl ship it all to Newport Beach.

"When I delivered the stuff to Newport Beach, I discovered that there was this huge warehouse almost the size of the Dodger Stadium," said Raúl. "They were gathering and collecting stuff from all over México and the United States for an exclusive residential development. I thought it was Malibu or Palm Springs, but to my astonishment, it was in Cabo San Lucas." Raúl later learned the purchases were for the Palmilla Hotel in Cabo San Lucas. The woman who purchased the items was the daughter of the owner of that famous hotel at the tip of the Baja peninsula.[140]

Raúl Luján's artistic abilities and ambition impressed the

woman's father. He asked Raúl if he wanted to join his daughter in business, move to Cabo, and work for them in the Cabo area. When Raúl declined the offer, the father said, "Will you build a house for one of my friends down in another place?"

"So, I went to build for a crazy group of three businessmen from Newport Beach," recalled Raúl, speaking of how he ended up at the secluded ranch where he met John Lyddon.

Raúl was ready to leave Rosarito Beach. "Rosarito Beach developed really crazy," said Raúl. "It was growing so bad that lower, middle-class, and some high-end investors and nice families who wanted to buy a place could only get condos."

All through the 1980s, Raúl watched as the once artisan town began to change. "The town started taking a direction of being a come-and-drink town, and I didn't want my kids to grow up there," Raúl recalled. "We always thought about going south. We thought about Bay of L.A. for a while, go there and do something fun, invest some money," he added. But it was a town further south along the Sea of Cortez where Raúl and his family chose to relocate.

"I was always attracted to Mulegé," said Raúl, fondly recalling the time he spent there on vacation as a boy. Raúl had a close friend who lived in Mulegé named Ricardo Castillo, who owned *Villas de Mulegé*. "He always told me about Chivato," Raúl recounted. "He was very good friends with Bill Alvarado. He delivered all the red roof tiles, clay tiles for Bill. I helped him buy it in Tecate and Rosarita Beach." Ricardo also told Raúl that "some crazy *gringos* were building big houses out there with no planning, no nothing."

Raúl's friend had earlier invited him to visit Punta Chivato, but Raúl was always too busy. "So, I never thought that I would some-day fly into Punta Chivato with my friend, John," said Raúl in an interview. "And that's how everything began."

Raúl did not immediately commit to building John Lyddon's vacation home in Punta Chivato. He was still working on the house at the exclusive ranch up north. In addition, Raúl's wife and children lived in Rosarita Beach, far from John's building location. Raúl recounted a call from John one Friday in autumn while he was home spending time with his family.

"I want to see you on Sunday around noon to see my blueprints," said John, calling from his boat moored at Cabo San Lucas.

Raúl knew John was not requesting his presence at Punta Chivato; he expected it. "To him, it is—'I'll see you there,'" said Raúl.

Raúl decided to take his sons with him. On a Saturday evening, Raúl, his son, Bobby, age 8, and his son, Jeffrey, age 5, boarded a public bus in Ensenada and headed south on Baja 1. The bus was to arrive in Mulegé at 9:00 Sunday morning. Raúl had arranged with his Mulegé friend, Castillo, to borrow a truck to drive to Punta Chivato to meet John, who would fly in from Cabo San Lucas. Raúl felt he was allowing plenty of time.

"The bus broke down somewhere in San Ignacio and was there for two or three hours," recalled Raúl. "It was very early in the morning, and it was freezing."

When the bus finally arrived in Mulegé, Raúl found the truck Castillo had left for him to use. The vehicle was far from ideal. "We get in this junk piece of truck to drive to Chivato," he recalled. "It was my first time I ever drove to Chivato."

The truck Castillo loaned to Raúl turned out to be as unreliable as the bus they had traveled in earlier that morning. They left Mulegé and turned off Baja 1 to Punta Chivato at Palo Verde. But only a short distance down the dirt road past Palo Verde, the truck abruptly stopped. "The truck broke down completely," said Raúl. "The engine threw a piston."

Twice within 24 hours, Raúl had faced unexpected delays in his journey. However, the tenacious builder was not one to give up. Raúl told the boys they would walk the rest of the way to Punta Chivato.

"We walked about 2-1/2 hours," Raúl remembered, thankful that it was not in the heat of summer.

Finally, Raúl saw John's King Air fly overhead toward Punta Chivato.

"We got it, kids. He's still there," Raúl encouragingly announced to his sons.

"We started to almost run," Raúl related. "I thought the kids were going to die on me. You know, with no water, no nothing. The kids were red."

When he spotted houses in the distance, Raúl decided to leave the old road and cut across toward them.

"We see a car, the hotel van, coming toward the airport and people getting in the airplane, and we started to run," Raúl continued. John was taxiing north to take off when he noticed the three figures running across the runway. "He saw us, and he turned around and took us back to the hotel and gave us lemonade," said Raúl. "He was very nice to my kids. He bought us lunch."

"What are you doing now?" John asked Raúl after they had finished lunch and discussed the blueprints.

"Well, we're going to go back to Mulegé and spend the night and go back to Tijuana in a couple days," Raúl answered.

"Forget the truck," said John, according to Raúl. "I'll give you 1,000 bucks, and you can buy him [Castillo] another one. Let's take your kids home. We'll go to Tijuana."

Bill's mechanic, Javier, picked up Castillo's broken-down truck while Raúl contacted his long-time friend and told him what had transpired. "He always jokes about it," Raúl laughed, recalling the truck his friend loaned him breaking down in the desert.

"We board the airplane, and we go back home," said Raúl. His wife, Kim, was surprised to see them so soon. "There were no phones then, no cell phones, no nothing," Raúl added, remembering those earlier times. After dropping off his sons, Raúl and John continued to Tijuana.

"It's very funny when I tell the story of Chivato, and my kids now are grown up and very active in Chivato," reflected Raúl about the first time he brought his sons to Punta Chivato. "It was exciting for the boys. They would never forget that weekend, especially the way John treated them."

"It took us about three months to design John's house," recalled Raúl, "and for me to make a decision to build it." By the fall of 1989, Raúl and John had agreed on how to build his house. "We came back several times to Chivato with him," Raúl added.

"John was very trustful, and he built his house with nothing," recalled Raúl, knowing the issues with leases at Punta Chivato. "He had a receipt on a napkin. That's all he had."

"You know, you have absolutely nothing," Raúl recalled telling John about this lease with Bill Alvarado. "You have a lease contract in somebody else's name but a different lot." Raúl pointed out to John that his lot number was 22 on the contract, but he had negotiated for lots 14 and 15.

"I don't care," John responded to Raúl's warnings. "I love the area, I love the view from my lot, I paid for it, I trust Bill. Build it."

"I started to build his house for him when he had nothing," recalled Raúl. "That was in 1990."

John believed in Bill Alvarado and in México and did not hesitate to have Raúl build his beautiful two-story dream home on the Sea of Cortez at Punta Chivato.

Chapter 73

RAÚL'S SKILLS NOTICED

After Raúl built John Lyddon's home at Punta Chivato, Frank "Scoop" and Bonnie Vessels hired him to construct their house.[141] Like John Lyddon, the Vessels had selected a double lot in Subdivision 1 near the short airstrip. The Vessels' land was initially leased to Billie Brush. They had Lots #16 and #17, and John Lyddon had Lots #14 and #15.

Raúl Luján impresses Americans eager to build homes at Punta Chivato.

From Nov. 1991 video by Bill Alvarado

Raúl's creativity and excellent artistry were evident in each home he built. These included several on the bluff north of Hotel Punta Chivato, all in Subdivision 2. Among these were Greg and Pam Joy's home on Lot #1 and three homes near the camping beach: Walter and Jeanne Fox's home on Lot #21, Bob and Bev Busse's home on Lot #14, and Colin and Penny Vowles's home on Lot #10.

"He did a very nice job on them," commented long-time Punta Chivato resident Harry Oxley. "He had a partner when he started out who was really a neat guy. Then, that partner went away. They had a disagreement or something."

Walter and Jeanne Fox leased a lot in Punta Chivato long before they decided to build their home. They applied the $2,000 they had given Bill Alvarado for a timeshare, which never materialized, to the lot. They also offered him their Boston Whaler.

The land Walter favored was a secluded point located north along the coast. Jeanne, however, preferred the lot where they would eventually build, located above the camping beach. Bill originally promised that lot to someone else but offered it to the Foxes when the investor did not come through with the down payment. "That's how we got the lot," Jeanne said during an interview at her home in Oregon years later. "I think that was the best lot out there."

At first, Jeanne did not want to have an entire house constructed in Punta Chivato. She felt more comfortable building a garage where they could stay when they visited the area. One of Walter's partners in oral surgery, Rick Shoemaker, and his wife, Patsy, had built a garage on the lot they leased near the boat launch ramp, Lot #1, Section 1.

"Shoemakers had a garage down there, and they were living in that, and that was working out just fine," recalled Jeanne Fox. "So, I said to my dear husband and Bill, 'Well, if it will help, we'll build a garage, and then we'll go from there.'"

Shoemaker's garage; later part of Casa Powell; Oberto's home (right); built and previously owned by Oregonians McVays, Nidiffers, and Hortons.
Courtesy George Powell

Walter contacted Chaparro, the builder others were using at that time in Punta Chivato.

"The next thing we get a phone call from Bill," said Jeanne Fox, who was then back in Oregon.

"Send money!" said Bill.

"Why?" asked Jeanne, wondering what their friend Bill was up to now.

"Well, Chaparro put in the foundation for your house," replied Bill.

"He'd seen Walter's plan, and Chaparro went ahead and built the foundation plus the garage," said Jeanne with a chuckle. "So, we were committed. That was '79."

It was not until Raúl Luján arrived in Punta Chivato ten years later that the Foxes started building their home on the bluff. "I was walking on the beach one day with one of my friends, and I saw the big white house down at the end," said Jeanne, referring to the home Raúl was building for John Lyddon. "I went up to the guys who were working, and I asked who was building it." It turned out that the person Jeanne asked responded to her in English. It was Raúl Luján himself. Jeanne asked Raúl if he would be interested in looking at their house plans.

"I didn't want a Chaparro house," said Jeanne. "I didn't want the kind of house he built. If I was going to build something, I wanted it to look nice."

After reviewing the Foxes' house plans, Raúl agreed to build it. "That's when we committed ourselves to it," Jeanne said.

Starting with the footprint of the house put in by Chaparro, Raúl began construction on the home in 1989. The Foxes were impressed by Raúl and his ability to keep things moving. In addition, he had an engineer on the job. "He was such a nice guy," Jeanne said. "Raúl had some good people working for him, a good crew."

Jeanne was particularly impressed by the resources and connections Raúl had both in the United States and Baja. Raúl suggested unique building materials, including timbers from the Roseburg Lumber Company in Oregon[142] large, wooden beams from the old copper mine in Santa Rosalía,[143] and fancy tile from Tijuana. Walter picked out the beautiful tile they used on the floors and walls. Raúl was able to get enough of the tile to finish almost all the bedrooms with it. He also used white tile left over from John Lyddon's home.

"Raúl, being Mexican, had connections with the Ejido," commented Harry Oxley. "He knew who to take care of. He made real good money off it, too. He didn't do this out of the kindness of his heart."

Jeanne Fox at newly constructed home in Punta Chivato.
From Nov. 1991 video by Bill Alvarado

Raúl and his crew completed Walter and Jeanne's home in close to six months. Bill Alvarado described his long-time friends' home as a "small hotel."

"We moved in in 1990," said Jeanne. "After '93, we started spending part of the winter down there and were able to do that for about eight or nine years. We started spending about five months of the year."

Fox home above camping beach at Punta Chivato.
From Nov. 1991 video by Bill Alvarado

View of camping beach from wrap-around porch of Fox home.
From Nov. 1991 video by Bill Alvarado

Chapter 74

ACCIDENTS IN PARADISE

Like his predecessors, Bill Alvarado witnessed several accidents involving airplanes at Punta Chivato. When such unfortunate mishaps occurred, Bill either observed them or was one of the first to be informed. As the hotel owner, he took responsibility for notifying the Mexican authorities and helping handle the immediate situation.

"A couple of them lost a wheel on takeoff," Bill recalled, noting most incidents were not life-threatening. Others had rough landings and incurred damage to their airplanes. "We had three guys who came in from Clearlake to fish. They crashed but were able to get their plane fixed so they could get it out of there."

"The only plane accident that involved fatalities at our place was the one with the two couples: the father, son, and their two girlfriends," Bill said. He indicated the man's "wife thought he and their son were just going to Punta Chivato on a little fishing trip" and "she had no idea they had ladies along."

Billie Brush was working at the hotel reception desk that day and shared her recollection of the incident. "The father had called ahead of time and made reservations for about ten or twelve rooms, and a whole group came in," she said. The two couples had breakfast at the hotel and then told Billie they planned to go to Mulegé to get fuel. "They were going to stay longer, so they hadn't checked out."

To Billie's surprise, they got into the plane, and rather than head south toward Mulegé, the pilot started flying around in circles. "Some of their friends were taking pictures of them," Billie recalled.

"I was in the room and heard RRMMM," added Bill. "What was that? I thought a car had run into a building."

When Billie heard the noise, she ran outside to the ravine between the hotel and Casa Grande. A cluster of people had already gathered, looking over the edge where the plane had rammed nose-first into the solid bluff above the water.

"It came absolutely dead straight in," Bill recalled of the sight before him. "The plane didn't tip over; it was still angled."

"I still to this day don't know what they were attempting to do because I didn't see it," said Bill, who speculated the pilot "got too close to the ground, couldn't pull it up and went into a stall."

"I think they were showing off because people were taking pictures," Billie surmised of the pilot's actions, which sadly proved fatal to all on board.

The passengers in the plane's back seat did not have seat belts and were thrown past the two occupants of the front seats and through the airplane's windshield. Initially, as the gathered crowd got the bodies out of the airplane, they noticed one of the women was still gasping. Someone administered CPR, but she did not survive.

Bill immediately called the authorities in Mulegé, and they eventually arrived to take the bodies. Dealing with the wreckage, however, turned out to be a challenging endeavor.

"It takes a long time to examine a wreck," Bill recounted. "The insurance company wanted to have a 24-hour guard there. I had one of my workers pick up extra hours," Bill added, willing to comply by paying for someone to stand watch over the damaged aircraft so nothing would be disturbed.

Bill was angry when it took several weeks for the Mexican insurance representatives to complete their investigation. "They wanted me to pay to remove the crashed airplane to Santa Rosalía," Bill said, still exasperated years later. "They didn't want to pay."

Although shocked by the accident, Billie was unhappy about the money they lost. Even the deposit check Billie received from the pilot bounced. "We were never about to recoup anything from any of those rooms or expense of anything. We could tell you horror stories about being cheated out of money," said Billie.

Many recalled a tragic boating accident that occurred near the island of Tortuga, approximately 27 miles northeast of Punta Chivato. The boat was owned in partnership by Mike Morse and a friend of his from San Diego, California. His friend, a private pilot, had flown down with his fiancée and another couple to enjoy the wonders of the area. Mike was up in the States when the two couples arrived at Punta Chivato.

Homeowner Barbara Silzle, who lived near Mike's garage, described Mike's partner as "nice, jovial, and happy-go-lucky. He had another guy with him and these two real cuties," recalled Barbara. "I think one of them was his wife and one was a girlfriend of the other."

Barbara remembers the foursome going out in the boat soon after they arrived. Upon their return to the launch ramp, Bill Silzle noted they appeared to have a problem with the boat. "My husband observed them taking all this water out of it."

"Boy, you've got to put a plug in that thing. It's really leaking," Barbara recalls her husband telling the young man.

"Oh, that's alright," the boat owner replied. "We just pull it up on the trailer and get the water out of it."

Barbara Silzle remembers seeing the two couples enjoying dinner that night at the hotel; the two guys appeared to have been drinking heavily. Bill Alvarado recalled they were also smoking pot. "It was about 10:00 or 11:00 at night when they left the hotel," Bill said.

Billie recalls one of the women returned to the hotel that night asking if they knew of anyone flying back to the States because she needed to get back home. "Her and her boyfriend had been fighting over drinking and drugs and stuff," Billie recalled, but she was not sure this was the reason the woman wanted to leave.

Bill and Billie knew Bill Silzle planned to fly out the following day and suggested the woman talk to him. They gave her directions to the Silzle home, but she never showed up. Instead, she joined the others who got into the boat late that night and went out toward Tortuga Island.

The next day, Barbara noticed the boat had not returned. Concerned, she went up to the hotel to tell Bill Alvarado.

"They were supposed to come back, and they haven't shown up and it's the next day," Barbara said. She recalled the sea was rough the previous evening and hoped the boaters had decided to go ashore somewhere.

Wasting little time, Bill got some homeowners together to begin a search. "I believe Bill and several others spent hours up in the air looking for them," Barbara recalled.

Homeowner Lee Cobb went searching with hotel boatman Miguel Romo. Eventually, the two women were found wearing their bathing suits and strapped together with floatable cushions. "It was a pretty good-sized boat," Barbara indicated. "Ours is 26, and it was every bit that big," she said. "As I remember, it had kind of a cab. I think it had bed cushions, and that's what the girls were probably strapped to," she added. In addition to the women, Miguel found a tin of hashish.

According to Barbara Silzle, the water was cooler than usual. "Bill said they died from hypothermia," she said, wondering if they could have been saved had they been spotted sooner.

One of the men was also found dead. The boat was eventually located on the bottom of the sea.

"I had to go to Santa Rosalía to identify the bodies," Bill recounted. "That was a horrible thing; I don't like to see dead people." Perhaps even harder was informing the next of kin. "That was a real chore to try to explain to their families," said Bill, who took on such unpleasant duties.

"They were nice kids," remarked Bill. "Especially the one couple we knew real well from San Diego. We knew the pilot and his fiancée because they were regular visitors down there."

Billie lamented the fact that children were left behind. "She left two children, a boy and a girl. He had a couple of boys and a daughter," she recalled.

However, the resident of Punta Chivato, who perhaps took the news of the drownings the hardest, was Mike Morse. "Mike felt guilty about it because there was definitely a leak in the boat somewhere, and he hadn't repaired it," remarked Bill. "But he hadn't used it that much to check on it. It was as much the other guy's boat as his."

"Mike, he was a little different after that," remarked another homeowner. "Quite a bit different. It changed him."

Some commented that Mike, once an avid fisherman, stopped going out on big fishing excursions after the death of his friends. "He stayed in the States for a long time before he came back," Barbara Silzle commented. "Alvarado told me, 'Mike feels guilty about that boat.'"

"The insurance investigator came and talked to me," recalled

Barbara. "I think he said he found out from the family that none of them knew how to swim except the guy that they never found." "The insurance man wanted to imply that they were on dope or something like that," Barbara added. "I gave very little information."

The search went on for another few years for the fourth person who went missing that night. There were supposed sightings of him in Via Constitución, in La Paz, and up near the border. "They'd come down and were absolutely certain that he was alive," said Bill. "They spent untold thousands of dollars hunting down all of these false leads." The missing man was never located.

For many years, a large cross was located at the top of a dune west of the camping beach. Barbara Silzle said it was a tribute to one of the of the campers, Russ, who brought a trailer to the beach after Bill removed the hump of sand in the road. "He was quite a diver," Barbara recalled. She never shared how her fellow diver died.

Bill was relieved of many emergency medical responsibilities after some medically trained individuals purchased lots and built homes in Punta Chivato.

Walter and Jeanne Fox, Bill Alvarado's long-time friends from Eugene, Oregon, stayed at Casa Grande for years before purchasing and building on the lot above the road to the camping beach. Walter, a retired oral surgeon, and Jeanne, a retired dental hygienist, were frequently called upon to help.

Jeanne recalled a person coming to their house after being shot in the mouth with an underwater speargun. "Walter operated on the table down there," she said.

Walter Fox. From Nov. 1991 video by Bill Alvarado

Medical professionals vacationing in Punta Chivato seemed to be "on call" for any medical emergency, even those unrelated to their field of expertise. "They used to be doing all kinds of surgery down there," Jeanne Fox laughed.

When Mary Morss was in Punta Chivato, she was in an accident in her dune buggy. "I was down at the beach checking to see if anyone needed things from town," recalled Mary. As she drove down the road toward Baja 1, she saw a cloud of dust, the indication of another vehicle. Unfortunately, the narrow dirt road made a curve at the point where the two would pass, and there was a blind spot. "I knew they were on the same road, so I was getting over as far as I could," said Mary. "I could see that they were smack dab in the middle of the road, not even getting over." Mary, who thought she had pulled far enough off the road, was surprised when the vehicle tagged her dune buggy, flipping it over and throwing Mary out.

"Fortunately, Walter's partner was down there at the time, Shoemaker, and he stitched Mary up," recalled Bill, referring to Walter Fox's oral surgery partner, Rick Shoemaker, who built a garage on Lot #1, Subdivision 1.[144]

Not prepared to perform surgery while on vacation, Rick Shoemaker was ill-equipped but willing to help Mary. "They were going to offer me a drink because they didn't have any anesthetic or anything like that," said Mary. She recalled some humor in the situation. One of the Mexican employees who was standing nearby observing Mary get stitched up requested a drink. Perhaps it helped steady his nerves while observing.

Homeowners Andy Adams and Greg Joy, both medical doctors, were unofficially considered "on call." Andy specialized in family practice, and Greg was an orthopedic surgeon from Placerville, California. Often, they received calls on the radio or heard a knock on their doors from individuals wanting medical intervention for themselves, a family member, or a friend.

"Both the patient and the doctor need equal amounts of anesthesia," Greg said with a deep chuckle. "If there's an imbalance, it's not going to work out."

Chapter 75

CHARITABLE HOMEOWNERS

Early camper Les Conner was a long-time employee of a Sears store in California. "We used to have access to a lot of clothes," Les explained. "If you go out of the building with Levis or a jacket or a pair of shoes and brought it back, they don't resell them. It goes in what they call the 'allowance.'" The Conners initially gathered and loaded up surplus items and drove them to Punta Chivato. "We used to come down and spend a couple of weeks," said Les, who first camped on the beach with his wife, Lucy, before building a home at Punta Chivato. After sizing the clothing and shoes, they would give them to the locals. "We got to know the Mexicans through that," Les added.

"We wanted an outlet for a lot of the clothing," said Lucy Conner. But simply giving the clothes away to the Mexicans felt "degrading" and "patronizing" to her. After years of giving the items away, they devised an alternate solution: having a bazaar.

In 1991, *Bazaar de Niños* (Children's Bazaar) was established. It would become a passion for the Conners and several other Punta Chivato homeowners, including Art and Dorothy Oberto, John and Gerry Fitzsimmons, and Dale and Julia Dryer. However, Les and Lucy Conner are credited with starting the charitable event that benefited local school children. The proceeds were used to support the maintenance and operation of San Bruno schools.

"Of all the original people who actually try and take part in the Mexican culture/community, by far the number one is Les and Lucy," John Fitzsimmons said in a later interview. "They're head and shoulders above whoever is second, third, and fourth. This bazaar is a big deal," he added, looking back at the event's history.

After getting permission from the president of the municipal of Santa Rosalía to hold the event, Lucy Conner had a brilliant idea. She met with Gertrudes, a local Mexican woman from San Bruno, and requested she write a letter to the official's wife asking her to attend.

"Write her a letter and ask her if she'll be our honorary chairperson for the first bazaar," Lucy told Gertrudes, handing her stationery imprinted with shell designs. To Lucy's surprise, the mayor's wife accepted the invitation and was present for the ribbon cutting of the first Bazaar de Niños held in 1991.

The bazaar made $2,000 the first year and $3,000 the second year. A designated bank account was set up in Santa Rosalía. The early projects funded by the money included installing toilets and a drinking fountain at the elementary school in Palo Verde. Previously, the students drank out of a garden hose.

Each year, the Bazaar Committee members brought items from the States to Punta Chivato. Les Conner remembers the Obertos often drove to their home in Southern California en route from Seattle, Washington to Punta Chivato. "We'd load up their Blue Bird," said Les. "The big carrier was the Blue Bird because we could get so much in. Dorothy would hide stuff in suitcases. They would stop by and stay the night. And we'd load up the next."

Once in Punta Chivato, all the donated items were stored in Art and Dorothy Oberto's garage.

A date was chosen to organize the clothing in preparation for the bazaar. After the first few years, locals were encouraged to participate in sorting and pricing the goods. "The committee consisted of about 70% Mexicans," remarked Les. "They feel like they're doing it themselves. They come out here and we separate it at Art and Dorothy's garage. Then we have a big spaghetti lunch."

Les shared a story of one American homeowner at Punta Chivato who initially just planned to drop his wife off to help with the sorting. "Barbara Wood came over to help and here comes Jim to drop her off. He says, 'I'm leaving.' And three hours later, he's still there because he got involved separating." The event turned into an avenue to not only help the school but a way to become better acquainted with other homeowners at Punta Chivato and local Mexicans.

The bazaar grew over the years. In time, it lasted for two days and included rides for the local children. Les recalled the effect the children had on them. "We've learned to really like a lot of those kids. We've had some happy memories. The kids get under your skin."

Art and Dorothy Oberto at Punta Chivato. Courtesy Harry Oxley

Art Oberto took a special interest in one six-year-old boy who always walked around with a scowl on his face. "He stood out because he was so mean," remembered Les. "He looked for trouble. It's recess, and he comes out of class, runs over, and this kid is standing by the fence. POW hits him in the back. No reason at all."

The first year of the bazaar, Les remembered meeting the boy. It was on a Saturday, the day before the bazaar. Les was sitting on the step of a bus, and the boy boldly approached him and demanded in Spanish, "Tomorrow you bring a bicycle." Les responded, "No way, José." Not losing a beat, the boy corrected him, "No way, Chewy." Les nicknamed him "No-Way Chewy."

Chewy thrived on the special attention the Conners and Art Oberto gave him. "We realized that he was one of those little troublemakers, one of those kids that could go either way," recalled Lucy Conner.

Whenever Art visited the school, he would select Chewy to help him with projects. "Man, that turned that kid's life around," said

Les. Art was so proud of Chewy and had high aspirations for the boy.

A publication by the Punta Chivato Homeowners' Association dated March 31, 1994, reported that $4,600 was raised at the annual Bazaar de Niños. Part of the proceeds was used to put in a concrete volleyball court at the primary school. "They were playing in dirt and slipping," recalled Les Conner, who said the girls preferred to play volleyball while the boys played soccer. "This is first through sixth grade, and they've got about 100 students." The money was also used to purchase swings for the kindergarten class and to plant gardens at the school.

"We get to know all the kids by sight, not by name," said Les, who recalled visiting the school at Palo Verde after the volleyball court was completed. "I'm sitting out there; it was recess. Here they come; they let them out. I felt like Dr. Schweitzer. They come running toward me, smiling and happy. Go right past me to the volleyball court. I thought we could film a commercial."

The bazaar fundraisers provided additional benefits for the primary school, including replacing windows, installing fans in the schoolrooms, laying concrete for a basketball court, and general maintenance. The kindergarten enjoyed the addition of a palapa to provide shade, painted tires, and a wading pool. All the children looked forward to the annual Christmas Party the Americans put on for the school. A homeowner would dress up as Santa and pass out gifts to children living in Punta Chivato, Palo Verde, and a nearby fish camp.

Initially, it was not a problem bringing items for the bazaar across the U.S.-Mexican border. However, the customs officials later became more restrictive. This surprised the Americans since they felt the new NAFTA agreement would lessen the constraints for bringing in items. One homeowner went as far as to call the officials in Washington, D.C. He was told they were allowed to bring in up to $1,000 of goods without tax. According to a PCHA publication, "The customs people at the border absolutely do not comply with this new regulation."[145]

As it became more difficult to transport quantities of donations across the border, the annual bazaar sometimes had to be postponed and rescheduled. "We've skipped," said Lucy Conner, regarding the gaps in event scheduling. "It's been every two years now for about three times."

In addition to the Bazaar de Niños, Les and Lucy Conner later suggested starting a scholarship program for children in grades 7 through 9. "We had kids that couldn't go past the sixth grade because there wasn't a seventh grade in San Bruno, and they couldn't afford to go to Santa Rosalía," said Les. Les spoke with the Fitzsimmons and Dryers, who eagerly agreed to help sponsor the program.

These couples each donated $200 to support a graduating San Bruno primary school child enrolling in school in Santa Rosalía for a period of three years. The total of each scholarship was $600. Initially, two students received the scholarship money, which covered their uniforms, books, lunches, and transportation. In 1995, with donations from others, enough was raised to purchase tires for the school bus that drove the students to and from Santa Rosalía.

As more Americans in Punta Chivato donated money to the scholarship fund, additional Mexican children were chosen. In 1998, fourteen Punta Chivato homeowners donated $200 each to fund scholarships for secondary school.

Receiving the tuition money was based on academic achievement. Students were chosen by the president of the *Padres de Familia*, which was like a Parent-Teacher Association (P.T.A.). A second scholarship was given based on need and determined by the school parent-teacher group.

The first scholarship recipient was easy to determine; the group chose the student who received the highest grades. Many students were motivated by this grant and studied more diligently. However, the second scholarship, based on need, soon began to pose a problem. To be eligible for this non-academic-based scholarship, students filled out an application reviewed by the local "P.T.A.," who would decide which child deserved to receive the tuition. Les recalled the arguments that arose among some selection committee members.

"Well, her father drinks," said one member of the decision group. "We can't give it to her."

Another interjected, "Yeah, and if one of these wins, their father is a fisherman and his motor is broken, and he's got seven children. So, guess where the money is going to go?"

"We had to then go back and get the guy who was the closest thing they had to a priest," said Les. "Years ago, Beto used to interpret at some of our meetings out here. He's very active in the Catholic church there. So, we had him distribute the money."

Eventually, a secondary school was built in San Bruno, and the scholarship money was used to create the new high school. In time, the Americans who had started the scholarship decided to close it down. The remaining $500 or $600 left in the fund was transferred to the Bazaar de Niños account established at the bank in Santa Rosalía.

Les was proud of the students who used the scholarship money to further their education. Several went on to graduate from college at the university in La Paz.

Another charitable event initiated by the homeowners at Punta Chivato was a wine-tasting party. The proceeds were given to the Red Cross in Santa Rosalía to buy an ambulance. Eventually, the Punta Chivato homeowners started other activities, including annual golf and fishing tournaments. The profits generated were used to improve the lives of the local Mexican population.

Chapter 76

GÜERO'S TIENDA

Ermenegildo Alaníz de Anda remembers Hotel Punta Chivato was in operation when he moved to San Marcos Tierra as a young man. He was nicknamed "Güero," pronounced "way-row" with the "G" silent. This translates to "fair-haired" or "blond" in English. Güero was born in 1955 in Aguascalientes on mainland México, north of Guadalajara. He relocated with his family to the small village north of Punta Chivato in 1972 at age 17.

Although aware of the resort at Punta Chivato, Güero knew little about it. Through word of mouth, he learned the hotel had shut down when the previous owner, Cleveland Crudgington, left the area. He also heard about another American who arrived in the late 1970s intending to resurrect the hotel. But Güero did not venture over to Punta Chivato and knew little about the operations or Americans there. "I don't remember Doc Lyons because I didn't live there at that time," said Güero during an interview. "I was working as a fisherman in San Marcos Tierra. I wasn't at the hotel."

Güero eventually married a local woman named Lola, and they moved to the nearby town of San Bruno. He and his wife and three children lived there for twenty years. In 1988, Güero purchased a ranch from an old ejidatario of the Ejido San Bruno. In buying the ranch, Güero acquired the right to become a member of the Ejido. The Ejido San Bruno had 27 members at that time. "It was very poor," he recalled.

Years later, Güero went to Punta Chivato to discuss with Bill Alvarado the possibility of starting a small *tienda* (store) to provide groceries to the homeowners and campers at Punta Chivato. Bill was thrilled with the idea. "Bill helped much," Güero said. "He provided me with electricity, with water, and many things."

To help subsidize his income while he started his business, Güero did carpentry work on the new homes being built in the early 1990s, including the home of Greg and Pam Joy.

Güero recalls it being difficult in the beginning. His car was a "lemon," and the tires did not last long on the washboard road from Baja 1 to Punta Chivato. He was grateful when the Americans bought tires for his car.

A building for the tienda was constructed across from the generator/laundry building inland from the hotel. This central location was within walking distance for hotel guests, homeowners, and beach campers. Güero added living quarters in the back of the store and eventually put a ramada in the front and over his hot dog cart at the side of the building.

On February 16, 1992, the long-awaited store opened its doors to customers. Those living at Punta Chivato were excited, heralding it as "a welcome addition to our community" and something that "has been needed for a long time."

Gloria standing at the entrance to tienda. Courtesy Greg Joy

Güero started with a cooler for milk, sodas, cheese, and a few canned goods. Gradually, he added a meat freezer and carried bread, fresh vegetables, and fruit. American shoppers were impressed to be able to buy fresh strawberries at the store in Punta Chivato.

Güero learned what items his customers wanted and did his best to accommodate them. In a short time, the store's shelves were well-stocked with food and other requested products, including rubber slippers, brooms, camera film, paper products, and razors. There were always "treats" available at the check-out counter for children of all ages. "It is truly amazing what he has in his inventory," one homeowner wrote. "It saves many of us a long, bumpy trip to town for a few items."

"The tienda was very important to the people in Punta Chivato," recalled Greg Joy during an interview with Güero. "I remember you sent your van into Santa Rosalía for beer and other things. It was good."

Güero concurred, "For all the people, it was good, not only for me but for all."

Gloria and Güero behind the counter in their tienda at Punta Chivato.
Courtesy Greg Joy

On February 28, 1996, Güero got married a second time to a local 31-year-old woman, Gloria Guadalupe Mendoza Ruíz. At that time, Güero was 40 years old. Their wedding was held at his ranch in San Bruno. Gloria soon became familiar to all in Punta Chivato since she was often behind the check-out counter at the tienda. Although quiet, she had a welcome smile. She would quickly total your purchases on a hand-held calculator and place your items into plastic bags. Gloria also became known for her singing voice. She and her father were often the entertainment at local fiestas.

Güero and Gloria left the tienda in 1997 and moved to a parcel of land further inland, off the road into Punta Chivato. In 1999, Güero started a warehouse with building supplies called *Materiales de Punta Chivato*.

Chapter 77

CHIVATO CHARLA

In February 1992, Punta Chivato homeowners received the first issue of a local newsletter, *Chivato Charla*, written and published by homeowner Marge Summers, the oldest daughter of Doc Lyons. Marge and her husband, Jere, built a home on the largest lot Bill presented to Doc, Lot #4 in Subdivision 2. They called it *Villa de los Veranos*, Summers' Villa.

"After our last visit to Punta Chivato in early February, I got the idea for a newsletter," Marge wrote in the introduction of the first publication. She explained *Chivato Charla* literally translated to "Goat or Kid Talk."

"This is an intermittent newsletter, published when there is enough news to fill a page," she wrote. Marge solicited information from anyone interested in contributing. She requested submissions be mailed to the Summers' post office box in Mulegé.

"Editor welcomes articles, comments, gossip, even unprintable stuff," Marge wrote in one early *Chivato Charla*. "This doesn't mean I'll print it; I just like to know what is going on."

"*La Golosina*," translated as "delicacy, fancy dish, tidbit," was a section Marge included in the first issue. "In this section we will feature new ways to prepare fish, local vegetables or other favorites," she wrote.

"*La Queja*" was a section Marge translated as "complaint or groan." She included examples in the March/April 1993 issue: "Don't drive on the airstrips!! They are for airplanes only. Also, with more twin-engine planes coming to the hotel, be sure you stop and look both ways at the runway crossing."

Several months after the first issue, Marge suspended publication when she and her husband packed up and moved from Arizona to become full-time residents at Punta Chivato. "NOTE: No June, July, Aug., Sept. or Oct. newsletters for 1992," she announced.

Later issues included updates on the medical condition of some homeowners, hints about dangers one might encounter at Punta Chivato, and remedies for medical situations.

The May/June 1993 issue of the *Chivato Charla* included the following:

We've killed over a dozen scorpions in our house the last 2-3 months.

Larry Lucore got hit by a stingray last month and said it was one hour of the most excruciating pain he's ever had. He kept his foot in HOT, HOT water until it subsided.

Lupe Alvarado (Jeff's wife) knows of several local plants that can be used to make poultices for bites and stings. For sting-rays, she said to boil leaves of a vine, Tripa de Aula, to put on the sting.

Another interruption in the publication occurred in 1994. When Marge resumed the newsletter, she cleverly wrote in the March/April 1995 issue:

Pen to paper, finger to key, dots to paper, we are back from a long hiatus. We missed reporting on terrific news items such as the takeover of the Hotel, 30-year lease offers and expenses thereof, and the Oxley-Lujan lease of Casa Grande and Punta Chivato Shores. But yesterday's news is good for paint spatters and litter boxes.

In the winter of 1998, Punta Chivato homeowner George Powell began to produce the *Chivato Charla* using his computer.[146]
By the Spring 2000 issue, the *Chivato Charla* had become available online.

The "web" is changing the world faster than most people realize. It is changing the way we do business, get information and communicate. Chivato Charla will change too. Own web site.

The Fall 2000 newsletter included the following:

"I Haven't Received a Charla in Ages. Whaaasup?" You wouldn't be asking if you were on-line. The easiest way to read the Charla is on the web.

Chapter 78

DESERT LYNX GOLF COURSE

Lee and Connie Cobb, a couple from Southern California, had a home built on Lot #19, Subdivision 1, at Punta Chivato, another parcel once held by Doc Lyons.[147] They loved living on the beach and the privacy of being at the end of the available lots west of the hotel. The Cobbs were avid golfers and were often seen hitting golf balls from the beach.

Several people who were interviewed take credit for the idea of putting in a golf course at Punta Chivato. However, all mentioned Lee Cobb as the course designer and driving force behind it. "Lee Cobb was one of the main instigators of it," said Billie Brush. "Lee put a lot of work in on it—determining where the holes would be."

Since water was at a premium in the arid land, a typical green golf course was out of the question. Instead, it was decided to put in a "desert course."

Bill Alvarado spoke with the Ejido San Bruno, and it was agreed the 9-hole course would be built on the property between the road to Punta Chivato and the short airstrip. This land was relatively level and sparsely vegetated. Ejidatario Julian Vargas had a small tractor that was used to knock down brush and cacti.

Bill was able to obtain AstroTurf for golf tee mats. Always resourceful, he found a golf course in San Diego that was replacing the mats at its driving range.

"I really need a bunch of mats," Bill said when he spoke with the golf course manager.

"What for?" the man asked, curious about what Bill planned to do with them. "Going to sew them together? They'd look terrible in your den," he added with a laugh.

After Bill explained his plan to use the squares of AstroTurf as driving mats for a desert golf course in Baja, the man told him, "Take a bunch of them."

Bill took ten of the used driving mats. He recalls being questioned at the border when returning to Punta Chivato. "Nobody knew what that was," he recalled. "What are we doing with squares of AstroTurf?"

The holes for the course were 12-inch cement nipples used for sewer pipe. "I tell you, a hole that big is still hard to hit," said Bill, who recalled playing on the completed course "at least three or four times a week" with Lee Cobb.

"Originally, it was only three holes over by the road," said Les Conner, who was also a golfer. These holes were short and flat and considered "easy." "I heard somebody say they were going to make a soccer field up there for the employees," said Les. That never happened. Instead, the desert course was expanded.

The February 1992 *Punta Chivato Charla* included the following update on the new project:

> *The GOLF COURSE work is progressing nicely. Nine holes are already laid out. The course is a little primitive at present but refinement and landscaping (or sandscaping) are in the works. It should be played with a club best described as a cross between a sand wedge and a broom.*

Finding an adequate substance to use for the "greens" around each hole proved more difficult. Les Conner remembered Lee Cobb suggested putting in a composition material. Several golfers contributed $100 apiece to pay for it. Les and Lucy Conner headed back to the States for a month, and when they returned, Les noted that the material had not yet been put in.

"Well, when are you going to put in the comp?" Les asked Lee when he saw him.

"Well, we put it in. It all blew away," Lee responded. He explained how a strong, northerly wind came in, and all the "greens" disappeared.

The next solution was to use sand and oil for the "greens." It was thought oil would keep the sand from blowing off. A barrel was set up in the arroyo between holes 1 and 9. Bill had oil drained from his generators and put into the drum.

"It was not a good idea," recalled Bill. "They were getting oil on everything."

"That was the Goddamnedest mess I ever saw in my whole life," remarked Kerry Kellogg. "You couldn't go home because you had all that oil all over your feet, shoes, socks, everything."

The sand and oil mixture was hauled off. Eventually, someone suggested using ground-up shells from Shell Beach. "That was the answer to the whole thing," said Kerry.

"We had to do some maintenance every year to the 'greens,'" recounted Bill, "but they're pretty good considering the amount of rain they get."

While the first three holes were considered "easy holes," the course became increasingly more challenging. Hole number 4 was longer with a dogleg to the right. Beginning with hole 5, the difficulty changed as these were laid out in undulating natural terrain with ocotillo, creosote bush, and other desert vegetation. Jackrabbits commonly darted from behind a bush or cactus when startled by a golf ball or a golfer searching for a lost ball. A sudden, unforeseen scurry often surprised the golfer. Connie Cobb was said to have screamed when she reached over to pick up an errant golf ball, and an unexpected jackrabbit took off from behind brush nearby.

In the spring of 1992, a "Name-the-Golf-Course" contest was held at Punta Chivato. To enter the competition, one needed to pay a $1.00 entry fee with each suggestion. There was no limit to the number of submissions one could make as long as each was accompanied by a payment of $1.00. The winner would receive half of the collected entry money. The other half would be allocated to the maintenance and improvement fund of the golf course.

Desert Lynx Golf Course at Punta Chivato. Courtesy Greg Joy

"Desert Lynx Golf Course" was the winning entry chosen by four local judges: Lee Cobb, Les Conner, Bob Hilbun, and Bill Alvarado. Kerry Kellogg said, "Montana," Bob Hilbun came up with the catchy name.

The April/May 1992 issue of the *Chivato Charla* credited Connie Cobb as the first person to make a hole-in-one on the new Desert Lynx Golf Course with an 81-yard shot. Other golfers mentioned in the issue included Bob Hilbun, Kerry and Penny Kellogg, Peggy Fodor, Lester Bell, Conna Melton, Billie Brush, Lucy Conner, and Walter Fox. The new recreational activity quickly became popular among many Americans at Punta Chivato.

That issue of the *Charla* also detailed a Casino Night event held the week before Easter 1992 at Casa Grande. The proceeds were targeted to maintain and upgrade the newly named Desert Lynx Golf Course. Both homeowners and beach campers participated in the evening event, which raised $1,258.

Lee and Connie Cobb worked hard to make the Casino Night a success. Penny and Kerry Kellogg chaired the Gaming Committee with Don and Joan Jacks. The Jacks made the tables and game cloths. Lynda Davis handled the ticket sales at the door. The tickets were exchanged for chips used for betting in adherence to Mexican Gaming laws of NO money on the tables. Lucy Conner did a fantastic job running the bingo table with one eye closed and her glasses as a magnifying glass. The craps table handled by Don Jacks generated the largest crowds, but the blackjack tables were the noisiest. Dealers were Lee Cobb, Larry Lucore, Les Conner, and Richard Fodor. Bob and Bobbie Hilbun ran the Silent Auction with many great items donated such as an Oxley fishing trip, a

John Lyddon flight, wine from Raúl Lujan from Santa Tomas vineyard, beautifully decorated T-shirt, fishing rods from Bill Alvarado and a quilt from Bobbie Hilbun. Penny and Colin Vowles had beautiful Desert Lynx T-shirts made and Bette Baker sold them. Walter and Jeanne Fox donated the nearly 100 wursts (hotdogs) and 3 gallons of chili, that Chef Walter prepared and sad to say, sold out of within the first hour. The crowd was much larger than anyone anticipated and decibel level inside Casa Grande was as high as everyone's spirits. Marilyn Oxley and daughters, Susie and Robin did a fantastic job of supplying drinks from the bar run by Hector.

The following year, Frank Vessels donated bright red flags for the golf course and purchased two ball washers. Soon, the newly formed golf committee had a sign made with the golf course name.

Sadly, the primary initiator of the golf course, Lee Cobb, lost his battle with pancreatic cancer in 1995 at age 51. Following is a note written by Lee and Connie's daughter, Heidi Cobb, which appeared in the summer *Chivato Charla*.

As you all know my father (Lee Cobb) passed away on February 5, 1995, after a long battle with pancreatic cancer. A memorial service was held on May 30th at the 5th tee of "The Desert Lynx Golf Course." This seemed the perfect place as he and Connie developed the course. Punta Chivato has always been my parents' favorite home. My father is still here in spirit and watching and smiling at everyone who plays on the course.

Connie knew her husband loved the desert course he helped create. After his passing, she got permission to place some of Lee's ashes on the course.[148]

The Cobbs donated a new Desert Lynx Golf Course sign. It was placed beside the road between the ninth hole and the first tee. Painted in white, turquoise, and pink, the colors stood out in contrast to the monotone desert terrain. Reyes Ramírez framed the attractive sign with rock from Mulegé.

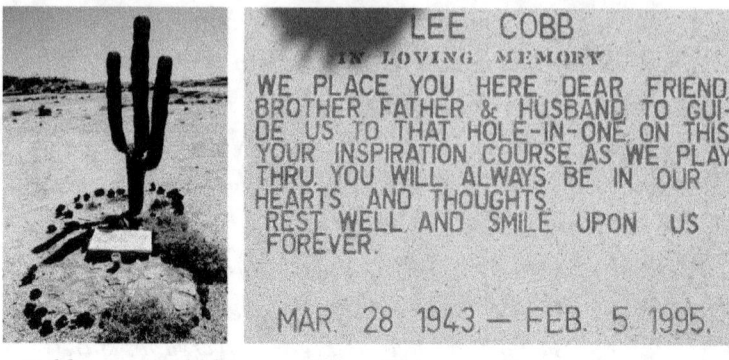

Lee Cobb memorial plaque at Punta Chivato golf course. Courtesy Greg Joy

In an article in the June/July 1995 issue, the *Chivato Charla* shared news of continued work to beautify and improve the golf course at Punta Chivato.

> *Bob Hilbun and Les Conner hired Amador Seretaño to transplant several nice cardón cactuses around the fairways and water them for 6 months until they are established and can survive on their own. Seretaño also located and moved large native rock to all the tees because many of the cement blocks that Lee Cobb had installed and painted white had been maliciously broken and strewn around. There is also new carbonate sand under the existing tee mats, making it better for tee shots. We hope to acquire new tee mats in the near future.*

Amador Seretaño. Courtesy Pam Oxley

In the spring of 1996, the *Chivato Charla* reported ongoing maintenance efforts.

> *Our Desert Lynx Golf Course looks great. The cardón cacti are doing well, Bob Hilbun and his "adopt-a-hole" group (Lou Razo, Kerry Kellogg, Ed Seabloom) have raked the "greens" clear of large pebbles and fresh carbonate has been spread at the tee-offs.*

Congenial groups played together, some making regular golf dates. Kerry Kellogg recalls joining a group of golfers at the desert course daily at 2:00 p.m. even if the winds were blowing. "We bet two pesos for whoever wins a hole and five pesos for the top score. That's twenty cents and fifty cents." He remembers playing with a group of nine and winning $4.60.

Lou Razo, a novice golfer, surprised a group when he shot par for the first time. Art Oberto's handicap won him a quarter from Les Conner one day. Jeanne Fox shot a hole-in-one, shocking herself and her golf partners. Doc Tonini and Jim Cavanaugh from Shell Beach became actively involved in the course.

For years, a Spring Scramble—a "Team Best Ball" tournament—was held. Forty-six golfers were recorded to have played in the annual event on March 19, 1999. A total of $1,774 was raised from entry fees, and the Golf Fund totaled $2,504.

In 2000, it was decided to rename the spring golf tournament the "Lee Cobb Memorial Golf Tournament" in honor of the man most responsible for starting the course enjoyed by so many at Punta Chivato.

The Second Annual Lee Cobb Memorial Golf Tournament occurred in March of 2001. A total of 90 golfers participated in the event. Some came from the nearby towns of Punta Arena, Mulegé, and San Bruno to join the Chivato golfers. In the Spring of 2001, *Chivato Charla*, it was reported that an auction and lunch were added following the tournament.

> *The food committee prepared a great lunch of salads, chili beans, and hot dogs. Les Conner conducted the auction of donated items to benefit the Palo Verde School. Proceeds from last year's auction made possible new drinking fountains, wash basins and lunch benches. More improvements will be made from this year's proceeds.*

Funds from the golf tournaments were used to build an outdoor classroom at the Palo Verde school. According to Les Conner, the structure cost $7,300. The teachers and students at the school appreciated the charitable donations, and the Americans at Punta Chivato enjoyed a fun afternoon of golf while feeling satisfied that they had helped improve the lives of the local people.

Chapter 79

BILL ALVARADO FLEES

Early one December evening in 1993, Jere and Marge Summers sat at a table in the Punta Chivato Hotel restaurant with Bill Alvarado and Billie Brush. The television was tuned to a station airing a baseball game. The Summers planned to leave for Tucson, Arizona, the next morning, where they intended to spend Christmas with their children and grandchildren. They had come to say goodbye and ask Bill and Billie if they needed anything from the States. The Summers planned to return to Punta Chivato after the holidays.

Suddenly, the Mexican employee managing the front desk hurried into the restaurant and headed toward their table.

"Señor Bill, *el teléfono*," he said in a quiet but anxious tone, indicating an urgent telephone call.

As the others continued their conversation, Bill stood and quickly walked to the office building across from the restaurant. Billie and the Summers grew concerned when he was gone longer than expected. By the time Bill finally returned, the baseball game had ended. His face was ashen, and he had a stunned expression. He clutched a sheet of paper.

"You don't look right," Marge said, surprised to see the sudden change in Bill's demeanor. "What happened? What's going on?"

"You won't believe this," Bill replied in a low voice, "but the telephone caller said to me, 'You don't know who I am. Your calls are being listened to. I will send you a fax.' Then he hung up."

Bill handed the fax to his friends. Marge recalled the fax as reading:

There are policemen right now in your dining room. They are going to arrest you tomorrow. They are there watching you at the request of the ejido. They're setting you up to arrest you. My advice is to get out of there.

Jere Summers remembered seeing a couple of unfamiliar Mexicans in the restaurant that evening. "In those days, the hotel was a favorite place to go because the prices were right, and everybody was welcome," said Jere. Most of the Mexicans who ate in the hotel were ejidatarios. "Bill always fed the ejidatarios," he added. "If they came in and had their meeting, they got dinner for free." But these men who sat at a table across the room were not ejidatarios. "We didn't know who they were," Marge said.

"Well, I don't know how we're going to get out of here," Bill said, his voice mirroring his fear. "They're watching."

Without hesitation, Jere Summers offered Bill a solution. "We're leaving in the morning, and if you want a ride out, you can go with us," he said. "Nobody's going to stop me. Nobody's going to take you out of my vehicle," Jere added emphatically.

The Summers were fond of Bill Alvarado. They knew how much he had meant to Marge's father, Doc Lyons, during his years in Baja. Jere was willing to do whatever he could to help his late father-in-law's long-time friend.

Bill relaxed a bit as he quickly responded, "That sounds like a plan."

This was not the first time Bill Alvarado felt threatened. He had been accused by the Ejido San Bruno of non-compliance with his contract. "They wouldn't renew his lease," said Billie at an interview years later. "Julian [Vargas] was trying to make it sound like Bill had not paid proper taxes, and he was going to have him put in prison."

Billie realized Bill was being watched "like a hawk" by the Ejido. "They started sending their goons out to stay at the hotel every night to watch him," Billie recalled. "They probably were afraid he was going to take off, so they started coming out day and night to watch everything."

According to Billie Brush, the fax Bill received came from an attorney friend in Oregon who was aware of the situation. Billie was afraid if the Ejido followed up on their threat and locked Bill up in a Mexican prison, he would die there.

The morning after he received the faxed warning, Bill packed a small duffle bag and climbed into his pickup. So as not to cause suspicion, he followed his regular routine. First, he drove to the camping beach and greeted the early risers. Someone offered him a cup of coffee, which he graciously accepted. Next, Bill checked on the pila on the hill above the hotel. Then, he motored by the new homes under construction at Punta Chivato to check on their progress. Since the main contractor, Chaparro, had recently died, the Americans often used Raúl Luján as their building contractor. Bill greeted Raúl's workers, who were known to arrive at the job around 7:30 in the morning and stop for breakfast close to 9 a.m. Everyone was used to seeing Bill make his rounds each morning for an hour or two. No one appeared to notice or consider it unusual when Bill turned into the Summers' driveway that morning.

Views toward the Sea of Cortez from pila (reservoir) on hill

View from covered pila in the foreground toward Hotel Punta Chivato in the distance (3 block homes in ravine seen middle, left of center).
From Nov. 1991 video by Bill Alvarado

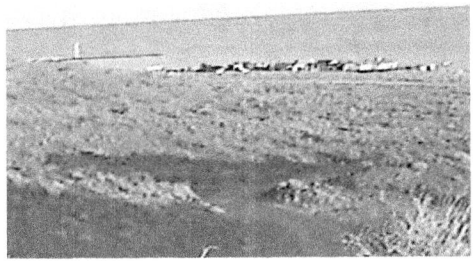

Taken from dirt road near pila toward Hammerhead/lighthouse (top left) and early homes in Subdivision 2. From Nov. 1991 video by Bill Alvarado

Earlier, Jere Summers had backed their motorhome out of the garage and parked it in front of the house for easier loading. "I had the right garage door open and room there," Jere remembered. "I didn't have quite as much stuff in the garage in those days," he added with a laugh.

Jere continued, "About half an hour after the workers went to breakfast, he [Bill] come wheeling down and zipped into the garage, and I closed the doors." With his bag in tow, Bill climbed into the Summers' motorhome and lay on the back floor.

As was typically the case, the Summers were not ready to depart on time. Marge was still packing food, clothes, presents, and other items they planned to take on their journey.

"I was in the garage doing something," said Jere, "when Marge comes out with an armful of clothes." The items were on hangers, and as Marge walked toward the closet at the back of the motor-home, she could barely see over the top of the bundle. Suddenly, she let out a squawk as the toe of her foot hit something. Marge had not seen Bill enter the motorhome and almost tripped over him. "Scared the hell out of her," Jere recalled.

Bill chuckled on hearing Marge's outburst, then put an index finger to his lips. "Shh," he said. "No one knows I'm here." Marge nodded and proceeded to hang up the clothes. Bill quietly remained on the floor as the Summers finished loading their motorhome. Their dog, Ralph, and their two cats were the last ones to board.

In the meantime, Billie Brush also followed her usual morning routine. Although she was not being threatened, she still wanted to play it safe. Billie left their room in the back section of the hotel and walked to the bathroom in the restaurant. Everyone knew the light in Billie's bathroom did not provide enough illumination for her to don her make-up and fix her hair. Then she had breakfast in the restaurant. After visiting briefly with the hotel cook and stopping by to greet Tony, an employee at the front desk, Billie turned to leave. "I've got to go down and see somebody," she casually remarked. With that, Billie left the office and headed toward her brown truck parked in the lot behind their hotel room.

Billie drove like she was going to visit one of the homeowners, then headed over to the main road out of Punta Chivato. As she bounced along the washboard road, Billie recalls passing a few Ejido members driving to work at the hotel. She calmly waved at them.

When she reached Palo Verde, Billie turned right onto Baja 1 and headed north toward Guerrero Negro on the west side of the Baja peninsula. Fortunately, no one noticed her the previous evening as she crammed as much as possible into the back of her pickup.

The plan was for Billie to meet up with the Summers in Guerrero

Negro. But Billie arrived hours earlier since they got off to a late start, and the motorhome traveled more slowly.

Bill remained in hiding when Jere pulled in to get gas in Santa Rosalía. It was not until they reached the grade of the *Tres Virgenes* mountains above the town that Bill felt comfortable getting up and moving forward in the motorhome to converse with the couple.

"Where have you been?" Billie asked as the motorhome finally pulled up at the designated meeting place in Guerrero Negro. Although angry about having had to wait so long, she was relieved to see Bill was safe with the Summers.

Bill remained with the Summers, and Billie followed behind them as the caravan continued north of Cataviña. There, they found a place to camp in the rocks for the night. Billie slept in her truck because she was allergic to cats, while Bill slept in the motorhome where there was more room to stretch out.

The next day, the vehicles continued north to Ensenada, where Bill felt it was finally safe to transfer from the motorhome to Billie's truck. He reasoned that Ensenada was in northern Baja California, a different state than Baja California Sur.

The couples parted company. Bill and Billie headed toward Tijuana en route to San Diego, and Jere and Marge Summers drove to Tecate headed for Tucson, Arizona and their family's Christmas.

Bill and Billie rented a room at the Budget Motel in San Diego, where they could get inexpensive weekly rates. They remained at the motel for three months while they decided on their next move.

When Jere and Marge Summers returned to Punta Chivato in January 1994, they were surprised to receive a telephone call one evening from Bill Alvarado. He was still in San Diego and sounded desperate for money, indicating he wanted to sell the truck he had left in the Summers' garage the previous month. Bill asked if Jere would consider driving the truck to San Diego.

"There's an extra gas tank on it, and both tanks are full," Bill instructed Jere. "There's a switch on the dash. When your regular tank starts getting down, you flip the other switch, and it'll pump it into the front tank. But you'll have to turn it off because it will overflow."

"In my earlier stupidity in those days, I said, 'O.K. I'll leave about 4:00 in the morning,'" Jere shared in an interview years later.

Jere decided to take another vehicle with him for transportation back from San Diego. "We had a little '83 Toyota that was light-weight and already set up to tow," he said, indicating he preferred to drive rather than take a local bus back down the Baja peninsula.

The following morning, Jere went out early to repair a problem with the lights on the Toyota. By the time he had the lights working, daybreak was upon him. Jere attached his Toyota to the hitch on Bill's truck, bid Marge a hasty goodbye, then climbed into the truck and drove along the dirt road toward Baja 1. Although he left later than expected, Jere figured it was still early enough to make it to San Diego later that day.

On the Punta Chivato Road, Jere noticed a campfire over to the side near San Marcos Tierra. Three Mexicans were standing near their broken-down car. Jere recognized one as Carlos Ramírez, a member of the local Ejido.

"I didn't slow down," recalled Jere. Moments later, he encountered Victor Velazquez, an ejidatario high up in the San Bruno organization, driving toward him from the opposite direction. "He swung around, and he's chasing me," Jere said. "The road was pretty good in those days, so I'm hauling ass, about 50." But when Jere reached the village of Palo Verde, he was forced to slow down. Victor pulled up next to him. *Well, I'm ready to do battle*, Jere remembered thinking, "but he just wanted to see who it was."

Jere was relieved the encounter with Victor had not amounted to anything. However, he knew Victor would tell the Ejido he saw Jere driving Bill's truck. No one except for the Summers had seen or heard from Bill Alvarado for a month.

Jere turned right onto Baja 1 and continued to Santa Rosalía, where he filled the tires with air at the Pemex gas station before continuing to San Diego. After delivering Bill's truck to him, Jere drove his own vehicle further north to Poway to visit Mike Morse. He shopped to restock their home in Punta Chivato before returning to Baja.

Nothing unusual transpired until a week after Jere was back at Punta Chivato. It was late in January 1994. Jere remembers seeing a car pull up on the walkway at the hotel when he drove there to check for mail. Several locals were sitting at the bar enjoying drinks. Jere returned home.

As the Summers were getting ready to sit down for supper at 7:30 that evening, the same car Jere had just seen at the hotel pulled up in front of their home. Three heavily armed, non-uniformed Mexicans soon stood at their door. They were the same men Jere had seen sitting at the hotel bar.

"You have to come to town and see our comandante," one of the men demanded, speaking in broken English and glaring at Jere.

"What's this about?" Jere gruffly replied. "How about in the morning?"

The speaker shook his head and indicated the comandante would tell Jere what it was about when they got to the station. "Make it hard or make it easy," the Mexican told Jere. Years later, Jere would chuckle as he remembered the comment, saying he thought the Mexican had watched too much television.

"We're not going until we eat," Marge told the Mexicans. "You can sit down." Surprisingly, the three men did not put up any resistance to the gringa's demand. They went into the living room and sat down; one played a little game while the others watched the television that was already turned on.

Trying to stay calm, Jere and Marge ate their dinner at the table in the adjoining dining room. Jere knew the men had already had dinner at the hotel.

"This is part of the way they do things down here—intimidation," Jere explained. "They wait until it gets dark. Then they go down and get a couple of free drinks off the hotel to build up their courage."

After the Summers finished their supper, the group spokesman, the only one who knew any English, stood and sternly addressed Jere, "O.K. You come."

"No, I'm not going with you," Jere responded. "I'll drive my own car 'cause I've got to have a way to come home. I'm not staying in town."

"No, you ride with us," the Mexican countered. "She can follow," he added, nodding in Marge's direction.

Marge was quick to speak her mind, "No way. I'm not doing that."

After a discussion amongst themselves in Spanish, the Mexicans finally agreed that Jere and Marge could follow them in their own vehicle.

It took about 45 minutes to reach the police station on the hill above the town of Santa Rosalía north of Punta Chivato. When the Summers were led into the comandante's office, the official first asked Jere if he spoke Spanish. When he said, "No," it was determined that an official translator was needed.

Jere and Marge patiently waited while María de los Ángeles was contacted and asked to come to the station and serve as the interpreter. The Summers had never met her, but she mentioned she knew Bill Alvarado from Punta Chivato.

"They had a stack of papers," Jere recalls. The Summers realized this was going to take time. "I listened to all their bullshit," Jere said.

"You're accused of stealing a truck that belongs to the Ejido and taking it north," María translated.

The only English-speaking official who had come to the Summers' home stood next to the desk. "Is this your name?" he asked Jere, slapping a paper down in front of him.

"I just looked at him," Jere recalled. "I wouldn't even talk to him."

But while Jere would not acknowledge that officer, he finally addressed the comandante. "I would like to know when and how the Ejido started registering vehicles in the state of Oregon?" Jere stated, "Because that vehicle is registered in Oregon, where Bill is from. So, I'd like to know how I can steal a vehicle from them [the Ejido] that is not theirs. How did they register it in Oregon?"

Jere could see that the comandante was growing uncomfortable. "He sat there for 15 beats or so and he looked at me and just kind of folded the papers up and said, 'Thank you for coming in,' and that was the end of it. Never heard any more about it. He knew it was bogus."

During a later interview, Billie said she and Bill felt terrible that Jere had to go to Santa Rosalía on their account. She said she assured Jere not to worry. "I've got the title to the car, and I'll get everything to you," she told him. "That's my pickup, and it has nothing to do with the hotel or Bill. The brown one was mine, too," Billie added, referring to the other vehicle she and Bill had together. But Billie's reassuring words from San Diego did nothing to keep Jere from being interrogated for stealing the vehicle. "They [the Mexican officials] scared Jere and Marge so bad they were afraid to ever do anything else on our behalf," Billie ruefully stated, "and I don't blame them. They had to live there."

Rumors quickly began to spread regarding Bill Alvarado and Billie Brush's disappearance. The Summers decided to remain tight-lipped about their involvement. "I wasn't really concerned about it at the time," Jere reflected. "It's just one of those things. It's a friend of mine. I gave him a ride."

The Summers hoped for the first few months that Bill Alvarado's issues with the Ejido would be straightened out and he could return to Baja. However, as time passed, their hopes dwindled.

"We were new to México," Jere later said in an interview. "We didn't understand the graft and corruption and illegalities and the bullshit that goes on down here to the extent that we do now, and I don't think we even scratch the surface now. I think there's a lot more. Every day, I hear something new that just boggles my mind. What these people, the government in general, and the people themselves can do to you."

Jere has no doubt Bill Alvarado would have ended up in a Baja jail if he and Marge had not helped him escape to the United States. "This is Napoleonic code," Jere expounded during an interview. "Anybody can make a charge against you, and you're guilty until you prove yourself innocent. People get in trouble and now I understand that they really were probably innocent. They were just picked up, and their lawyers would suck $20,000 or $30,000 or whatever they could get out of the families and never do anything. It's just a very crooked criminal justice system."

"I'm not saying that Bill was absolutely perfect and on the up and up," Jere continued. Bill was a promoter, a glad-hander; he loved everybody, and everybody loved Bill." Jere pointed out one of Bill's faults: he was not "on top of management."

"The cooks were stealing him blind," said Jere. "A lot of Mexicans and even some *gringos* were getting drinks on the cuff." Jere surmised Bill was losing money where he should have been making it. "Your bar should turn a good profit; your restaurant should turn a good profit," said Jere.

Bill had even hired a consultant for advice on managing the restaurant and bar better. For days, the man sat in the dining room and just watched. He noted the bartender was "a little heavy-handed with mixing drinks." Americans at Punta Chivato knew that a couple of Pedro's margaritas could put you flat on your back. One of the consultants recommended, "If your profit is going out the back door, you need to put controls on the bar."

Jere credits Bill for his persistent dream and eventual success resurrecting Hotel Punta Chivato. "He [Bill] was putting everything he had into trying to get the hotel viable," said Jere. In a ten-year period, it was finally beginning to turn a profit." Jere noted Bill continued to pour any profit he made back into the hotel operation. "I suspect he cut corners; he had to. He was getting no support from the Ejido."

Unlike his predecessors, Bill kept the hotel open in the summer to develop a "summer crowd." "The fishing was fantastic, particularly in those days," Jere remarked. As a result, Punta Chivato once again became a popular fishing resort with guests arriving year-round. "Had they [the Ejido] left him [Bill] alone and let him proceed for the next twenty years, in all likelihood, all of them would have realized a substantial amount of money," Jere speculated.

Meanwhile, while residing in the Budget Motel in San Diego, Bill and Billie had not lost hope. Like Cleveland Crudgington, the previous owner of Hotel Punta Chivato, who had also suddenly left México and later hoped to take back the hotel, Bill expected to return to his beloved dream in Baja.

Desperate, they went to Tijuana and hired a Mexican attorney. "He was supposedly going to be able to get the hotel back for us," recounted Billie. "He had all these influential people in México City that he knew."

However, Billie said the attorney wanted Bill to go after his Mexican accountant. "The Ejido found out that Bill hadn't been stealing from them and hadn't been doing anything illegal, so they tried to go after his accountant, who was dishonest." Bill's accountant was observed to have acquired several new pickups. "They figured that he was the one that was the bad guy," Billie added. Their Tijuana attorney suggested shifting the focus to Bill's accountant. "The attorney wanted Bill to put him in prison."

Bill wanted nothing to do with this plan. "He's a family man with young children," said Bill. "He's a nice guy. I'm not doing it. I'm not going to send him to jail. And we didn't."

After spending $6,500 on his services, Bill and Billie ended their association with the attorney. The only result they got was going further into monetary ruin. "That ended us as far as any kind of financial future," Bill sadly recalled. "God, I didn't want to leave."

"I loved it as much as he did," Billie said. "That's why I put in so damn much of my own money."

Ironically, while still in San Diego, Bill heard from a member of the organization that caused him to flee Punta Chivato. "The Ejido called me about a month after all this happened," Bill recalled, "and said, 'We have no ill feelings about you. We just want some money.'" Billie was still outraged. "After they kicked us out, they still wanted money from us. It was horrible. It was worse than horrible. We have never been back."

"Gee, I wish you could break in and get my records that are still down there," Bill lamented during a later interview, not realizing that whatever he had left at Punta Chivato was long gone.

"I don't know what they did with all of our stuff in our room," added Billie, still distraught over their hasty exit.

Bill and Billie got married in 1995 and lived in San Diego, in a "dinky" apartment consisting of two rooms and a bath, according to Billie. She was 58 years old; Bill was 59. Ironically, they were exactly a year apart, both born on the same day, September 29.

Life for the couple was difficult, both financially and health-wise. "Bill couldn't get Social Security for five years because of his age," said Billie. He had a long history of diabetes and began to experience complications due to poor circulation in his legs. "He couldn't get disability because he had been out of the country for too long and hadn't paid into the system the last ten years," Billie shared. Billie dealt with arthritic pain, and soon after their marriage, she suffered a stroke. "It was just downhill from there," she bemoaned.

When they were able, Bill drove them to Eugene, Oregon, where they visited Bill's sons and grandchildren. They also stopped to visit a long-time friend Bill had met when he worked for the Eugene newspaper, *The Registered Guard*. The two men shared a love of football and fishing. "Every time we came up and visited with them, they kept after us to come up here," recalled Billie. "Then they started looking around for places for us in case we might want to come up."

In 1999, their Oregon friends showed Bill and Billie a few places available for purchase. One was in a mobile home park in Oakridge, Oregon. "I liked it," said Billie. It was open and roomy." The Alvarados bought the mobile home but delayed their move until 2000 due to continued medical issues. "The only reason that I hated to leave San Diego," said Billie, "was leaving all my doctors down there and the care that I got."

Although Billie felt uneasy about finding new physicians in Eugene, she enjoyed living in the small mountain community."

"I love the country; the people are wonderful," said Billie. "It's nice to have some family real close." In addition to being closer to his sons and grandchildren, Bill now lived close to mountain streams and lakes where he could get back into fishing. Despite losing both his legs in 2002 due to complications from diabetes, Bill continued to find a way to get out and fish in the nearby streams.

During an interview in 2003, at their mobile home in Oakridge, Oregon, Bill and Billie Alvarado reflected on Bill's ongoing legacy in Baja. Bill shared an incident that occurred in 2000 when his son, Arnie, went to Loreto, a town south of Punta Chivato. "I told him about a couple of places that are good to eat down there," said Bill.

Bill's son chose one, entered the restaurant, and sat down.

"Do I know you?" the establishment owner asked before taking his order.

"No. It's my first time in the restaurant," Arnie replied.

"You look so much like a really good person that I know," said the restaurant owner. "His name was Bill Alvarado, and I haven't seen him in years."

"It's my dad," said Arnie.

"Oh my God, everything is on the house: your dinner, booze, drinks, whatever you want."

Bill said, "That made me feel good."

Billie remembers Bill was beloved by everybody. "I cannot tell you the thousands of dollars that he never collected from anybody that needed anything that came down there," Billie reflected. "Hippies, poor people, anybody who broke down, their rigs were fixed, they could stay on the beach, they could come in and eat or drink. He never turned away a soul. That's just the way he is with everybody."

Bill quickly added, "Oh, I was not loved by everybody...Well, I feel good about the number of people that I helped down there."[149]

PART IV

Chapter 80

EJIDO TAKES OVER HOTEL

After Bill and Billie left Punta Chivato, some San Bruno ejidarios moved in and took over the hotel's administration. Julian Vargas, Victor Velasquez, and Lupe Mendoza were the main members involved.

In retrospect, Jere Summers felt the Ejido had planned to get Bill out so they could take over Hotel Punta Chivato. "The last year or two before Bill left, the Ejido kept saying, 'Oh no, don't worry, we're going to renew the contract,'" recalled Jere. But Bill seemed to have "an inkling" that something was not right. "Bill went down and got a judge to issue some legal document, saying that they [the Ejido] couldn't come in and that he would have time to negotiate. This went on for a year."

"The Ejido would keep saying, 'No, no, no problem, we're going to negotiate,'" Jere remembered Bill stating. The Ejido had found another judge to overrule Bill's. "That's when the stuff came out that they were going to arrest him."

The Ejido's attorney pointed out that it was well past the contract period with Bill Alvarado, and no new contract had been signed. "At some point, the Ejido said, 'Well, we think there's money being stolen,'" recalled Jere. "The Ejido sent a couple of people out. One guy was supposed to be a bookkeeper, and everything was supposed to go through him. They set up a special cash register, so you had to go over there and pay them instead of the bar. That was kind of an irritant, but then they were stealing the money. It was just a vicious circle."

"Victor Velasquez was supposed to be monitoring it," said Jere. "Well, Victor's stupid; a real asshole. He'd sleep in. He took over a truck and claimed it as his own. He was riding around. He'd go down and eat for free and invite people in." Bill complained that the truck Victor was using belonged to the hotel, but Victor claimed it was his. Bill did not win that battle, either.

After Bill left Punta Chivato, the Ejido picked managers.

"Victor was manager for a while, Julian had it for a while; there were two or three different managers," recalled Jere. "They would all buy a new car at the end of the year. They were all skimming off the top. They all owed their allegiance to Julian [Vargas]," Jere added.

With Bill gone, the Ejido increased the hotel room rates. A 1995 Automobile Club of Southern California publication listed the rates as $45-$55 with $10 per extra person.

Mike Morse became an asset to the Ejido after Bill left. It had been ten years since he first arrived at Punta Chivato, and he was well-known by American homeowners and Mexicans. Mike and his wife, Magdalena, lived in one of the buildings in the ravine near the hotel. He spoke both English and his version of Spanish, which, surprisingly, was understood by the locals.

"After Bill left, the Ejido asked me to stay and work at the hotel," Mike shared in an interview. "I also 'set the hook' for property sales."

"He survived down there in a very interesting way," commented Lee Links. "[Mike] worked for everybody that would give him a project to do, even Raúl. He's probably the only guy that made any money out of Raúl that I know."

Due to their hasty departure, Bill and Billie had to leave their pet bobcat, Macho, behind at Punta Chivato. "When we left there and had to leave him, it just about killed me," Billie lamented during an interview. "But there was no way we could get him into California because even though I had the paperwork where I bought him, you're not going to have those in the state of California. Besides, we didn't have a place to live where we could keep him. So, there was no choice."

When the Ejido took over Hotel Punta Chivato, they tore down the large fenced-in area home to Macho and Rammie and removed the tree supporting the fence. They rebuilt a much smaller cage but left the door open, allowing the bobcats to roam freely. They did not provide them food or water as Bill had, expecting the wild animals to forage independently.

If the homeowners at Punta Chivato were disgruntled by the

bobcats when Bill and Billie were there, they became even angrier after the Ejido took over the hotel and allowed the animals to run loose.

"I was afraid of Macho," remarked homeowner John Fitzsimmons. His wife, Gerry, remembers hearing Macho walk across their roof in the middle of the night.

"Macho was sleeping around on the porches and chasing the cats," said Lucy Conner, who enjoyed sitting on the veranda of their ocean-front home. "I looked up one day and there he is sitting on the roof looking down on the house."

Many residents who had pets at Punta Chivato grew particularly irritated with the bobcats on the loose. When three nursing cats were killed within six months, some questioned whether coyotes or bobcats were the culprits.

The following complaint written by Marge Summers appeared in the Sept./Oct. 1995 issue of the *Chivato Charla*:

> *The hotel does not seem to care that we are bothered by the cats being out. They both return to the hotel for food, but they are now living in Silzle's yard, on Adams' roof, and roaming free. We know they come around our house because Ralph [Jere and Marge Summers' dog] hears them and bounds out of the house at 2 AM, barking and carrying on. Other home-owners have similar complaints. WE have tried to get in touch with someone so they can make arrangements to put them into a wild animal type refuge, then the cats can be captured and hauled northward.*

One of the homeowners decided to take matters into his own hands after Macho got into his garden. The angry resident retrieved his BB gun and fired at the bobcat to scare him away. The result was Macho lost sight in one eye.

Eventually, Julian Vargas, then president of the Ejido San Bruno, decided to have Macho captured and taken to a zoo in La Paz. Several homeowners later reported visiting Macho there.

The other bobcat, Rammie, just seemed to disappear. Some speculate she got pregnant, went off, and had her kittens. Although she was never seen again, there were reported sightings of young, wild bobcats on the beach at Punta Chivato.

Years later, during an interview in Oakridge, Oregon, Bill and Billie still spoke fondly of their bobcats, especially Macho.

"For years, he [Bill] couldn't even think about him without crying," said Billie. "It was as bad as losing one of his kids. He was so attached to him. I worried about him [Macho] starving to death."

Mike Morse, who stayed in touch with the Alvarados after they left Punta Chivato, shared with them how much Macho missed them. "You should have heard him [Macho] at night. The moaning and the carrying on he did," Mike told the couple. Of course, this only broke their hearts more.

"Macho was used to us making our shopping trips, but then we'd come back," Billie said, remembering when they left Punta Chivato for good. "That time we didn't come back. We never saw him again."

"I hope that the zoo that he's in is taking care of him," Billie remarked when the author spoke with her in July 2003.

Chapter 81

THIRD LEASE

In August 1993, before Bill Alvarado fled Punta Chivato, a new agrarian law was enacted in México. According to this new law, communal lands of the ejido could now be leased for thirty years.

Some say the change resulted from internal political conflict in México City. The ejidos throughout México represented 13% of the vote. They had tremendous power when they suddenly became the swing vote. "People didn't want to cross the ejido at that time, state-wise, nation-wise, because PAN[150] wanted them, PRI[151] wanted them, and nobody was going to go against them," recalled Les Conner, referring to México's main political parties.

Whatever the reason behind the enactment of the new law, it appeared it would also benefit those who built homes in Punta Chivato. Under their current contract with the Ejido, the term of their leases was twenty years. Now, it would be extended to thirty years.

Another individual who would benefit from the new agreement was Raúl Luján Soberanes, the young local home builder who had arrived in Punta Chivato just four years earlier. During this brief time, Raúl's status had risen from a home builder to a powerful, influential individual in the area, including Santa Rosalía and Mulegé. Surprisingly, he was the intermediary between the Ejido San Bruno and the American homeowners in negotiating their new leases. This was only a foreshadowing of how Raúl would eventually become more involved in the future of Punta Chivato.

Dennis Peyton,[152] an attorney licensed in México and the United States, was hired by the PCHA to review the old and new contracts. He acknowledged the advantages of the extended lease but suggested they ask the Ejido to execute a promissory agreement to grant the additional 30 years upon termination of the current lease. This sounded like a good idea to the homeowners since most of them had many years left on their previous twenty-year lease. It was advantageous to extend the length of their investments in Punta Chivato for the longest period possible.

As with all contract negotiations, it took several months before a final new lease was agreed upon. On December 26, 1993, association president Harry Oxley sent a letter to the members of the PCHA. The following excerpts from this letter reveal his sentiments about the new lease and Raúl Luján:

> *I think the news that we received this week about the avail-ability of the new lease has to be the highest point in the year, at least for me. I can't imagine a better gift.*

> *Each Asociado[153] pays $15,000.00, $5,000.00 being paid immediately and an additional $10,000.00 being paid on or before January 20th and we receive a guarantee of a 30-year lease.*

> *Raul Lujan has been handling all the details with the Ejido. The payment so far has been made to Raul and he has taken care of paying the Ejido.*

> *As I have explained to you the agreement calls for a 10% com-mission to be paid to Raul Lujan for his services. Raul has told me that this can be settled after January 20th. I have probably received to date 20 phone calls from Raul keeping me advised as best he can of every facet of these negotiations. My feeling is that we could have never put this agreement together without him.[154]*

> *I will be very glad when the 20th has come and gone and we can look forward to our new leases and living happily ever after in Punta Chivato.*

A year later, in early October of 1994, Harry Oxley wrote another letter to the homeowners at Punta Chivato conveying news of the completion of the thirty-year leases. He stated ejidatario Julian Vargas had confirmed the registration of all the new contracts via a letter he received from Franco Domínguez, director of the National Agrarian Registry in La Paz, Baja California Sur.[155]

Once again, there was no written confirmation that the leases were ever legally registered in the Agrarian Department in México City, only in La Paz in Baja California Sur. Such documents need to be registered in México's capital city. Approval in La Paz was not enough. Were the Americans once again moving forward in blind faith?

Chapter 82

PUNTA CHIVATO SHORES

As president of the PCHA, Harry Oxley spent many hours with Raúl Luján discussing the proposed homeowners' thirty-year leases. As a result, the two became friends. Soon they decided to join in a business venture.

In 1994, Harry and Raúl formed Punta Chivato Shores, S.A. de C.V. The partnership's aim was to develop property for future homes in Punta Chivato. Harry would contribute money for the land, and Raúl would function as the building contractor and general administrator of the company.

Their first proposal was to purchase the land between the hotel and Casa Grande. They intended to build upscale homes on this property, mainly along the waterfront. They also planned to restore Casa Grande and turn it into a bed-and-breakfast or corporate get-away.

The following was recorded in the Punta Chivato Homeowners' Association annual meeting minutes on March 31, 1994, regarding Punta Chivato Shore's proposed refurbishing of Casa Grande:

Construction to begin immediately at the Casa Grande with a target opening date of July this year. They will shortly begin a professional video and send a press kit to magazine publications, travel clubs, and travel agencies, which will serve to inform people of the new plans for the area and help promote the hotel as well. Harry said the present water supply system and the hotel sewage system are of the utmost importance to the new project and are under study now.

A promotional brochure produced by Punta Chivato Shores read as follows:

Punta Chivato Beach Front Home Sites
Baja California's most beautiful vacation destination is under new management and ready to fill the needs of both visitors and residents interested in the ultimate Baja vacation experience.

Through an exclusive agreement between landowners, Ejido San Bruno and leaseholders, Punta Chivato Shores, a limited number of beach front home sites are now available through long-term leases! 25 new parcels, ranging from 8,000 sq. ft. to 16,000 sq. ft. in size recently have become available on 30-year leases, with a renewal option for another 30 years.

Longtime homeowner and Punta Chivato Shores President Harry Oxley has teamed with contractor Raul Lujan to make the dream of owning property in this planned community a reality. The latest properties join some 25 homes already completed by North Americans on parcels of land that became available 12 years ago. Many of the new home sites have beach frontage. Punta Chivato Shores is a planned community which features attractive limited development.

Renown for world class fishing and miles of sparkling beaches as well as sharing the restaurant and entertainment offered by the Hotel, the new land parcels have the amenities of resort living combined with the isolation of the tropics. The area is considered by many to be Baja's most desirable.

Another excerpt from the 1994 Punta Chivato Shores promotional brochure prematurely touted the completion of part of their envisioned project, Casa Grande.

Punta Chivato's crown jewel is the newly renovated Casa Grande. The Casa Grande, which has served as the center of operations for over 25 years, has been completely renovated to offer groups of up to 20, the solitude of Baja with the comforts of home. A huge dining room, living room complete with vaulted ceilings, volcanic fireplace and 6 private guest rooms make the Casa Grande a perfect family or corporate get-away. The private dock offers boating, diving and fishing charters as well as wind-surfing lessons in season. Wind surfing tours are available with either the Hotel Punta Chivato or the Casa Grande. Two incredible new suites have been redecorated to assure that even the most discriminating guests will feel pampered. These beautiful private rooms include gourmet meals, private bath, laundry, maid and chef. Cocktails are served in the living room or on the incredible patio area overlooking the Sea of Cortez and Bahia Conception (you are welcome to bring your favorite refreshments). Special group and monthly rates available.[156]

Harry's partnership with Raúl in Punta Chivato Shores created unrest among some of the other homeowners at Punta Chivato, who felt his business interest might adversely affect his ability to represent them. Harry decided it was best to resign as president of the PCHA. He sent the following letter, dated January 10, 1995, to all the members of the association:

From President, Harry Oxley

In my recent dealing with the Ejido, on behalf of the Asociados, it has become apparent that there are some conflicts between my position as President of the Punta Chivato Asociados, and my business with Punta Chivato Shores.

I therefore would like to tender my resignation as President. After discussions with some of the Asociados, including members of the board, I intend to ask Bob Davis to fill out the remainder of my term.

I honestly feel that the goals I set when I took the position of President have been obtained with our new 30-year lease, and I know Bob Davis can do an excellent job as Interim President.

But the partnership with Raúl did not work out as Harry had hoped. Eventually, he decided to step away from his involvement in Punta Chivato Shores. "I had to get out of it," Harry said at a later interview. "I could see tax problems. I could see problems with a lot of things. I didn't want to be involved in it anymore."

Although Harry helped get buyers for the lots between the hotel and Casa Grande, he indicated he did not get any compensation for the transactions. The money went to Punta Chivato Shores, and Raúl never paid him once he left the partnership. "He didn't buy me out," said Harry. "I just basically ate it."

The waterfront property between the hotel and Casa Grande was sold as two separate parcels, one to Jimmy and Barbara Wood from Madera, California, and the other to Gordon Campbell and Maria Ligeti from the Bay Area. Raúl built large, beautiful homes for both couples.

In 1999, Raúl sold Casa Grande to the Campbells, who had purchased the adjoining lot. Gordon Campbell was asked about his plans for the once-grand house at the homeowners' meeting that spring. He said he was seriously considering turning Casa Grande into an executive retreat.[157]

Work was started on renovating Casa Grande. The outside was re-stuccoed, and Raúl gutted the inside. However, the renovation stopped there. "They tore everything out," said Bob Davis during an interview in 2002, "and that's it. They never put anything back in."[158]

Raúl, the sole owner of Punta Chivato Shores, eventually sold the company to the Campbells.[159] The business was later renamed Techfarm.

Raúl Luján and the Campbells began a business venture together, building a restaurant west of the long airport runway. They planned to call it Pilots Club Steak House. The October 3, 2000, *Chivato Charla* issue reported on the restaurant's progress.

> *Construction is continuing, with opening likely before year end. The cylinder on top will be an observation tower-cocktail area. Access will be upstairs in the structure on the right, then across a walkway. The design is quite unique. The view is incredible.*

In December 2003, an internet site stated that Raúl and the Campbells had plans to build palapa-style units nearby for overnight accommodation. A second restaurant was planned for the point northeast of the camping beach. The design would be like the steak house, but this restaurant would specialize in seafood.[160]

Chapter 83

PRIVATIZATION OF EJIDO LAND

The disparity between México's social classes remained apparent long after the Mexican land reform laws were enacted in the 1960s. Throughout the country, but especially in Baja, the inequity was pronounced. The intention of México's earlier laws for redistributing the land among the Mexican peasants had so far failed, doing little to solve the country's rural poverty.

As the Mexican government recognized the developmental potential and value of ejido properties, especially those located along her borders and coastlines, an amendment to México's constitution was enacted.[161] Under this 1992 amendment, the Mexican government gave ejidatarios the ability to have legal entitlement to their current designated property. Using a system called "privatization," the ejidos could now take their community land, convert it to private property, and make a profit by selling or leasing it to eager foreign investors.

It was not until early 1997 that action on this amendment would begin in Punta Chivato. Bob Davis, then president of the PCHA, wrote to inform the American association that the Ejido San Bruno was in the process of completing the necessary paperwork to put their land into private ownership.

For those Americans who held leases to the parcels on which they had built homes, it sounded like a dream come true. Would they truly soon be rid of their questionable and possibly illegal land leases and finally have the security of owning both their home and land in México?

Unlike in the United States, a foreigner wanting to purchase property in México had to do it in conjunction with a Mexican Corporation or through a Bank Trust (called a *fideicomiso*). "As I understand it," Bob Davis's letter explained, "non-citizens of México can own a Mexican Corporation. It is no longer necessary for a corporation to be 51% owned by a Mexican citizen."

In his letter, Bob Davis wrote:

*It has been suggested that perhaps the best way for all of us
will be to form a corporation and purchase all of the properties
we occupy. We will continue to explore the situation and will
keep you informed of the progress. It is most important that
we all work together and strive to make this a fair and equitable deal for both the Homeowners and our friends the Ejido
San Bruno.*

*I have been assured that when the proper time comes, we will
be notified and will have the first chance to purchase our lots.
None of this, to my knowledge, will affect our current leases
and we will have the option to continue as we are on the
remaining twenty-seven years or purchase the land.*[162]

The Americans knew the process of acquiring ownership would
not happen quickly. It had already been five years since the Mexican
amendment had been enacted. To explore their options, the PCHA
formed a Land Acquisition Committee to gather information on
attaining their leased lands from the Ejido San Bruno. The committee consisted of Harry Oxley, Bob Davis, Les Conner, and Tom
Rosen.

On June 24, 1997, the Land Acquisition Committee sent a
letter to the Ejido asking that negotiations begin for the Homeowners' Association to acquire ownership of their leased lots. By
October of that year, the Ejido notified them they would vote to
approve negotiating with the Americans at their October 25, 1997,
General Assembly Meeting. As a result of that meeting, the 27
members of Ejido San Bruno became unified in their decision to
privatize. By doing so, each of the ejidatario families would be able
to own land parcels and could, in turn, sell/lease them.

The Ejido stated they preferred dealing with the PCHA as a
group rather than with each homeowner. Therefore, the transaction
was approached as a group through the PCHA Land Acquisition
Committee members, although those who chose to obtain a fideicomiso would later sign individual documents.

The Land Acquisition Committee retained the services of attorney Dennis Peyton, who lived in the United States but had a law
office in Tijuana. Mr. Peyton recommended the transaction be
individually executed by bank trusts. He also advised setting up a

preliminary contract with the Ejido San Bruno to confirm they would fulfill all the requirements to sell the lease to the Americans. The objective was to have the sale "legally tied up" before any funds were given to the Ejido San Bruno.

Acquiring bank trusts required patience and a sizeable outlay of money by each American household for appraisal fees, surveys, bank set-up fees, and attorney fees. The agreed-upon cost of the land was $7.00 U.S. per square meter.[163] In addition, the homeowners would be responsible for paying a 2% Mexican acquisition tax. Much of the money was collected upfront, even years before the fideicomisos were finalized. This caused unrest among the homeowners, especially those who had retired. Some did not have liquid funds readily available.

The American homeowners hoped the trusts would be completed by the end of 1998. However, the Ejido San Bruno continued to cite necessary delays due to difficulties obtaining all the required documentation. At the suggestion of attorney Dennis Peyton, the homeowners entered into a promissory agreement with the Ejido, creating an irrevocable trust for the transfer of the Ejido property. They paid one-third of the sale price in exchange for the Ejido's commitment to finalize the Bank Trusts as soon as possible.

In 1998, on the advice of its attorney, the PCHA took steps to become a legal entity in México. The organization became known as "Punta Chivato Homeowners' Association, Civil Association," which was abbreviated "A.C." Formalizing the Association through this process was thought to strengthen the Americans' position. They hoped by doing this, their goal of land ownership would be realized more quickly.

However, the Bank Trusts continued to be delayed by the Ejido. In August 1999, the Land Acquisition Committee wrote a letter to update the still-hopeful Americans on the unresolved issues. One problem was the lots where the Americans had built homes, had never gone through the process of becoming legal subdivisions under Bill Alvarado, who had first begun leasing the lots. Now, the Ejido San Bruno was faced with completing this legal process, called "regularization," where the Ejido land with homes on it was subdivided into parcels. Regularizing a subdivision took more time. The procedure ultimately conveyed private title for parcels of Ejido land to a Mexican Corporation or trust, which could then sell the property to non-Mexicans.

Another document called a *memoria descriptiva* had to be written up describing the entire area, including roads, green areas, boat ramps, and parcels with homes. The Mexican government would not sign off on bringing the subdivision legally up to date without this document. Yet another delay cited by the Ejido was their need to obtain a new attorney.

As the new millennium arrived, the Americans at Punta Chivato were still anxiously awaiting word about their fideicomisos. At the April 13, 2000, PCHA annual meeting, Harry Oxley gave an update on the status of these documents. He indicated all but five of the permits were received by the notary in Santa Rosalía. However, until those five remaining fideicomisos were complete, the papers would not be available for signature.

Chapter 84

PLAYA CONCHA (SHELL BEACH)

South of the hotel, past the longer airport runway, stood a large section of land not included in the original agreement between the hotel's original owner, Dixon Collins, and then-President Mateo in México City. Unlike the property around Hotel Punta Chivato, this area was undeveloped. After the members of Ejido San Bruno voted to privatize their land, they began the process of creating regular subdivisions on this land.

The area was split between ejidatario households. If the head of the family decided to convert the family's specified land into parcels for sale, the request first had to be made before the Ejido general assembly, during which a two-thirds vote of approval was necessary. Members were expected to make their intentions known and give the other ejidatarios the first right of refusal before selling a parcel to a third party outside the Ejido San Bruno.

The March/April 1995 edition of the *Punta Chivato Charla* announced the formation of this new subdivision south of the hotel:

> We have a new subdivision in our midst. Ejido San Bruno has divided much of their land into parcels and each ejidatario has received 3 parcels, one waterfront and two inland lots. Güero Alaniz, our tienda owner, has subdivided his parcel into several 15-18-meter-wide lots and is leasing them on an annual basis.
>
> A contest was held and after much consideration the name "Playa Concha" (Shell Beach) was chosen. Richard Fodor won a 2-day free trip to that new resort area by submitting the winning name. Other names submitted were Linda Vista, Chivato Oeste, Tortilla Flats.

"The laws began to change," commented Güero during an interview years later. "They gave us the land and titles so one could sell. Now, it is beneficial to be an ejidatario. Many benefited." As an ejidatario, Güero took advantage of the new opportunity to own land at Punta Chivato.

"I began to develop this," Güero continued, indicating he built the first ramada on the bluff above Shell Beach, a property he would later sell to Bill and Janine Waggener of Placerville, California. Güero and his wife, Gloria, had their new home and warehouse built on some of his property.

A few long-time campers from the beach decided to lease or purchase lots from Güero. Among them were Mike and Conna Melton, Lester and Betty Bell, and Helmut and Edith Zwick.

"Güero came up to me and said he was going to make another camping beach over there," said Mike Melton during an interview. "He said he had some land for sale."

Mike had never been on that bluff and seen the Sea of Cortez from there. After he visited the first time, he told Güero he knew at least ten other people who might want to buy lots. "And that's how it started," said Mike.

On January 22, 1995, campers Lester and Betty Bell moved onto property above Shell Beach. They built a 40' by 40' palapa and lived in a trailer on their parcel. "We were there [the camping beach] for many a windstorm. That's what drove us out of there," Betty said about living on the camping beach. Mike and Conna Melton purchased a trailer from Bill and Barbara Silzle, who no longer needed it after building their home in Punta Chivato. The Meltons parked it on the lot they leased next to the Bells. Steve and Rusty Howland also put a trailer on property in the same neighborhood. "All three of us came on the same day," recalled Betty Bell in an interview.

"All the people who originally bought at Shell Beach were from the camping beach," remarked early camper and homeowner Les Conner.[164]

Lee and Lynn Links were among those who considered leaving the camping beach. Lynn described living on the beach as hard work. "I felt I wasn't enjoying it as much as I did earlier," Lynn said. "We were getting older. The beach was too close for me. I wasn't having the privacy that I wanted. There were too many people too close together. Too many people always cleaning too many fish. Too many people always walking back and forth behind my windows."

However, Lynn did not want to rush into leaving the camping beach, although she experienced strong peer pressure from fellow campers who had left. "I saw a lot of people going to a lot of places, but they weren't places that I wanted to go," said Lynn, referring to those who had relocated above Shell Beach. The Linkses felt the lots at Shell Beach were too small. "People were just cramming in there. I had more space down on the beach," Lynn added, "I didn't find anything that would give me more privacy. That was why we didn't leave the beach earlier when the rest of the beach left."

Lynn's husband, Lee, voiced concern about their delay in selecting a piece of property. "You're going to wait too long. You're not going to find anything," he said.

But Lynn Links was adamant. "We're going to wait and find what we want," she told Lee. "I don't want to go to something that I don't like."

Lee and Lynn finally found a piece of property they both liked. It was on a bluff above the Sea of Cortez. A beautiful arroyo beside it was unbuildable, offering privacy to their selected property. The area was large enough for their camping trailer, the construction of an outdoor kitchen and dining area, a garage, and a storage room. In addition, the space was perfect to accommodate a garden, one of Lynn's passions. The only problem was they did not know who owned the parcel or if it was for sale.

During this time, in September 1998, a hurricane hit Punta Chivato. Lee and Lynn were fortunate to pull their trailer off the camping beach in time. Bob and Lynda Davis offered to let them park their rig next to their home on the bluff while they were away. Soon, Lee noticed that water and mud had seeped into the Davis's home. Due to the house being on lower ground than the adjacent residences, the runoff from the rainstorm traveled down the driveway and entered their home, flowing under the garage and house doors. "It came in every place," said Lynn. "It was in Bob and Lynda's bedroom, in their bathroom, and in the main part of the house." They measured the mud line in the garage—six inches.

Much of the muddy water ran through the house and out again, but the sliding glass doors had an inch-wide lip that held the water inside. Lynn and Lee worked for hours cleaning up the Davis's home. Fortunately, they were able to obtain a wet vac to speed up the process.

In the aftermath of that storm, the Linkses were even more intent on locating the ejidatario who owned the parcel they had seen.

"That was why we stayed so long up at the Davis's house," Lynn recalled. "We were trying to find the man who owned the parcel. He was like incognito."

Mike Melton, who, along with his wife, Conna, had already moved from the camping beach to Shell Beach, offered to assist the Linkses in their search for the owner. At the time, Mike worked as a broker for a local real estate business, *Dos Amigos* Realty (Two Friends Realty). The two friends who owned the business were local ejidatarios, Güero Alaníz and Julian Vargas. Mike's job was to help sell Ejido lots to Americans eager to buy.

Mike found out who owned the land the Linkses wanted, but the owner had no intention of selling it. Although Mike Melton did not represent the couple, he agreed to hold their money in case the ejidatario owner, Adan Mendoza Murillo, changed his mind. In time, he did.

Conna and Mike Melton at Punta Chivato. Courtesy Harry Oxley

"Mike was instrumental in convincing Adan he should develop his parcel," said Lynn, "that he could get some money doing it."

Adan not only sold the Linkses the parcel they wanted but also ended up selling nearby lots where homes were later built by Bruce and Jeri Sue Jacobson, Dave and Renee Beck, Jim and Sherry Butch, and Lynne Weiser.

"Mike didn't earn a nickel from us," said Lynn, who later referred to the parcel they chose as "absolute paradise." "For all the work he did in helping to arrange sales of Ejido land, Mike earned very little."

Mike Melton would later be falsely accused of fraud by the president of the Ejido San Bruno, Victor Manuel Velazquez Meza, who indicated Mike was forcing ejidatarios to sign documents to sell their land to Americans. Mike and Conna Melton were deported from México due to not having up-to-date immigration status, according to an article in a La Paz newspaper.[165]

The new development on Shell Beach was not welcomed by all. One of the earlier homeowners nearer the hotel commented, "Until the Shell Beach people came in, I think we were just one happy community. The trouble was the Shell Beach people brought in another element that was not as dedicated to ownership as all of us were and helping each other like we were. They were more just part-time people."

"Shell Beach was like an upscaled campground," remarked Harry Oxley regarding the first parcels that were built on. "Then they leased their lots, and now they're buying their lots. And they're changing from trailers to houses. It's evolving."

An article in the January 1997 issue of the *Chivato Charla* commented on the new Shell Beach residents. The article intended to help unify the community at Punta Chivato—the old and the new residents.

> *There are many new lot owners at Shell beach that we don't know, so we welcome all of you. There are many new palapas and houses and more construction going on, spreading westward along Shell Beach.*

Hoping to promote goodwill among those celebrating America's Independence Day while in Punta Chivato, Mike and Conna Melton decided to continue a tradition they started while still living on the camping beach—a Fourth of July fish fry and fireworks display. An article in the Summer 1998 *Chivato Charla* extolled this community event:

4th of July Fish Fry and Fireworks at Shell Beach

The July 4th fish fry has been an annual event at the Melton's for a few years. This was the first time at their home on Shell Beach. This year's event will be a tough act to follow.

About 50 people attended. Who would have thought there were that many people at Chivato in July? In addition to the excellent beer-batter fish and onion rings Mike is famous for, there was tri-tip barbecue with all the trimmings.

The fireworks display was impressive. And Mike showed what a gutsy guy he is by setting off fireworks upwind of his thatch roof.

Chapter 85

DORADO TOURNAMENT

Even as the Americans struggled to acquire legal ownership of their land in Baja, their love and enjoyment of the area continued. In the summer of 1997, a new charitable event began in Punta Chivato. Deemed the 1st Annual Punta Chivato Dorado Tournament, it lasted for three days, July 5-7. Homeowners Harry Oxley and Bob Davis, both avid fishermen, came up with the idea and decided to try it.

"I've always been in the promotion business," Harry said. "I thought, 'God, we ought to put on a dorado tournament.'" The premise was to have a fun time and raise money for local charities.

According to Harry, six principals volunteered to take on the brunt of the work, which entailed getting sponsors, advertising, organizing, and hosting the event: Harry and Pam Oxley, Bob and Lynda Davis, and Lou and Dee Razo.

Harry solicited sponsors who donated prizes for the winners in several categories: first and second-place finishers in the men's and women's divisions, "Largest Fish," and "Most Caught & Released." On the final evening of the tournament, a dinner was hosted for all participants. Acting as emcees, Harry and Bob announced the winners in each category. Amid whoops and hollers, tired but happy fishermen and fisherwomen went forward to receive their prizes and accolades.

The first tournament was a success, and the three couples decided to host it again the following year. The 2nd Annual Bulls Only Dorado Tournament was held in May 1998. The entry fee was $40 per person, and early registration was advised due to the event's popularity the previous year. On Friday night, May 22, 1998, a captains' meeting and kickoff party were held at the Punta Chivato Hotel restaurant.

The following day, before 7:00 a.m., captains and crew launched their crafts from the boat ramp and eagerly awaited the "shotgun" start. At the blast, boats of all sizes and speeds suddenly were under full throttle, heading out in all directions, leaving a flurry of jumbled waves as they went in search of the trophy fish.

On Sunday morning, there was a four-hour free-for-all, the largest-fish-of-any-kind contest. That evening at the awards banquet, the following winners were announced by Harry Oxley:

1st place overall largest fish–Pam Oxley

Men's 1st Place–Will Willett

Men's 2nd Place–Tom Rosen

Women's 1st Place–Pam Kelley

Women's 2nd Place–Patty McCaffrey

Most Releases–Larry Lucore

2nd Day "Anything Goes"–George Kelley

Bob Davis said the net amount brought in after expenses was $950. Chairman Harry Oxley held the tournament proceeds as a fund for local medical emergencies at Punta Chivato. Homeowners approached by a local Mexican for a charitable donation were directed to refer the individual to the Oxleys for consideration on behalf of the association.

Harry Oxley and daughter, Laurie, next to fishing tournament results.
Courtesy Harry Oxley

In subsequent years, this popular fishing tournament was held in June, a month when the dorado arrived, and the sea's southern swell had not yet fully developed. The event quickly became a highlight in the fast-growing Punta Chivato community. Many scheduled their vacations around the tournament. It was an exciting time for homeowners and campers at Punta Chivato and fishermen who arrived from surrounding towns. Registrants came by car, camper van, motorhomes, private planes, and boat. Facilities in Santa Rosalía and Mulegé, as well as Punta Chivato, were utilized by the influx of those who loved to fish and hoped to win a prize.

Harry increased the number of sponsorships as the entry total grew each year. "It's growing like crazy," said Harry Oxley during an interview. "We have a lot of interest from sponsors, and I think it's just going to get better and better. We don't necessarily want a lot more entries. We're going to keep the entries under 150." Harry was able to line up sponsorships and prizes from such well-known companies as Yamaha Marine, Corona, Seeker rods, O'Boy Oberto, Tag and Brag, Fisherman's Landing, Maxima America, Shimano, and Fish Trap Lures.

In 1999, 29 boats with 82 anglers participated in the dorado tournament. The following was reported in the Spring 1999 issue of the *Chivato Charla*:

Third Annual Bulls Only Tournament held June 11-13, 1999

It took over an hour for Bruce Lynn (from Bakersfield), fishing with Rick Rhodes on El Charro to land a 38.5 pounder 6 miles off Punta Inez on 30# line.

Results:

Men's Division:
1st Place   *Tom Cunningham on Palapa Papa*
2nd Place   *Bob Davis on Sunshine*

Women's Division:
1st Place   *Pam Kelley (also was winner last year)*
2nd Place   *Lynda Davis on Sunshine*

Most Releases:
Two young men from the camping beach fishing from Dauntless. Names not available.

2nd Day Anything Goes:
Craig Brewer caught a BIG blue marlin. Other fish caught in-
cluded: sailfish by Dennis (Red's friend) aboard Speedbump; sailfish
by Jeff Koch on Wood Eye; sailfish by Eric Franklin (Davis' grand-
son) on Sunshine. The day before, when it didn't count, Jeff Adams
caught a nice marlin.

Lots of money made for worthy causes (almost $1900). The Red
Cross representative was given $400 at the Awards Banquet.

As mentioned in a later *Charla* article, the kindergarten in San
Bruno received $50 of the third annual tournament's earnings.

Twenty-seven boats with seventy anglers, including twenty-four
women, registered for the 4th Annual Bulls Only Dorado Tournament held June 16-18, 2000. Registration and the banquet were
held at a new restaurant under construction west of the long airport
runway. Cerveza Corona co-sponsored the event and erected large
tents with tables and chairs on Art and Dorothy Oberto's lot next
to George and Diane Powell's lot. Saúl's restaurant from Mulegé catered the captains' meeting dinner, offering a choice of lobster or
steak for entrées.

Unfortunately, rough sea conditions and a lack of fish prompted
all boats to return early. Due to the swells at the boat launch ramp,
getting the vessels back onto their trailers without damage proved
challenging. That day, Jeffrey Luján from Mulegé caught the only
dorado and won the overall first prize.

The following Sunday, June 25, a makeup day was scheduled
for the remaining awards. That day, 14 boats with 30 anglers headed
out into calm seas. Fishers were excited to find dorado everywhere—
172 were caught and released. Ralph Millar, on a boat from Mulegé,
won the Men's Division with a 38-pound bull. Kathleen Flick won
first place in the Women's Division with a 22-pounder. Bob and
Lynda Davis, aboard their boat, *Sunshine*, registered "The Most
Releases" with 32 fish. The "Anything Goes" category was won by
Karen Moranville, who caught a sailfish and a 127-pound tuna and
released several dorado. The best fish story was by Peggy Fodor, who
related how her husband, Richard, happened to have his trunks off
when a 34-pound bull hit. It put up a tremendous fight, but he
finally landed it—in the buff. The tournament that year raised over
$3,000 to support local charities.

In a subsequent year, the net profit from the tournament grew to as much as $6,000. Recipients of funds raised by the tournament over the years included the Santa Rosalía Red Cross, Casa Hogar (C.R.E.E.A.D., a drug rehab program), and several local Mexicans who desperately needed money to have operations, cancer treatment, and other medical services.

When interviewed in 2002, Harry Oxley reflected on the tournament he helped found. "The tournament's doing what it was designed to do," he said. "It is helping local people. We don't want it to go out of our local area. It's doing a good job. It's getting better and better. We'll get to the point where we really don't advertise it. On top of everything, the dorado tournament is fun."

When asked about the amount of work the principals put into running such an event year after year, Harry replied, "We enjoy doing the cooking. We enjoy the work. Every year after it's done, we go, 'Oh man, we're not going to do that again next year. We're going to get other people to help.' And then we end up doing it."

Many were surprised when the tournament, scheduled for June 2004, was suddenly canceled by the tournament committee. Following are excerpts from a letter sent to prior tournament registrants:

> *Our wonderful Paradise has been temporarily destroyed with barbed wire fences and open trenches blocking the launch ramp to the point where it is very difficult to launch a boat.*
>
> *In addition, the ramp and adjacent area are in total disrepair as the damage sustained in the hurricane in September has not been repaired and we are not being "allowed: to arrange for the repairs ourselves."*
>
> *We were holding out hope that the situation would change... it hasn't.*

The tournament committee realized it was impossible for the forty-plus boats signed up for the event to all launch at the appropriate time. It was not worth putting the anglers in danger. Since they could not resolve the situation in time for the tournament, it was canceled. The sponsors for the event also had to be notified:

We are working hard to resolve this terrible situation and hope that next year things will return to normal in Punta Chivato and we can continue with our Tournament.

The problem was eventually resolved, and the annual fishing tournament continued.

Chapter 86

SOCIAL SCENE

From the 1960s, vacationers who came to Punta Chivato hoped to escape the unrest and pressures of life in the United States. They looked at the seaside hide-away as an ideal place to temporarily disappear, a place where there were no rules, where one could do as he or she pleased and get away with it. However, as more people found the secluded vacation spot, socializing with others became hard to avoid.

Campers developed interpersonal relationships often out of necessity. The harsh reality of setting up camp on a desolate beach far from the comforts of home, encountering challenging weather conditions and unfamiliar dangers from the land and the sea brought them together.

For some, it was the camaraderie of sharing stories with like-minded adventurers who had also braved the long drive from the United States down the Baja peninsula and successfully navigated the washboard dirt road leading from Baja 1 to Punta Chivato. It was as if there was an unspoken badge of honor to be one of those adventurous souls who dared travel to the unknown and "conquer" it.

The social scene began to change as homes were built at Punta Chivato. Those early homeowners who had not started out camping on the beach chose not to interact much with others.

"We just came down for three or four or five days at a time and didn't have time to socialize with the homeowners, much less the camping beach," said John Fitzsimmons. "We were very much into ourselves. We came down for weekends."

Other early homeowners, like the Oxleys and Adamses, not only started out at the camping beach but had the luxury of staying at Punta Chivato for longer stretches of time. They maintained relationships with fellow campers and developed new social connections with the homeowners.

According to some, as more homes were built, the social scene at Punta Chivato became a two-class society—the beach people and the homeowners. "The people on the camping beach weren't necessarily included that much in social events unless it was something that was going on at Bill's place," said one camper, referring to functions Bill Alvarado hosted at the hotel.

Long-time camper Lynn Links remembered, "When we were on the beach, we weren't invited up to a lot of things up in the houses." The exceptions were those homeowners, like the Oxleys, with whom they had developed an earlier connection as beach campers.

The social scene changed even more at Punta Chivato as the rate of home construction accelerated at the end of the 1990s and into the new millennium. Many of the early homeowners retired and were able to spend consecutive months there. A few decided to make Punta Chivato a permanent residence.

Lynn Links stated she noticed a change after moving from the camping beach to their lot at Shell Beach. "Shell Beach area and the whole community came together more socially and also the beach people who were there in the winter," she said, referring to the Kelloggs and Seablooms, who continued to trailer camp on the beach during the wintertime. "They are part of our community and take part in our community activities and contribute to the community," Lynn added. "There's a difference between just coming and being a beach camper and coming and staying a length of time and coming into the community, such as the Seablooms and the Kelloggs."

Many short-time beach campers were never included in the social life at Punta Chivato. "They were only transient people, and our community didn't reach out," said Lynn Links. If those individuals eventually built a home, as the Acostas did, they became part of the "group."

There were frequent parties at the Oxley home, including the annual New Year's party, which celebrated both the coming year and Harry's birthday.

As the area's population increased, regular social events were scheduled, some weekly and some annually. Often, the annual events were held as fundraisers for local Mexican causes.

In addition to the charitable Annual Bulls Only Dorado Tournament, which began in 1997, and the Annual Lee Cobb Memorial Golf Tournament and Auction, which commenced in 2000, several other annual events were started in the late 1990s and early 2000s by Punta Chivato homeowners who shared like interests.

Bev and Bob Busse began the Annual Wine Extravaganza after they hosted a dinner party and served their own homemade wine. Homeowner Lynda Davis wrote in the May 3, 2002, issue of the *Chivato Charla:*

> *It was such a hit with the group (we drank their entire supply) and they decided to 'challenge' others in Punta Chivato to make wine, too.*

Potential winemakers were encouraged to begin the hobby: "Save your bottles and go to the nearest wine and beer supply store for your wine-making supplies."

The Busses' challenge quickly caught on as other homeowners developed their own wine-making techniques, bottled their libations, named their "winery," and prepared creative labels. Some of the labels were Zorro Winery (Walter and Jeanne Fox),[166] Davis Pointe (Bob and Lynda Davis), Summercrest (Jere and Marge Summers), Chateau Chivato (George and Diane Powell), Cactus Corner Cellars (Harry and Pam Oxley), Longears Vineyards (Joel and Connie Slaughter), B & D Fine Wines (R.B. and Doc Tonini), Tres Arcos Vintners (John and Gerry Fitzsimmons), and Viento Sur Cellars (Ben Pierce and Leslie Sullins-Pierce).

At the annual wine-tasting affair, each wine was rated for clarity, bouquet, and taste. The only rule for entrants was that they must have made their own wine. Both red and white wines were produced. In subsequent years, as the number of entries grew, the tasting had to be scheduled for two separate days. "Punta Chivato has proven to be a vintners' paradise," Lynda Davis announced in the May 3, 2002, *Charla.*

Card games also became regular pastimes for many Punta Chivato homeowners. Bunco, poker, and "O Hell" were some of the favorites. In 1998, the first Annual "O Hell" Tournament took place. Up to twenty people assembled at the designated host's home, where a minimal "entry fee" was collected. After a fun-filled afternoon, the first-place winner was given a monetary reward. The one with the lowest score was presented with a bottle of wine. This became humorously known as the Lee Links Loser Award or the Lynx Sportsmanship Award.

At an annual Punta Chivato Homeowners' meeting during Easter week in 1999, when the topic of fixing the boat ramp was being discussed, Bob Davis offhandedly suggested forming a separate entity to address boating-related issues. The Punta Chivato Yacht Club (PCYC) was founded.

An organizational meeting was held at the hotel in May 1999, and thirty people attended. Fifteen put up $50 each to become charter members. Bob Davis was elected Commodore of the Yacht Club. The club's goals were: "In cooperation with the hotel, improve and maintain the boat launch, promote boating interest and safety, and encourage social interaction among Chivato residents."

Interest grew as word spread about this new club. Fifty people showed up at the next meeting, and the total membership increased to sixty-two. A logo was created that consisted of an anchor silhouetted against a setting sun over three squiggly, blue lines depicting water. Knit shirts, heavy Lucite beer mugs, and highball glasses with the logo were produced for sale.

Punta Chivato Yacht Club (PCYC) beer mug created for sale. Photo taken by author

Money from the Yacht Club was used to repair and extend the dock at the boat ramp, making it easier and safer to get on and off one's boat. Plans were also made to extend the concrete launch ramp.

In addition to supporting the launch ramp at Punta Chivato, the Yacht Club organized social events, including an annual Mother's Day brunch at Ray's Restaurant in Conception Bay. Some traveled there by boat, and others drove.

The Spring 2000 issue of the *Chivato Charla* carried an article that reported membership in the Punta Chivato Yacht Club had grown to 135 individuals! It became one of the most popular groups in Punta Chivato.[167]

Women at Punta Chivato developed other social events, such as the Annual Home and Garden Tour. Each year, different residents opened their homes to fellow homeowners. The first home on the tour often provided coffee, juice, and pastries, while lunch was provided at the final stop.

In 2000, a committee headed up by Pam Oxley collected over 300 recipes from residents and published a cookbook entitled *Las Cocinas de Chivato*. Bev Busse designed the colorful book jacket and section separators. Many hours were put into the project, which included layout, typing, and proofing. The first printing of 300 copies sold out the first week. Sale proceeds went into a community benevolent fund.

Another local fundraiser was an annual Punta Chivato calendar that included photographs of the picturesque sea, land, sunsets, and unique flora and fauna of their beloved Baja paradise.

Through the formation of these social activities, the growing community at Punta Chivato shared comradery and supported causes important to the local Mexican population.

Chapter 87

WHALE PROJECT

In late winter and early spring of 1999, those who visited Punta Chivato were entertained by several young gray whales (*ballena gris*) frolicking in the waters just off the point. They were so close that one could row a kayak out and pet them. "The babies would swim all around the kayaks and just play," recalled one witness.

Then, around Easter, one of the baby whales became entangled in a gill net set out by local Mexican fishermen. As the whale struggled to free itself, the fishing net wrapped more tightly around its tail. Sadly, the whale, estimated to be two years of age, drowned and eventually washed up on Deadman's Beach.

While residents at Punta Chivato mourned the loss of the once-friendly, 32-foot gray whale, one enterprising couple decided to use it as a learning experience, particularly for their grandchildren.

In May, when Andy and Bunnie Adams' daughter and her four children arrived from Montana for a two-week visit, Bunnie drove them to Deadman's Beach to look at the whale. *Perhaps it would provide a good school project*, she thought.

When they arrived, Bunnie noticed the dead whale had already dried out from sun exposure and was cracked open along its spine, revealing its vertebrae and ribs. "Andy suggested that we use the whale as a school experiment and collect all the bones before people started taking them to decorate their houses," shared Bunnie.

The following day, Bunnie, Andy, and all four grandkids, aged nine to fifteen, headed back to Deadman's Beach. Starting at one end, they sawed through the thick, dried flesh and meticulously extracted each bone from the bloody tissue. Every bone was laid out on the sand exactly as it came out of the whale. "It was still smelly as hell," Bunnie recalled. "The flies were incredible."

The determined group carried on. One granddaughter, Bethany, opted to take photographs rather than get closer to the whale. "Lindsay drew pictures of the whale as we worked," said Bunnie, "and Rayanna and Jessie helped us get the bones all out." It took only two hours to retrieve all the bones, but according to Bunnie, "it was two intensive hours!" They got used to the smell.

Once the whale's bones had been removed, the crew decided not to leave them on the beach where wild animals or curious collectors could take them. Determined to keep all the bones together in anticipation of eventually reconstructing the skeleton, the Adamses carefully placed the young gray whale's bones in their Suburban and slowly drove back to their beach-front home at Punta Chivato.

The Adamses consulted with a local Mexican who worked as the caretaker for John Lyddon's property nearby. Ruben, who had training in marine biology, told them they would need to bury the bones with lime. The lime would absorb the oil out of the bones and preserve them. The Adamses had Mexican workers dig a 37-foot-long trench. Then, they purchased bags of lime, which José Luis Benson and Ruben sprinkled over the bones.

As the workers threw dirt back over the limed-covered bones, Ruben inquired, "Where are the arm bones, the flippers?" Bunnie admitted they had left the flippers on Deadman's Beach, not realizing they had bones in them. After retrieving the large bones from the flippers, another hole had to be dug so they could also be buried with lime.

The bones remained underground for four months, during which time only a few of the whale's digits disappeared. Bunnie suspected the neighbor's dog had dug them up and reburied them elsewhere.

"Then we started pulling parts out and cleaning off the rest of the meat and bleaching them and then laying them in the sun to dry," stated Bunnie. The porous bones readily absorbed water, and some of the larger pieces became difficult to lift. "It took weeks for the water to all drain out of them," Bunnie recalled. With each step in this process, the Adames were careful to keep the bones in order. They were pleased they had taken the time initially to number each one. Then, they painted each bone.

Due to Mexican laws that regulate the removal of certain plants and animals from the country, it was necessary to get authorization from the Mexican government before proceeding. Andy applied for the federal zone, the beach in front of their home. According to Bunnie Adams, Ruben was able to obtain a permit from the Mexican Fish and Game Department official in Santa Rosalía to erect the whale skeleton there. However, as Punta Chivato residents had discovered in relation to their home leases, documents approved locally generally were not valid until signed in México City.

A large frame was built on the federal zone in front of the Adams's home, and they began to assemble the whale bones.

Ruben suggested the Adamses ask the school children in Santa Rosalía to come out and name the whale. "They were going to bus the children out to see it, but they never did do it," said Bunnie. She suggested it might have had something to do with issues the homeowners at Punta Chivato were having at the time with the Mexican government. Bunnie vowed that when the skeleton was completed, she would return and ask the children to visit and give the whale a name. They even spoke of someday relocating the whale skeleton from the federal zone to a "green area" between the Adams's home and the airplane taxiway.

A partially completed whale skeleton remained on the beach for about a year and a half. "The reason it never got completed is when we put the ribs on it was so heavy that it sagged," said Bunnie. A piece of wood was used as a brace, but they refrained from putting up the rest of the bones until a permanent solution could be found. "We're going to completely redo it and repaint so that it won't rust, and we're putting the ribs all back on and connecting them permanently," said Bunnie when interviewed in December 2002. "That's January's goal."

Although initially, the whale project and its odor were not popular with some homeowners who lived nearby or wanted to enjoy a leisurely stroll along the beach, the whale eventually became a tourist attraction. George Powell even posted it on the Punta Chivato website. "People would come to Punta Chivato and ask, 'Where is the whale?'" said Bunnie with a smile.

Eventually government officials demanded the whale be removed.[168]

Chapter 88

EJIDO SELLS HOTEL

Hotel Punta Chivato continued to thrive for a short time under the management of Ejido San Bruno. But according to one home-owner, "right after they took over and found out there wasn't all this money and no secret bank accounts, the Ejido began to struggle."

Homeowners who regularly ate breakfast at the hotel continued to do so out of habit. They liked the wait staff and enjoyed the food and good service. But gradually, things began to change as long-time employees left Punta Chivato. One of these, Saúl, left to open a restaurant of his own in Mulegé. First named La Palapa, the name was later changed to Sr. Gecko Restaurant.

Saúl Zuñiga, owner of Sr. Gecko Restaurant in Mulegé 2024.
Courtesy Pam Oxley

Having enough money to pay their employees at the hotel be-came a major problem for the Ejido. Jere Summers, who, along with his wife, Marge, oversaw reading the residential water meters, recounted their urgency in providing the hotel with each month's water payment on behalf of the American homeowners.

Victor would be there on the afternoon of the first wanting the money for the water. They were depending on the money that we were paying for the water, not to pay the taxes but to pay the hotel employees. That's where the money went. So, we would read the meters, we'd do the figures, write a check and take it down to the hotel. We never held them up on that because that's what they were using to pay the help. We did what was proper and right, we paid the people that supposedly controlled the water which was the hotel.

As the number of experienced employees at Hotel Punta Chivato dwindled, the quality of the service fell, too. The hotel rooms were not being maintained.

People would fly in and request a room but be told there were no rooms available. Noticing the scarcity of guests, they would insist on being shown a room. "Well, it'd be dirty," said one homeowner. "They didn't have rooms because they weren't cleaned." Perhaps the Ejido thought the hotel restaurant and the bar were going to support it.

Some people had made room reservations at the hotel prior to Bill's departure and did not know the owner had left. "Where's Bill?" inquired the return guests, incredulous that the gregarious *gringo* who worked so hard to restore the hotel had gone. When the private pilots' association put the word out that Bill was no longer at Punta Chivato, several fly-in groups canceled their reservations.

Although first-time hotel guests still came to Punta Chivato after hearing about the fishing and easy access to the Sea of Cortez, business for the Ejido gradually dropped off as regulars chose not to return. "It just kept going down and down and down until people weren't coming anymore," commented one homeowner. "It kept getting worse and worse to the point that they could not stay open."

Unable to keep Hotel Punta Chivato viable, the Ejido San Bruno tried to sell it. They received several offers. One was from "a serious Japanese buyer" who apparently pulled out over concern that the water supply was inadequate.[169] Another was from homeowners Art and Dorothy Oberto.

"The Obertos came in and looked at the books, made an offer," recalled Jere Summers, sharing the following dialog.

"No, no, we want $5 million," replied the Ejido.

"It's not worth $5 million," said Art Oberto. "Is the whole land and everything included?"

"No, no, it's just the hotel," said the Ejido.

"No, there's too much work to be done," Art replied, deciding it was futile to try to negotiate further.[170]

Another bid to purchase the hotel came from a man out of Reno, Nevada. His offer was also rejected. The Ejido held firm to their asking price—$5 million."

"They should have jumped on it," said Jere Summers, recalling the bids the Ejido received for the hotel, "because one of them, I think, was a couple of million, and one was a million and a half or something like that." But the Ejido San Bruno would not budge. "No, no, no, $5 million." Hotel Punta Chivato remained closed and continued to deteriorate as the Ejido attempted to find someone who would meet their asking price.

Jere remembered attending a "final hurrah" dinner at the hotel restaurant on July 18, 1999, the evening before the hotel closed. The date was memorable to him since it was the same day he and Marge acquired a new dog they named Rita. Sadly, it was also the day one of the residents of Shell Beach, Will Willett, had a heart attack and died while doing what he loved—fishing with a couple of buddies from a boat in the Sea of Cortez off Punta Chivato. "It was kind of a damper," said Jere, "but we did; we all went down [to the hotel]."

For that last hotel dinner, the homeowners requested the staff order enough hamburgers and buns for all the people who were at Punta Chivato that humid summer day—twenty in all.

In August of 1999, the hotel was sold to Giuseppe Marcelletti Pandolfi, an Italian who owned and operated two other hotels in Baja California Sur, one in La Paz and the other in Loreto. According to one homeowner, who said he spoke to the new hotel owner, the Ejido agreed to sell him the hotel for $800,000. The sale included the road in front of the hotel and both airplane runways.

Homeowner Harry Oxley, who had been reelected president of the PCHA, received the following letter dated August 13, 1999:

Giuseppe Marcelletti (left) and Lou Federico (right) 2000.
Courtesy Lou Federico

Mr. Harry Oxley

Representative of Homeowners and lessees of the tourist area of Chivato Point

By means of the present we notify you that Mr. Giuseppe Marcelletti Pandolfi is the new owner of the installations previously called Hotel "Punta Chivato," therefore new administrator of the landing fields.

In view of the foregoing we ask you to notify all residents of Punta Chivato in order that good harmony and coordination prevails in this tourist area.

Nothing more for the moment, we remain sincerely,
C. Julian Vargas Limon
C. Victor M. Velasquez Meza
C. Carlos Ramirez Ramirez

Marcelletti renamed the resort *Posada de las Flores* (Inn of the Flowers) the same as his other Baja hotels. He intended to convert the hotel into a Five-Star establishment. The rooms were renovated, some being made into small suites. All were elegantly decorated with new furnishings. The entire facility got a facelift, including the restaurant, bar, kitchen, and pool area. New landscaping around the hotel enhanced the Mexican colonial architecture. The extensive project took a year to complete.

On August 1, 2000, the hotel officially reopened. As posted on the hotel's website, *www.posadadelasflores.com*, Posada de las Flores Punta Chivato sat on 7.5 acres and offered twenty units, including ten standard rooms, six sea views, four garden views, and ten junior suites. A newly built tennis court available for guests was located behind the hotel. The opening of a hotel gym was anticipated for January 15, 2002.

With the hotel finally completed, homeowners at Punta Chivato expected guests would once again flock to the idyllic area. Strangely, they noted very few people stayed at the restored hotel. Fishermen who requested rooms were often turned away.

One homeowner reported he got into a conversation with the owner of a hotel on mainland México in the Yucatan. After mentioning that he lived in Punta Chivato, the man indicated he was familiar with the new hotel owner. "Oh yeah, that boy over there," the man said, referring to Marcelletti, "He's a good friend. He's in the Mafia, you know." This could have been the start of a rumor about Marcelletti's relationship with the Mafia and that Punta Chivato's Posada de las Flores was used for money laundering.

Chapter 89

RAÚL BUYS LARGE PARCEL

In the summer of 1999, while the early Punta Chivato homeowners were wondering if they would ever receive their fideicomisos and legally own the land where they had built their homes, they received further news that caused their hopes to waver. PCHA President Harry Oxley shared a letter he received from the board of Ejido San Bruno. The notice, dated August 10, 1999, informed the Americans of the sale to Mr. Raúl Luján Soberanes of a large parcel of Ejido property (referred to as parcel 121) at Punta Chivato:

> By means of this letter we notify you that the group of 27 co-owners of the undivided parcel no. 121 have, …based on rights (provisions) mentioned in article 84 of the current agrarian law, unanimously decided to sell and dispose of to Mr. Raul Lujan Soberanes and his companies said parcel.…
>
> In view of above stated, the service of supplying water that the well supplies to the aqueduct as well as the service of cleaning, etc. will be administrated as much in their supply as in their distribution by the new owner.

With the exclusion of Hotel Punta Chivato and property purchased by the hotel (considered parcel 120), Raúl's newly acquired parcel spanned from one mile west of the long runway to Deadman's Beach and included the camping beach.

Parcel 121 initially included all the lots Bill sold to the Americans. However, in Ejido San Bruno's agreement with Raúl, they cut out the properties built on by the Americans who were in the process of obtaining their fideicomisos. Fortunately for the Americans, the Ejido firmly held to its commitment to allow the Americans on parcel 121 to move forward in buying their land.

The Land Acquisition Committee of the PCHA would later learn that a major reason for the delay in receiving their fideicomisos was Raúl Luján's involvement. It appeared he was still intent on obtaining all of parcel 121 for himself. Some believed he wanted control over the Americans by holding their leases.

"Raúl was going to get control of the land at Punta Chivato and then develop it and sell the lots," speculated one homeowner during an interview. "I think that's been his goal all along…I know that's what he thought was the thing to do out at Punta Chivato. Get it away from the Ejido, which he really did fairly successfully."

Raúl would later complain that some Americans were using more land than their fideicomisos designated. Outbuildings, including airplane hangars, were cited. Some Americans along the waterfront had built on the federal zone, which Raúl was also trying to control. He came up with fees he would collect from these offenders.

Anyone in parcel 121 who chose to remain under the lease would now have Raúl Luján as a landlord. Raúl continued to enforce a clause, initially set up by the Ejido, regarding future home construction on parcel 121. This clause stated those who held property leases were required to begin construction of their homes within three years, and the construction had to be completed within five years.[171]

Word was circulated that the fideicomisos were "lost" by an official in Santa Rosalía. However, after a meeting with Raúl Luján held in San Diego with PCHA attorney Dennis Peyton and homeowners Greg Joy and Tom Rosen, the fideicomisos magically reappeared and were finally officially signed. By the autumn of 2000, most Americans received their fideicomisos. The transaction took more than three years.

Soon after Raúl acquired parcel 121, he raised the fee to camp on the beach. At $10/night, some decided to look for another location in Baja to camp. Several long-timers begrudgingly paid the higher fee to continue to enjoy their special vacation spot.

Lynn Links speculated the Internet played a role in changing the camping beach at Punta Chivato. "The beach has definitely changed because there are not the number of short-term campers there used to be. You know, two-week campers. I think it was all the bad publicity about our beach on the Internet—that it was going to be closed and we weren't going to be able to camp there.

People didn't even want to come in because they didn't know if the beach was even going to be open. People went other places. When the beach was open finally, the price had doubled."

Other seasoned campers at Punta Chivato seriously considered leaving the camping beach and investing in the new parcels opening at Shell Beach. "Victor [Velasquez] was the key to getting a lot of camping people interested in buying in Shell Beach," remembered Lynn Links.[172] "Victor told everybody the beach was going to be closed because they were going to build condominiums." When word spread that Raúl intended to close the beach, camping regulars began to get scared.

Long-time camper Dennis Gardner shared the following memory of his final day on the camping beach at Punta Chivato:

> *The last day that I was on the camping beach, I was sitting there. I had my trailer out there and I had like 10 chairs kind of in a half circle. I'm sitting there in the middle with all my imaginary friends. Nobody else on the camping beach anywhere. I spent the last week down there by myself. I knew that that day was supposed to be the last day and I had everything all packed up. Somebody came along, it might have been Mike Morse, and he said, "You know it's time to get off the beach. I'll give you another hour." But the wind was blowing like crazy. It was just blowing sand in your hair and sand in everything, and it was just a nasty day. It had been blowing for about 24 hours.*

Dennis had just closed a deal to purchase a lot with a trailer on Shell Beach from Char Willett. Her husband, Will, had died the past year of a heart attack while fishing with friends in the Sea of Cortez. The sad event left many stunned, especially those who were fishing with him that day. Dennis recounted the following:

> *I think I talked to Mike Melton, Güero, or somebody. Char and I made a quick deal on this place. Pam and Harry [Oxley] kind of vouched for me. I had my business for sale, and I had my house for sale, and I signed a note basically saying whichever sold first she [Char] would get the balance of her money. Pam and Harry basically called her up and told her I was an integrous person and I would be good for my*

*word, and she didn't have to worry about it. I sold the house
and the business 3 or 4 months later and cashed her out on
the balance. Of course, we're not talking about an enormous
amount of money.*

Dennis Gardner recalled it was October 3, 2000, when he closed
the deal with Char Willett and moved from the camping beach to
Shell Beach.

*As I closed up the trailer and picked up the chairs and came down
here [Shell Beach], [I] parked the trailer somewhere in the back.
No sand blowing here. I thought, this is kind of nice. I liked it here,
but I knew it was going to take a little getting used to. Two weeks
later I realized that I could probably never go back to the camping
beach. I definitely felt comfortable and happy here.*

An update on the camping beach appeared on that same date in
the October 3, 2000, issue of the *Chivato Charla*:

*If you haven't checked out the camping beach recently, you are
in for a pleasant surprise. Sr. Lujan wants it to be an upscale
family-oriented area…no more boisterous holiday drinking
parties. It has been cleaned up and new showers built. It ties
in with the master plan that Punta Chivato be an upscale
development.*

"Most of the people who were camping there now have homes,"
said long-time camper and early homeowner Harry Oxley, "homeowners in our development and homeowners in Shell Beach."

Many who relocated to Shell Beach eventually became year-
round residents at Punta Chivato. Soon, more people were residing
on the Shell Beach parcels than those who had built homes on Bill
Alvarado's original lots.

Kerry and Penny Kellogg were among the few long-time
campers who chose not to relocate to Shell Beach. Although they
missed their friends who left the beach, they noted one positive con-
sequence—it was easier for them to find a campsite for their large
camping rig. "We used to have a hard time getting in here," said
Kerry. "So, it's been really a godsend for those of us who stayed on
the beach. We can always get a spot down here now."

The Kelloggs were among the "snow-bird crowd" who resided

on the camping beach in Punta Chivato during the winter months. They initially paid to store their rigs in San Bruno when they returned north to California. Later, they rented a space behind Güero's hardware store. "We rented a spot from him, and we put a chain-link fence all the way around it with gates on it," said Kerry. "Güero made us such a nice offer. Güero really did us a nice thing."

Information on the Internet was more positive years later, as noted in the following December 2003 article:

> *The Campground next to the Hotel is presently open for a fee of $10/day, improvements are being made, new roofs being installed at the showers and a new waterline has been put in. There are also plans to build a restaurant later by the same group that is building one now next to the Airstrip. It does not look that it will be closed permanently later. There is no gate, but one may be installed soon. The latest news is that the campground may stay open. No other development is presently planned at the beach east of the Hotel. An RV Park and campsites will be available at shell beach soon. We will try to keep you posted of any future developments, just check back often.*

Raúl's involvement at Punta Chivato rapidly escalated in the years following his first introduction to the area by John Lyddon in 1989. From a residential builder to a major landholder, Raúl's name was soon renowned by both Americans and Mexicans in the area. He appeared to have contacts in the government and the financial means to influence the direction of issues affecting the Punta Chivato homeowners and the local Mexicans.

With his acquisition of parcel 121 and the water supply to Punta Chivato, Raúl had tremendous control over the potential development and future of the Baja paradise. He claimed he owned the water and the well but could not produce the documents confirming this.

The Ejido was already supplying water to the parcels being developed on Shell Beach. But would the water supply be able to sustain the rapid growth Raúl planned for parcel 121? Water availability would always be a concern in an arid land like Punta Chivato. The issue of future development hinged on having an adequate water supply.

Some locals referred to Raúl as a "fox" and contended his cunning was as crucial to his success as his intelligence. Whatever motivated Raúl's drive and influence on this once-unknown coast of eastern Baja California Sur, México, he was now positioned to take it to the next level. Gated communities, green golf courses, floating casinos…he is in the driver's seat, and he has dreams to paint the future picture of a once remote area.

This book has tried to capture the development of Punta Chivato over the first forty years. It all started with one man's vision of building a fishing resort. Successive individuals influenced the direction of Hotel Punta Chivato and the surrounding land. More development is destined to occur as time marches on, and others dream of owning a piece of Baja that was and still is considered "paradise."

Epilogue

I stumbled upon the idea of writing a history of Punta Chivato in the late 1990s. At a beach party in Punta Chivato, I asked Marge Summers if she knew how the area started. She was uncertain but shared her father's involvement. I suggested that someone should write a book about the beginnings of Punta Chivato. She replied, "Why don't you write the book?" Always willing to take on another project, I accepted the challenge. I never anticipated it would take over 20 years to complete this endeavor!

The earliest history was a mystery to everyone I initially spoke to at Punta Chivato. Some speculated that the Spreckels Sugar Company was involved. Therefore, I was fortunate to meet Lou Federico one day in 2000 when he was visiting Punta Chivato. After our initial conversation, we had several interview sessions at his home in Folsom, California. Lou had drafted articles about his life and graciously shared his stories and photographs with me. However, his urgency to publish his personal story and my desire to back up information by contacting as many individuals as possible led him to move forward, hire a ghostwriter, and complete his book, *One Hell of a Ride: The Life and Times of Lou Federico*, which was published in 2004.

Overall, the interview process was both exciting and frustrating. Some potential interviewees were challenging to find. Some key individuals had, unfortunately, passed away. Letters were sent to all the celebrities mentioned in the story, but none responded due to an unwillingness to share or perhaps never having received my correspondence. Others, like Mim Crudgington, who lived in Tucson, Arizona, adamantly expressed disinterest in being interviewed. Fortunately, Cleve's adopted son, also named Cleveland, and his mother, Phyllis, an earlier wife of Cleveland Sr., graciously invited me into Cleve Jr.'s Monrovia home and shared stories and photos of Cleve Sr.'s involvement at Punta Chivato.

Dixon Collins invited me to interview him at his home in Angels Camp, California but acted suspicious of my visit when I first arrived. After photocopying my driver's license and asking several questions, he slowly warmed up as he shared his early experiences in Baja. I felt fortunate to spend several hours interviewing the man who first dreamed of building a resort at Punta Chivato.

My husband and I made multiple trips to Oregon to interview Bill and Billie Alvarado, Mary Morss, and Jeanne Fox. I also located others in parts of California, Oregon, and Washington and interviewed them in their homes. Having a home at Punta Chivato through 2004 allowed me considerable time to capture stories from those who had camped and built homes in the area. All interviewees were recorded on tape, and they kindly gave me their written consent to use their recollections and photographs.

I practiced my Spanish with local Mexicans willing to recount their tales of the area. Particularly memorable visits included an interview with Doña Chuy in San José de Magdalena regarding Luis Sui Qui, meetings with early hotel workers Florencio and Marcos Aguilar, speaking with Chema, and sessions with Pedro and Aurelia Molina, and Güero Alaníz.

I entitled this book *The Elusive Dream* because many people in Punta Chivato's history worked hard to follow a dream that seemed out of reach. Some would say it was a dream come true to build a home next to the Sea of Cortez. However, not realizing the Mexican "way" caused much anxiety to the early hotel owners and those who trusted they were given legal leases to the land on which they built homes.

For me, the elusive dream was collecting and dovetailing the interview information into an interesting, chronological story rather than a history book. Most of the dialogue in the book is word-for-word, as described to me by an individual. I did not correct the use of incorrect grammar or misspelled words in letters, documents, or interviews to depict the characters for the reader more accurately.

Part of the delay in completing the book was concern about conflicting stories. Some individuals still held grudges against others they had met in Punta Chivato. For example, Lou Federico once exclaimed that if he ever saw Dixon Collins again, he would "shoot him between the eyes." Since I was interviewing them both around the same time, I felt I needed to be cautious not to reveal I knew where Dixon Collins resided.

The perfectionist part of me wanted to "get each story right," which led to more questions and considerable research. I realized everyone has a story to tell, and each would see it from his or her own perspective. This history is a conglomeration of people's remembrances. There may not be a "right story." The truth may lie somewhere in the middle.

Once I stopped working full-time as a physical therapist, time opened up to write this book. However, as the queen of procrastination, I could always find something else to do with my time. In my mind, I always knew I would one day make the push to finish this project.

In 2020, Covid-19 was the impetus for me to move ahead and refocus on completing this book. During these years of uncertainty, one thing remained constant: this story needed to be told. I realized I may be the only person who had collected such a vast amount of first-hand information about the early days of Punta Chivato. It was time to share it.

Much has changed at Punta Chivato over the past forty years. Many old timers have moved, some have died, roads have changed, more homes have been constructed, and the hotel is once again abandoned. My hope is that someone else will pick up the baton and be willing to carry the evolving story of this Baja paradise on into the future.

Acknowledgments

I'm grateful to everyone who agreed to be interviewed for this book. Without you, it could not have been written. Thank you for sharing your fond remembrances and challenges of being in Punta Chivato during the early years.

Many thanks to Marge Summers for sharing information, letters, diaries, and an autobiography written by her father, Doc Lyons. I am indebted to her and Jere Summers for their openness and honesty about their long history with the area. Thank you to Jim Lyons for clarifying information about his father.

Thanks to Harry and Pam Oxley, Rich Ream, Tom Rosen, Betty Bell, Marge Summers, George Powell, Craig Cove, Mike Morse, Dave Jacobson, Yolanda Acosta, and Peter McLaughlin for sharing their Baja references with me and giving permission to use their photographs. Much gratitude to George Staples for sharing Bill Alvarado's 1991 narrated video of progress in Punta Chivato after George left. I could never have used photos from this amazing slice of history without the help of Robert Joy, who introduced me to "the snipping tool!"

For your editing assistance, I want to thank Jennifer Fosgate, Tom Rosen, Tanya Lee (and my college friend Gwen Davidson for introducing me to Tanya), and El Dorado Writers Guild members.

Thanks to Kim Rogers for your expertise and attention to detail in creating the maps, book cover, and formatting this book.

A special thanks to my Santa Cruz childhood friend, Dina Stolman, M.D., who reached out to her long-time friend, author Penny Paine. Penny contacted me from her home in England and subsequently referred me to author and president of To Press & Beyond, Gail Kearns, in North Carolina. Gail and her friend, book designer Peri Gabriel, worked closely with Kim Rogers and me to make my dream of publishing a reality. Your expertise, prompt assistance, and honesty were much appreciated following my recent negative experience with an unprofessional independent publishing group.

Many special individuals supported me throughout my long journey to complete this book. To my incredible friends who encouraged me year after year: Debbie Trybom, Ruth Hoedemaker, Jennifer Fosgate, Deb Kellerman, Carol Evans, Julie DePaul, Carol Croce, Melody Nichelson, Laurie Eskew, Marian Fitzpatrick, Don and Eileen Keesler, Deb Betley, Carol Brachna, Jan Cole, Ellen Fishman, and Alyssa Goard. Thanks to all my P.E.O. sisters, especially Beth Fellman, Ann Royal, Roz Boscia, Sue Cantlin, Kay Smith, and Gaelyn Keith.

Thank you to my many B.S.F. and Summer Sisters for their ongoing prayers, especially June Shepard, Denise Heitman, Carol Spicer, Rena Gonzales, Joan Scoville, Carole Brinckman, Diane Dennis, Arline Sault, and Rita Rogers.

A huge thank you to Pam and Harry Oxley, long-time residents of Punta Chivato, for information about the early days of P.C., photos, updates, and keeping after me to get this book out! Also, thanks to Lynne Weiser for her support while doing local interviews.

Finally, I cannot thank my family enough for their unwavering support: Greg Joy, Mike and Joyce Joy, Max and Hana Mizel, Aki Joy and Anju Samuelson, Robert and Lili Joy, Monica Joy, Willie Caldwell, and Lauren Joy. What a blessing to have their unconditional love! And my brother's children: my nephew, William Jacob Roach, my nieces Taylor Marie White and Malea Danielle Roach– you are all so precious to me!

Notes
Chapter 1

1. Not until the 1960s did Aeronaves de México offer direct DC-6 flights between Los Angeles, California, and La Paz, Baja California Sur, México, three times a week and roundabout DC-3 flights to Santa Rosalía and Loreto. Later Capitán Francisco Muñoz started Servicio Aereo Baja, which offered eight-passenger flights from Tijuana to Mulegé and the Bay of Los Angeles on the eastern Baja peninsula.

2. John Bonfante married Ines Rocca in 1932. Her parents started Rocca's Market in San Martin, California, and John soon became involved in the business. In 1961, John and his brother, Mike Bonfante, established the first Nob Hill Foods market in Morgan Hill, north of Gilroy, California. When Mike died in a plane accident in 1977, Mike's son, also named Michael, took over the business, which he developed into 27 stores. The chain was later sold to Raley's in 1997. The younger Michael eventually created an amusement park and gardens in Gilroy and named the facility Bonfante Gardens. In 2008, the city of Gilroy purchased the park, and the name was changed to Gilroy Gardens. John Bonfante died in San Martin, California, on September 8, 2000, at 89.

3. Don Johnson, renowned for later owning Hotel Serenidad in Mulegé, also grew up in San Jose. During an interview, Don described John Bonfante as being "tight as hell." He added, "But that's the way John was. I grew up with Italians. I know how Italians are. I've eaten more spaghetti than most Italians. I felt very much at home with Italians because I either grew up with Italians, Portuguese, or Mexicans. That was my type of people. You know what's interesting? I think, at times, we're not progressing. We're going backwards. In those days, we never discussed what nationality a man was. It was either Pete or Pedro or whatever his name was. But nationality never came into the picture, ever. We were all friends. And even today, I'm still friends with these people. Doesn't make any difference to me what nationality they are."

Chapter 2

4. It was a surprisingly humane and progressive penal system. Many say it worked because an escaped prisoner would have had difficulty surviving on the arid land surrounding Mulegé. The main restrictions were: "free" inmates could not enter places where liquor was sold, they could not dance, and they had to be back at the prison at 6 p.m. each evening. The caretaker at the prison would blast a conch shell horn, beckoning them to return. The prisoners and guards would then drift in from all directions. Roll was called, the prisoners marched into prison, and the door was closed. The prisoners had few amenities back inside, sleeping with only a blanket on the hard, bare ground. The conditions were also far from sanitary. Generally, the townspeople in Mulegé treated the prisoners well, as if they were just like anyone else. Only a few ever betrayed that trust. In the 1960s, one prisoner stole some clothes from a store in town. For this, all the prisoners had their rights rescinded for a while. The peer pressure not to abuse the system must have been enormous. The old prison building is now a museum.

5. Purchased in 1964 by Alfonso Cuesta, it became known simply as Hotel Hacienda.

6. *Baja Sea Guide, Volume II* by Leland R. Lewis and Peter E. Ebeling, SEA Publications, Inc., Newport Beach, California, 1971, p. 488.

7. Building of Hotel Rancho Loma Linda is detailed in Lou's book, *One Hell of a Ride: The Life and Times of Lou Federico*, published in 2004.

8. John Wayne, nicknamed "The Duke," was born Marion Robert Morrison. The 6'4" American actor became a star during Hollywood's Golden Age, especially in Western and war movies. He passed away on June 11, 1979, at age 72.

9. Jane Mansfield, born Vera Jayne Palmer, was an American actress on stage, screen, and television. With her sexy figure and bleached, platinum-blonde hair, she was considered one of the early "blonde bombshells," along with Marilyn Monroe. She tragically died at age 34 in a traffic accident en route to New Orleans, Louisiana, with her family in 1967.

10. Samuel Yorty was the mayor of Los Angeles from 1961-1973. He died in Los Angeles in 1998 at age 88.

11. Swedish-born actress, singer, and dancer Ann-Margret Olsson was born in 1941. Professionally known simply as Ann-Margret, she acted in many movies, including *Bye-Bye Birdie* (1963), *Viva Las Vegas* (1964), and *Carnal Knowledge* (1971).

12. Kirk Douglas, a Hollywood movie star during the Golden Age of film, died in 2020 in Beverly Hills, California, at age 103.

13. Cuca Gorosave was Don Johnson's wife's aunt.

14. Serenidad Hotel initially offered a 4,000-foot airstrip and gas to refuel airplanes. In 1968, with partners Fernando del Moral and Chester Mason, Don Johnson purchased Serenidad. Later, Johnson and his wife became sole owners. The popular Saturday-night Pig Roast at Serenidad, which Johnson began, still draws big crowds, especially private pilots. The traditional dinner often features folkloric dancers, mariachis, one margarita, and all the roast pig you can eat. In 1980, Johnson was appointed American consul in Mulegé, a job he held for 13 years. Don's wife, Nancy Ugalde Gorosave de Johnson, passed away in 2016 at age 71. Don passed away in 2020 at age 94. The couple was married for over 50 years. The well-known Serenidad Hotel remains in the family to this day.

15. Dick Stockton's company, South Gate Manufacturing (SOGAM), made parts for satellites.

16. Over the years, the resort was known by other names, including Hotel Mulegé and Vista Hermosa.

17. In 1965, Dick Stockton stopped making payments to Bonfante and Ortiz for the hotel. Although they were still owed $80,000 in U.S. currency, the two decided not to fight for it. Paul Ortiz claimed it would be a losing battle due to the politics involved. With Stockton's inability to come up with the money to pay taxes in México City, Frank Chaves took over the hotel in Mulegé. Stockton later went bankrupt, lost everything, and went to work for Howard Hughes as a negotiator, per Lou's account.

466 J. M. Joy

18. Dave Galloway, who owned a crane hoist company in Southern California, took over Club Aero Mulegé. He renamed the resort *Hotel Mulegé*. Following a legal battle between Dave Galloway and Frank Chaves, Galloway was put in jail in México City. After he was released, Galloway started drinking heavily. He died of a heart attack at the resort in 1968, less than a year after buying the hotel. His wife, Paula, took over, renaming the hotel *Vista Hermosa* (Beautiful View). The Mulegé Ejido eventually took over this once well-known, quaint fishing resort on the hillside. Later, it fell into disrepair and was never resurrected.

Chapter 3

19. Jonathan Kandell, *La Capital: The Biography of México City*. Random House, New York, 1988, p. 397.

20. Knight, Alan. "The History of the Mexican Revolution." *History Today,* Vol. 30, Issue 5, May 1980, *historytoday.com/archive/Mexican-revolution*

21. Obregón, a symbol to the peasants of disillusionment and shattered dreams, was assassinated in 1928 after leaving office.

Chapter 4

22. Another version is an Englishman named Peter Davis, came to the area in the 1800s and married a local.

23. Saúl, a prominent figure in the hotel's history in Mulegé, was born on Davis Street in Loreto. Some people have Davis four times in their names. One may hear other English names in Loreto, including "Smith" and "Green." Saúl, a bartender at Club Aero Mulegé, stepped up as the hotel manager after Lou Federico left. Later, he was encouraged to teach English at the local school. Despite not being a teacher by profession, Saúl was one of the few locals who spoke English. He taught in Mulegé for 15 years. In the mid-1980s, he ventured out and started his own business, a grocery store named Saúl's. Well known by all in Mulegé, Saúl and his family continue to operate this successful business where many clients are American expatriates.

Chapter 6

24. In 1906, Mark Honeywell invented the mercury seal generator and founded Honeywell Heating Specialty Company in Wabash, Indiana. Over the years, the company has grown through acquisitions and mergers and has several specialty divisions.

25. Franklin Otis Booth Jr., a former *Los Angeles Times* executive and businessman, died in 2008 at 84.

26. In 1952, the Northern Territory of Baja became a state, *Baja California,* and government officials were locally elected. However, the southern half of Baja remained a federal territory, and its governor and officials were appointed from México City. All permits in *Baja California Sur* (south Baja) had to be issued from México City. The title papers Bastida and Yee held had government stamps on every page. But the stamps were from Baja California Sur government offices in La Paz and Santa Rosalía, not México City. This discrepancy rendered their papers illegal. It wasn't until October 8, 1974, that *Baja California Sur* was recognized as a state of México.

27. According to Lou, Dixon paid $60,000 for 4,000 acres.

28. In an interview, Dixon said it was 4,000 hectares, just under 10,000 acres (1 hectare = 2-1/2 acres). He stated he had a 30-year lease: 10 years at $4,000/year, 10 years at $8,000/year, and 10 years at $16,000/year.

Chapter 8

29. San Marcos Island appeared on early charts of the gulf as Isla de Galápagos and was, and sometimes still is, referred to as Galápagos Island because of the large number of marine turtles frequently found in the waters surrounding the island. A small tribe of Indian fishermen initially inhabited it. In the latter part of the 1800s, during the height of a land promotion scheme on the nearby Magdalena Plain, the off-lying island was referred to as San Marcos Island after the name of the model community proposed for the prospective coastal colonists. The highest elevation is 890 feet above sea level. An outlying but smaller island 22 miles off the coast is called Isla Tortuga, yet another

Spanish word for turtle. The highest point of Tortuga is 1,020 feet above sea level. This island is covered with dark lava rocks, and the volcano's broad crater occupies the center. There is very little vegetation. The waters surrounding the island became a popular fishing spot.

30. In 1978, with the new Mexican mining laws requiring that most of a company's capital be Mexican, Kaiser decided to sell its interests to the Canadian company Domtar. A partnership was developed with Companía Mexicana Occidental, A.A., (CPMSA), which had acquired mining rights for the island.

31. Lou Federico, "Tale of Two Cities," *Discover Baja*, September-October 1993.

Chapter 9

32. According to Florencio Aguilar, who worked at the hotel years later, "Octavio Llano only visited P.C. one or two nights." His primary interest appeared to be the "ladies."

33. Per an interview with Lou Federico: "For a journeyman laborer, for a square meter of rock work was $4.00/sq. meter, American money. I was paying journeyman laborers, non-piece work, $4.00/day. I was paying peons $2.00/day."

34. When interviewed years later, Dixon still spoke fondly of Luis Sui Qui, describing him as one of the most honorable men he had ever met, a man whose integrity he greatly admired. Luis Sui Qui died in June 2001.

Chapter 10

35. Otis Chandler was a second cousin of Franklin Otis Booth, Jr., Dixon's wife's previous husband. Ironically, two of Otis's sons, Norman Brant Chandler and Harry Brant Chandler, graduated from Stanford University in the author's class in 1975. Sadly, Norman, who followed Otis into the news business, preceded his father in death, passing away in 2002 at the age of 49. Four years later, Otis Chandler died at the age of 78.

36. Otis hoped to eventually achieve a "Grand Slam," i.e., obtaining all four North American wild sheep: the Mountain Bighorn, Dall, Stone, and Desert Bighorn.

37. Ricardo easily found work back in Mulegé. As a master designer and woodworker, many sought his skills to construct boats and furniture. Sadly, cancer cut his life short at the age of 50.

Chapter 11

38. Lou Federico's "Tale of Two Hotels" article was published in *Discover Baja* in September-October 1993.

39. On October 9, 1967, now living back in California, Lou and Lana had a second child, a son they named Tony Dean. Lou eventually was put in charge of the American Sportsman Club in California and later opened a club of his own, Golden Ram Sportsman Club. He retired and lived with his wife, Lana, in Folsom, California, until he died in 2010 at age 85.

Chapter 12

40. The original booklet is now out of print.

41. In January 1996, Arnold Senterfitt sold Baja Bush Pilots to Jack and Karen McCormick.

42. The only Mexican law intended to separate air traffic and avoid collisions was a requirement to fly at different altitudes depending on the direction of navigation.

43. MSL stands for mean sea level, an acronym pilots and air traffic controllers use to measure elevation.

44. The fuel might not yet have been available at the time of Senterfitt's visit, but Dixon had plans to include it. They probably decided that by the time the supplement went to print, there would be aviation fuel at Punta Chivato.

45. *Private Pilot* article, Feb. 1967, p. 501. (When Bob Said wrote this article, runway lights were discussed but not yet present. Not until late 1967 were lights installed along the shorter east-west strip, Runway 9. Although part of Dixon's dream, lights were never put in along the north-south airstrip, Runway 31. Neither runway was ever paved with asphalt.)

46. Chema (José Espinoza) interview.

47. Lacy founded Clay Lacy Aviation, one of the oldest jet charter

companies in the United States. In 1988, Lacy broke the record for flying around the world in a Boeing 747SP, completing the journey in 36 hours and 54 minutes. Lacy was also one of the first pilots to fly the Pregnant Guppy.

48. Conroy's company, Aero Spacelines International, expanded to include various Guppy aircraft.

49. In the 1980s, he started the Elephant Bar chain. Carrows was bought by Catalina Restaurant Group, Inc. in 2002.

50. Erle Stanley Gardner, *Off the Beaten Track in Baja*. William Morrow & Company, 1967, pp. 496-497.

51. Erle Stanley Gardner wrote seven books about his adventures in Baja, the last one published just months before his death in 1970 at age 80.

52. John Davison "Jay" Rockefeller IV served on the West Virginia House of Delegates (1966-1968), was elected governor of West Virginia (1977-1985), and served as a United States senator from West Virginia (1985-2015).

Chapter 13

53. This section of the beach, with its abundance of various shells, would later be called "Shell Beach."

54. Eventually, railway tracks from the copper mines in Santa Rosalía were laid to aid in pulling boats out of the water for repair or before an approaching storm. A cart with steel wheels ran down the tracks. Equipped with an engine and a winch, the cart could pull boats as long as 32 feet up the track.—per Bob Davis.

55. Bob Said, "The Good Life: A Piper under the Sun," *Private Pilot*, February 1967, pp 16-23.

Chapter 14

56. Florencio's brother, José Marcos, worked in the hotel restaurant for ten years.

Chapter 15

57. In 1958, Andrew Lococo founded an elite, 210-room hotel, The Cockatoo Inn, in Hawthorne, California, after a fire destroyed his popular chicken-and-rib drive-in restaurant established in 1946 at that same site—the corner of Hawthorne Boulevard and the Imperial Highway. The Cockatoo Inn soon became a popular destination for the elite of Los Angeles. The politicians and Hollywood actors who were guests at the Cockatoo Inn were Betty Grable, Mickey Rooney, John F. Kennedy, Robert Kennedy, and Marilyn Monroe. Frank Lococo, Andrew's cousin, worked as the inn's manager. He recalled, "all the limos that used to pull up out front with congressmen and councilmen from all over." Other frequent guests at the grand establishment were members of the American Mafia. Andrew Lococo was referred to as "a notorious" and "prominent" member. At that time, the U.S. attorney general's office tagged him as a major organized crime figure. In 1970, Andrew Lococo was convicted during a grand jury trial of perjury, horse-race fixing, and violating interstate gambling laws. He died in 1973 at age 55.

58. Florencio continued working in Punta Chivato through Dixon's era and into Crudgington's time at the hotel. He left the hotel in 1972.

Chapter 16

59. The first president of Ejido San Bruno was Don Fortino Piñera.

60. Ben Hunter, *The Baja Feeling*, Ontario, California: Brasch and Brasch Publishers, Inc., 1978, p. 18.

Chapter 17

61. Chema (José Espinoza) worked at Borrego de Oro for only three months before starting his own hotel. When asked what working at Punta Chivato was like, he replied, "So alone. I didn't want to stay there." In 1968, Chema and his brother, Rubin, started constructing the now well-known El Morro Hotel in Santa Rosalía. It was built slowly in sections, not all at the same time. It did not open until 1975.

62. The author found no other mention in references or interviews of Dixon Collins having a pilot. He seemed to be his own pilot.

Chapter 18

63. In 1837, two brothers-in-law, William Procter and James Gamble, became business partners in a small soap and candle startup called Procter & Gamble. The company eventually became known for manufacturing household brands such as Ivory soap, Crisco, Tide, Crest, and Pampers.

64. Olivia Procter Benedict was the granddaughter of William Procter, one of the founders of Procter & Gamble. She lived to be 91, passing away in 1959. When she died, she was considered one of the wealthiest women in Ohio, with $6 million in assets.

65. During an interview, Cleveland Crudgington's later wife, Phyllis, shared this information. However, the author was unable to verify this family connection. Elisha Graves Otis (1811-1861) invented a safety device that prevented elevators from falling if the hoisting cable failed. He founded Otis Elevator Company when he was forty years old.

66. Mary Cunningham Stephenson (later LeBlond) was a wealthy woman fond of horses. She owned Jay Trump, who won the Grand National Steeplechase in 1965. In 1969, she purchased Turner Farm in Indian Hill, Ohio, which she planned to subdivide and leave to her heirs.

67. A year after Bonnie's birth, her mother, Elizabeth Stephenson Crudgington, married George R. Drew. They divorced in 1953. Elizabeth Stephenson Crudgington Drew died only three years later in 1956. Bonnie was raised by her maternal grandmother, Mary Cunningham Stephenson.

68. Shared with the author during an interview with Cleveland Benedict Crudgington's third wife, Phyllis.

69. Phyllis was Gerald Rudolph Ford, Jr.'s girlfriend long before he became the thirty-eighth president of the United States (1974-1977). Blonde and blue-eyed, Phyllis was a student at Connecticut College, and Ford was at Yale Law School when they met. They dated for a few years before WWII; Ford was considering marriage and even took her home to meet his parents. Although they never married, the two stayed in touch over the years. Phyllis and her later husband, Dean Phillips, were active in Ford's

1976 presidential campaign. Gerald Ford died in 2006 at the age of 93.

70. Karl Breckenridge, "Jus'kiddin' on the Keyboard," *Reno Gazette Journal,* December 23, 2014.

71. Bonnie married Yoshiaki Mitsui in 1969, but they would later divorce. They had two children: a daughter, Natsu, and a son, Charles. Bonnie moved back to Ohio and Turner Farm in the early 1990s after raising her children in California. She acquired Turner Farm in the upscale city of Indian Hill, Ohio, a suburb of the Greater Cincinnati area, where she created a successful organic farm that continues to this day, offering tours, workshops, and conferences. She stipulated that the 230-acre parcel never be developed. Bonnie died in Ohio in 2013 at age 69.

72. Five years after her divorce from Cleveland Crudgington, Sr., Phyllis married Dean Phillips on June 12, 1969, in Virginia City, Nevada. They resided in Reno, where he was a real estate developer.

Chapter 20

73. Dwight Dixon Collins would continue to be involved in property development in the U.S. and abroad. He died at home in Angels Camp, California, in 2014 at the age of 79.

Chapter 21

74. According to John Fitzsimmons' flight logbook, he also traveled to Punta Chivato in February 1972, January 1973, February 1974, and May 1974. All were during Crudgington's era. John Fitzsimmons letter December 25, 2003.

Chapter 26

75. Bob Davis and his wife, Lynda, eventually built their dream home on that lot.

Chapter 27

76. Concurrently, in December 1973, México increased the price

of gasoline by 100%. This made the cost of 94-octane gas 64 cents a gallon; 80-octane was 45 cents a gallon. At that time, México produced all its gasoline except the 7% brought in from Venezuela.

77. The first official Baja 1000 started in Tijuana before switching to Ensenada as the starting point. In addition to the point-to-point race, some entered the loop race that began and ended in Ensenada.

Chapter 29

78. This T-shaped formation would later be referred to as "hammerhead," its formation reminiscent of a hammerhead shark.

Chapter 30

79. Luis Sui Qui died in June 2001, per Chema.

80. Mim moved to Tucson, Arizona. The author made several attempts to obtain her story, but she declined to be interviewed and did not want to contribute to the book.

81. The author attempted to interview Nathan Crudgington at a listed residence in La Paz. His wife, Francisca, answered the phone and refused to provide any information other than to indicate that Nathan was in South America and would be returning to San Diego. Francisca said she would give Nathan the message and ask him to return the call. He never did.

82. Cleveland B. Crudgington's third wife, Phyllis, died at age 97.

Chapter 32

83. During her interview in 2003, Barbara Silzle said she and her husband, Bill, had been married for 57 years, which would be 79 years in 2025! Barbara shared the following advice for a long marriage: "Realize that you never have to be right. Keep your mouth shut and listen."

84. Ben Hunter, *The Baja Feeling*. Ontario, California: Brasch and Brasch, Publishers, Inc., 1978, p. 20.

Chapter 33

85. The early pangas (skiffs) were rowboats. Later, the term referred to small boats with a raised bow powered by an outboard motor. They are used in many Third World countries. Initially constructed of wood, they would later be made of fiberglass.

Chapter 35

86. The Quarterdeck Restaurant, earlier called the Captain's Table, was in business from 1976 to 1982. Later, the site would become a McDonald's.

87. The Town Club of Eugene was an Oregon Domestic Non-Profit Corporation established in 1950.

88. Founded in 1914, The United States Power Squadrons is a non-profit educational organization that aims to improve maritime safety and enjoyment through classes in seamanship, navigation, and related subjects.

Chapter 37

89. In 1974, the Territory of Baja California Sur finally became the State of Baja California Sur. Its capital is the city of La Paz.

90. Bill said at another interview it was 7%.

Chapter 40

91. Pedro later recalled Bill Alvarado was "45 or 46" years old and had only been at Casa Grande since "May or June of 1979."

92. During an interview with the couple on October 10, 2003, Pedro was 51, and Aurelia was 45. The following year, 2004, they celebrated their 25th anniversary.

93. Miguel Romo died in a car accident in 1991 when Luis was only 12 years old.

94. In a letter by Doc Lyons in July 1980, he mentions letting Alberto go.

95. While staying at this fly-in resort in the 1960s, Dixon Collins first dreamed of building a hotel in Punta Chivato.

Chapter 43

96. A baked or fried turnover consisting of pastry filled with meat from the cabrilla fish, a sea bass.

97. Ana would later become known for her gift shop, Ana's, in Mulegé. When interviewed on November 10, 2004, Ana particularly remembered two regular customers who came to her store from Punta Chivato, Connie Cobb and Marilyn Oxley. She fondly recalled Marilyn as tall, blond, well-dressed, and someone who bought a lot from her.

Chapter 45

98. This would later be the lot where Doc's eldest daughter, Marge, and her husband, Jere Summers, would build a home.

99. The Oxleys would later lease Lot #9 in Subdivision 2.

Chapter 46

100. This lot was sold for $27,000 to Lee and Connie Cobb in 1989 by Marge and Jere Summers, who had obtained the parcel as heirs of Doc Lyons.

101. McVay interview, September 5, 2004.

102. A *palapa* is a simple, open-sided sunshade shelter with a thatched roof of dried palm fronds.

103. Kellogg interview, March 10, 2005.

Chapter 47

104. According to minutes from a homeowner's meeting.

105. The Federal Electricity Commission's high-tension lines fed the population in Mulegé, but they were located 15 kilometers away, a little over nine miles.

106. *Sunshine* was Bob and Lynda Davis's boat. Harry Oxley's boat was nicknamed *Taco*.

Chapter 49

107. Article in *México West,* February 1983.

108. Doc Lyons note, April 26, 1983.

109. Doc Lyons note, May 2, 1983.

110. Doc Lyons note, May 10, 1983.

111. Doc Lyons letter, June 12, 1983.

Chapter 50

112. Sonora is a Mexican state located directly south of Arizona. Drug smugglers frequently use this border.

113. Robert "Russell" Brown started shaping surfboards in 1967 and owned a shop near the Newport Beach pier in Southern California.

Chapter 51

114. Doc Lyons July 5, 1983, letter.

Chapter 52

115. Doug became a regular camper at Punta Chivato after being introduced to it by childhood friend Dennis Gardner. Both grew up in Bend, Oregon.

Chapter 54

116. One of the buildings in Palo Verde fronting Baja 1 became a store. Another landmark, on the corner of Baja 1 and the new road to Punta Chivato, was surrounded by fruit trees. Eventually, it became known for the ostriches kept in the backyard. Years later, a primary school was built in Palo Verde along the new section of the road near Baja 1. The population of Palo Verde grew after a tomato farm was established further down the road.

117. The term "honey wagon" refers to a vehicle used to collect the contents from RV sewage tanks.

Chapter 55

118. Kellogg interview, March 19, 2005.

119. At this time, the author and her husband, Greg Joy, who lived next door to the Davises, met Lee and Lynn Links.

Chapter 57

120. In 1992, *The San Diego Union* and *The San Diego Evening Tribune* merged. The newspaper is currently *The San Diego Union-Tribune*.

121. Mike Morse, a long-time resident of Punta Chivato, lost his battle with liver cancer on October 4, 2018.

Chapter 58

122. *Chivato Charla*, Nov./Dec. 1992.

123. Doc Lyons passed away at the end of that year, December 1984, from squamous cell carcinoma.

Chapter 61

124. PCHA June 2, 1986, letter.

125. PCHA June 2, 1986, letter.

126. Participating Ejido members included Ejido President Lupe Mendoza, Victor Velasquez, Nello Romo, and Carlos Ramirez.

127. Homeowner participants varied, but early on included Homeowners' Association President Harry Oxley, Walter Fox, Richard Fodor, and Les Conner.

Chapter 62

128. Richard "Rich" Ream passed away in 2008 in Wilson, Wyoming, at age 90.

Chapter 63

129. The Flying Samaritans is a non-sectarian, non-profit volunteer organization dedicated to providing medical and educational services to the rural areas of Baja, México.

Chapter 64

130. Born in New York in 1954, Denzel Hayes Washington Jr. is a successful and respected American screen and stage actor, producer, and director.

131. Olivia Newton-John died in 2022 at age 73 from cancer.

132. Information on Larry Hagman from an interview with Robin Converse. Larry Hagman died in 2012 at age 81.

Chapter 66

133. Bill recalled that Deadman's Beach, located north of Punta Chivato, got its name from fishermen who, years earlier, had died off that beach. According to Bill, the legend was that fishermen who died at sea were "thrown overboard because the crew still had another month and a half before they had to go back to Guaymas with their shrimp."

Chapter 69

134. Harry Oxley's letter to Punta Chivato lot leasees dated November 15, 1987.

135. Mexican law describes the Federal Maritime Zone as a 20-meter strip of land next to the beach that is passable and has an inclination of no greater than 30 degrees. Neither Mexican citizens nor foreigners are allowed to own it. However, they may request a temporary concession to use the land, which will require a renewable fee.

136. The Ejido eventually agreed to date all leases September 22, 1987, the date Hotel Punta Chivato and the Ejido San Bruno signed the master lease.

Chapter 70

137. *Chivato Charla*, Feb. 1992.

138. Walt Peterson, *The Baja Adventure Book*, Berkeley, California. Wilderness Press, 1987, 1992, pp. 179-180.

Chapter 71

139. According to information obtained by the author, Bill Alvarado had a visa but not a work permit. He later got his FM3, a non-immigrant visa required of those staying in México for longer than six months. Renewable annually, this document allowed limited work in specific situations.

Chapter 72

140. The initial 15-room hacienda at the tip of the Baja Peninsula was conceived by Abelardo Luis (Rod) Rodríguez M., the son of former President Abelardo Rodríguez L. of México (1932-1934), as a getaway for him and his American wife, actress Lucille Bremer. Born and raised in California in the United States, Rod became an experienced pilot. He first spotted the 400-acre property from the air in the 1940s. Built in 1956, Palmilla Hotel would become a lavish hotel, catering to the rich and famous. Early well-known guests included Lucille Ball, John Wayne, and Dwight D. Eisenhower. Rod retired from the resort business in 1965. He died on his birthday in 2018 at the age of 100. In 2004, the resort underwent a major $90 million expansion and was renamed One&Only Palmilla.

Chapter 73

141. Owners of the Vessels Stallion Farm in Bonsall, California, the Vessels were well-known breeders of American Quarter Horses. Frank's grandfather, Frank Vessels, Sr., founded Los Alamitos Racecourse in Cypress, California. "Scoop" was an American off-road truck racer who won the Baja 1000 desert off-road race in 1977. He acquired the nickname "Scoop" as a boy because he cleaned up his grandfather's horse stalls. Sadly, Scoop passed away in 2010 at age 58 while piloting his twin-engine Aero Commander 500.

142. In 1936, Kenneth Ford purchased the Roseburg Lumber Company outside Roseburg, Oregon. As the company expanded and added locations, it reorganized in 1985 and became Roseburg Forest Products Company.

143. Raúl Luján also used large wooden beams from the copper mill in Santa Rosalía to construct the Vessels and Joy homes in Punta Chivato.

Chapter 74

144. This lot eventually became the home of George and Diane Powell of Fresno, California.

Chapter 75

145. PCHA minutes, March 31, 1994.

Chapter 77

146. *Chivato Charla*, Spring 1999.

Chapter 78

147. Marge Summers, Doc's eldest daughter, inherited the parcel lease from her father and was paid $27,000 for the lot by the Cobbs.

148. Connie Cobb passed away in 2023 at the age of 77.

Chapter 79

149. William "Bill" Ralph Alvarado died in 2006 at age 70.

Chapter 81

150. PAN, an acronym for *Partido Acción Nacional*, National Action Party, is one of México's main political parties. Founded in 1938, it is a conservative party. Vicente Fox and Felipe Calderón were successful PAN candidates, elected back-to-back for six-year terms as México's president (2000-2012).

151. PRI, an acronym for *Partido Revolucionario Institucional*, Institutional Revolutionary Party, changed names twice after being founded in 1929. This party held uninterrupted power for over 70 years until 2000.

152. Dennis John Peyton was born and raised in Wisconsin. He earned his law degree in México City and is fluent in English and Spanish. Located in Southern California, he specializes in litigation and real estate transactions in México.

153. PCHA December 26, 1993, letter regarding 3rd lease. *Asociado* means homeowner in this letter.

154. Raúl Luján was to be paid $1,500 per participation lot for his services.

155. Ejido letter, September 21, 1994.

Chapter 82

156. Whether this Punta Chivato Shores brochure was ever distributed is in question. Casa Grande, the once-beloved "big house" at Punta Chivato, was never refurbished.

157. PCHA meeting minutes, April 2, 1999.

158. Casa Grande was a dwelling for the Mexican military for a while but never became a retreat.

159. Harry Oxley interview.

160. Baja Links. *Punta Chivato*, 22 December 2003, *www.baja-web.com/punta-chivato/pt-chiva.htm* (site no longer available; the author has printed copy.)

Chapter 83

161. An amendment to Article 27 of the Mexican Constitution of 1917.

162. PCHA letter, January 14, 1997.

163. For example, a 1,012 square meter parcel (0.25 acre) would cost $7,084 U.S. dollars. Per a February 24, 1998, Land Acquisition Committee letter: "This would result in an approximate price of $6,700 for the lots to the west of the hotel and $10,00 for the lots to the east of the hotel." After several meetings, Ejido San Bruno agreed to reduce their asking price. They initially placed a value on the property of $45.00 U.S. per square meter.

Chapter 84

164. Leslie "Les" Conner passed away in 2016 at age 85.

165. Felipe Zúniga Meza, *El Forjador* (La Paz, B.C.S. newspaper), May 28, 2003.

Chapter 86

166. Walter Fox passed away in 2005 at the age of 82. Jeanne Fox passed away in 2016 at the age of 89.

167. Robert "Bob" Davis died in 2021 in Wichita, Kansas, at age 92.

Chapter 87

168. Bunnie Adams passed away in October 2018.

Chapter 88

169. October 17, 1997, PCHA Water/Steering Committee meeting minutes.

170. Art Oberto, known as "Seattle's Sausage and Jerky King," passed away in 2022 at age 95. His wife of 58 years, Dorothy Oberto, passed away in 2013, just two days before her 79th birthday.

Chapter 89

171. *Chivato Charla*, Fall 1999.

172. Lynn Links passed away in 2014 after a battle with pancreatic cancer.

Character Reference

Acosta Mesa, Yolanda – daughter of Ricardo Acosta Munguia, building supervisor of Borrego de Oro for Dixon Collins; visited building site as a teenager; later hired by Bill Alvarado as hotel manager.

Acosta Munguia, Ricardo – hired by Dixon Collins as construction foreman at Punta Chivato; left before hotel was completed and returned to Mulegé.

Adams, Andy and Bunnie – couple from Bonsall, California who drove their family to Punta Chivato in the early 1970s, arriving after Cleve Crudgington left; long-time beach campers at Punta Chivato; later built home in Subdivision 1 west of Punta Chivato Hotel.

Aguilar, Florencio – worked at Borrego de Oro as a young man; hired by Rice family to oversee Casa Grande.

Aguilar, Hector and Mari – local Mexican couple who befriended many Americans at Punta Chivato.

Aguilar, Marcos – brother of Florencio, worked as waiter at Borrego de Oro.

Aguilar, Pedra de Fernando – Ricardo Acosta's sister-in-law; hired by Dixon Collins as cook for workers constructing Punta Chivato.

Alaníz, Güero – Member of Ejido San Bruno, with his wife, Gloria, opened a *tienda* (store) at Punta Chivato

Alvarado, Bill – from Oregon; partner in home at La Posada on Conception Bay; first visited PC by boat in late 1970s and met Don Zacarías; restored and ran Hotel Punta Chivato; eventually smuggled out of México.

Anaya, Jorge – bookkeeper/accountant hired by Dixon Collins for work at Punta Chivato.

Apodaca, Mateo – boyfriend of Yolanda Acosta Mesa; moved into Casa Grande with Yolanda in 1980.

Bastida - government fishing inspector in Santa Rosalía; claimed to own land at Punta Chivato with Gilbert Yee.

Bell, Lester and Betty – ran a sporting goods store in Lee Vining, California; introduced to Punta Chivato by their neighbors, Kerry and Penny Kellogg; moved to lot above Shell Beach.

Bonfante, John – American from California Bay Area who became successful entrepreneur in the grocery store business; avid fisherman who had the idea of building the first fly-in, fishing resort in the town of Mulegé, Baja California Sur.

Brush, Billie (Alvarado) and Dick – couple who first camped at Punta Chivato in 1985; Billie would become Billie Alvarado in 1995, years after her first husband, Dick, passed away.

Burr, Aaron – employee of Dixon Collins; his photo was used in several places in Dixon's hotel promotional brochure.

Busse, Bob and Bev – from Colorado; leased a lot at Punta Chivato in Subdivision 2 and built a vacation home.

Chandler, Otis – Publisher of family-owned *Los Angeles Times* (1960-1980); second cousin to Franklin Otis Booth, Jr.

"Chema" – nickname for José Espinoza; early manager at Borrego de Oro; with his brother, Rubin, opened El Morro Hotel in Santa Rosalía in 1975.

Cobb, Connie and Lee – avid golfers from Southern California; built home on Lot 19, Subdivision 1; Lee designed and promoted building Desert Lynx Golf Course at Punta Chivato

Collins, Barbara – (*see* Honeywell, Barbara).

Collins, Dwight Dixon - referred to as "Dixon," – American from Southern California who was the visionary behind Punta Chivato Hotel in the 1960s. Named it Borrego de Oro.

Collins, Sibyl – Dixon Collins' mother.

Conner, Les and Lucy – early campers at Punta Chivato; eventually built home in Subdivision 1 west of Hotel Punta Chivato.

Converse, Robin – early camper at Punta Chivato (1970s); eventually built home in Subdivision 1 west of Hotel Punta Chivato.

Cortes, Manuel – high government official from México City; also known as Ingeniero Manuel Cortes or Ing. Manuel Cortes. (The title before his name indicates an advanced degree, especially in engineering.)

Crudgington, Bonnie – Cleveland and Mary Crudgington's daughter.

Crudgington, Cleveland "Cleve" Benedict – Heir to American company Procter & Gamble; second proprietor of hotel at Punta Chivato.

Crudgington, Cleveland Benedict, Jr. – biological son of Phyllis and adopted son of Cleveland Crudgington, Sr.; name at birth was John Gardner Ricksen.

Crudgington, Mary – Cleveland Crudgington's first wife; purported heiress to Otis Elevator Company.

Crudgington, Mel – Cleveland Crudgington's second wife; they had one daughter together.

Crudgington, Mary "Mim" – née Mary Williams; Cleveland Crudgington's fourth wife; heiress to Dow Chemical Company.

Crudgington, Phyllis – Cleveland Crudgington's third wife; mother of John Gardner Ricksen, whose name was legally changed to Cleveland Benedict Crudgington, Jr. after she married Cleveland Benedict Crudgington, Sr.

Dalziel, Bill – architect for Borrego de Oro who worked for Beverly Hills, B.A. Burkess and Associates and was hired by Dixon Collins.

Davis, Bob and Lynda – Bob was an early investor in Punta Chivato hotel during Crudgington era; helped start Punta Chivato Yacht Club and Dorado Tournament. Both active in PCHA; next door neighbors to the author and her husband in Subdivision 2 at Punta Chivato.

Davis, Saúl – originally from Loreto, Baja California Sur; worked at first fly-in hotel in Mulegé with Lou Federico; later opened a grocery store in Mulegé called Saúl's.

Don Zacarías – elderly Mexican caretaker of Hotel Punta Chivato after Cleve Crudgington abandoned it; hired by the Ejido San Bruno; resided in Casa Grande.

Dryer, Dale and Julia – early visitors to P.C.; partners in home with Fitzsimmonses in Subdivision 1 in Punta Chivato.

Federico, Lana –– née Lana Green; Miss San Francisco of 1961; married Lou Federico December 8, 1963; they resided in Mulegé and Punta Chivato.

Federico, Lou – introduced to Baja by friend John Bonfante in 1950s; part owner of fly-in resort built in Mulegé, Hotel Rancho Loma Linda (Pretty Hill Ranch Hotel); showed Dixon Collins land where Borrego de Oro would be built in Punta Chivato; involved in construction of hotel.

Fitzsimmons, John and Gerry – flew to Punta Chivato during both Dixon Collins' and Cleve Crudgington's hotel eras; later built home in partnership with the Dryers in Subdivision 1 west of Hotel Punta Chivato.

Fox, Walter and Jeanne – townhouse neighbors of Bill Alvarado in Eugene, Oregon; introduced to P.C. by Bill and often stayed in Casa Grande until leasing Lot 21 in Subdivision 2 and building Casa Zorro above camping beach.

Galloway, Dave – third American owner of first fly-in resort (1966) in Mulegé after Stockton and Bonfante; renamed it Hotel Mulegé.

Galloway, Paula – wife of Dave Galloway; took over Hotel Mulegé after her husband died in late 1960s; renamed it Vista Hermosa.

Gardner, Dennis – early camper at Punta Chivato; later moved to trailer above Shell Beach.

Harris, Hazel – single, older woman who camped at Punta Chivato; known for collages she made from shells found on Shell Beach.

Henthorn, Jerry – early camper at Punta Chivato beach; retired fireman; married local woman, Adela; eventually, they moved to San Bruno, Baja Sur.

Heron, Jack – auto mechanic from Merced, California; arrived at Punta Chivato by private plane during Dixon's era; stayed and offered his skills as a mechanic and his plane for transportation.

Hielo, Don – a local Mexican Bill hired to help with gardening after Don Zacarías and Doc Lyons were gone.

Hilbun, Bob and Bobbie – from Montana, early beach campers at Punta Chivato; later built home in Subdivision 1 west of Hotel Punta Chivato.

Honeywell, Barbara – heiress to Honeywell Corporation; married Dixon Collins after divorcing Franklin Otis Booth, Jr.

Horton, Don and Marge – building contractor from Oregon; built second home at Punta Chivato in partnership with Archie and Doris McVay, and Ray and June Nidiffer in Subdivision 1.

Jacobson, Dave and Norma – campers at Punta Chivato beach (late 1970s).

Johnson, Don – early friend of Lou Federico in San Jose, California; partner in fly-in resort in Mulegé with John Bonfante and Lou Federico and worked as assistant manager; purchased Serenidad Hotel in Mulegé in 1968, another fly-in resort, later became sole owner with his wife, Nancy Ugalde Gorosave, a Mulegé local; lived and worked there until his death in 2020 at age 94.

Joy, Greg – camper, physician, built home in Punta Chivato in 1990 with first wife, Pam, in Subdivision 2, north of Casa Grande, the author's husband.

Kellogg, Kerry and Penny – early campers on Punta Chivato beach from Lee Vining, California.

Larsen, Jack and Bunnie - friend of Bill Alvarado's in Eugene, Oregon, where he owned jewelry store; often flew Bill down to Baja; financier for Bill in resurrecting Hotel Punta Chivato; died in airplane crash in May 1980, en route from Punta Chivato to their home in Eugene, Oregon.

Leyua, Ana Bertha Duran – became acquainted with campers at Punta Chivato who visited her store in Mulegé, *Regalos Ana*; occasionally visited P.C. and shared her cooking skills at Casa Grande during Bill Alvarado's era.

Links, Lee and Lynn – Lynn and her first husband camped at Punta Chivato beach in 1980; after they divorced, Lynn camped there as a single woman for many years; married Lee Links, and the two camped on the beach until they built on a lot above Shell Beach.

Llano, Octavio – involved in Punta Chivato with Dixon Collins; part of affluent, powerful Llano-Zaragosa family; had large family-owned supermarket and building company in Guaymas, and financial interests throughout México.

Lococo, Andy – financed the building of Casa Grande in 1960s; friends with David Rice; speculated to be involved with American Mafia.

Lucore, Larry and Kathy – introduced to camping at Punta Chivato beach in 1970s by Andy and Bunnie Adams; later built home in Subdivision 1 west of Hotel Punta Chivato.

Luján, Raúl – Mexican who built many homes in Punta Chivato; became powerful landowner in the area.

Lyddon, John – instrumental in introducing builder, Raúl Luján, to Punta Chivato where he constructed many homes, including John's vacation home on Lots #14 & #15 in Subdivision 1.

Lyons, William "Doc" – 77-year-old roommate of George Staples in Oregon; joined partnership with four others in house in Posada south of Mulegé; moved into Casa Grande with Bill Alvarado; financier and right-hand man for Bill during hotel restoration; avid gardener; father of four children; daughter Marge Summers would later build a home with her husband, Jere, on one of her father's parcels at Punta Chivato.

McElrath, Frank – from San Diego, California; purchased lot in Subdivision 2 at Punta Chivato where he built a home.

McVay, Archie and Doris – from Brookings, Oregon; built second home at Punta Chivato in partnership with Don and Marge Horton, and Ray and June Nidiffer in Subdivision 1.

Melton, Mike and Conna – first camped at Punta Chivato in April of 1983; camped full-time until moving to lot above Shell Beach.

Molina, Pedro and Aurelia – local Mexican couple who moved to Punta Chivato and found employment with Bill Alvarado in 1979, soon after they married; long-time employees in various capacities at P.C. Like family to many.

Moranville, Doug – friend of Dennis Gardner's from Bend, Oregon; owned a t-shirt printing business; produced many "Punta Chivato" t-shirts sold at Hotel Punta Chivato gift store by Mike Morse.

Moreno, Manuel – owned property near first well used for water for Punta Chivato; Bill Alvarado and an English woman purchased the property and used the water from that well; after Mr. Moreno died, the property was held by Lupe Navarro, Bill's son's girlfriend at the time and later wife. Eventually, the Moreno family repurchased the property.

Morse, Mike – from Poway, California, east of San Diego; house painter; first visited Punta Chivato in 1983 when he was 34 years old; avid fisherman and enamored of Punta Chivato; moved to Punta Chivato to help Bill Alvarado; later worked for Raúl Luján; eventually married a local woman.

Morss, Mary – Bill Alvarado's long-time friend from Oregon; joined Bill to help restore Hotel Punta Chivato.

Navarro, José María "Chaparro" – worked on restoration of Punta Chivato Hotel during Bill Alvarado's era; built several homes at Punta Chivato.

Navarro, Lupe – daughter of José María Navarro (Chaparro); eventually married Jeff Alvarado, one of Bill Alvarado's sons.

Nidiffer, Ray and June – Ray was private pilot from Oregon; owner of C&K Markets which operated grocery stores including Shop Smart, Price Less Foods, and Ray's Food Place; built second home at Punta Chivato in Subdivision 1 in partnership with Archie and Doris McVay, and Don and Marge Horton.

Oberto, Art and Dorothy – couple from Seattle, Washington, who grew Art's father's sausage business into a multimillion-dollar company; bought second home built at P.C. from three Oregonians; very involved in P.C. charity functions, especially to benefit local Mexican school children.

Olachea – head immigration officer in La Paz, Baja California Sur.

Ortíz, Pablo – Mexican national whose name was on title to resort property Hotel Rancho Loma Linda in Mulegé.

Oxley, Harry and Marilyn – early camping family at Punta Chivato (1974); first to lease lot in Subdivision 2 on the bluff south of the camping beach; Harry frequently served as president of the PCHA; the driving force behind Annual PC Dorado Tournament.

Oxley, Pam – Harry's second wife after passing of Marilyn; with her first husband, Greg Joy, built home in Subdivision 2 in 1990; gracious host with her husband, Harry, of numerous fiestas at Punta Chivato; Harry and Pam are some of the longest ongoing American residents at Punta Chivato.

Parr, William Matt "Bud" – Partner with Abelardo "Rod" Rodriguez in first hotel, La Palmilla, in Cabo San Lucas in 1950s; owner of Hotel Cabo San Lucas in 1970s which attracted wealthy American fishermen and celebrities.

Peyton, Dennis – attorney licensed in both México and the United States; hired by the Punta Chivato Homeowners' Association.

Powell, George and Diane – from Fresno, California; built home in Subdivision 1, adding on to garage built earlier by Shoemakers.

Ream, Rich – friend of Jeanne Winters; along with Jeanne and Sam Southwick, leased lot and built first home in Punta Chivato.

Rice, David and Trini – from Long Beach, California; partners in Casa Grande with Andy Lococo; speculated to be involved with American Mafia.

Romero, Rudolfo – hired by Dixon Collins as captain for his fleet of "Barbaras;" seen in Dixon's hotel promotional brochure wearing his sunglasses and signature captain's cap.

Romo, Miguel – with his wife, Angelita Sandoval, and two-month-old son, Luis, joined Angelita's sister and brother-in-law, Pedro and Aurelia Molina, to work in Punta Chivato.

Salzman, Walter "Red" and Nancy – early beach campers at Punta Chivato in 1973; introduced the Silzles to the area.

Sandoval, Angelita – with her husband, Miguel Romo, and two-month-old son, Luis, joined her sister and brother-in-law, Pedro and Aurelia Molina, to work in Punta Chivato.

Senterfitt, Arnold – pilot; published spiral-bound manual diagraming runways in Baja entitled *Airports of Baja California*; organized Baja Bush Pilots.

Sherwood, Don – popular radio disc jockey in the 1950s and 1960s for radio station, KSFO, in San Francisco, California.

Shoemaker, Rick and Patsy – couple from Eugene, Oregon; partner with Walter Fox in oral surgery practice; leased lot in Subdivision 1 at Punta Chivato and built a garage.

Siboreal, John – early camper at Punta Chivato beach; later built home in Subdivision 1 west of Hotel Punta Chivato.

Silzle, Bill and Barbara – avid surfers and divers; early campers at Punta Chivato; later built a home in Subdivision 1 in Punta Chivato.

Sordo, Dr. – a physician-pilot who flew from mainland México to Punta Chivato; helped promote weekly dinners at Casa Grande for Bill Alvarado.

Souther, Phil and Nellie – introduced to Punta Chivato by friends Andy and Bunnie Adams in 1970s; leased Lot 12, Subdivision 2 at Punta Chivato.

Southwick, Sam – piloted Jeanne Winters and Rich Ream to Punta Chivato in November 1978; along with Jeanne and Rich, purchased lot and built first home in Punta Chivato in Subdivision 1.

Staples, George – friend of Bill Alvarado's in Eugene, Oregon, law student; partner in house in Posada near Mulegé; fluent in Spanish language; joined Bill at Casa Grande and helped refurbish Hotel Punta Chivato and sell lots.

Starr, Bob – a promoter out of Costa Mesa, California, who expressed an interest in investing in Punta Chivato during Bill Alvarado's era but never followed through.

Stockton, Dick – purchased Hotel Rancho Loma Linda, in Mulegé and renamed it Club Aero Mulegé.

Sui Qui, Luis – laborer of Chinese-Mexican heritage who worked for both Dixon Collins and Cleve Crudgington at Punta Chivato.

Summers, Jere and Marge – Marge's father was the notorious "Doc" Lyons of Posada and Punta Chivato during Bill Alvarado's era; inherited her father's leased parcels of land; they built on one of the parcels in Subdivision 2; Marge started the local newspaper, *Chivato Charla*.

Tansy, Herb – owner of popular fly-in fishing resort in Baja Sur, Rancho Buena Vista.

Velasquez Meza, Victor Manuel – member of the Ejido San Bruno.

Vessels, Frank "Scoop" and Bonnie – owned thoroughbred race-horse breeding business in Southern California; purchased two lots in Punta Chivato where Raúl Luján built them a home.

Winters, Jeanne – small-plane pilot; along with Rich Ream and Sam Southwick leased a lot and built first home in Punta Chivato – Lot 18 Subdivision 1; left Punta Chivato due to health issues.

Yee, Gilbert - chef at Club Aero Mulegé; claimed ownership of Punta Chivato with Bastida.

Zwick, Helmut and Edith – early couple to purchase a parcel above Shell Beach.

Timeline

1521 – Spanish conquer México; previously Aztec land; two-class system

1700s – Jesuit missionaries establish mission in Mulegé, Baja California Sur

1810 – Spanish rule of México overthrown; México City replaced Madrid as the ruling hub

1907 – Austere prison, *Carcel de Cananea*, built on hillside in Mulegé

1910 – (Nov. 20) Mexican Revolution of 1910, middle-class protest against long-standing dictatorship of Porfirio Diaz (1876-1910)

1917 – Mexican Constitution drawn up with promise to restore land to native people

1920 – Álvaro Obregón elected first president of México

1929 – Political party (PRN) formed in México; later renamed PRI

1934 – Ejido system reinstated in México under President Lázaro Cárdenas

1950s – John Bonfante and Lou Federico meet in San Jose, California

1952 – Northern Territory of Baja becomes a state of México, named *Estado de Baja California*

1956 – First hotel constructed in Cabo San Lucas, Baja California Sur, México, called Palmilla Hotel.

1959 – John Bonfante and Lou Federico discuss purchasing fly-in resort in Baja

1961 – Hotel Rancho Loma Linda built in Mulegé, financed by John Bonfante, Lou Federico and Don Johnson

1961 – Leroy Center builds Serenidad Hotel, a fly-in resort near the mouth of the river in Mulegé

1961 – Dick Stockton takes over Hotel Rancho Loma Linda and renames it Club Aero Mulegé; Lou Federico stays on as hotel manager

1962 – Saúl Davis moves to Mulegé from Loreto; gets job as bartender at Hotel Rancho Loma Linda

1963 – Lou Federico takes Dixon Collins to see potential building site at undeveloped Punta Chivato; Lou Federico weds Lana Green, December 1963; they live in Mulegé

1964 – Ferry line established between mainland town of Mazatlán and La Paz in southern Baja

1965 – Construction of hotel at Punta Chivato begins; financed by Dixon and Barbara Collins

1966 – Borrego de Oro, Dixon's luxury resort in Punta Chivato officially opens

1966 – Club Aero Mulegé (previously Hotel Rancho Loma Linda) leased to Dave Galloway

1966 – Ejido San Bruno established by the federal government in México City (June 23)

1968 – Don Johnson and partners purchase Serenidad Hotel; originally built by Leroy Center

1968 – Cleveland Benedict Crudgington takes over Hotel Borrego de Oro (renames it Punta Chivato Hotel) and Casa Grande

1973 – Transpeninsular Highway down Baja completed October 17

1973 – Ferry line established between mainland city of Guaymas and Santa Rosalía, Baja Sur

1974 – Cleveland Crudgington leaves Punta Chivato in summer and does not return in the fall

1974 – Baja California Sur recognized as a separate state of México (October 8)

1975 – El Morro Hotel in Santa Rosalía opens

1978 – William "Doc" Lyons becomes roommate of law student, George Staples, in Eugene, Oregon

1978 – Bill Alvarado joins friend, Jack Larsen, on fishing trip to Baja; they stay at Serenidad Hotel; Bill first notices abandoned Punta Chivato Hotel from the air

1978 – George Staples, Tom Miller, Phil Clapp, Bill Alvarado and later Doc Lyons become partners in Posada property near Mulegé.

1978 – (November) Rich Ream and Jeanne Winters first visit Punta Chivato by plane; they found the hotel abandoned; only caretaker present

1979 – Bill Alvarado decides to move into Casa Grande with dream of restoring Hotel Punta Chivato

1979 – William "Doc" Lyons first visits Punta Chivato with Bill Alvarado

1979 – Newlyweds Pedro & Aurelia Molina move to Punta Chivato to work for Bill Alvarado; soon followed by Aurelia's sister, Angelita Sandoval, brother-in-law, Miguel Romo, and 2-month-old nephew, Luis Romo Sandoval

1980 – Posada partner, George Staples, joins Bill Alvarado and Doc Lyons at Casa Grande

1980 – Yolanda Acosta Mesa and boyfriend, Mateo Apodaca move into apartment at Casa Grande; Yolanda works for short time as manager of Hotel Punta Chivato

1980 (May) – Jack and Bunnie Larsen tragically die in airplane accident near Cajon Pass while flying from Punta Chivato to their home in Oregon

1980 – (June-August) Bill Alvarado drives to Eugene, Oregon for Larsen funeral; stays to promote idea of time shares at Punta Chivato; Doc Lyons in charge at Punta Chivato during this time

1980 – Jeanne Winters leases first lot at Punta Chivato from George Staples while Bill Alvarado is in Oregon; Lot #18, Subdivision 1; partner, Rich Ream hires, Pedro Molina to construct small home which is completed in three months

1980 – Raúl Luján marries Kim, an American he met in Rosarito Beach while building a home for her parents

1980 – Lynn Links camps at Punta Chivato for first time with her first husband

1980s – Oregonian partners, Archie and Doris McVay, Ray and June Nidiffer, and Don and Marge Horton, build home at Punta Chivato in Subdivision 1

1981 – Mary Morss, Bill's friend from Eugene, Oregon, moves to Punta Chivato to help Bill with hotel restoration project

1982 – Construction of Oxley home in Subdivision 2 commences

1983 – Mike Morse, a housepainter from Poway, California, first arrives at Punta Chivato; assists Bill Alvarado in restoring Hotel Punta Chivato; became a permanent resident; married a local woman, Magdalena

1984 – Tile factory and icehouse at Punta Chivato; pig farm project

1984 – Americans who leased parcels at Punta Chivato informed their leases were invalid

1985 (Easter week) –- Punta Chivato Homeowners' Association (PCHA) formed

1985 – Dick & Billie Brush first camp on Punta Chivato beach

1986 – Archie and Doris McVay, Ray and June Nidiffer, and Don and Marge Horton decide to leave Punta Chivato; they release their home to Art & Dorothy Oberto from Seattle, Washington

1986 – Mary Morss moves from Punta Chivato back to Oregon

1986 (Fall) – Hotel Punta Chivato officially opens under proprietor, Bill Alvarado

1987 – Group of Punta Chivato homeowners plot to take over hotel from Bill

1987 – Americans who leased lots from Bill Alvarado and built homes at Punta Chivato were told the leases were illegal; new leases drawn up by end of year

1989 – Billie Brush and Bill Alvarado's sons forced to leave Baja due to lack of proper work papers

1989 – Raúl Luján first visits Punta Chivato; introduced by John Lyddon, an American who asked the young man to build him a home there

1990 – Billie Brush gains access back into Baja after obtaining valid paperwork

1990 – Raúl Luján builds home for John Lyddon on Lots #14 and #15, Subdivision 1, the first of many homes he would construct for Americans at Punta Chivato

1991 – Ream-Winters-Southwick home on Lot #18 of Subdivision 1 sold to two pilots from Northern California, Tom Rosen and Tom Ryan

1991 – *Bazaar de Niños* (Children's Bazaar) established by benevolent homeowners at Punta Chivato, Les and Lucy Conner; soon joined in their efforts by Art and Dorothy Oberto, John and Gerry Fitzsimmons, Dale and Julia Dryer and others

1992 – Güero Alaníz opens *tienda* (store) at Punta Chivato

1992 – First issue of *Chivato Charla* comes out, a local Punta Chivato newsletter, written and published by homeowner, Marge Summers

1992 – Desert Lynx Golf Course, a 9-hole course established at Punta Chivato inspired by homeowners Lee and Connie Cobb

1992 – Amendment to Mexican Constitution allowing ejidos to convert their land into private property and sell it. Called "privatization," it would be almost ten years before realized at Punta Chivato

1993 – New agrarian law enacted in México allowing communal lands of ejidos to be leased for 30 years

1993 – Bill Alvarado leaves Punta Chivato after threat of being put in jail

1994 – American lot and homeowners in Punta Chivato sign new leases after new agrarian law enacted in August 1993, increasing ejido land leases to thirty years

1994 – Harry Oxley and Raúl Luján form partnership, Punta Chivato Shores, to develop property for future homes in Punta Chivato

1995 – Mike and Conna Melton, Lester and Betty Bell, and Steve and Rusty Howland move to neighboring parcels above Shell Beach

1995 – Bill Alvarado and Billie Brush get married in San Diego and eventually move to Oregon

1996 – Güero Alaníz marries Gloria Guadalupe Mendoza Ruíz

1997 – The 1ˢᵗ Annual Punta Chivato Dorado Tournament held at Punta Chivato

1998 – The 1ˢᵗ Annual "O Hell" Tournament held at Punta Chivato

1998 – *Chubasco* (hurricane) hits Punta Chivato causing damage

1999 – Adams' whale project at Punta Chivato

1999 – Raúl Luján sells Casa Grande to Gordon Campbell and Maria Ligeti, who had built a large complex on adjacent parcel

1999 – Punta Chivato Yacht Club (PCYC) started by Bob Davis who served as the group's first commodore

1999 – Unable to locate a buyer willing to pay their asking price, Ejido San Bruno closes Hotel Punta Chivato (July)

1999 – Italian, Giuseppe Marcellotti Pandolfi, purchases Hotel Punta Chivato from Ejido San Bruno; he renames the hotel *Posada de las Flores* and begins to make improvements (August)

2000 – The 1st Annual Lee Cobb Memorial Golf Tournament and Auction held at Punta Chivato

2000 – Committee headed by homeowner, Pam Oxley, creates and publishes *Las Cocinas de Chivato,* a cookbook with over 300 recipes from residents at Punta Chivato

2000 – Remodeled *Posada de las Flores Punta Chivato* officially opens under new owner, Giuseppe Marcellotti Pandolfi (August)

2000 – Ejido sells large parcel 121 at Punta Chivato to Raúl Luján

2000 – Raúl Luján and the Campbells again partner to begin construction of *Pilots Club Steak House* west of the long airport runway at Punta Chivato

2000 – After a delay of nearly three years, American homeowners at Punta Chivato receive their fideicomisos

Sources

INTERVIEWS

Acosta Mesa, Yolanda – February 27, 2003, at El Patrón, her sister's restaurant on the beach in Mulegé

Adams, Andy and Bunnie - December 6, 2002, at Casa Adams with Phil and Nellie Souther

Aguilar, Florencio - November 6, 2003, at Hotel Morro in Santa Rosalia, June 1, 2004, at his home in Santa Rosalia with Marcos Aguilar

Aguilar, Marcos - June 1, 2004, at Florencio's home in Santa Rosalia

Alaníz, Güero - November 6, 2004, at Guero and Gloria's home in Punta Chivato

Alvarado, Bill - September 3, 2004, West Linn, Oregon with Mary Morss and Jeanne Fox, September 4, 2004, West Linn, Oregon with Mary Morss and Jeanne Fox, July 28, 2003, Alvarado home in Oakridge, Oregon, with Billie Alvarado

Alvarado Billie - July 28, 2003, at Alvarado home in Oakridge, Oregon, with Bill Alvarado

Bell, Lester and Betty - January 4, 2003, at Bell home in Punta Chivato

Collins, Dixon - November 21, 2002, at his home in Angels Camp, California

Conner, Les and Lucy - October 29, 2003, at Punta Chivato, with Dale and Julia Dryer and John and Gerry Fitzsimmons

Converse, Robin - November 1, 2003, at his home in Punta Chivato

Crudgington, Cleveland Jr. and his mother, Phyllis - November 29, 2002, at Cleveland Crudgington Jr.'s home in Monrovia, California

Davis, Bob - November 1, 2002, in Punta Chivato at Casa Davis, December 29, 2003, in Punta Chivato at Casa Davis, January 2004, in Punta Chivato at Casa Davis

Davis, Saúl - February 27, 2003, on the porch next to his store in Mulegé

Dryer, Dale and Julia - October 29, 2003, at Punta Chivato, with Les and Lucy Conners and John and Gerry Fitzsimmons

Espinoza, José M. "Chema" - December 5, 2002, at El Morro Hotel, Santa Rosalía

Federico, Lou - October 9, 2002, at his home in Folsom, California; November 20, 2002, at his home in Folsom, California; November 26, 2002, at his home in Folsom, California; January 29, 2003, at his home in Folsom, California

Fitzsimmons, John and Gerry - October 29, 2003, at Punta Chivato, with Les and Lucy Conners, and Dale and Julia Dryer

Fox, Jeanne - September 3, 2004, at her home in West Linn, Oregon, with Bill Alvarado and Mary Morss, September 4, 2004, at her home in West Linn, Oregon, with Bill Alvarado and Mary Morss

Gardner, Dennis - October 22, 2003, at his home in Punta Chivato

Johnson, Don - November 4, 2003, at Serenidad Hotel, Mulegé, December 28, 2003, at Serenidad Hotel, Mulegé

Kellogg, Kerry and Penny - March 10, 2005, at Punta Chivato camping beach

Leyua, Ana Bertha Duran - November 10, 2004, at Regalos Ana, Mulegé

Links, Lee - July 27, 2003, at a campground near Oakridge, Oregon, with Lynn Links

Links, Lynn - December 5, 2002, at Casa Joy in Punta Chivato. July 27, 2003, at a campground near Oakridge, Oregon, with Lee Links

Luján, Raúl – July 3, 2005, at his office in Mulegé

Lyons, Jim – July 27, 2024, telephone conversation between Jim Lyons and Greg Joy

McVay, Archie and Doris – September 5, 2004, at their home in Harbor, Oregon

Melton, Mike – November 2, 2002, at Punta Chivato

Molina, Pedro & Aurelia - October 22, 2003, at Casa Joy in Punta Chivato

Morse, Mike - December 31, 2003, at Punta Chivato, 2004, at Punta Chivato

Morss, Mary - September 3, 2004, at Fox residence in West Linn, Oregon, with Bill Alvarado and Jeanne Fox, September 4, 2004, at Fox residence in West Linn, Oregon, with Bill Alvarado and Jeanne Fox

Oxley, Harry - December 23, 2002, in Placerville, California, January 2004, in Punta Chivato

Peyton, Dennis - April 12, 2004, at his home in Eastlake/Chula Vista, California

Seretaño, Amador - November 9, 2004, on front porch of Casa Joy in Punta Chivato

Silzle, Barbara - June 2, 2004, at Casa Silzle in Punta Chivato

Souther, Phil and Nellie - December 6, 2002, at Casa Adams in Punta Chivato with Andy and Bunnie Adams

Staples, George - September 23, 2005, at his home in Eugene, Oregon

Summers, Jere - June 2, 2004, at Summers' home in Punta Chivato, with Marge Summers

Summers, Marge - November 7, 2003, in Punta Chivato, January 2004, in Punta Chivato

LETTERS/DIARIES/CORRESPONDENCE

Alvarado, Bill – letter to Doc Lyons, February 28, 1984; Bill narrated videotape taken in Nov. 1991/Jan. 1992 in Punta Chivato and mailed as a Christmas gift to George Staples, then shared with the author

Bonfante, John – brief history of Rancho Loma Linda, no date (shared by Lou Federico)

Booth, Otis, Jr. – letter to the author, March 12, 2003

Bulls Only Dorado Tournament letter – May 5, 2004

Chandler, Harry – emails to the author, January 16, 2003, February 24, 2003

Chandler, Otis – letter to the author, December 9, 2003

Collins, Dixon – emails to the author, November 7, 2002, February 23, 2003

Crudgington, Mary R. – letters to the author, December 19, 2002, May 12, 2003

Domingues, Franco, Director of the National Agrarian Registry in La Pax – letter to Julian Vargas Limon, President of the Ejidal Commissary – September 21, 1994

Ejido Letters – to Punta Chivato Homeowners' Association, September 5, 1994, August 10, 1999, August 13, 1999

Federico, Lana – letters to Lou Federico April 30, 1967, June 1, 1967 (shared by Lou Federico)

Federico, Lou – letter to Dave Galloway May 17, 1967 (shared by Lou Federico) and written notes by Lou Federico shared with the author

Fitzsimmons, John – emails to the author, January 16, 2003, December 26, 2003, letters to the author, December 25, 2003, March 11, 2004

Gerwick, Ben C. Jr. – email to the author, August 2, 2004

Gorosave, Cesar – letter to Luis Federico, January 2, 1969

Head, Dale – email to Mike Melton (shared by Mike Melton), November 5, 2002

Jacobson, David and Norma – letters to author, July 18, 2004, July 29, 2004

Lyons, William "Doc" – (shared by his daughter, Marge Summers)

    Autobiography
    Letters to his daughter, Jo
        Sunday, July 6, 1980, Monday July 7, 1980, August 17, 1980, Friday, September 12, 1980, Saturday, September 13, 1980

Letters to his daughter, Marge
    May 3, 1983, June 12, 1983, July 5, 1983, Tuesday at
    the Pickwick, San Diego
Letter to his daughter, Ann
    July 5, 1983, Tuesday at the Pickwick, San Diego
Notes from diary of William Lyons
    Apr. 25, 1983, Monday
    Apr. 26, 1983, Tuesday
    Apr. 27, 1983, Wednesday
    Apr. 28, 1983, Thursday
    Apr. 29, 1983, Friday
    Apr. 30, 1983, Saturday
    May 1, 1983, Sunday
    May 2, 1983, Monday
    May 3, 1983, Tuesday
    May 10, 1983, Tuesday
    July 5, 1983

Morss, Mary E. – email to the author, August 13, 2004, August 17, 2004

Peyton, Dennis – letter to Harry Oxley, April 20, 1993

Punta Chivato Homeowners – letter to Punta Chivato Homeowners' Association Board (PCHA Board), March 3, 1987

Punta Chivato Homeowners' Association – letters to PCHA homeowners: June 2, 1986, November 15, 1987, November 18, 1987, November 27, 1987, June 9, 1992, June 1993, December 26, 1993, January 31, 1994, January 10, 1995, April 27, 1995, January 14, 1997, April 15, 1997, October 1, 1997

Punta Chivato Homeowners' Association meeting minutes: March 31, 1994, April 2, 1999, November 27, 1999

Ream, Richard – letters to the author, November 20, 2002, January 22, 2003, November 18, 2003

Rosen, Tom – email to the author, May 23, 2018

Salzman, Milton "Red" – letter to the author, November 25, 2003

Sherwood, Don – letter to Lana Federico, February 12, 1967 (shared by Lou Federico)

BOOKS, BROCHURES, MAGAZINE ARTICLES, NEWSLETTERS

Automobile Club of Southern California. Baja California. 1995, pp. 78-79 and 197.

Baja California, Hotel Punta Chivato – early brochure showing photos from Dixon's era (no date).

Bernhardson, Wayne. *Lonely Planet: Baja California.* Lonely Planet Publications, 1998, p. 321.

Breckenridge, Karl. "Jus'kiddin' on the keyboard," *Reno Gazette Journal,* December 23, 2014.

Burkhart, John and Terry. "From the Editors' Desks," *Flight Log: The Pilot's Travel Newsletter.* Fullerton, California: Wordsworth, September 1991.

Cannon, Ray. *The Sea of Cortez.* Menlo Park, California: Lane Magazine & Book Company, 1966.

Cannon, Ray. "Cortez Tournament 'Played by Ear,'" *Western Outdoor News,* November 22, 1968.

Chivato Charla – February 1992, March 1992, April/May 1992, November/December 1992, March/April 1993, May/June 1993, July/August 1993, September/October 1993, March/April 1995, June/July 1995, September/October 1995, March/April 1996, January 1997, Winter 1998, Spring 1998, Summer 1998, Fall 1998, Spring 1999, Summer 1999, Fall 1999, Spring 2000, Fall 2000, October 3, 2000, Spring 2001, July 2, 2001, November 19, 2001, May 3, 2002.

Cross, Cliff. *Baja California, Mexico.* Tucson, Arizona: H.P. Books, 1974.

Dewyze, Jeannette. "Francisco Muñoz and his spectacular friendship with Erle Stanley Gardner," *San Diego Reader,* 21 September 1995.

Discover Baja Travel Club. "Punta Chivato News," December 1993.

Harper, Laurie. *Don Sherwood: The Life and Times of "The World's Greatest Disc Jockey."* Rocklin, California: Prima Publishing & Communications, 1989, p. 326.

Excursions Extraordinaires brochure. Windsurf Baja at Punta Chivato. Eugene, Oregon, 1990.

Federico. Lou. "A Tale of Two Hotels," *Discover Baja,* September/October 1993.

Federico, Lou. *One Hell of a Ride: The Life and Times of Lou Federico.* Livingston, MT: Word Wrangler Publishing, Inc., 2004.

Gardner, Erle Stanley, *Off the Beaten Track in Baja.* New York: William Morrow & Company, 1967, pp. 300-304.

Gerhard, Peter and Howard E. Gulick. *Lower California Guidebook: A Descriptive Traveler's Guide.* Glendale, California: The Arthur H. Clark Company, 1970.

Hotels Posada de las Flores, México, Baja California brochure (no date)

Hunter, Ben. *The Baja Feeling.* Ontario, California: Brasch and Brasch, Publishers, Inc., 1978.

Isla San Marcos: Una Empresa, Una Comunidad, Un Reto. (San Marcos Island: A Company, A Community, A Challenge), 1997.

Kandell, Jonathan. *La Capital: The Biography of Mexico City.* New York: Random House, 1988.

Kira, Gene S. *The Unforgettable Sea of Cortez: Baja California's Golden Age 1947-1977: The Life and Writings of Ray Cannon.* Cortez Publications, 1999.

Krutch, Joseph Wood. *The Forgotten Peninsula: A Naturalist in Baja California.* Tucson, Arizona: The University of Arizona Press, 1961.

Lewis, Leland R. and Peter E. Ebeling. *Baja Sea Guide, Volume II.* Newport Beach, California: SEA Publications, Inc., 1971, 1973.

McCormick, Jack. "Arnold Senterfitt," *Baja Bush Pilots Journal.* Chandler, Arizona: Baja Bush Pilots, April 2004.

McMahan, Mike. *There It Is: Baja! México's Puzzling Peninsula.* Northridge, California: Brooke House, 1974.

McDougal, Dennis. *Privileged Son: Otis Chandler and the Rise and Fall of the L.A. Times Dynasty.* Cambridge, Massachusetts: Perseus Publishing, 2001, pp. 234-235.

México West; Baja California, Sea of Cortez, México's West Coast. Vol 9, Number 2, June 1983, p. 3-4.

Miller, Tom and Elmar Baxter, *The Baja Book II: A Complete New Map-Guide to Today's Baja California.* Huntington Beach, CA: Baja Trail Publications, Inc., 1982.

Miller, Tom and Carol Hoffman. *The Baja Book III: A Complete New Map-Guide to Today's Baja California.* Huntington Beach, CA: Baja Trail Publications, Inc., 1992.

Minch, John and Thomas Leslie. *The Baja Highway: a geology and biology field guide for the Baja Traveler.* San Juan Capistrano, California: John Minch and Associates, Inc., 1991.

Niemann, Greg. *Baja Legends: The Historic Characters, Events, and Locations that Put Baja California on the Map.* San Diego, California, Sunbelt Publications, 2002, p. 260.

Otterstrom, Kerry G. *Manual de Mulegé, Baja California Sur, México: The Complete Tourism, Souvenir, and Historical Guide of Mulegé.* A Publication of Elizabeth Yee de Otterstrom, 1992.

Peterson, Walt. *The Baja Adventure Book.* Berkeley, California: Wilderness Press, 1987, 1992.

Punta Chivato Shores promotional brochure, "Join Us Punta Chivato Shores Baja," San Clemente, California, (no date, estimated 1994).

Said, Bob. "The Good Life: A Piper under the Sun," *Private Pilot*, February 1967.

Senterfitt, Arnold D. *Airports of Baja California.* San Diego, California, Summer-Fall 1966.

Senterfitt, Arnold D. *The Baja Pilot.* San Diego, California, 1966.

Stone, Joe. "Homes Envisioned on Baja Gulf Coast," *San Diego Union*, February 19, 1966.

Stanford Magazine. "Class Notes 1970s" – Norman Brant Chandler. November/December 2002.

Sunset. "The Surprises of Baja." November 1963.

Sunset Editorial Staff with Ken and Caroline Bates. *Baja California.* Menlo Park, California: Lane Magazine & Book Company, 1971.

Williams, Jack. *Baja Boater's Guide, Volume II – Sea of Cortez. The Definitive Guide for the Coastal Waters of Mexico's Baja California.* Sausalito, California: H. J. Williams Publications, September 1988.

Zúniga Meza, Felipe, "Presionan a inversionistas para que abandonen Punta Chivato," *El Forjador* (La Paz, B.C.S. newspaper), May 28, 2003.

INTERNET WEBSITES

"Abelardo Luis Rodriguez M. Obituary." *San Diego Tribune,* October 28, 2018. *www.legacy.com/obituaries/name/abelardo-rodriguez-m-obituary?pid=190592060*

"Aero Spacelines Pregnant Guppy." *Wikipedia*, Wikipedia Foundation 31 July 2023, *en.wikipedia.org/wiki/Aero_Spacelines_Pregnant_Guppy*

Andersen, Steve. "Scoop Vessels dies in plane crash," *Daily Racing Form*, 12 August 2010, *drf.com/news/scoop-vessels-dies-plane crash*

"Ann-Margret." *Wikipedia*, Wikipedia Foundation, 1 October 2023, *en.wikipedia.org/wiki/Ann-Margret*

"Benjamin Archie McVay." Redwood Memorial Chapel, Brookings, Oregon, 2016, *www.tributearchive.com/obituaries/900014/Benjamin%20Archie%20McVay*

Bobonick, Eliza. "A horse lover's legacy nourishes the community and provides an elegant home for events," *Soapbox Cincinnati*, 20 August 2019, *www.soapboxmedia.com/innovationnews/Meshewa-House-Turner-Farm.aspx*

"Carrows." *Wikipedia*, Wikipedia Foundation, 5 October 2023, *en.wikipedia.org/wiki/Carrows*

Cheek, Martin. "The History of Nob Hill, a Famous Local Author and Gavilan vs. Gabilan," *Gilroy Dispatch*, 29 December 2006, *gilroydispatch.com/the-history-of-nob-hill-a-famous-local-author-and-gavilan-vs-gabilan*

"Clay Lacy." *Wikipedia*, Wikipedia Foundation, 14 August 2023, *en.wikipedia.org/wiki/Clay_Lacy*

Connelly, Laylan. "Iconic Newport surfboard shaper "Russell" dies," *The Orange County Register*, Orange County, California, 22 August 2021, *www.ocregister.com/2011/08/22/iconic-newport-surfboard-shaper-russell-dies*

County Courts: "Apartment A Cocktail Bar, Wife's Divorce Charge," *Cincinnati Enquirer*, Cincinnati, Ohio, 16 May 1944, p. 19, *https://cincinnati.newspapers.com/search/results/?date=1944-05-16&keyword=county+courts&publication-ids=844*

"Dixon Collins." *Calaveras Enterprise*, 7 November 2014, *www.calaverasenterprise.com/news/dixon-collins*

"Dr. Walter H. Fox." *The Oregonian*, 22 March 2005, *obits.oregonlive.com/us/obituaries/oregon/name/walter-fox-obituary?id=19547610*

"Erle Stanley Gardner." *Wikipedia*, Wikipedia Foundation, 4 July 2024, *enwikipedia.org/wiki/Erle_Stanley_Gardner*

"Flying club." *Wikipedia*, Wikipedia Foundation, 27 June 2023, *en.wikipedia.org/wiki/Flying_club*

"Franklin Otis Booth, Jr." *Wikipedia*, Wikipedia Foundation, 21 August 2023, *en.wikipedia.org/wiki/Franklin_Otis_Booth_Jr.*

Goy, Dan & Lisa. "Hotel Serenidad and Baja Legend Don Johnson," *Discover Baja Travel Club*, 18 July 2013, *discoverbaja.com/2013/07/18/hotel-Serenidad-baja-legend-don-johnson*

Greene, Lauren. "Elephant Bar Restaurant Chain," *WorthPoint*, *www.worthpoint.com/dictionary/p/advertising/restaurants-chains/elephant-bar-restaurant-chain*

"Harvey Gross, 78, a Pioneer in Lake Tahoe Gaming Clubs." *The New York Times*, 3 November 1983, *nytimes.com/1983/11/03/obituaries/harvey-gross-78-a-pioneerin-lake-tahoe-gaming-clubs.html*

"History of the Baja Bush Pilots International." *Bush Pilots International*, 2010-2023, *bushpilotsinternational.com/page.php?name=history*

"Honeywell." *Wikipedia*, Wikipedia Foundation, 26 September 2023, *en.wikipedia.org/wiki/Honeywell*

Indian Hill Historical Society. "Remembering Bonnie Mitsui," *Indian Hill Village Bulletin,* 28 June 2023, #6, p. 22, *https://indianhill.gov/wp-content/uploads/2023/06/Bulletin-06-28-23.pdf*

"Jay Rockefeller." *Wikipedia*, Wikipedia Foundation, 4 July 2024, *en.wikipedia.org/wiki/Jay_Rockefeller*

"Jayne Mansfield," *Wikipedia*. Wikipedia Foundation, 30 June 2024, *en.wikipedia.org/wiki/Jayne_Mansfield*

"Jeanne Dignan Daniels Fox." *The Oregonian*, 8-14 December 2016, *obits.oregonlive.com/us/obituaries/oregon/name/jeanne-fox-obituary?id=20551454*

"John Wayne," *Wikipedia*, Wikipedia Foundation, 1 July 2024, *en.wikipedia.org/wiki.org/wiki/John_Wayne*

"Kirk Douglas." *Wikipedia*, Wikipedia Foundation, 4 July 2024, *en.wikipedia.org/wiki/Kirk_Douglas*

Knight, Alan. "The History of the Mexican Revolution," *History Today,* Vol. 30, Issue 5, May 1980, *historytoday.com/archieve/Mexican-revolution*

"Larry Hagman." *Wikipedia*, Wikipedia Foundation, 20 September 2023, *en.wikipedia.org/wiki/Larry_Hagman*

"Leslie H. 'Les' Conner." *Bakersfield Californian*, 18 November 2016, *legacy.com/us/obituaries/bakersfield/name/leslie-conner-obituary?id=15822534*

"Losing a Baja Legend: Don Johnson from Hotel Serenidad in Mulegé." *Discover Baja Travel Club*, 18 September 2020, photos by Brown McPherson, *discoverbaja.com/2020/09/18/losing-a-baja-legend-don-johnson-from-hotel-Serenidad*

Martina. "The Baja Storyteller: The Heydays of Hollywood Baja Style." *Baja Bound Mexican Insurance*, prior to 15 September 2020, *bajabound.com/bajaadventures/bajastoryteller/donjohnson*

"Mary Elizabeth 'Bonnie' Mitsui." *legacy.com/us/obituaries/cincinnati/name/mary-mitsui-obituary?id=22700300*

Morgan, KT. "The Hotel Pioneers of Los Cabos." *Cabosfinest,* 2004, *cabosfinest.com/the-hotel-pioneers-of-loscabos*

New York Daily News, New York, New York, 9 May 1971, p. 108, *https://nydailynews.newspapers.com/search/results/?date-end=1979&date-start=1970&keyword=Cleveland+B.+Crudgington*

"Olivia Newton-John." *Wikipedia*, Wikipedia Foundation, 25 September 2023, *en.wikipedia.org/wiki/Olivia_Newton-John*

"Otis Worldwide." *Wikipedia*, Wikipedia Foundation, 8 October 2023, *en.wikipedia.org/wiki/Otis_Worldwide*

"Park History & Timeline: A Dream Becomes a Reality." *Gilroy Gardens*, 2023, *gilroygardens.org/explore/park-history*

Peterman, Keith. "Flying to Baja in the 1970's & 1980's" *Cabovillas.com*, 14 June 2016

"Politics of México." *Wikipedia*, Wikipedia Foundation, 8 October 2023, *en.wikipedia.org/wiki/Politics_of_México#:~:text=Revolution%20in%201920.-,Major%20Political%20Parties.National%20Regeneration%20Movement%20(Morena)*

"Procter & Gamble." *Wikipedia*, Wikipedia Foundation, 10 October 2023, *en.wikipedia.org/wiki/Procter_%26_Gamble*

"Reno Pair Married in Virginia City." *Nevada State Journal,* June 12, 1969, *www.pinterest.com/pin/550987335647388872*

"Richard Frank Ream." *Salt Lake Tribune*, 10 February 2008, *legacy.com/us/obituaries/saltlaketribune/name/richard-ream-obituary?id=28757047*

"Rocca's Market: Rocca's History." 2010, *roccasmarket.isoars.com/-/history.html*

"Roseville Forest Products." Company-Histories.com, Roseburg Forest Products Company, (source) *International Directory of Company Histories*, Vol. 58. St. James Press, 2004, *company-histories.com/Roseburg-Forest-Products-Company-Company-History.html*

"Sam Yorty." *Wikipedia*, Wikipedia Foundation, 6 October 2023, *en.wikipedia.org/wiki/Sam_Yorty*

Sandell, Scott. "Landmark Cockatoo Inn Strives to Recapture the Glory of Its Past." *Los Angeles Times*, 21 April 1994, *latimes.com/archives/la-xpm-1994-04-21-hd-49226-story.html*

"The accidental billionaire." *Forbes*, 12 October 1998, *forbes.com/global/1998/1012/0114028s1.html*

"The Cockatoo Inn (site) (Hawthorne, California)." *Wikimapia*, *wikimapia.org/1174528/The-Cockatoo-Inn-site*

"The Flying Samaritans." *Wikipedia*, Wikipedia Foundation, 2 October 2022, *en.wikipedia.org/wiki/The_Flying_Samaritans*

"The San Diego Union-Tribune." *Wikipedia*, Wikipedia Foundation, 29 September 2023, *en.wikipedia.org/wiki/The_San_Diego_Union-Tribune*

"Town Club of Eugene." *Bizapedia*, Oregon Office of the Secretary of State Business Registration, 21 April 2016, *bizapedia.com/or/town-club-of-eugene.html*

"United States Power Squadrons." *Wikipedia*, Wikipedia Foundation, 14 December 2022, *en.wikipedia.org/wiki/United_States_Power_Squadrons*

"William Ralph Alvarado." *Family Search*

INDEX OF MAIN CHARACTERS

V

Vargas Limon, Julian, 345, 348-350, 356-357, 387, 396, 411-413, 416, 428, 448, 504

Velazquez Mesa, Victor Manuel, 241, 313, 400, 411-412, 429, 446, 448, 452, 478, 494

Vessels, Bonnie, 366, 494

Vessels, Frank "Scoop," 366, 391, 480-481. 494, 512

W

Weiser, Lynne, 75, 428, 462

Willett, Char, 293, 452-453

Willett, Will, 293, 432, 447, 452

Winters, Jeanne, 226-230, 232, 235-236, 309, 312, 315-316, 342-345, 348, 492-494, 497-498

Wood, Barbara, 377, 419

Wood, Jim "Jimmy," 377, 419

Y

Yee, Gilbert, 19-21, 119-121, 485, 494

Z

Zacarías, 169-172, 177, 183, 187, 189, 193, 196-197, 199, 227, 250, 298, 308, 337, 485, 487-488

Zuñiga, Saúl, 434, 445